School Rumble

⑫

Jin Kobayashi

TRANSLATED AND ADAPTED BY
William Flanagan

LETTERED BY
HudsonYards

DEL REY

BALLANTINE BOOKS • NEW YORK

School Rumble volume 12 is a work of fiction. Names, characters, places, and incidents are the products of the author's imagination or are used fictitiously. Any resemblance to actual events, locales, or persons, living or dead, is entirely coincidental.

A Del Rey Manga/Kodansha Trade Paperback Original

Published in the United States by Del Rey Books, an imprint of The Random House Publishing Group, a division of Random House, Inc., New York.

Del Rey is a registered trademark and the Del Rey colophon is a trademark of Random House, Inc.

Publication rights arranged through Kodansha Ltd.

First published in Japan in 2006 by Kodansha Ltd., Tokyo.

ISBN 978-0-345-50563-7

Printed in the United States of America

www.delreymanga.com

9 8 7 6 5 4 3 2 1

Translator and adapter: William Flanagan
Lettering: HudsonYards
Cover Design: David Stevenson

Honorifics Explained

Throughout the Del Rey Manga books, you will find Japanese honorifics left intact in the translations. For those not familiar with how the Japanese use honorifics and, more important, how they differ from American honorifics, we present this brief overview.

Politeness has always been a critical facet of Japanese culture. Ever since the feudal era, when Japan was a highly stratified society, use of honorifics—which can be defined as polite speech that indicates relationship or status—has played an essential role in the Japanese language. When addressing someone in Japanese, an honorific usually takes the form of a suffix attached to one's name (example: "Asuna-san"), is used as a title at the end of one's name, or appears in place of the name itself (example: "Negi-sensei," or simply "Sensei!").

Honorifics can be expressions of respect or endearment. In the context of manga and anime, honorifics give insight into the nature of the relationship between characters. Many English translations leave out these important honorifics and therefore distort the feel of the original Japanese. Because Japanese honorifics contain nuances that English honorifics lack, it is our policy at Del Rey not to translate them. Here, instead, is a guide to some of the honorifics you may encounter in Del Rey Manga.

-san: This is the most common honorific and is equivalent to Mr., Miss, Ms., or Mrs. It is the all-purpose honorific and can be used in any situation where politeness is required.

-sama: This is one level higher than "-san" and is used to confer great respect.

-dono: This comes from the word "tono," which means "lord." It is an even higher level than "-sama" and confers utmost respect.

-kun: This suffix is used at the end of boys' names to express familiarity or endearment. It is also sometimes used by men among friends, or when addressing someone younger or of a lower station.

-chan: This is used to express endearment, mostly toward girls. It is also used for little boys, pets, and even among lovers. It gives a sense of childish cuteness.

Bozu: This is an informal way to refer to a boy, similar to the English terms "kid" and "squirt."

Sempai/Senpai: This title suggests that the addressee is one's senior in a group or organization. It is most often used in a school setting, where underclassmen refer to their upperclassmen as "sempai." It can also be used in the workplace, such as when a newer employee addresses an employee who has seniority in the company.

Kohai: This is the opposite of "sempai" and is used toward underclassmen in school or newcomers in the workplace. It connotes that the addressee is of a lower station.

Sensei: Literally meaning "one who has come before," this title is used for teachers, doctors, or masters of any profession or art.

Onee-san/Onii-san: Normally older siblings are not called by name but rather by the title of older sister (*Onee-san*) or older brother (*Onii-san*). Depending on the relationship, "-chan" or "-sama" can also be used instead of "-san." However, this honorific can also be used with someone unrelated when the relationship resembles that of siblings.

Obaa-san/Ojii-san: Japanese grandparents are called by their titles rather than by name. Grandmothers are called "Obaa-san" (or "Obaa-sama" to imply added respect and distance, or "Obaa-chan" for more intimacy). Likewise grandfathers are called "Ojii-san," "Ojii-sama," or "Ojii-chan."

-[blank]: This is usually forgotten in these lists, but it is perhaps the most significant difference between Japanese and English. The lack of honorific means that the speaker has permission to address the person in a very intimate way. Usually, only family, spouses, or very close friends have this kind of permission. Known as *yobisute*, it can be gratifying when someone who has earned the intimacy starts to call one by one's name without an honorific. But when that intimacy hasn't been earned, it can be very insulting.

Cultural Note

To preserve some of the humor found in *School Rumble*, we have elected to keep Japanese names in their original Japanese order— that is to say, with the family name first, followed by the personal name. So when you hear the name Tsukamoto Tenma, Tenma is just one member of the Tsukamoto family.

School Rumble

12

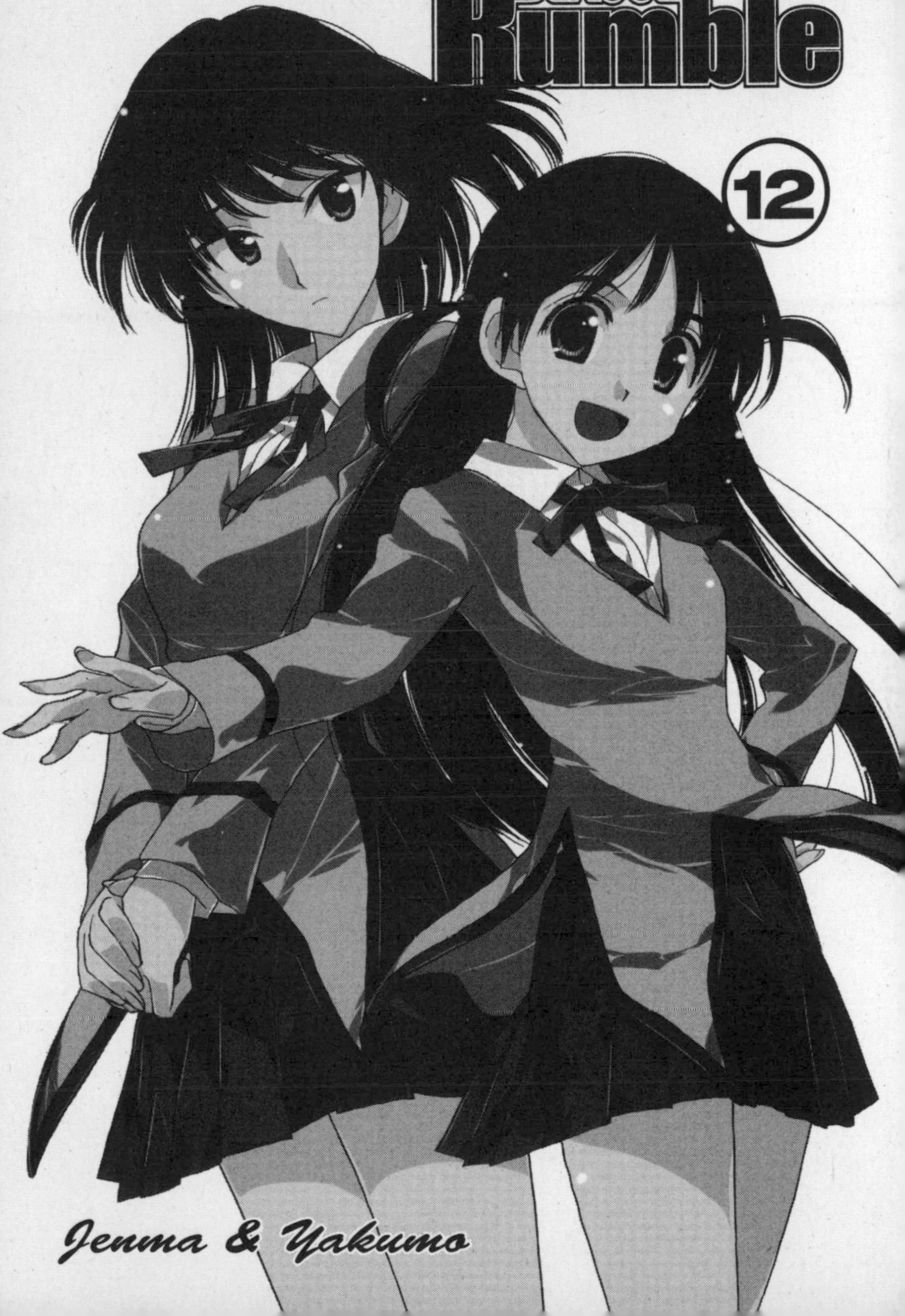
Jenma & Yakumo

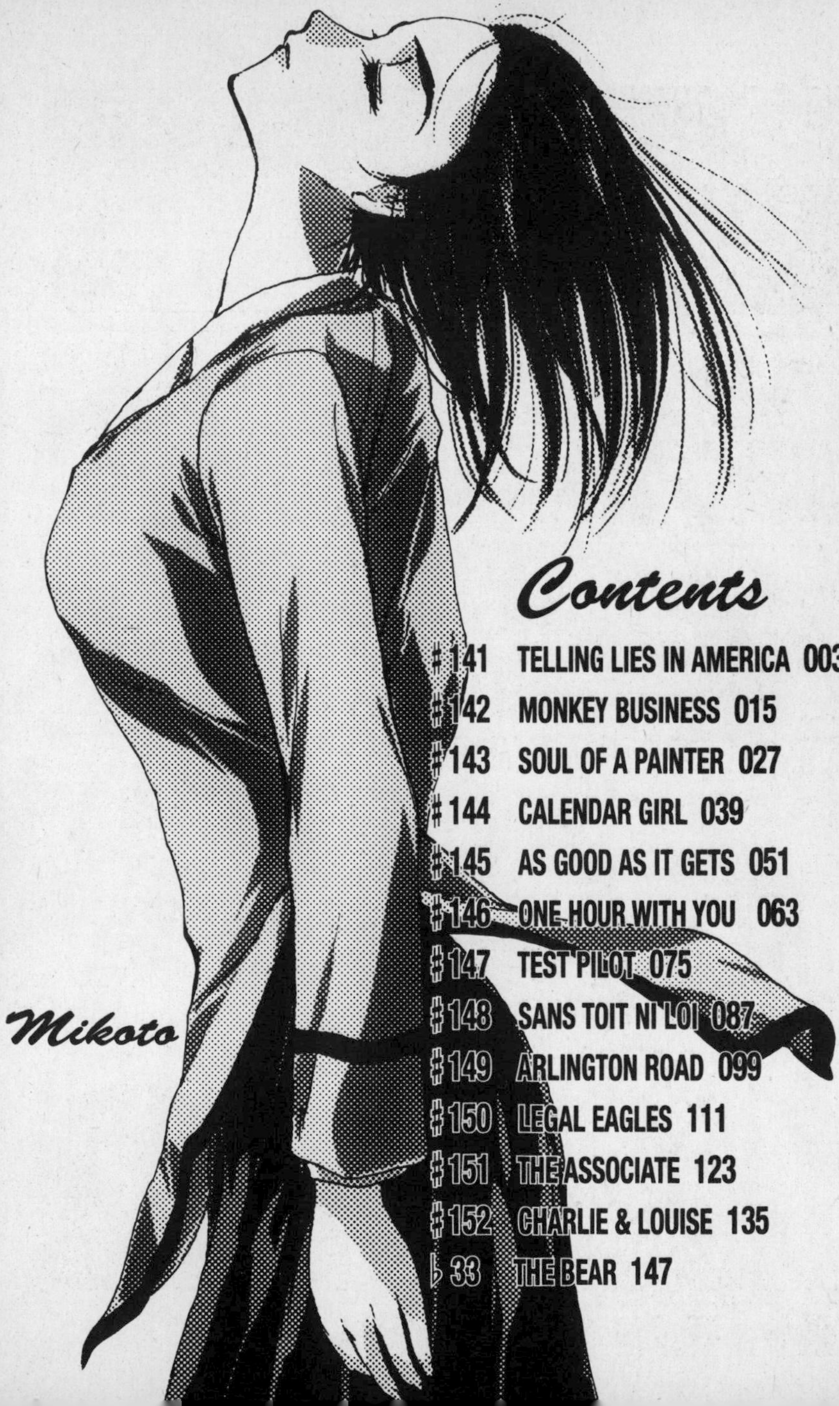
Mikoto

Contents

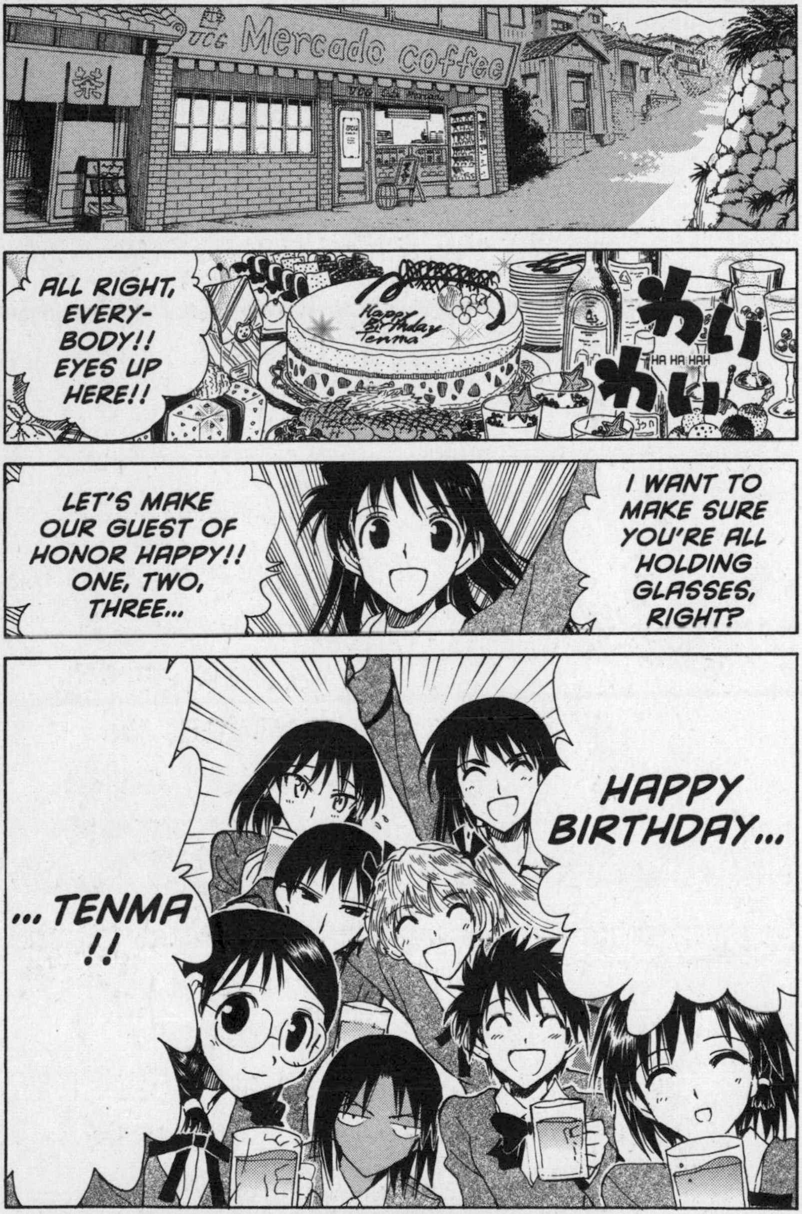
UCG Mercado coffee
わいわい
HA HA HAH
ALL RIGHT, EVERYBODY!! EYES UP HERE!!
Happy Birthday Tenma
I WANT TO MAKE SURE YOU'RE ALL HOLDING GLASSES, RIGHT?
LET'S MAKE OUR GUEST OF HONOR HAPPY!! ONE, TWO, THREE...
HAPPY BIRTHDAY...
...TENMA !!

#141 TELLING LIES IN AMERICA

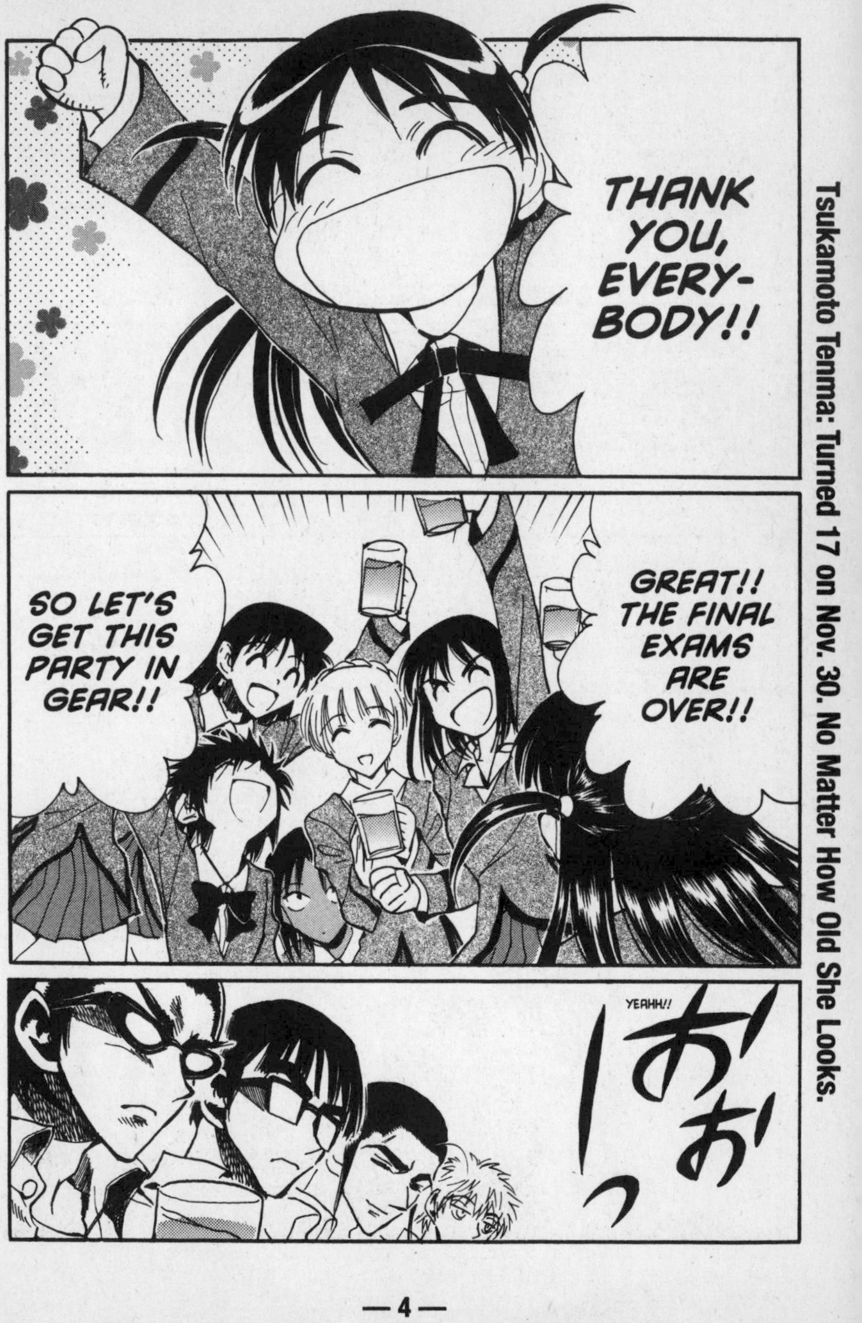
THANK YOU, EVERY-BODY!!
GREAT!! THE FINAL EXAMS ARE OVER!!
SO LET'S GET THIS PARTY IN GEAR!!
おおーっ
YEAHH!!

Tsukamoto Tenma: Turned 17 on Nov. 30. No Matter How Old She Looks.

Sawachika Eri: We Have Found a Weakness.

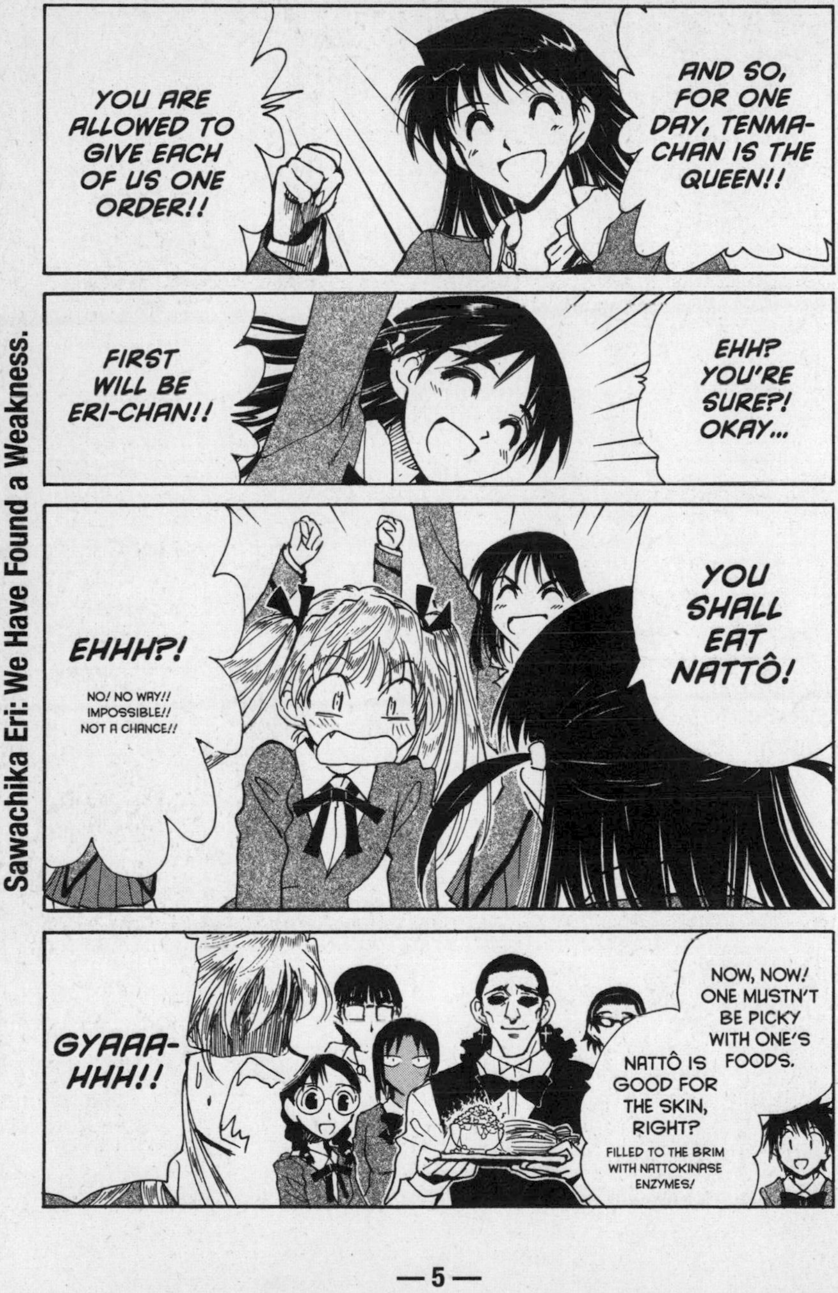
AND SO, FOR ONE DAY, TENMA-CHAN IS THE QUEEN!!
YOU ARE ALLOWED TO GIVE EACH OF US ONE ORDER!!
EHH? YOU'RE SURE?! OKAY...
FIRST WILL BE ERI-CHAN!!
YOU SHALL EAT NATTÔ!
EHHH?!
NO! NO WAY!! IMPOSSIBLE!! NOT A CHANCE!!
NOW, NOW! ONE MUSTN'T BE PICKY WITH ONE'S FOODS.
NATTÔ IS GOOD FOR THE SKIN, RIGHT?
FILLED TO THE BRIM WITH NATTOKINASE ENZYMES!
GYAAA-HHH!!

Sagano: Gets an Exemption as Master of Ceremonies.

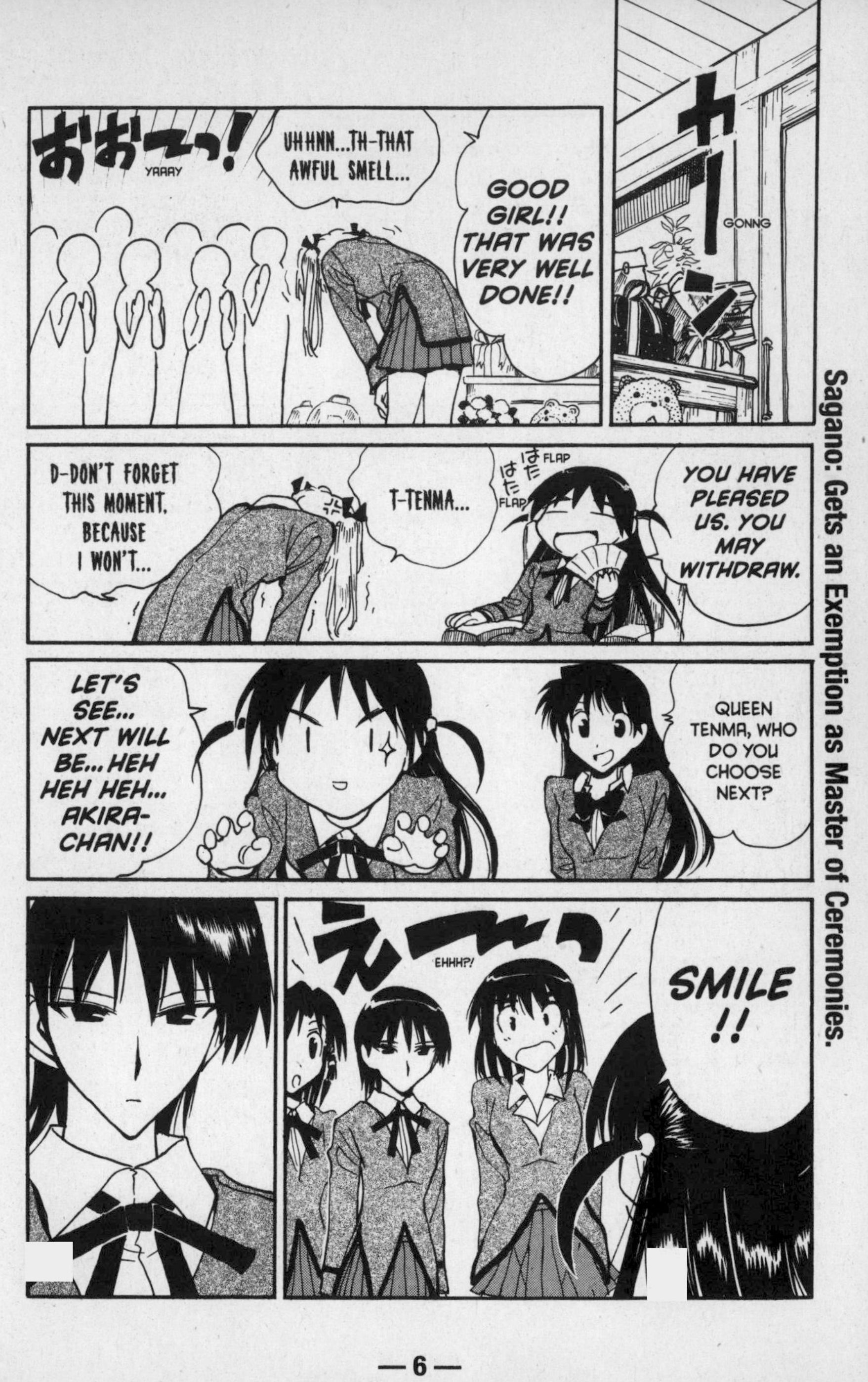
GONNG
GOOD GIRL!! THAT WAS VERY WELL DONE!!
UHHNN...TH-THAT AWFUL SMELL...
おおーっ!
YARRY
YOU HAVE PLEASED US. YOU MAY WITHDRAW.
はたはた
FLAP FLAP
T-TENMA...
D-DON'T FORGET THIS MOMENT, BECAUSE I WON'T...
QUEEN TENMA, WHO DO YOU CHOOSE NEXT?
LET'S SEE... NEXT WILL BE... HEH HEH HEH... AKIRA-CHAN!!
SMILE !!
えーっ
EHHH?!

Mikoto: Tenma's Elder by Four Months.

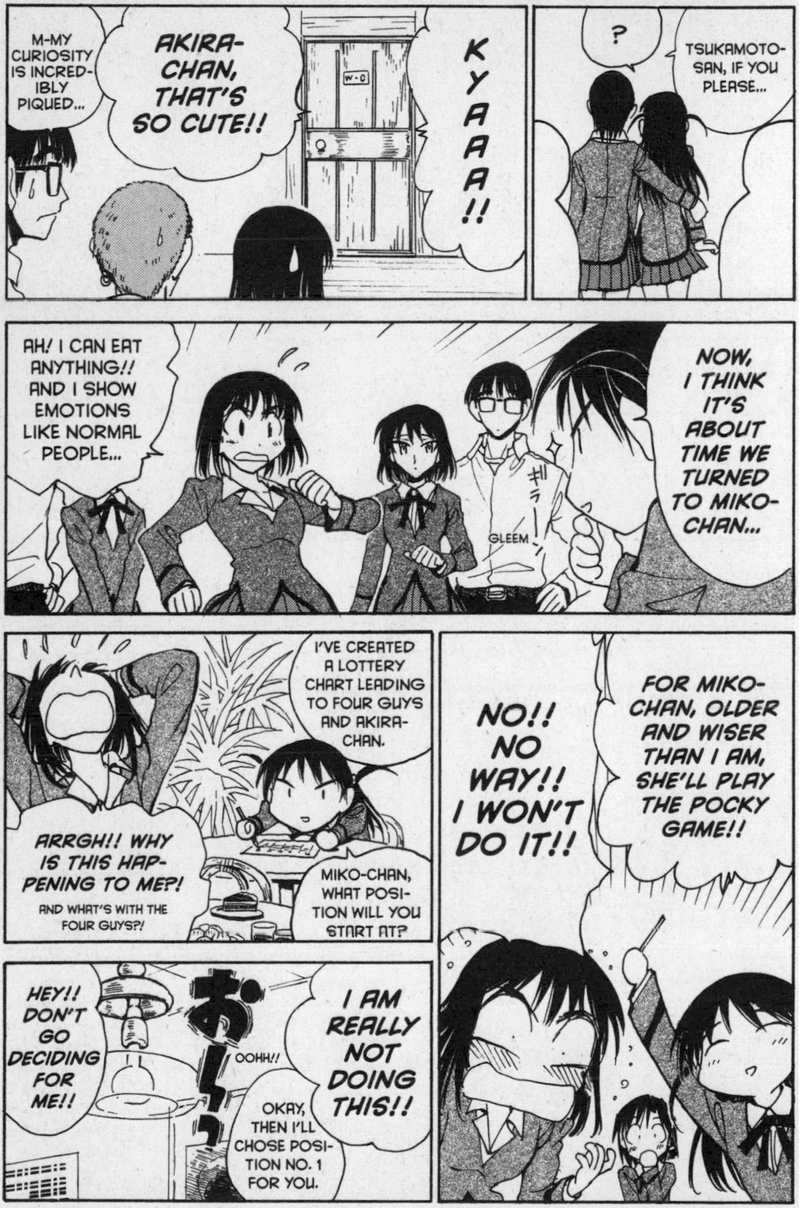
?
TSUKAMOTO-SAN, IF YOU PLEASE...
M-MY CURIOSITY IS INCREDIBLY PIQUED...
AKIRA-CHAN, THAT'S SO CUTE!!
KYAAAA!!
W·C
NOW, I THINK IT'S ABOUT TIME WE TURNED TO MIKO-CHAN...
GLEEM
AH! I CAN EAT ANYTHING!! AND I SHOW EMOTIONS LIKE NORMAL PEOPLE...
FOR MIKO-CHAN, OLDER AND WISER THAN I AM, SHE'LL PLAY THE POCKY GAME!!
NO!! NO WAY!! I WON'T DO IT!!
I'VE CREATED A LOTTERY CHART LEADING TO FOUR GUYS AND AKIRA-CHAN.
ARRGH!! WHY IS THIS HAPPENING TO ME?!
AND WHAT'S WITH THE FOUR GUYS?!
MIKO-CHAN, WHAT POSITION WILL YOU START AT?
I AM REALLY NOT DOING THIS!!
OOHH!!
HEY!! DON'T GO DECIDING FOR ME!!
OKAY, THEN I'LL CHOSE POSITION NO. 1 FOR YOU.

Sagano Megumi: Now on Friendlier Terms, So She Can Call Tenma "Tenma-chan."

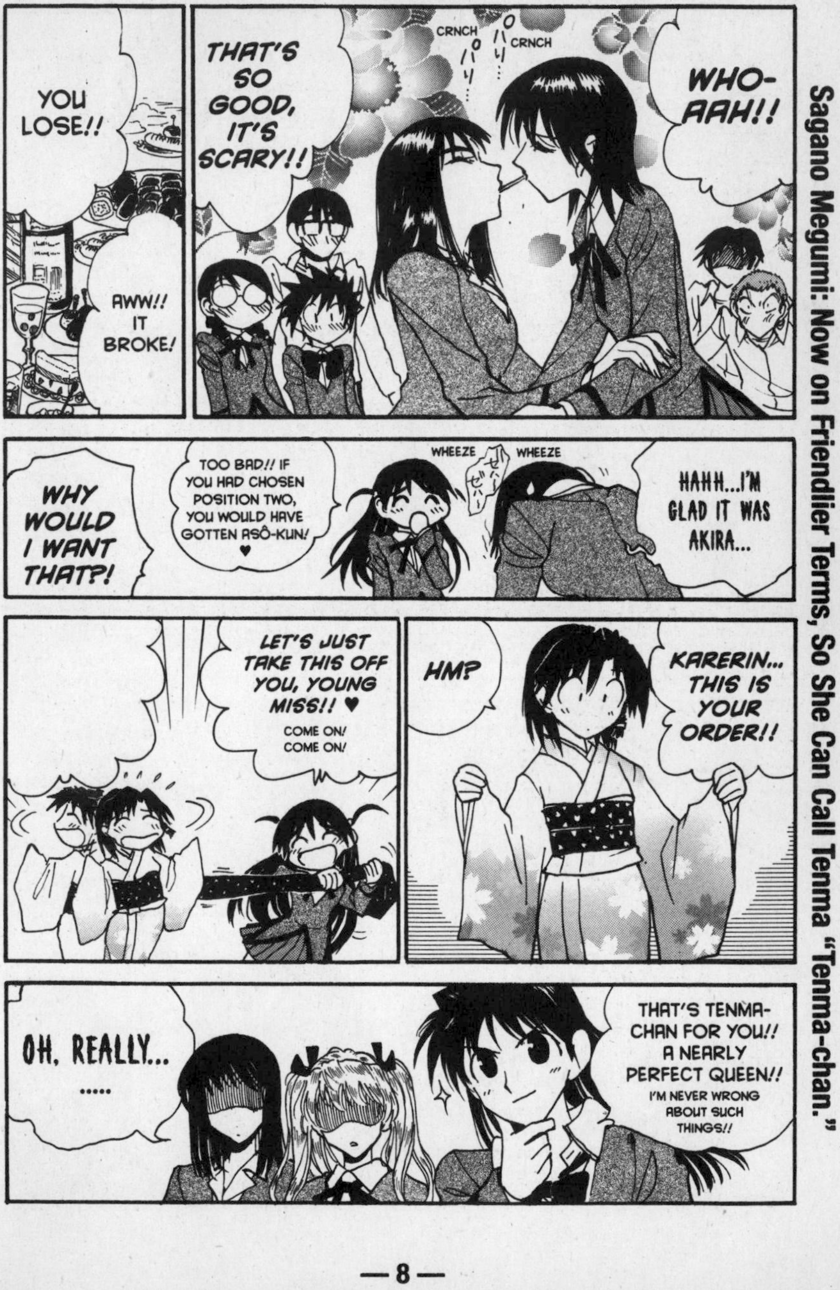
WHO-AAH!!
CRNCH
CRNCH
THAT'S SO GOOD, IT'S SCARY!!
YOU LOSE!!
AWW!! IT BROKE!
HAHH...I'M GLAD IT WAS AKIRA...
WHEEZE
WHEEZE
TOO BAD!! IF YOU HAD CHOSEN POSITION TWO, YOU WOULD HAVE GOTTEN ASÔ-KUN! ♥
WHY WOULD I WANT THAT?!
KARERIN... THIS IS YOUR ORDER!!
HM?
LET'S JUST TAKE THIS OFF YOU, YOUNG MISS!! ♥
COME ON! COME ON!
THAT'S TENMA-CHAN FOR YOU!! A NEARLY PERFECT QUEEN!!
I'M NEVER WRONG ABOUT SUCH THINGS!!
OH, REALLY...
.....

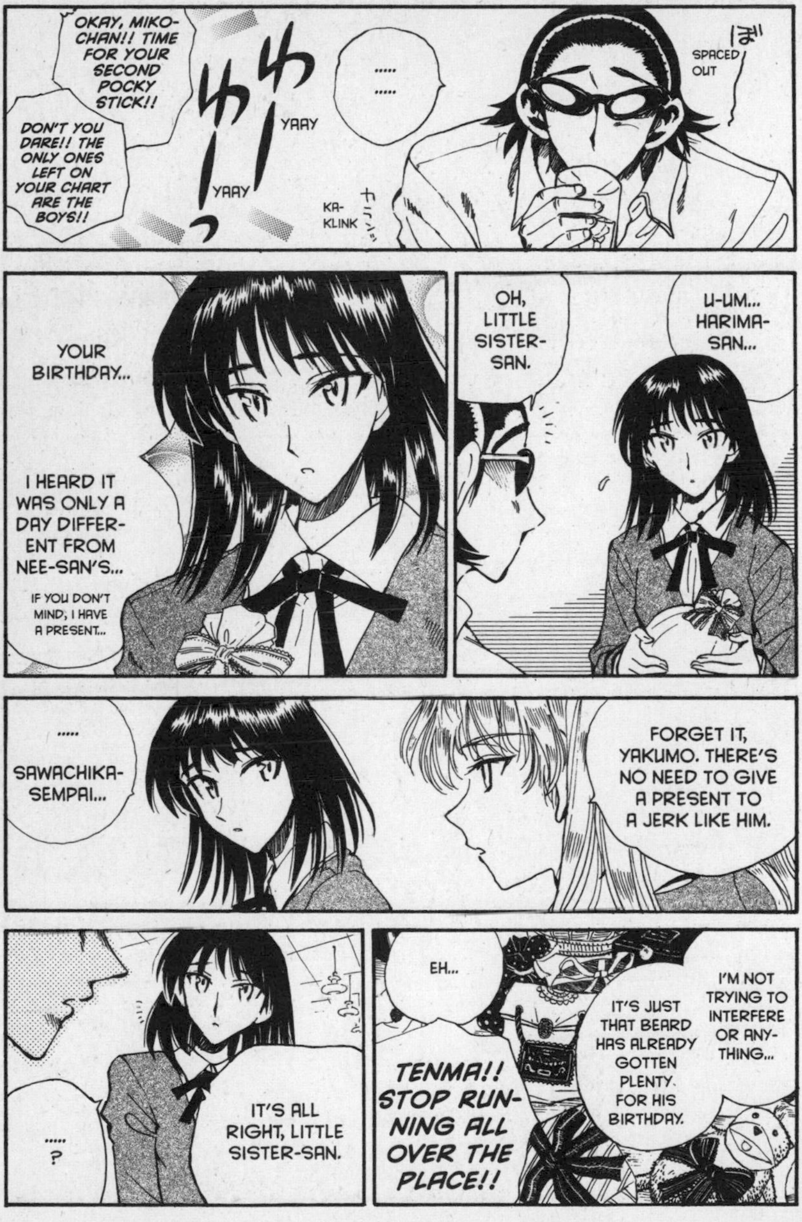
ぼ
SPACED OUT
....
YAAY
YAAY
KA-KLINK
OKAY, MIKO-CHAN!! TIME FOR YOUR SECOND POCKY STICK!!
DON'T YOU DARE!! THE ONLY ONES LEFT ON YOUR CHART ARE THE BOYS!!
U-UM... HARIMA-SAN...
OH, LITTLE SISTER-SAN.
YOUR BIRTHDAY...
I HEARD IT WAS ONLY A DAY DIFFER-ENT FROM NEE-SAN'S...
IF YOU DON'T MIND, I HAVE A PRESENT...
FORGET IT, YAKUMO. THERE'S NO NEED TO GIVE A PRESENT TO A JERK LIKE HIM.
..... SAWACHIKA-SEMPAI...
I'M NOT TRYING TO INTERFERE OR ANY-THING...
IT'S JUST THAT BEARD HAS ALREADY GOTTEN PLENTY. FOR HIS BIRTHDAY.
EH...
TENMA!! STOP RUN-NING ALL OVER THE PLACE!!
IT'S ALL RIGHT, LITTLE SISTER-SAN.
..... ?

Harima Kenji: On December 1, Turns 17 Years Old.

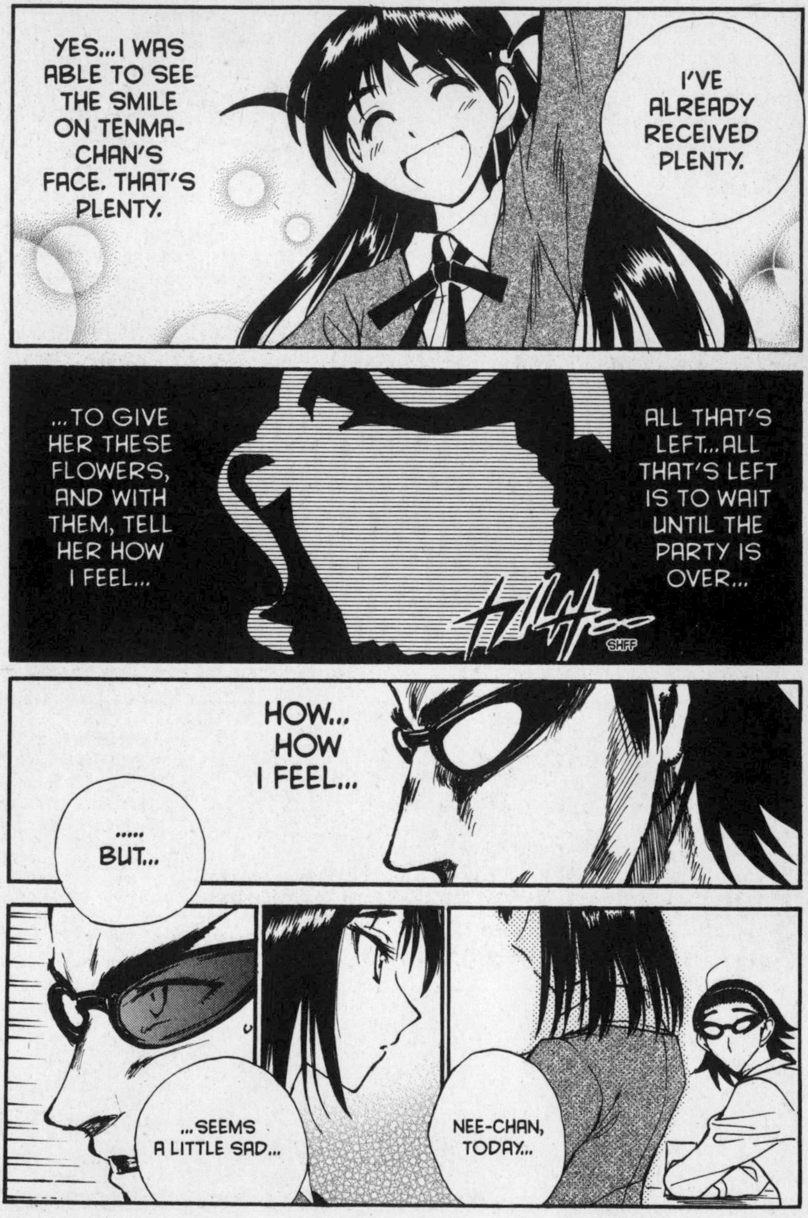
I'VE ALREADY RECEIVED PLENTY.
YES...I WAS ABLE TO SEE THE SMILE ON TENMA-CHAN'S FACE. THAT'S PLENTY.
ALL THAT'S LEFT...ALL THAT'S LEFT IS TO WAIT UNTIL THE PARTY IS OVER...
...TO GIVE HER THESE FLOWERS, AND WITH THEM, TELL HER HOW I FEEL...
SHFF
HOW... HOW I FEEL...
..... BUT...
NEE-CHAN, TODAY...
...SEEMS A LITTLE SAD...

Harima Kenji: Tries to Take One Step Toward Adulthood...

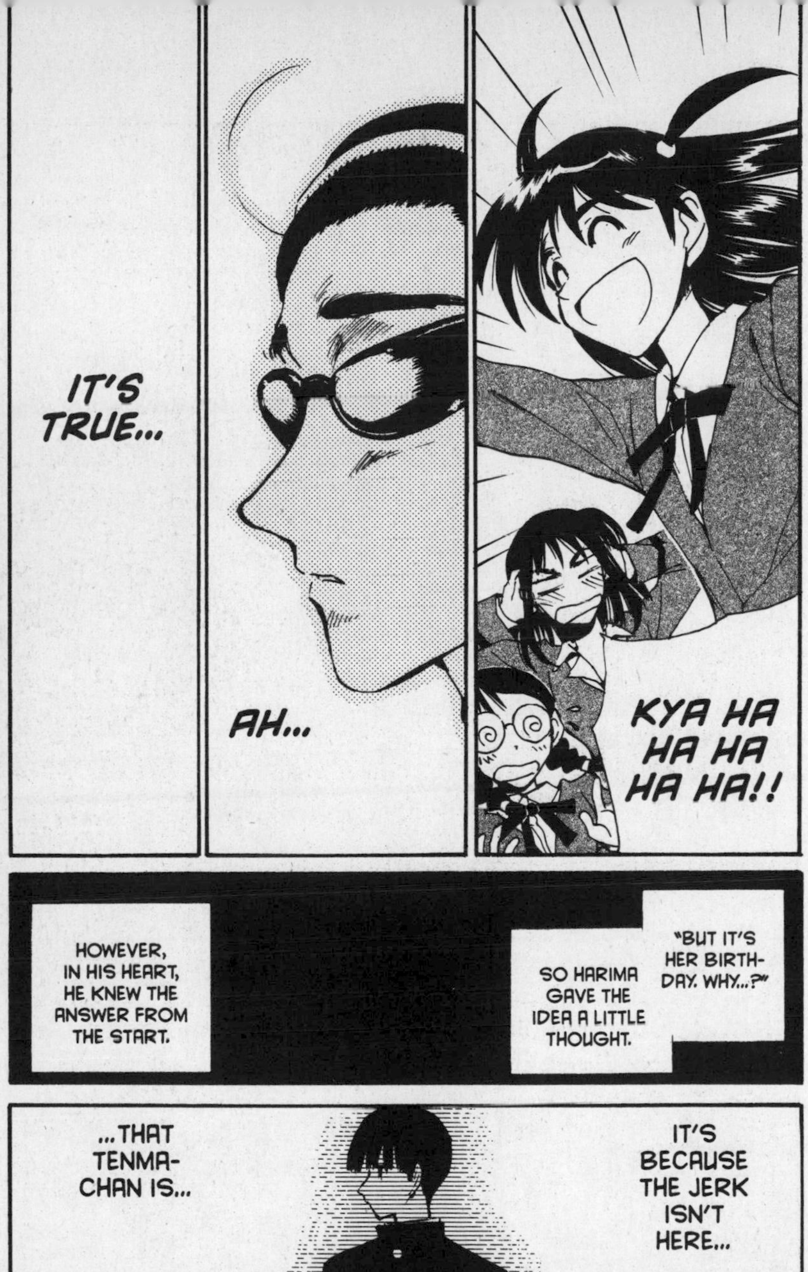
KYA HA HA HA HA HA!!
AH...
IT'S TRUE...
"BUT IT'S HER BIRTH-DAY. WHY...?"
SO HARIMA GAVE THE IDEA A LITTLE THOUGHT.
HOWEVER, IN HIS HEART, HE KNEW THE ANSWER FROM THE START.
IT'S BECAUSE THE JERK ISN'T HERE...
...THAT TENMA-CHAN IS...

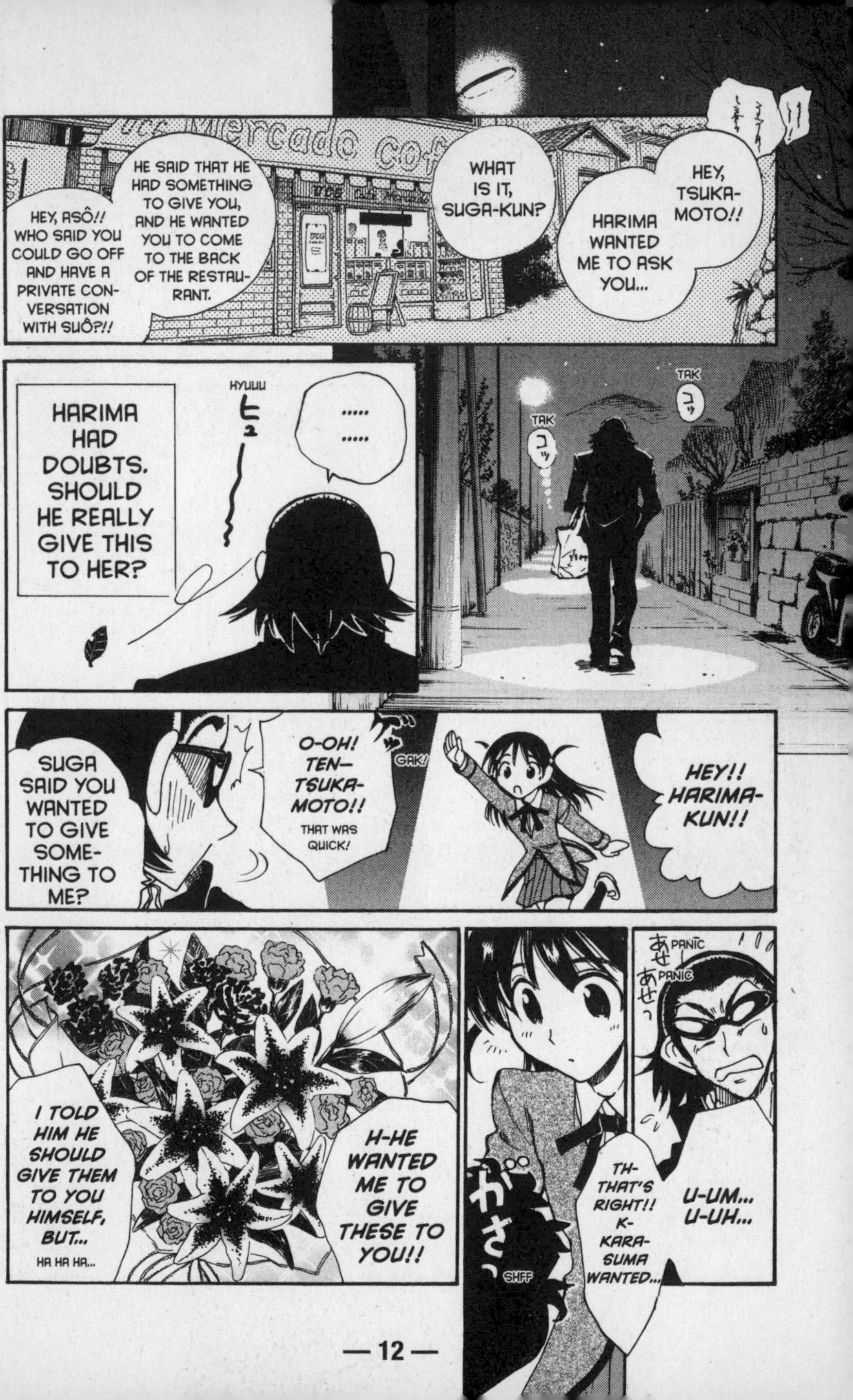
HEY, TSUKA-MOTO!!
HARIMA WANTED ME TO ASK YOU...
WHAT IS IT, SUGA-KUN?
HE SAID THAT HE HAD SOMETHING TO GIVE YOU, AND HE WANTED YOU TO COME TO THE BACK OF THE RESTAU-RANT.
HEY, ASÔ!! WHO SAID YOU COULD GO OFF AND HAVE A PRIVATE CON-VERSATION WITH SUÔ?!!
TAK
コッ
TAK
コッ
......
......
HYUUU
ヒュ
HARIMA HAD DOUBTS. SHOULD HE REALLY GIVE THIS TO HER?
HEY!! HARIMA-KUN!!
GAK!
O-OH! TEN— TSUKA-MOTO!!
THAT WAS QUICK!
SUGA SAID YOU WANTED TO GIVE SOME-THING TO ME?
あせ
PANIC
あせっ
PANIC
U-UM... U-UH...
TH-THAT'S RIGHT!! K-KARA-SUMA WANTED...
かさっ
SHFF
H-HE WANTED ME TO GIVE THESE TO YOU!!
I TOLD HIM HE SHOULD GIVE THEM TO YOU HIMSELF, BUT...
HA HA HA...

Karasuma Is Spelled with the Kanji for "Raven," Not "Bird."

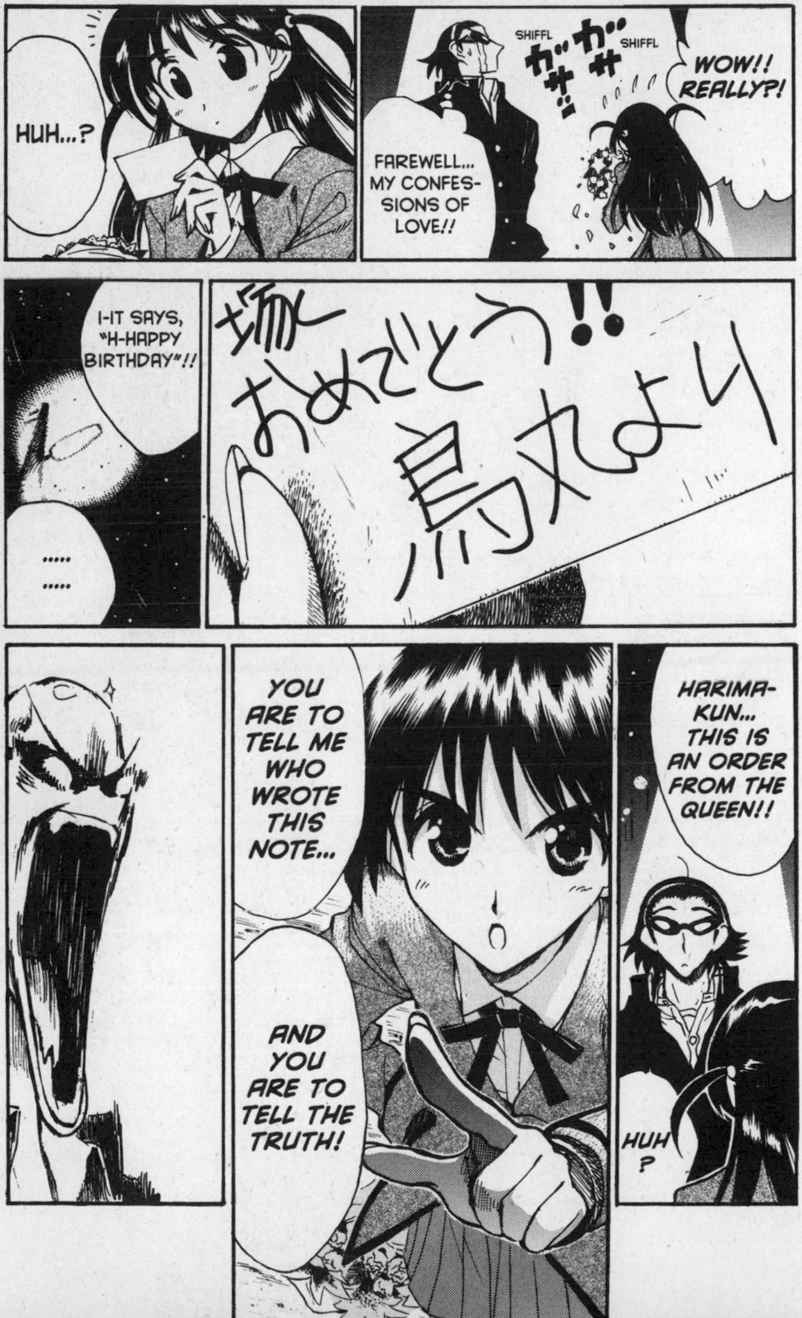
SHIFFL
ガサ
ガサ
SHIFFL
WOW!! REALLY?!
FAREWELL... MY CONFES-SIONS OF LOVE!!
HUH...?
おめでとう!!
鳥丸より
I-IT SAYS, "H-HAPPY BIRTHDAY"!!
.....
.....
HARIMA-KUN... THIS IS AN ORDER FROM THE QUEEN!!
HUH ?
YOU ARE TO TELL ME WHO WROTE THIS NOTE...
AND YOU ARE TO TELL THE TRUTH!

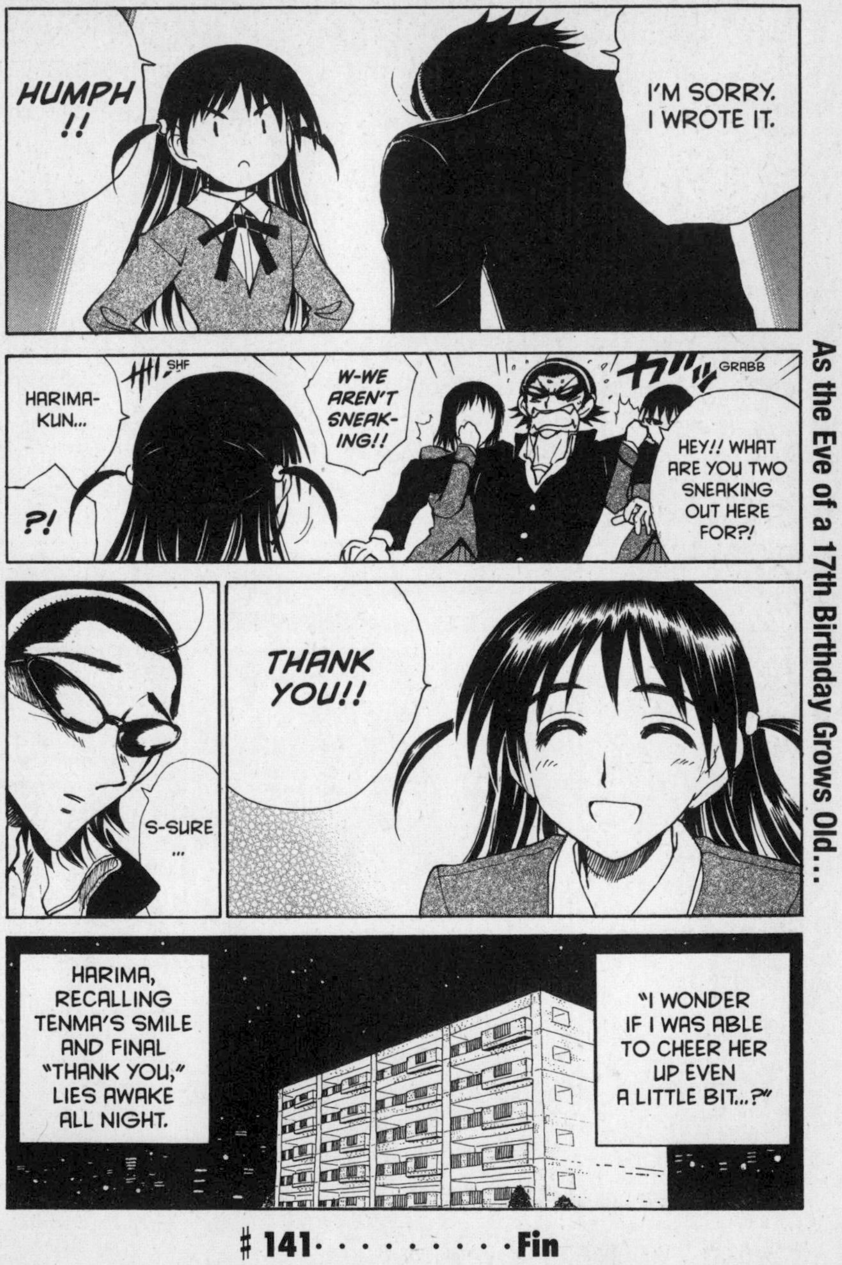
I'M SORRY. I WROTE IT.
HUMPH !!
GRABB
HEY!! WHAT ARE YOU TWO SNEAKING OUT HERE FOR?!
W-WE AREN'T SNEAK-ING!!
SHF
HARIMA-KUN...
?!
THANK YOU!!
S-SURE ...
"I WONDER IF I WAS ABLE TO CHEER HER UP EVEN A LITTLE BIT...?"
HARIMA, RECALLING TENMA'S SMILE AND FINAL "THANK YOU," LIES AWAKE ALL NIGHT.

As the Eve of a 17th Birthday Grows Old...

 # 141· · · · · · · · ·Fin

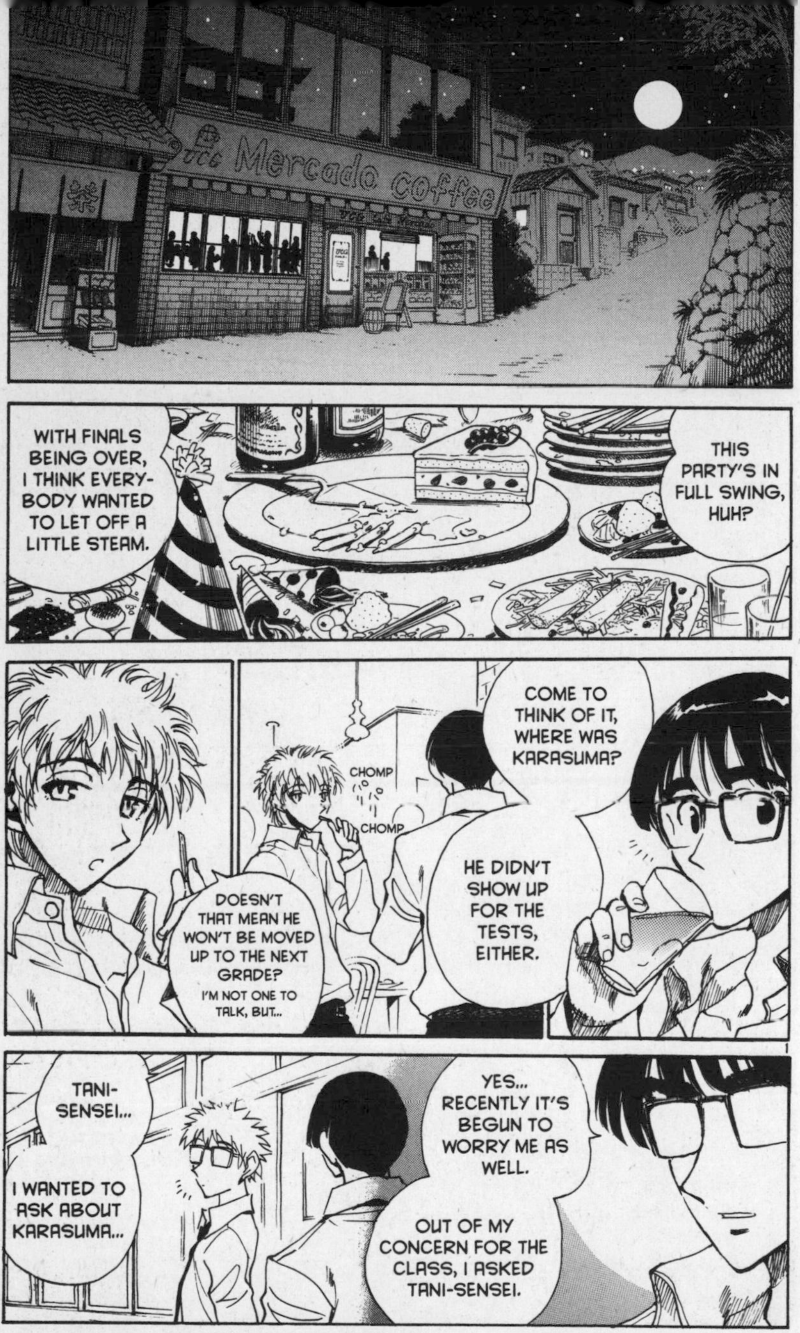
Mercado coffee
THIS PARTY'S IN FULL SWING, HUH?
WITH FINALS BEING OVER, I THINK EVERY-BODY WANTED TO LET OFF A LITTLE STEAM.
COME TO THINK OF IT, WHERE WAS KARASUMA?
HE DIDN'T SHOW UP FOR THE TESTS, EITHER.
CHOMP
CHOMP
DOESN'T THAT MEAN HE WON'T BE MOVED UP TO THE NEXT GRADE?
I'M NOT ONE TO TALK, BUT...
YES... RECENTLY IT'S BEGUN TO WORRY ME AS WELL.
OUT OF MY CONCERN FOR THE CLASS, I ASKED TANI-SENSEI.
TANI-SENSEI...
I WANTED TO ASK ABOUT KARASUMA...

#142 MONKEY BUSINESS

Hanai Haruki: His Responsibility as Class Representative.

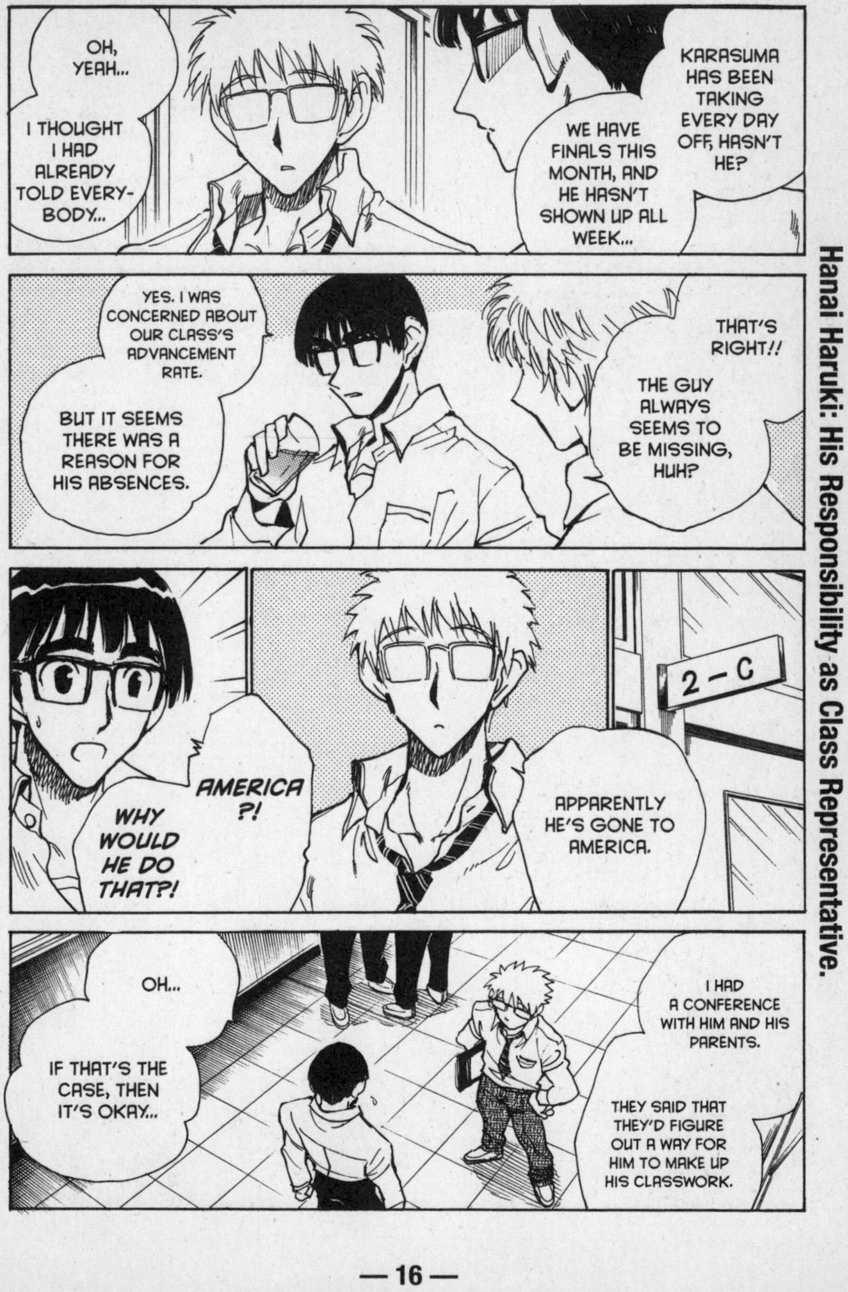
KARASUMA HAS BEEN TAKING EVERY DAY OFF, HASN'T HE?
WE HAVE FINALS THIS MONTH, AND HE HASN'T SHOWN UP ALL WEEK...
OH, YEAH...
I THOUGHT I HAD ALREADY TOLD EVERY-BODY...
THAT'S RIGHT!!
THE GUY ALWAYS SEEMS TO BE MISSING, HUH?
YES. I WAS CONCERNED ABOUT OUR CLASS'S ADVANCEMENT RATE.
BUT IT SEEMS THERE WAS A REASON FOR HIS ABSENCES.
2 – C
APPARENTLY HE'S GONE TO AMERICA.
AMERICA?!
WHY WOULD HE DO THAT?!
I HAD A CONFERENCE WITH HIM AND HIS PARENTS.
THEY SAID THAT THEY'D FIGURE OUT A WAY FOR HIM TO MAKE UP HIS CLASSWORK.
OH...
IF THAT'S THE CASE, THEN IT'S OKAY...

Karasuma Ōji: Transfers Away in March. Just to Remind You.

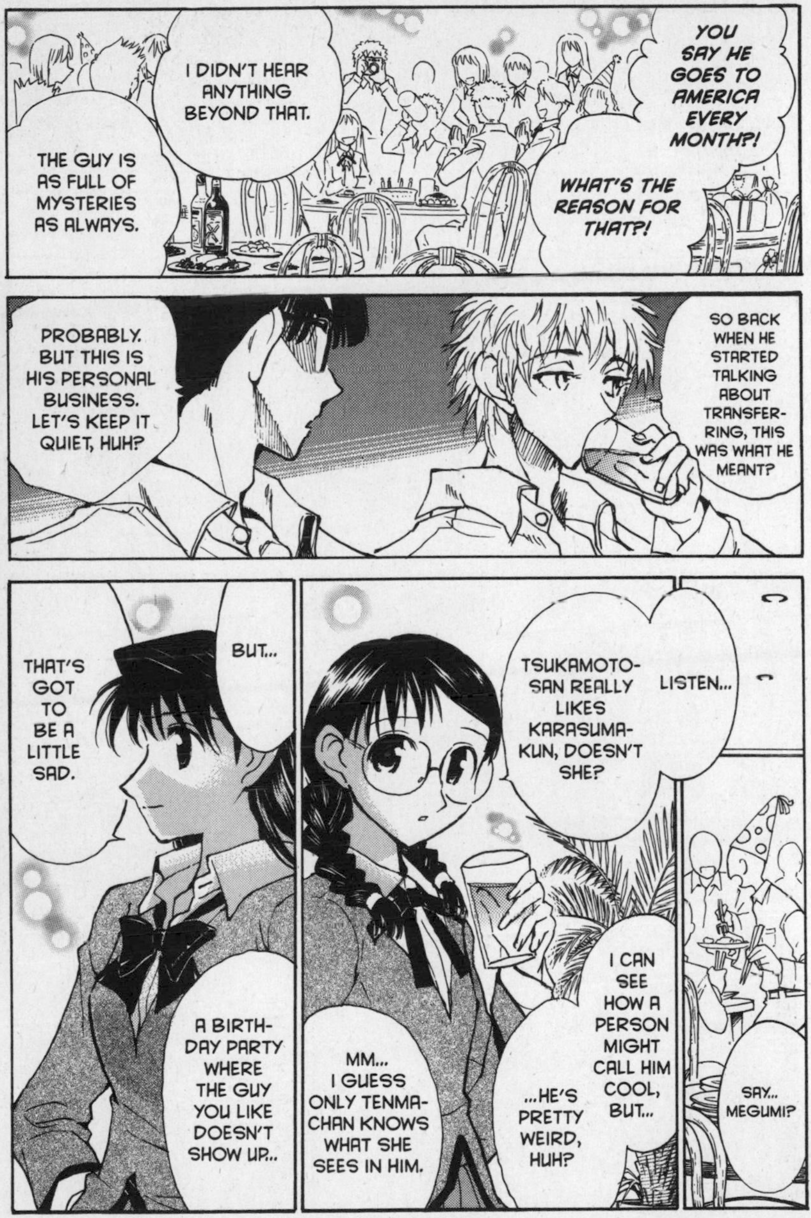
YOU SAY HE GOES TO AMERICA EVERY MONTH?!
WHAT'S THE REASON FOR THAT?!
I DIDN'T HEAR ANYTHING BEYOND THAT.
THE GUY IS AS FULL OF MYSTERIES AS ALWAYS.
SO BACK WHEN HE STARTED TALKING ABOUT TRANSFERRING, THIS WAS WHAT HE MEANT?
PROBABLY. BUT THIS IS HIS PERSONAL BUSINESS. LET'S KEEP IT QUIET, HUH?
SAY... MEGUMI?
LISTEN...
TSUKAMOTO-SAN REALLY LIKES KARASUMA-KUN, DOESN'T SHE?
I CAN SEE HOW A PERSON MIGHT CALL HIM COOL, BUT...
...HE'S PRETTY WEIRD, HUH?
MM... I GUESS ONLY TENMA-CHAN KNOWS WHAT SHE SEES IN HIM.
BUT...
THAT'S GOT TO BE A LITTLE SAD.
A BIRTHDAY PARTY WHERE THE GUY YOU LIKE DOESN'T SHOW UP...

Harima: Made a Stop at Home, and Came Back to the Party.

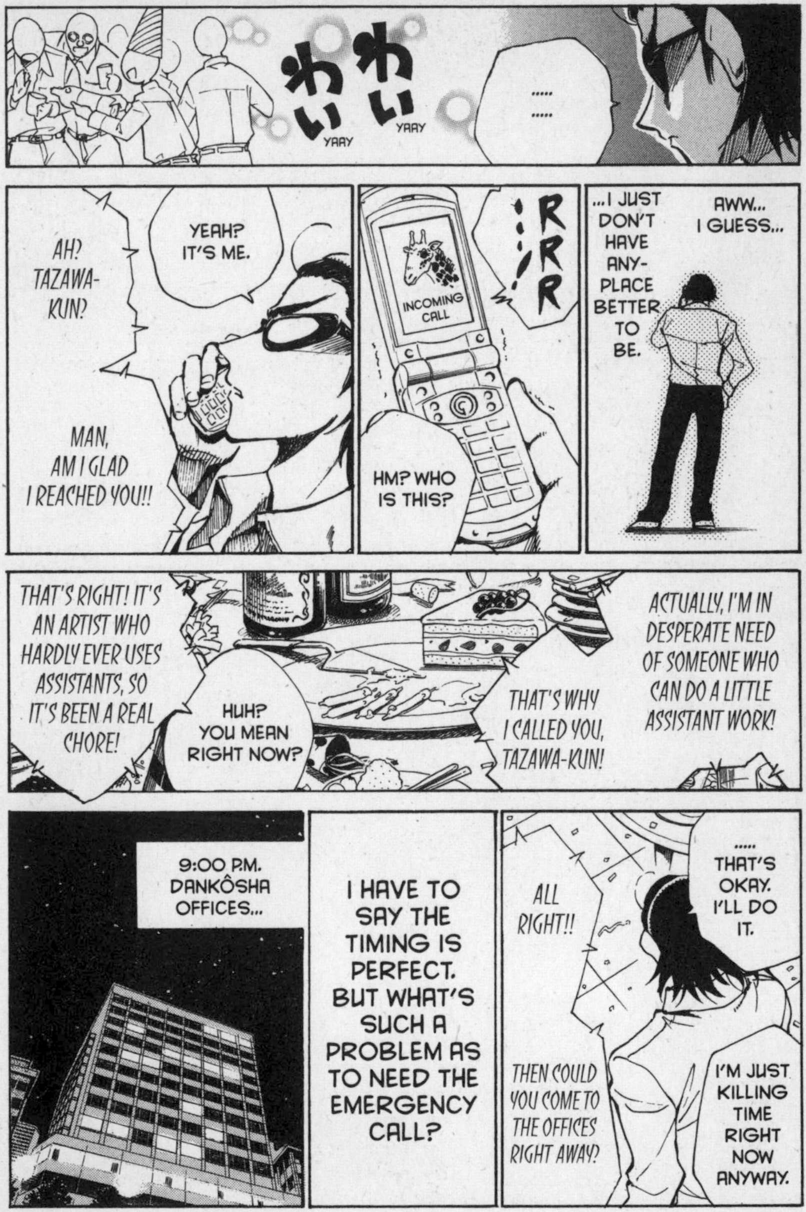
.....
.....
わいわい
YAAY
YAAY
AWW... I GUESS...
...I JUST DON'T HAVE ANY-PLACE BETTER TO BE.
RRR
!!
INCOMING CALL
HM? WHO IS THIS?
YEAH? IT'S ME.
AH? TAZAWA-KUN?
MAN, AM I GLAD I REACHED YOU!!
ACTUALLY, I'M IN DESPERATE NEED OF SOMEONE WHO CAN DO A LITTLE ASSISTANT WORK!
THAT'S WHY I CALLED YOU, TAZAWA-KUN!
HUH? YOU MEAN RIGHT NOW?
THAT'S RIGHT! IT'S AN ARTIST WHO HARDLY EVER USES ASSISTANTS, SO IT'S BEEN A REAL CHORE!
..... THAT'S OKAY. I'LL DO IT.
ALL RIGHT!!
I'M JUST KILLING TIME RIGHT NOW ANYWAY.
THEN COULD YOU COME TO THE OFFICES RIGHT AWAY?
I HAVE TO SAY THE TIMING IS PERFECT. BUT WHAT'S SUCH A PROBLEM AS TO NEED THE EMERGENCY CALL?
9:00 P.M. DANKÔSHA OFFICES...

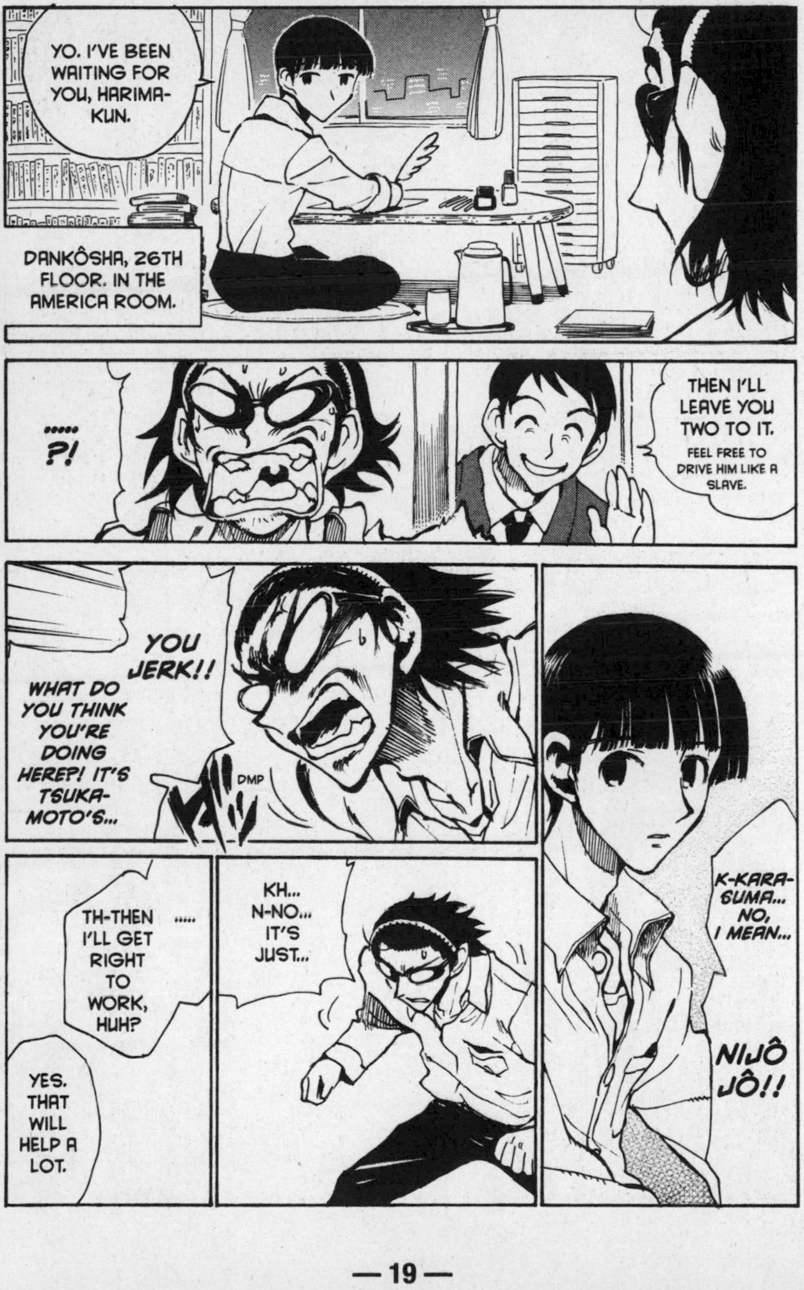
YO. I'VE BEEN WAITING FOR YOU, HARIMA-KUN.
DANKÔSHA, 26TH FLOOR. IN THE AMERICA ROOM.
THEN I'LL LEAVE YOU TWO TO IT.
FEEL FREE TO DRIVE HIM LIKE A SLAVE.
.....
?!
K-KARASUMA... NO, I MEAN...
NIJÔ JÔ!!
YOU JERK!!
WHAT DO YOU THINK YOU'RE DOING HERE?! IT'S TSUKAMOTO'S...
DMP
KH... N-NO... IT'S JUST...
TH-THEN I'LL GET RIGHT TO WORK, HUH?
.....
YES. THAT WILL HELP A LOT.

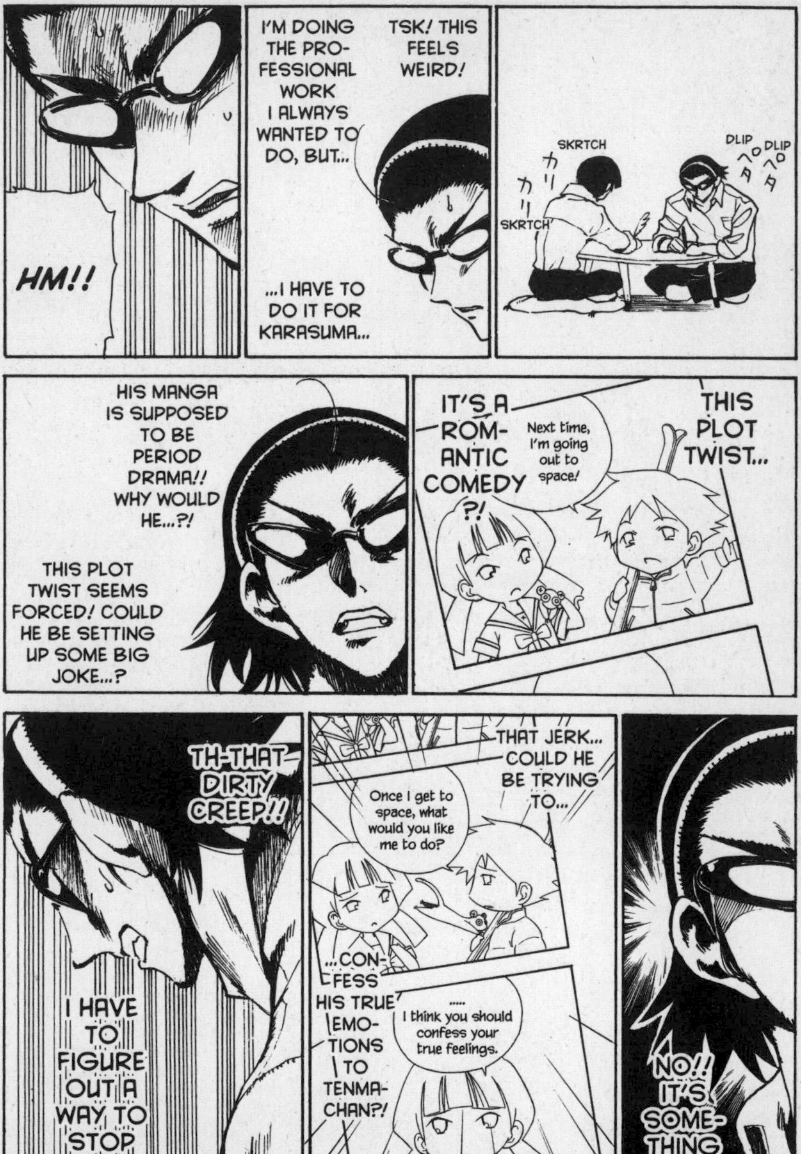

DLIP DLIP
SKRTCH
SKRTCH
TSK! THIS FEELS WEIRD!
I'M DOING THE PRO-FESSIONAL WORK I ALWAYS WANTED TO DO, BUT...
...I HAVE TO DO IT FOR KARASUMA...
HM!!
THIS PLOT TWIST...
IT'S A ROM-ANTIC COMEDY?!
Next time, I'm going out to space!
HIS MANGA IS SUPPOSED TO BE PERIOD DRAMA!! WHY WOULD HE...?!
THIS PLOT TWIST SEEMS FORCED! COULD HE BE SETTING UP SOME BIG JOKE...?
NO!! IT'S SOME-THING ELSE!!
THAT JERK... COULD HE BE TRYING TO...
Once I get to space, what would you like me to do?
..... I think you should confess your true feelings.
...CON-FESS HIS TRUE EMO-TIONS TO TENMA-CHAN?!
TH-THAT DIRTY CREEP!!
I HAVE TO FIGURE OUT A WAY TO STOP HIM!!

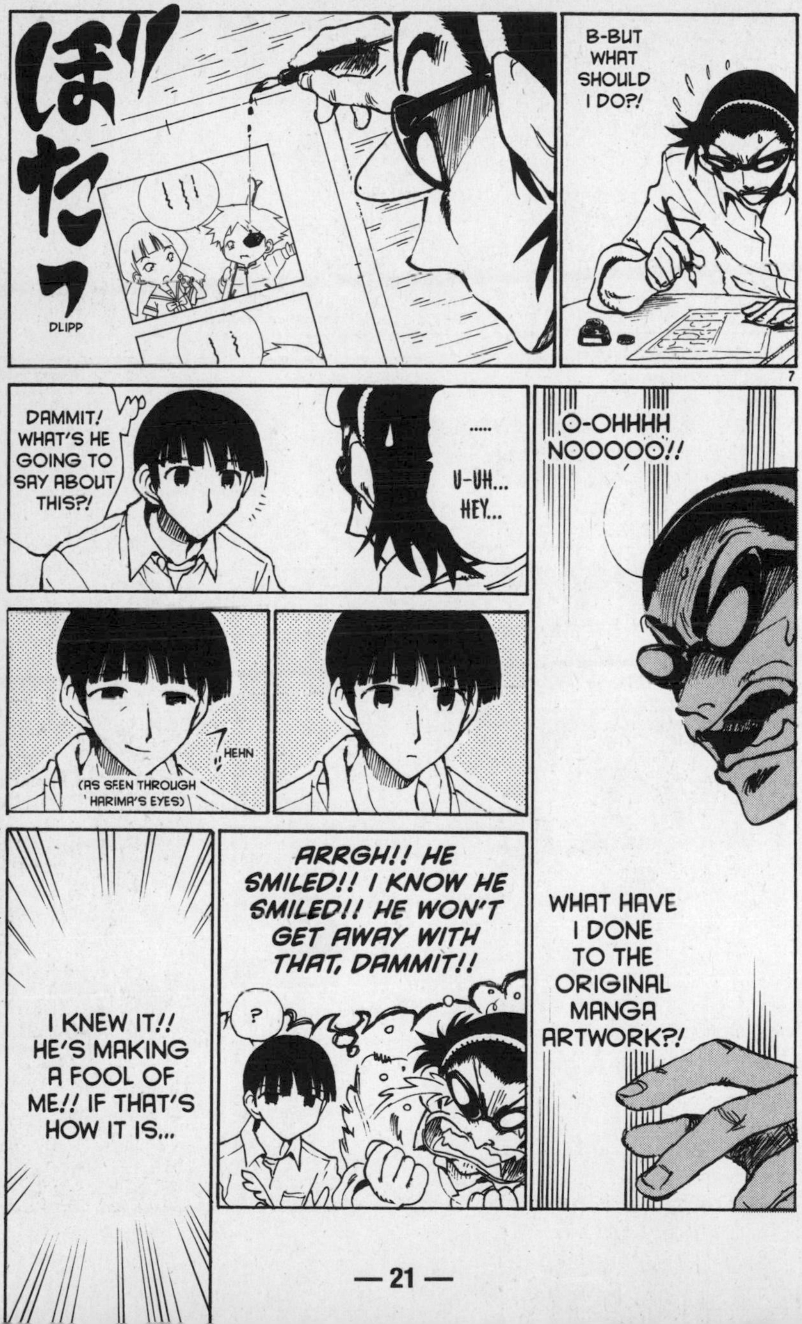
B-BUT WHAT SHOULD I DO?!
ぽたっ
DLIPP
O-OHHHH NOOOOO!!
WHAT HAVE I DONE TO THE ORIGINAL MANGA ARTWORK?!
.....
U-UH... HEY...
DAMMIT! WHAT'S HE GOING TO SAY ABOUT THIS?!
HEHN
(AS SEEN THROUGH HARIMA'S EYES)
ARRGH!! HE SMILED!! I KNOW HE SMILED!! HE WON'T GET AWAY WITH THAT, DAMMIT!!
?
I KNEW IT!! HE'S MAKING A FOOL OF ME!! IF THAT'S HOW IT IS...

Harima Kenji: Thinks "Gonna" Makes a Person Cool.

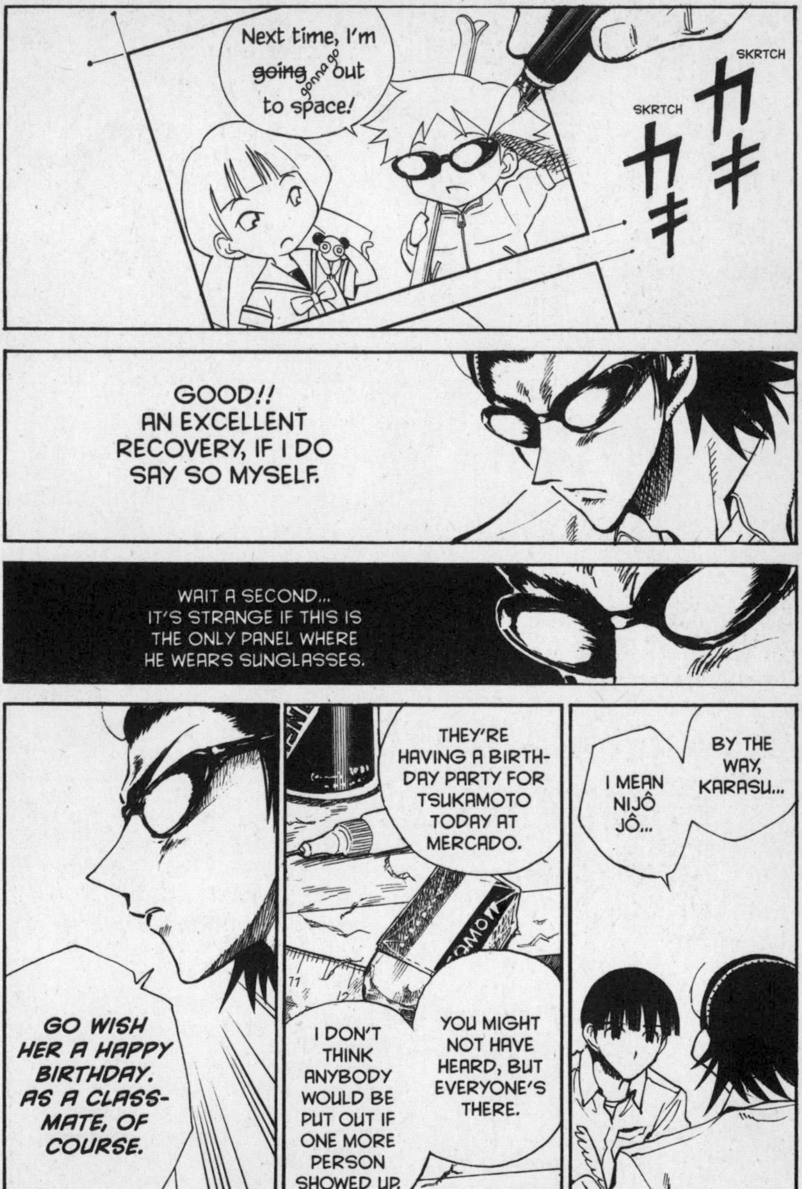
カキ SKRTCH
カキ SKRTCH
Next time, I'm ~~going~~ gonna go out to space!
GOOD!! AN EXCELLENT RECOVERY, IF I DO SAY SO MYSELF.
WAIT A SECOND... IT'S STRANGE IF THIS IS THE ONLY PANEL WHERE HE WEARS SUNGLASSES.
BY THE WAY, KARASU...
I MEAN NIJÔ JÔ...
THEY'RE HAVING A BIRTH-DAY PARTY FOR TSUKAMOTO TODAY AT MERCADO.
YOU MIGHT NOT HAVE HEARD, BUT EVERYONE'S THERE.
I DON'T THINK ANYBODY WOULD BE PUT OUT IF ONE MORE PERSON SHOWED UP.
GO WISH HER A HAPPY BIRTHDAY. AS A CLASS-MATE, OF COURSE.

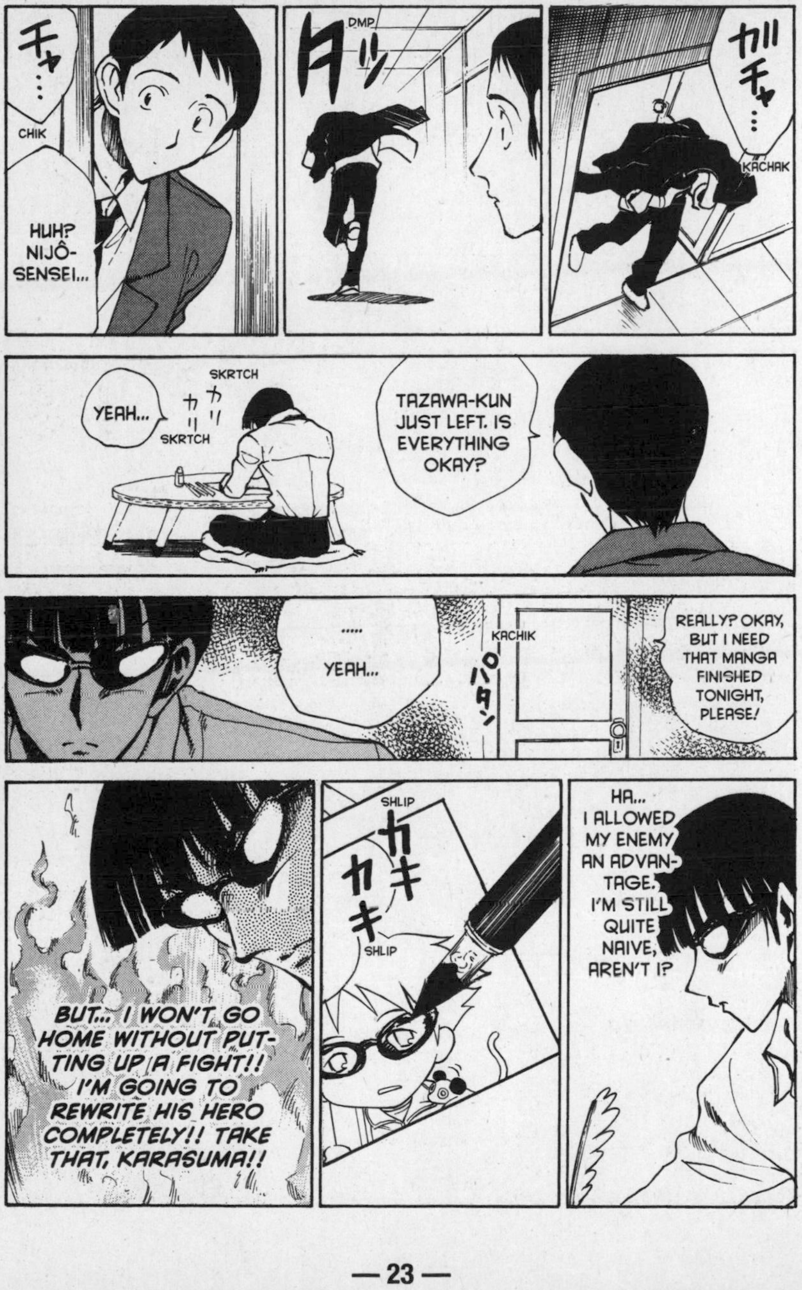
ガチャ…
KACHAK
タッ
DMP
チャ…
CHIK
HUH? NIJÔ-SENSEI...
TAZAWA-KUN JUST LEFT. IS EVERYTHING OKAY?
カリカリ
SKRTCH
SKRTCH
YEAH...
REALLY? OKAY, BUT I NEED THAT MANGA FINISHED TONIGHT, PLEASE!
パタン
KACHIK
..... YEAH...
HA... I ALLOWED MY ENEMY AN ADVANTAGE. I'M STILL QUITE NAIVE, AREN'T I?
カキカキ
SHLIP
SHLIP
BUT... I WON'T GO HOME WITHOUT PUTTING UP A FIGHT!! I'M GOING TO REWRITE HIS HERO COMPLETELY!! TAKE THAT, KARASUMA!!

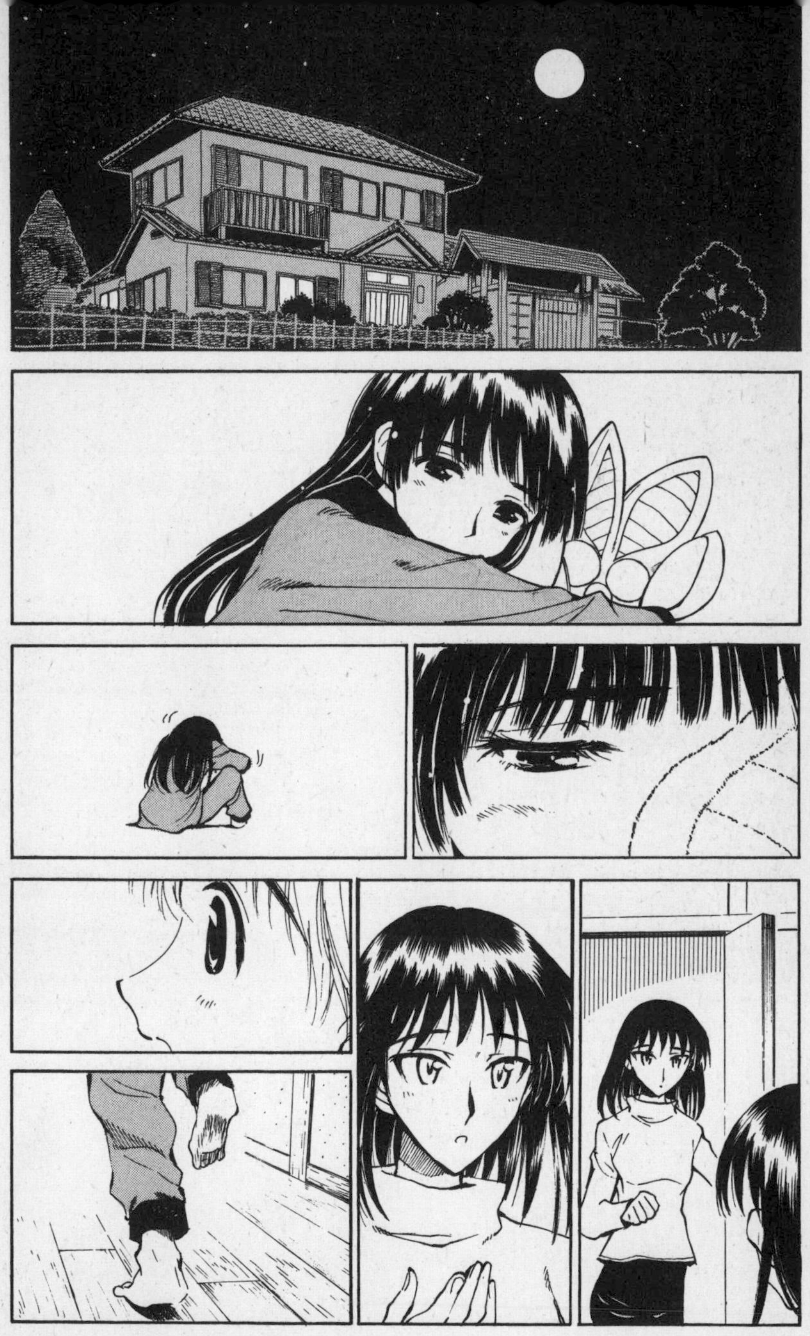

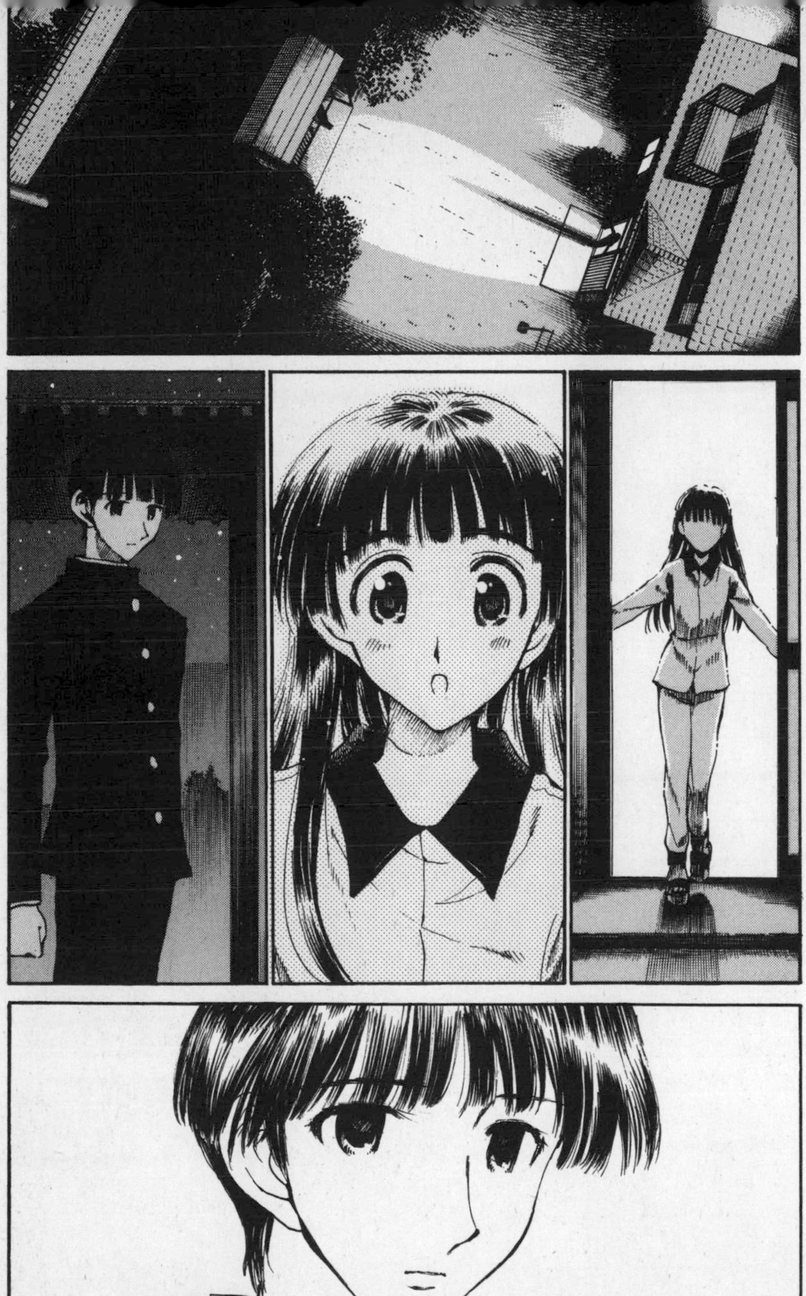

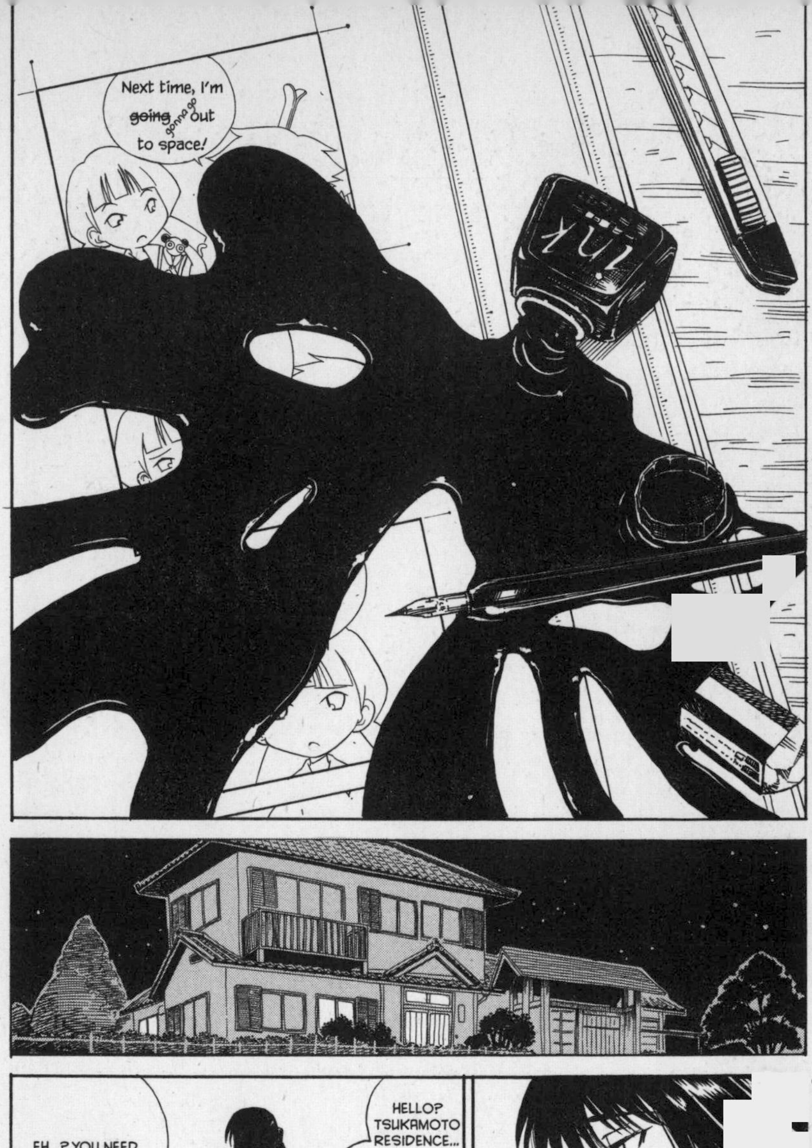
Next time, I'm ~~going~~ gonna go out to space!
ink
THAT'S GREAT FOR YOU, NEE-SAN...
ジリリーン
RRINNG
HELLO? TSUKAMOTO RESIDENCE...
AH... HARIMA-SAN...
EH...? YOU NEED HELP RIGHT AWAY...?

Meanwhile, What's Going on at the Office?!

 # 142· · · · · · · · ·Fin

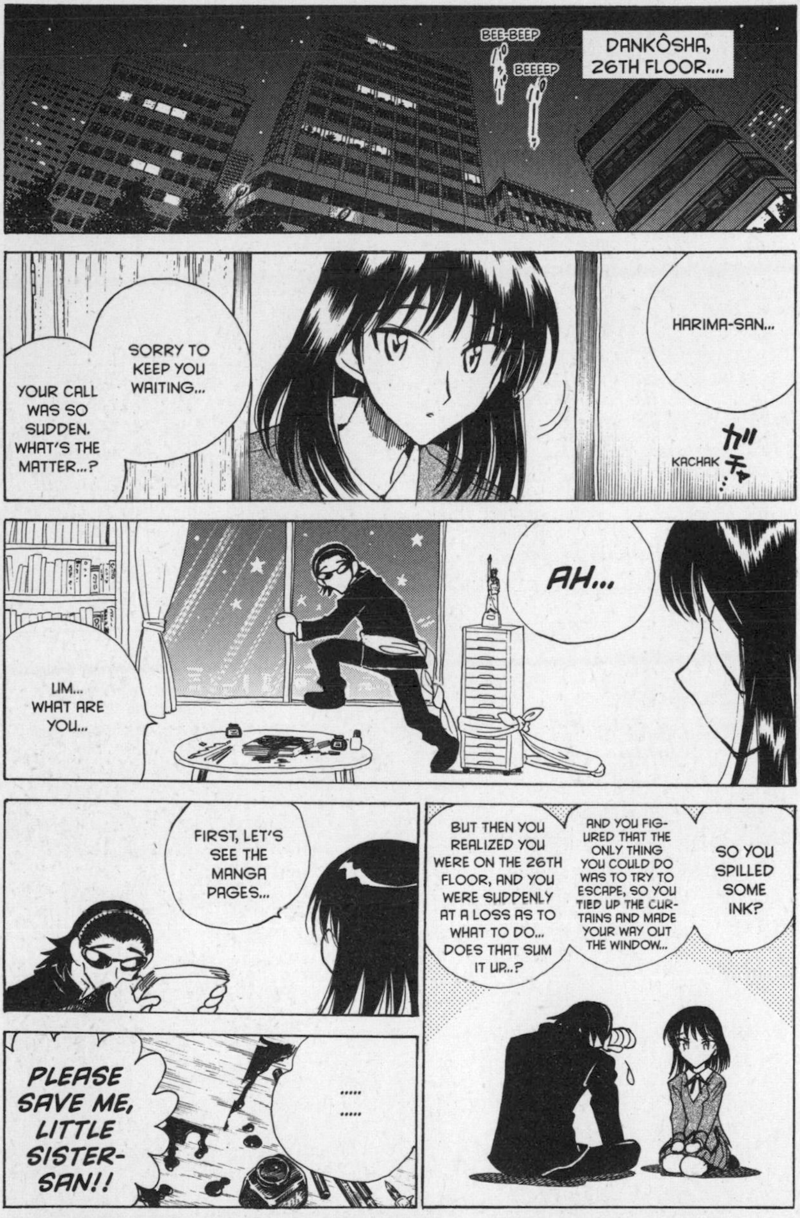
DANKÔSHA, 26TH FLOOR....
BEE-BEEP
BEEEEP
HARIMA-SAN...
KACHAK
SORRY TO KEEP YOU WAITING...
YOUR CALL WAS SO SUDDEN. WHAT'S THE MATTER...?
AH...
UM... WHAT ARE YOU...
SO YOU SPILLED SOME INK?
AND YOU FIGURED THAT THE ONLY THING YOU COULD DO WAS TO TRY TO ESCAPE, SO YOU TIED UP THE CURTAINS AND MADE YOUR WAY OUT THE WINDOW...
BUT THEN YOU REALIZED YOU WERE ON THE 26TH FLOOR, AND YOU WERE SUDDENLY AT A LOSS AS TO WHAT TO DO... DOES THAT SUM IT UP...?
FIRST, LET'S SEE THE MANGA PAGES...
....
PLEASE SAVE ME, LITTLE SISTER-SAN!!

143 SOUL OF A PAINTER

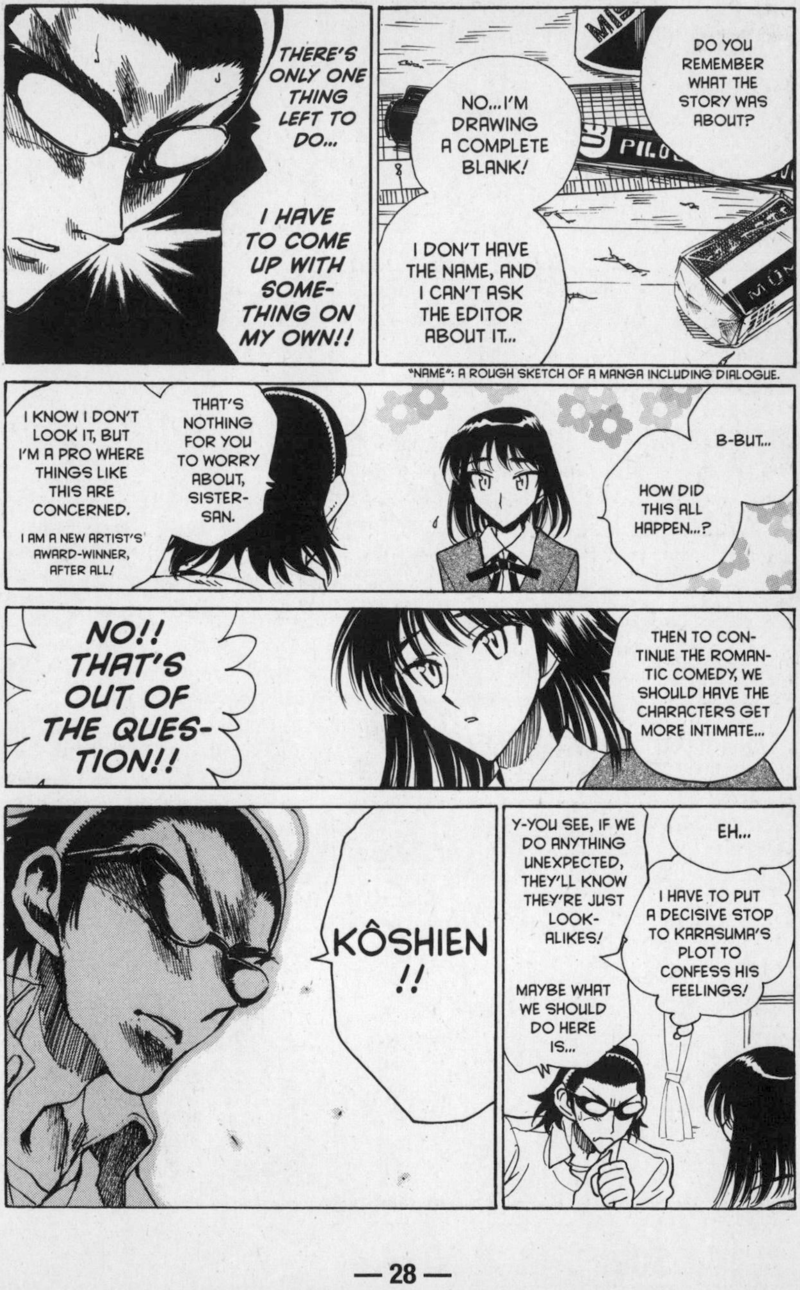
DO YOU REMEMBER WHAT THE STORY WAS ABOUT?
NO...I'M DRAWING A COMPLETE BLANK!
I DON'T HAVE THE NAME, AND I CAN'T ASK THE EDITOR ABOUT IT...
THERE'S ONLY ONE THING LEFT TO DO...
I HAVE TO COME UP WITH SOME-THING ON MY OWN!!
"NAME": A ROUGH SKETCH OF A MANGA INCLUDING DIALOGUE.
B-BUT...
HOW DID THIS ALL HAPPEN...?
THAT'S NOTHING FOR YOU TO WORRY ABOUT, SISTER-SAN.
I KNOW I DON'T LOOK IT, BUT I'M A PRO WHERE THINGS LIKE THIS ARE CONCERNED.
I AM A NEW ARTIST'S AWARD-WINNER, AFTER ALL!
THEN TO CON-TINUE THE ROMAN-TIC COMEDY, WE SHOULD HAVE THE CHARACTERS GET MORE INTIMATE...
NO!! THAT'S OUT OF THE QUES-TION!!
EH...
I HAVE TO PUT A DECISIVE STOP TO KARASUMA'S PLOT TO CONFESS HIS FEELINGS!
Y-YOU SEE, IF WE DO ANYTHING UNEXPECTED, THEY'LL KNOW THEY'RE JUST LOOK-ALIKES!
MAYBE WHAT WE SHOULD DO HERE IS...
KÔSHIEN!!

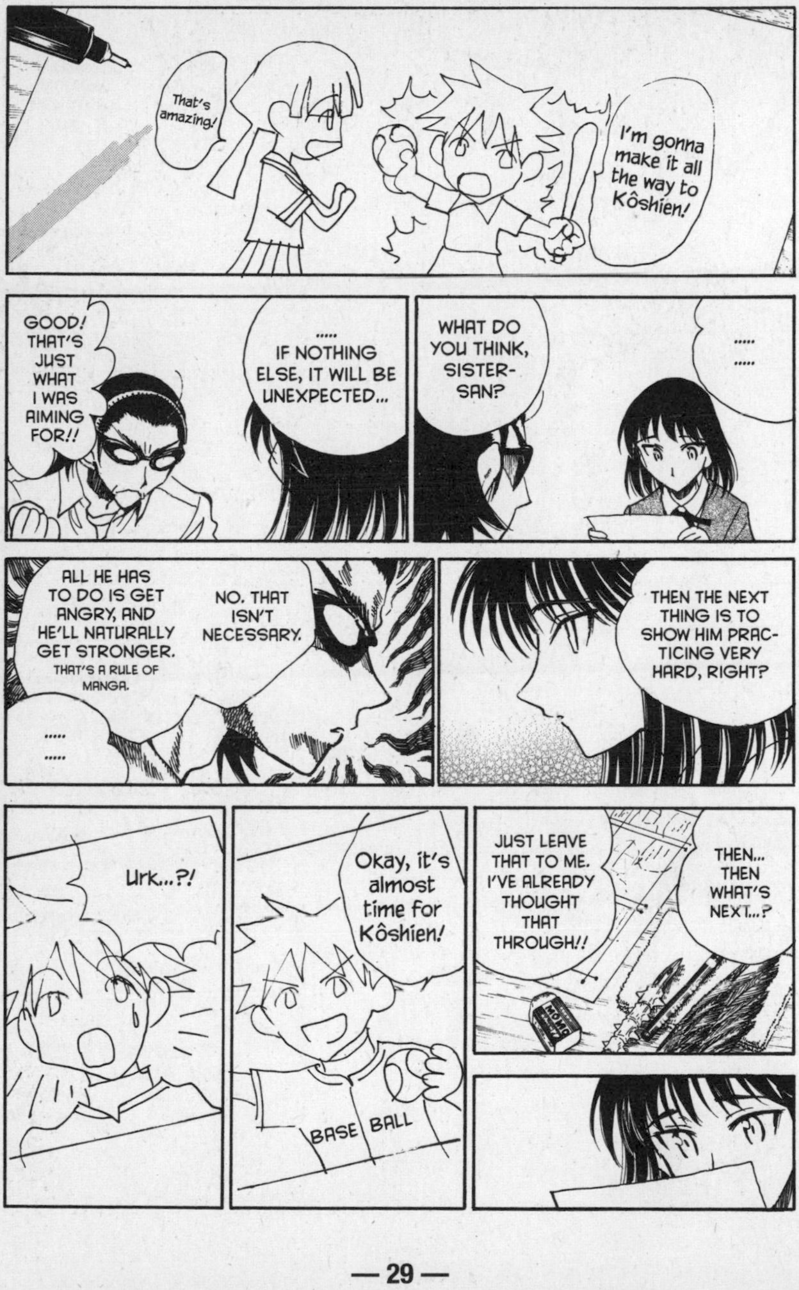
I'm gonna make it all the way to Kôshien!
That's amazing!
.....
.....
WHAT DO YOU THINK, SISTER-SAN?
..... IF NOTHING ELSE, IT WILL BE UNEXPECTED...
GOOD! THAT'S JUST WHAT I WAS AIMING FOR!!
THEN THE NEXT THING IS TO SHOW HIM PRACTICING VERY HARD, RIGHT?
NO. THAT ISN'T NECESSARY.
ALL HE HAS TO DO IS GET ANGRY, AND HE'LL NATURALLY GET STRONGER.
THAT'S A RULE OF MANGA.
.....
.....
THEN... THEN WHAT'S NEXT...?
JUST LEAVE THAT TO ME. I'VE ALREADY THOUGHT THAT THROUGH!!
Okay, it's almost time for Kôshien!
BASE BALL
Urk...?!

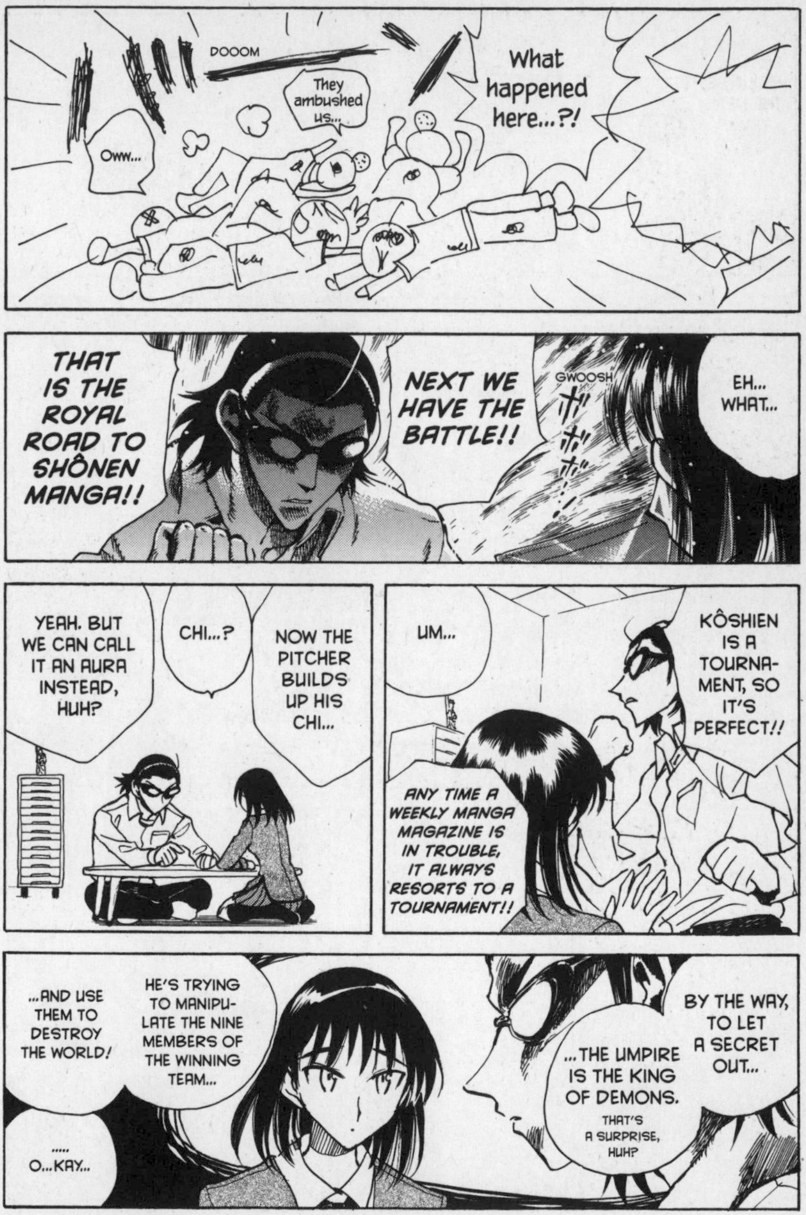

What happened here...?!
DOOOM
They ambushed us...
Oww...
EH... WHAT...
GWOOSH
NEXT WE HAVE THE BATTLE!!
THAT IS THE ROYAL ROAD TO SHÔNEN MANGA!!
KÔSHIEN IS A TOURNAMENT, SO IT'S PERFECT!!
UM...
ANY TIME A WEEKLY MANGA MAGAZINE IS IN TROUBLE, IT ALWAYS RESORTS TO A TOURNAMENT!!
NOW THE PITCHER BUILDS UP HIS CHI...
CHI...?
YEAH. BUT WE CAN CALL IT AN AURA INSTEAD, HUH?
BY THE WAY, TO LET A SECRET OUT...
...THE UMPIRE IS THE KING OF DEMONS.
THAT'S A SURPRISE, HUH?
HE'S TRYING TO MANIPULATE THE NINE MEMBERS OF THE WINNING TEAM...
...AND USE THEM TO DESTROY THE WORLD!
..... O...KAY...

Right, and Where's the Basis for That?

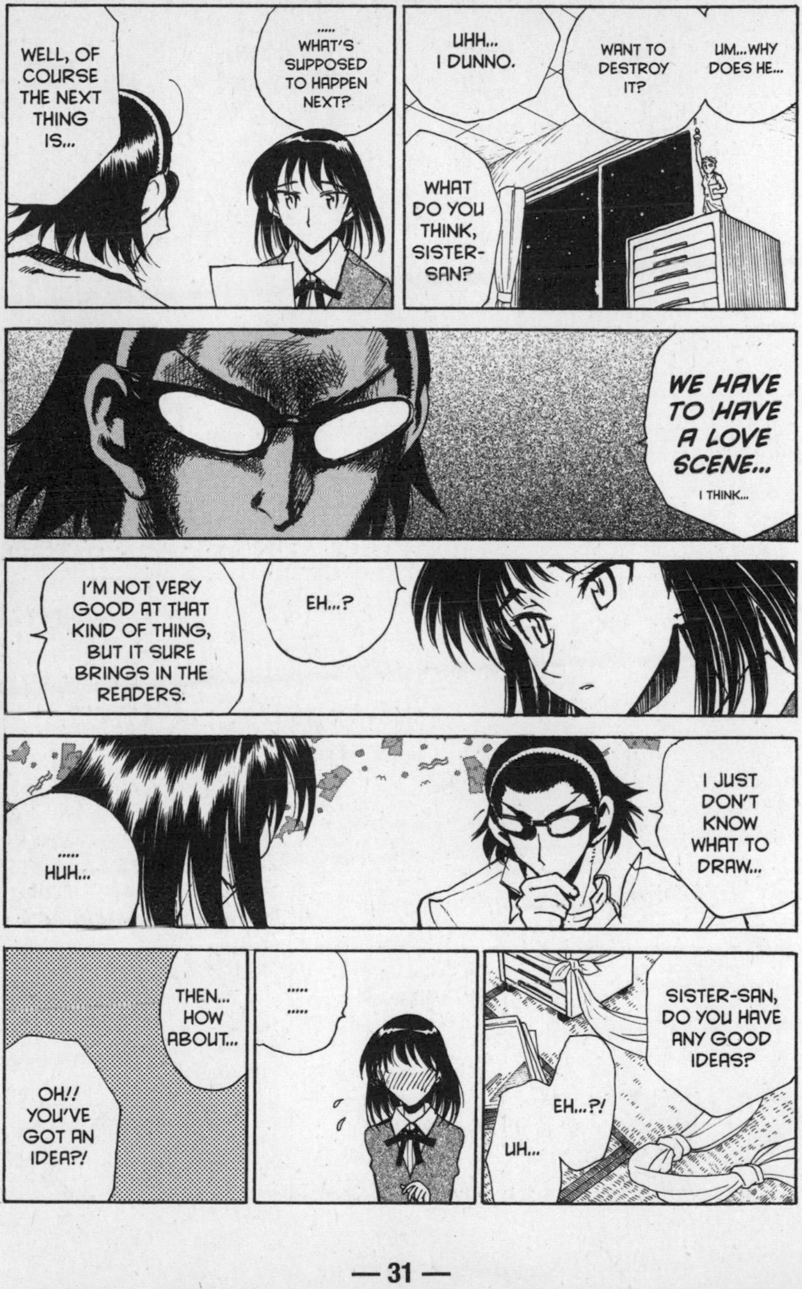

UM...WHY DOES HE...
WANT TO DESTROY IT?
UHH... I DUNNO.
WHAT DO YOU THINK, SISTER-SAN?
..... WHAT'S SUPPOSED TO HAPPEN NEXT?
WELL, OF COURSE THE NEXT THING IS...
WE HAVE TO HAVE A LOVE SCENE...
I THINK...
EH...?
I'M NOT VERY GOOD AT THAT KIND OF THING, BUT IT SURE BRINGS IN THE READERS.
I JUST DON'T KNOW WHAT TO DRAW...
..... HUH...
SISTER-SAN, DO YOU HAVE ANY GOOD IDEAS?
EH...?!
UH...
....
THEN... HOW ABOUT...
OH!! YOU'VE GOT AN IDEA?!

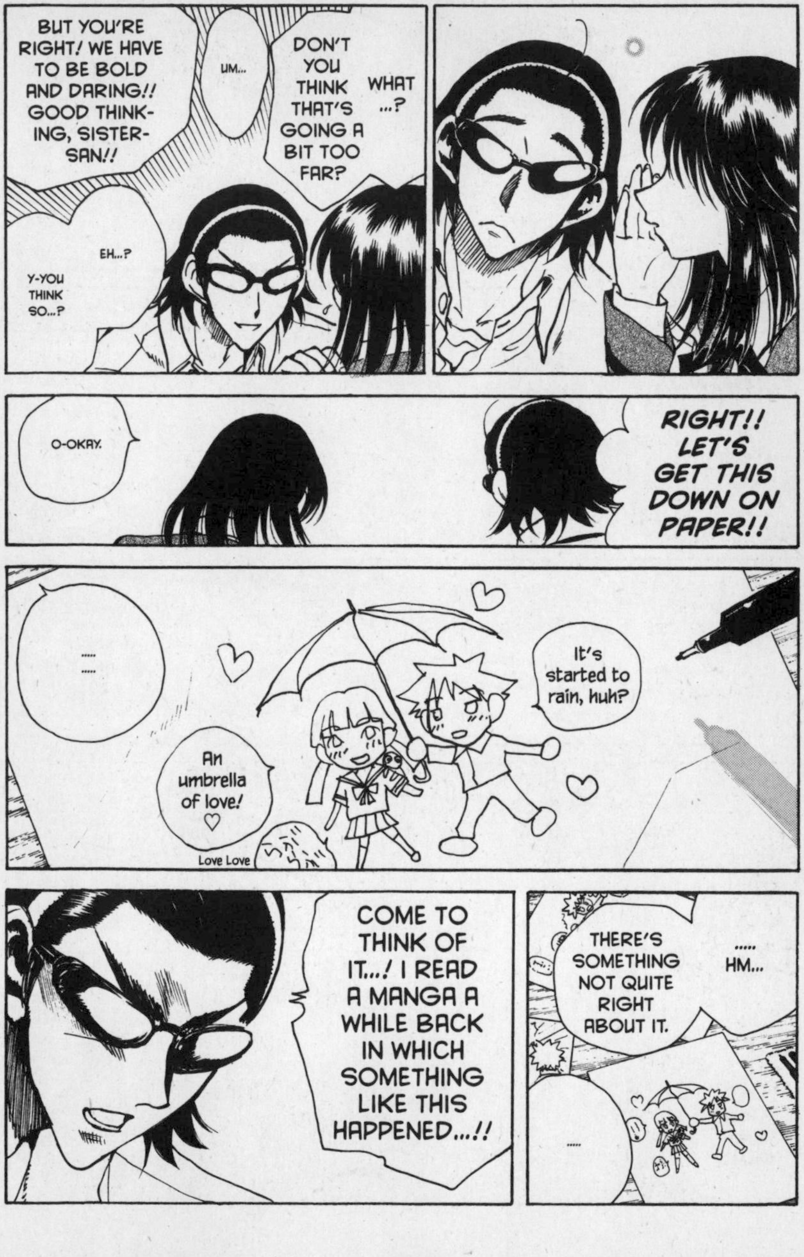
WHAT ...?
DON'T YOU THINK THAT'S GOING A BIT TOO FAR?
UM...
BUT YOU'RE RIGHT! WE HAVE TO BE BOLD AND DARING!! GOOD THINKING, SISTER-SAN!!
EH...?
Y-YOU THINK SO...?
RIGHT!! LET'S GET THIS DOWN ON PAPER!!
O-OKAY.
It's started to rain, huh?
An umbrella of love! ♡
Love Love
....
..... HM...
THERE'S SOMETHING NOT QUITE RIGHT ABOUT IT.
.....
COME TO THINK OF IT...! I READ A MANGA A WHILE BACK IN WHICH SOMETHING LIKE THIS HAPPENED...!!

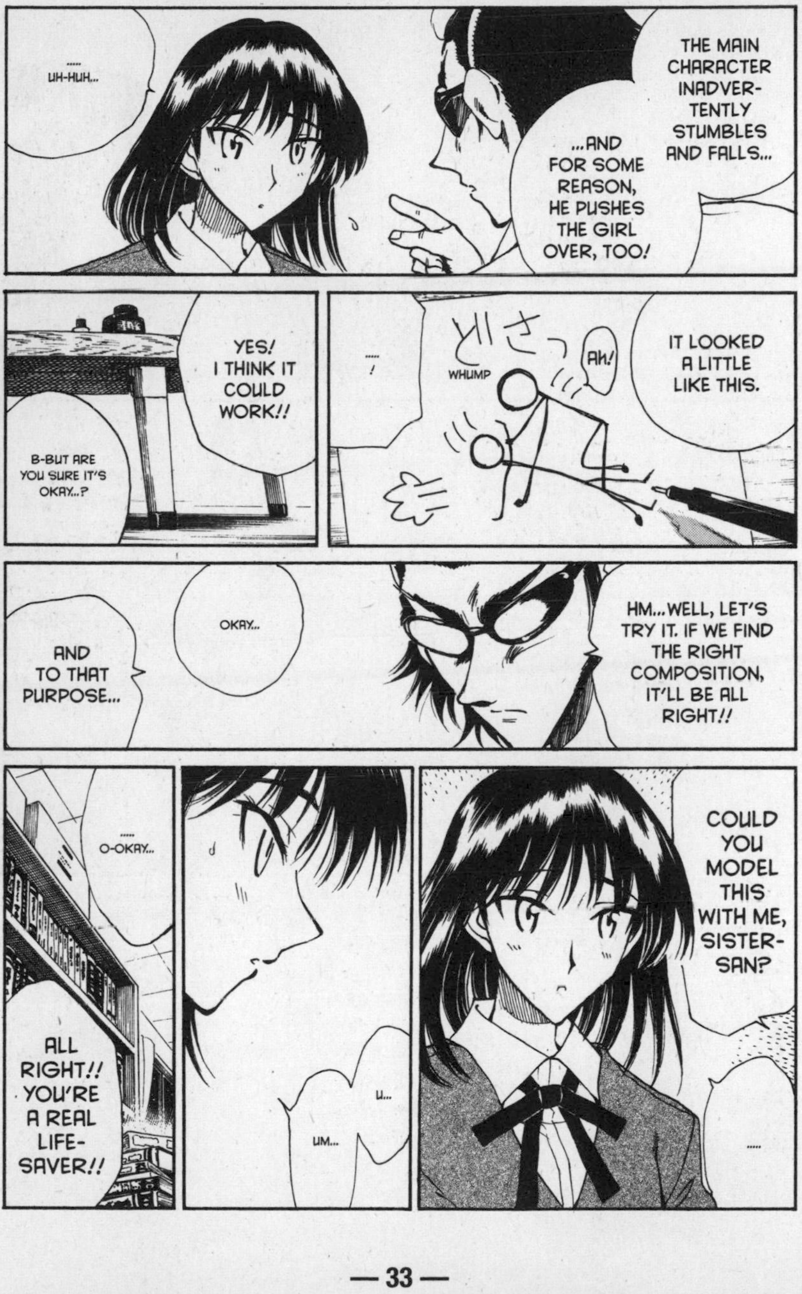
THE MAIN CHARACTER INADVERTENTLY STUMBLES AND FALLS...
...AND FOR SOME REASON, HE PUSHES THE GIRL OVER, TOO!
...... UH-HUH...
IT LOOKED A LITTLE LIKE THIS.
AH!
どさっ
WHUMP
......!
YES! I THINK IT COULD WORK!!
B-BUT ARE YOU SURE IT'S OKAY...?
HM...WELL, LET'S TRY IT. IF WE FIND THE RIGHT COMPOSITION, IT'LL BE ALL RIGHT!!
OKAY...
AND TO THAT PURPOSE...
COULD YOU MODEL THIS WITH ME, SISTER-SAN?
......
U...
UM...
...... O-OKAY...
ALL RIGHT!! YOU'RE A REAL LIFE-SAVER!!

He's Below...?

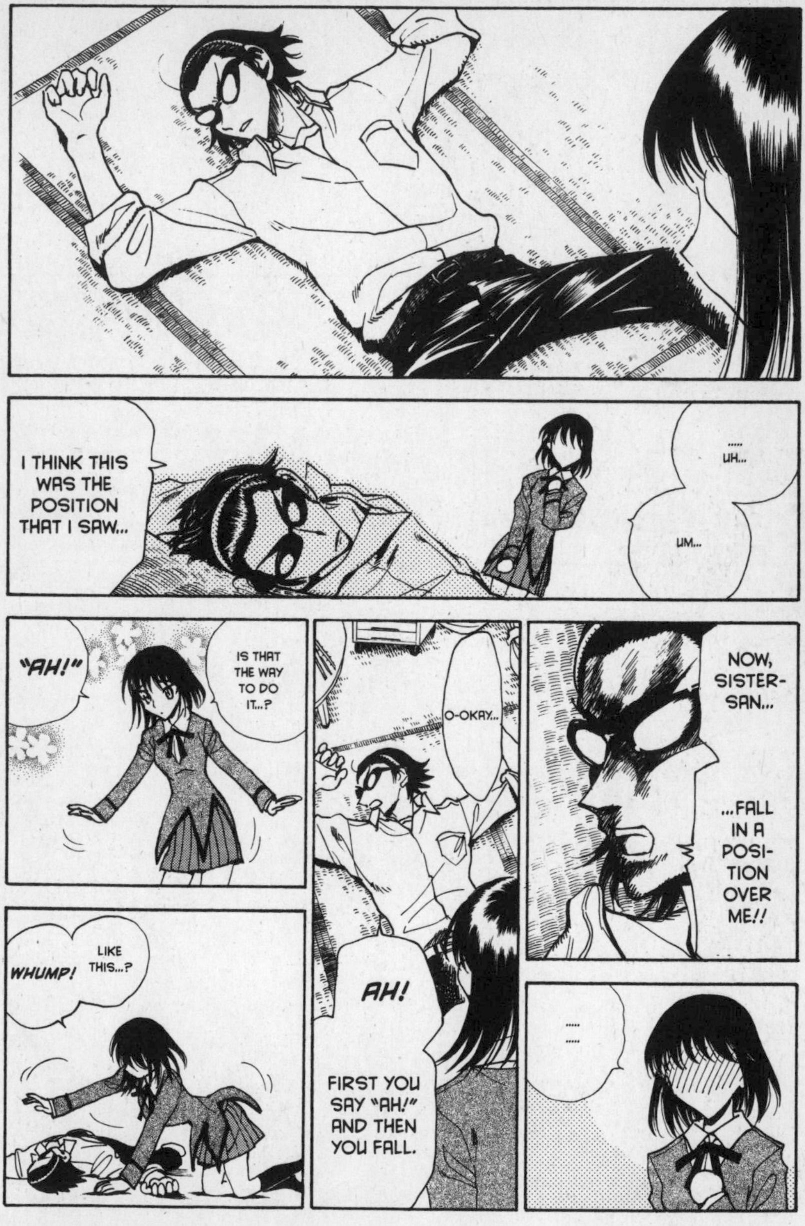

.....
uh...
um...
I THINK THIS WAS THE POSITION THAT I SAW...
NOW, SISTER-SAN...
...FALL IN A POSITION OVER ME!!
.....
.....
O-OKAY...
AH!
FIRST YOU SAY "AH!" AND THEN YOU FALL.
"AH!"
IS THAT THE WAY TO DO IT...?
WHUMP!
LIKE THIS...?

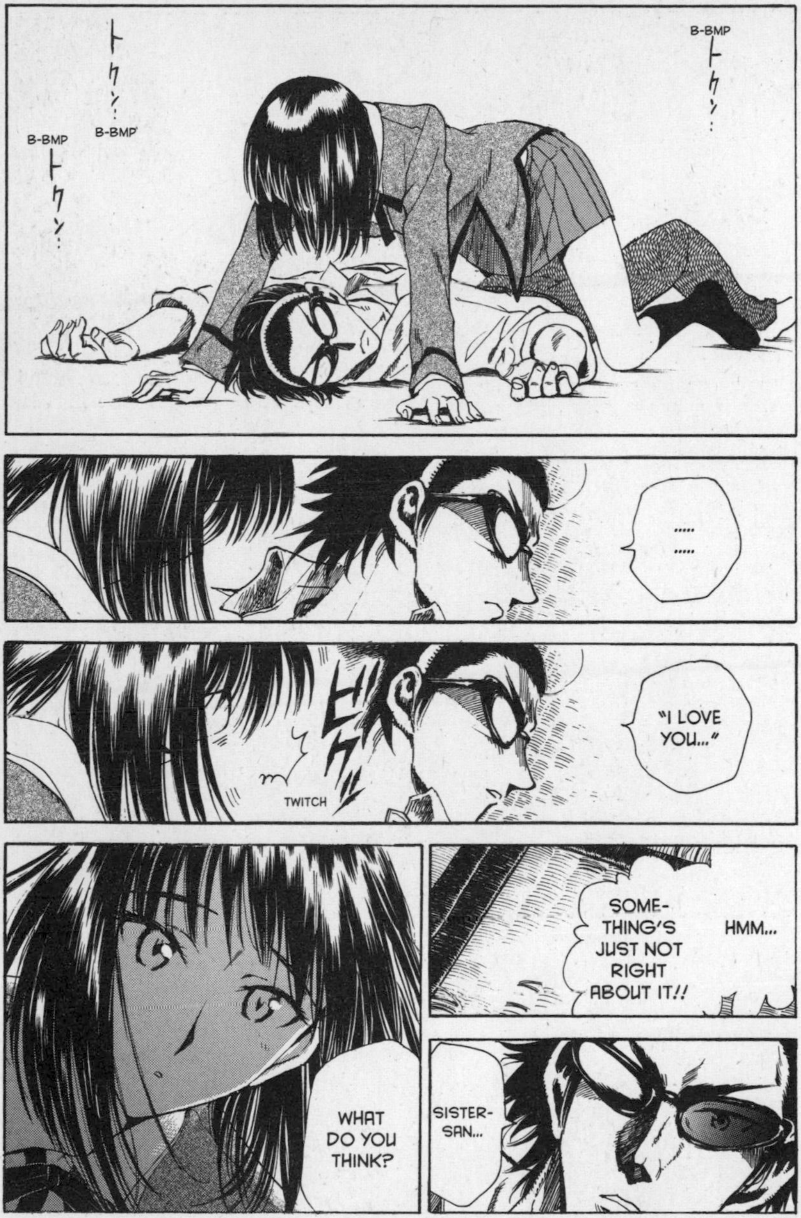

B-BMP
トクン‥
B-BMP
トクン‥
B-BMP
トクン‥
…… ……
"I LOVE YOU..."
TWITCH
HMM...
SOME-THING'S JUST NOT RIGHT ABOUT IT!!
SISTER-SAN...
WHAT DO YOU THINK?

Harima's Pen: Momentarily Has a Soul Residing in It.

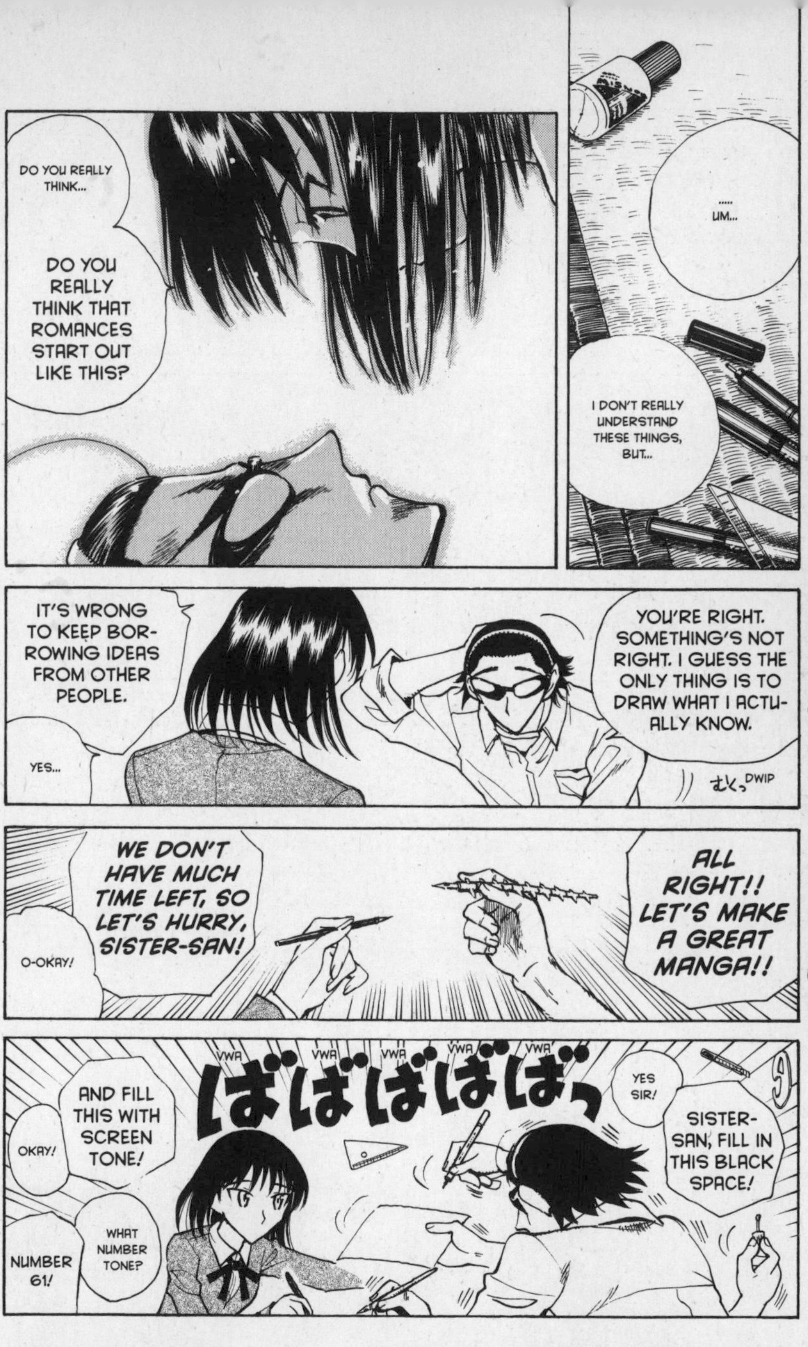

..... UM...
I DON'T REALLY UNDERSTAND THESE THINGS, BUT...
DO YOU REALLY THINK...
DO YOU REALLY THINK THAT ROMANCES START OUT LIKE THIS?
YOU'RE RIGHT. SOMETHING'S NOT RIGHT. I GUESS THE ONLY THING IS TO DRAW WHAT I ACTUALLY KNOW.
むくっ DWIP
IT'S WRONG TO KEEP BORROWING IDEAS FROM OTHER PEOPLE.
YES...
ALL RIGHT!! LET'S MAKE A GREAT MANGA!!
WE DON'T HAVE MUCH TIME LEFT, SO LET'S HURRY, SISTER-SAN!
O-OKAY!
VWA VWA VWA VWA VWA
ばばばばばっ
YES SIR!
SISTER-SAN, FILL IN THIS BLACK SPACE!
AND FILL THIS WITH SCREEN TONE!
OKAY!
WHAT NUMBER TONE?
NUMBER 61!

Editor: Doesn't Notice that Karasuma Isn't There.

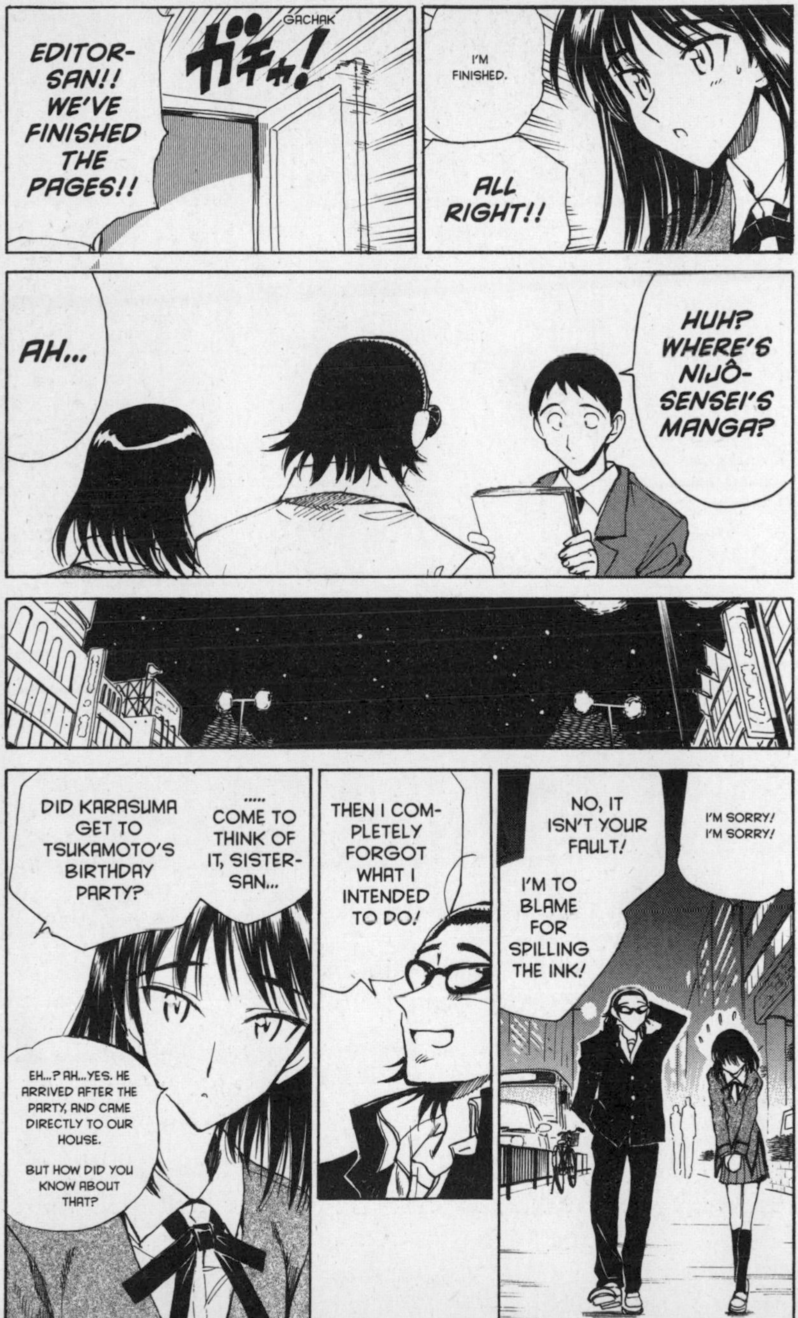
I'M FINISHED.
ALL RIGHT!!
GACHAK
ガチャ!
EDITOR-SAN!! WE'VE FINISHED THE PAGES!!
HUH? WHERE'S NIJÔ-SENSEI'S MANGA?
AH...
I'M SORRY! I'M SORRY!
NO, IT ISN'T YOUR FAULT!
I'M TO BLAME FOR SPILLING THE INK!
THEN I COMPLETELY FORGOT WHAT I INTENDED TO DO!
...... COME TO THINK OF IT, SISTER-SAN...
DID KARASUMA GET TO TSUKAMOTO'S BIRTHDAY PARTY?
EH...? AH...YES. HE ARRIVED AFTER THE PARTY, AND CAME DIRECTLY TO OUR HOUSE.
BUT HOW DID YOU KNOW ABOUT THAT?

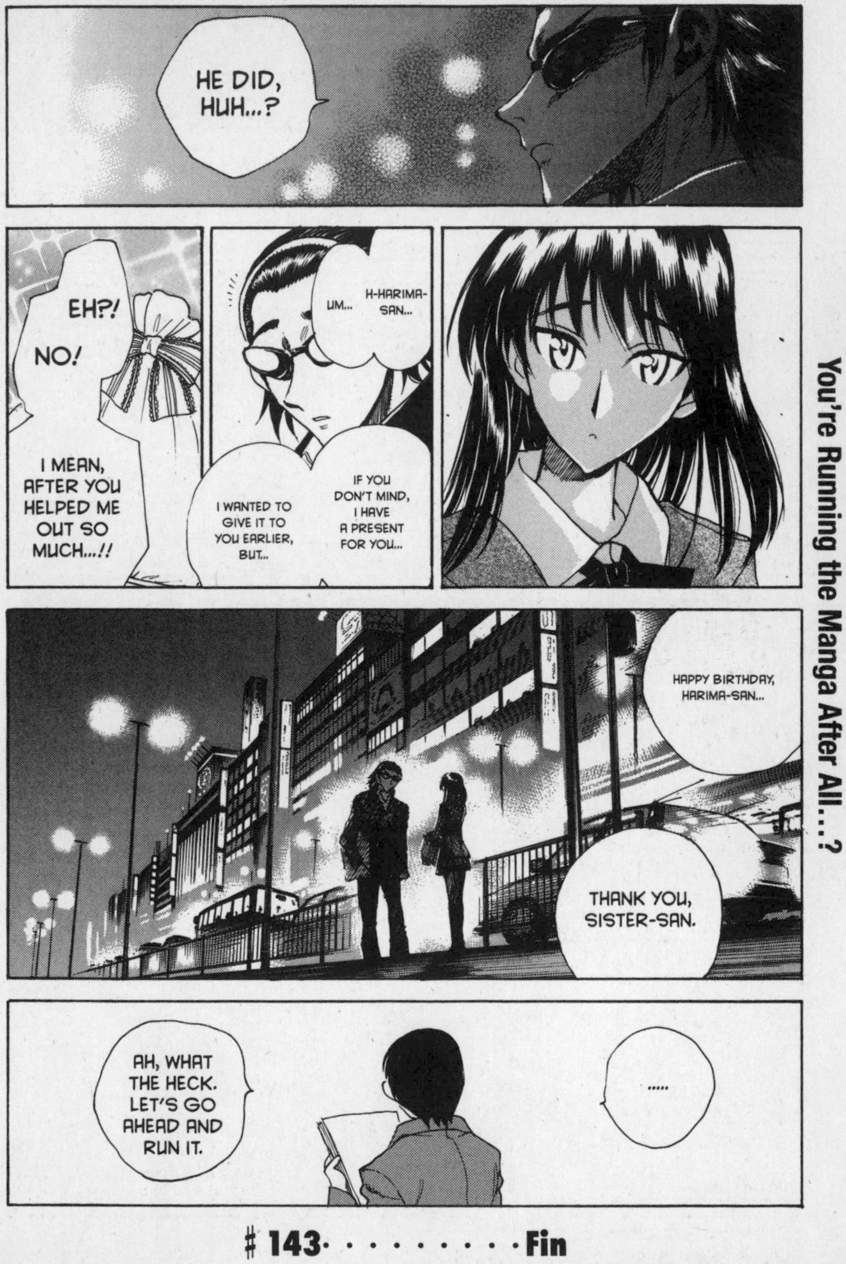
HE DID, HUH...?
UM... H-HARIMA-SAN...
IF YOU DON'T MIND, I HAVE A PRESENT FOR YOU...
I WANTED TO GIVE IT TO YOU EARLIER, BUT...
EH?!
NO!
I MEAN, AFTER YOU HELPED ME OUT SO MUCH...!!
HAPPY BIRTHDAY, HARIMA-SAN...
THANK YOU, SISTER-SAN.
.....
AH, WHAT THE HECK. LET'S GO AHEAD AND RUN IT.

You're Running the Manga After All...?

 # 143· · · · · · · · · Fin

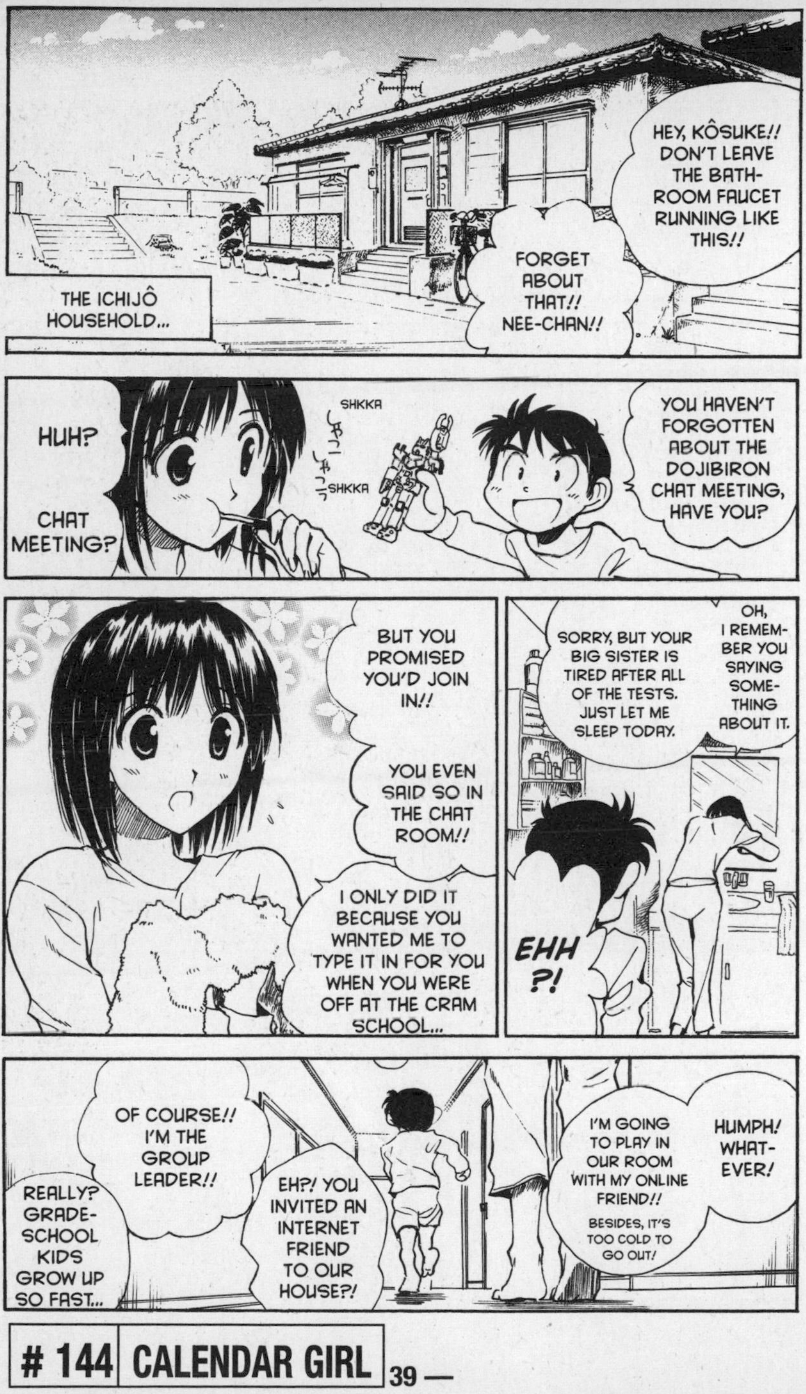
HEY, KÔSUKE!! DON'T LEAVE THE BATHROOM FAUCET RUNNING LIKE THIS!!
FORGET ABOUT THAT!! NEE-CHAN!!
THE ICHIJÔ HOUSEHOLD...
YOU HAVEN'T FORGOTTEN ABOUT THE DOJIBIRON CHAT MEETING, HAVE YOU?
SHKKA
SHKKA
HUH?
CHAT MEETING?
OH, I REMEMBER YOU SAYING SOMETHING ABOUT IT.
SORRY, BUT YOUR BIG SISTER IS TIRED AFTER ALL OF THE TESTS. JUST LET ME SLEEP TODAY.
EHH?!
BUT YOU PROMISED YOU'D JOIN IN!!
YOU EVEN SAID SO IN THE CHAT ROOM!!
I ONLY DID IT BECAUSE YOU WANTED ME TO TYPE IT IN FOR YOU WHEN YOU WERE OFF AT THE CRAM SCHOOL...
HUMPH! WHATEVER!
I'M GOING TO PLAY IN OUR ROOM WITH MY ONLINE FRIEND!!
BESIDES, IT'S TOO COLD TO GO OUT!
EH?! YOU INVITED AN INTERNET FRIEND TO OUR HOUSE?!
OF COURSE!! I'M THE GROUP LEADER!!
REALLY? GRADE-SCHOOL KIDS GROW UP SO FAST...

144 CALENDAR GIRL

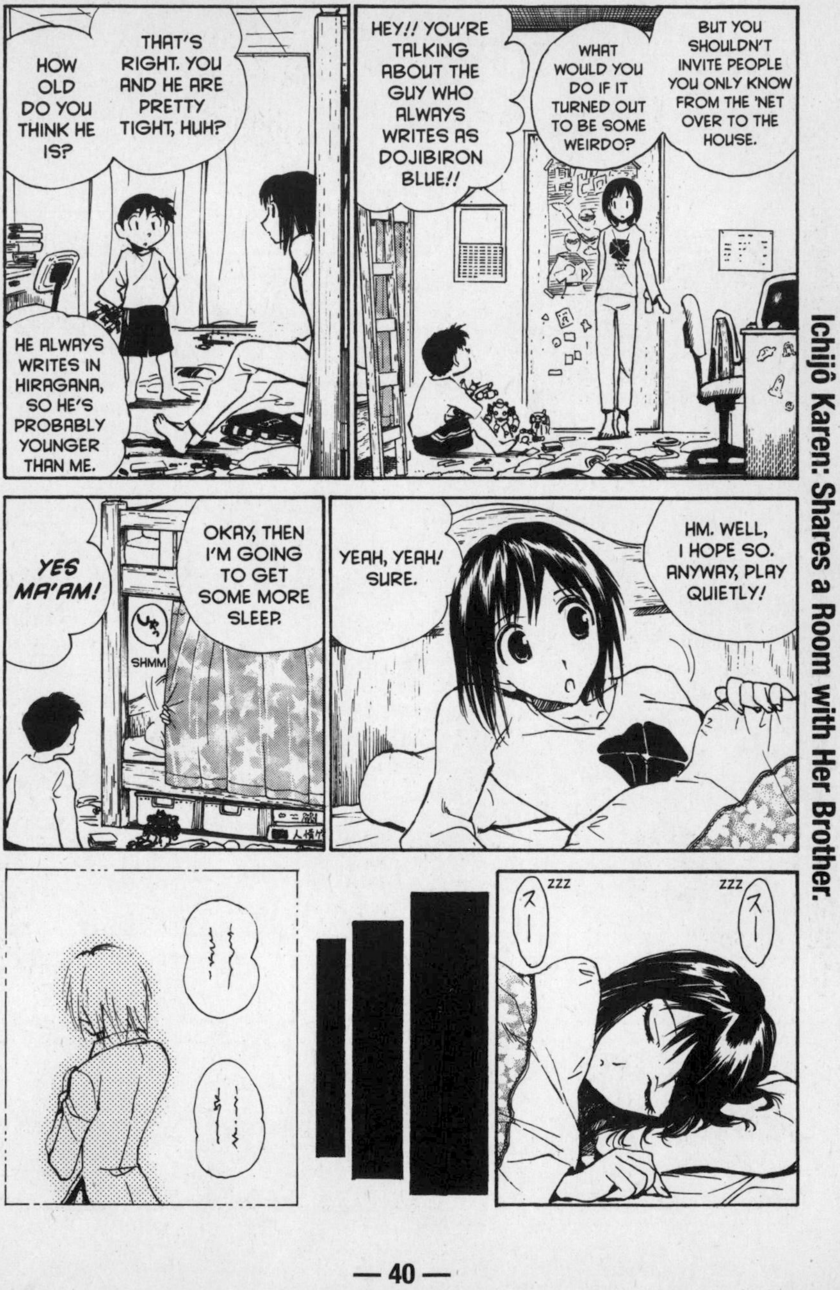
BUT YOU SHOULDN'T INVITE PEOPLE YOU ONLY KNOW FROM THE 'NET OVER TO THE HOUSE.
WHAT WOULD YOU DO IF IT TURNED OUT TO BE SOME WEIRDO?
HEY!! YOU'RE TALKING ABOUT THE GUY WHO ALWAYS WRITES AS DOJIBIRON BLUE!!
THAT'S RIGHT. YOU AND HE ARE PRETTY TIGHT, HUH?
HOW OLD DO YOU THINK HE IS?
HE ALWAYS WRITES IN HIRAGANA, SO HE'S PROBABLY YOUNGER THAN ME.
HM. WELL, I HOPE SO. ANYWAY, PLAY QUIETLY!
YEAH, YEAH! SURE.
OKAY, THEN I'M GOING TO GET SOME MORE SLEEP.
YES MA'AM!
SHMM
ZZZ
ZZZ

Ichijô Karen: Shares a Room with Her Brother.

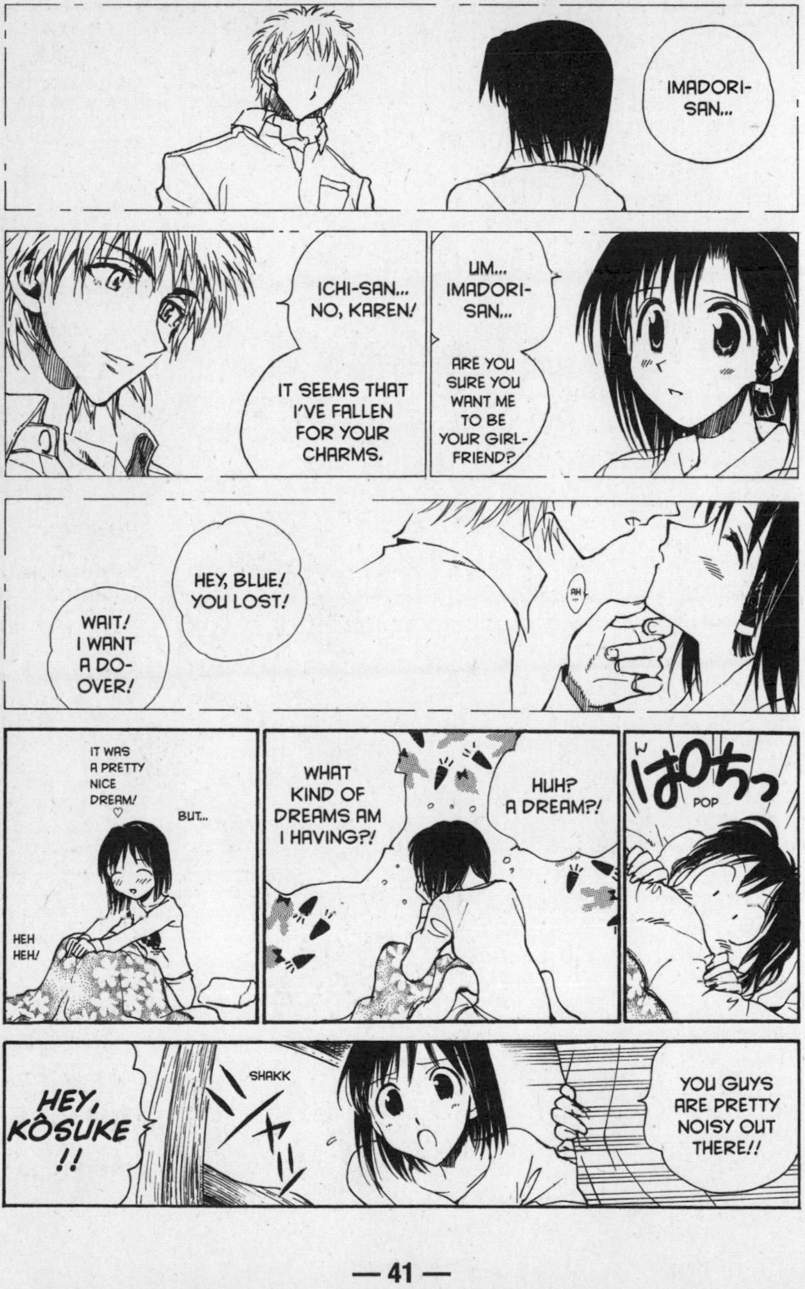
IMADORI-SAN...
UM... IMADORI-SAN...
ARE YOU SURE YOU WANT ME TO BE YOUR GIRL-FRIEND?
ICHI-SAN... NO, KAREN!
IT SEEMS THAT I'VE FALLEN FOR YOUR CHARMS.
AH...
HEY, BLUE! YOU LOST!
WAIT! I WANT A DO-OVER!
ぱちっ
POP
HUH? A DREAM?!
WHAT KIND OF DREAMS AM I HAVING?!
IT WAS A PRETTY NICE DREAM! ♡
BUT...
HEH HEH!
YOU GUYS ARE PRETTY NOISY OUT THERE!!
SHAKK
HEY, KÔSUKE!!

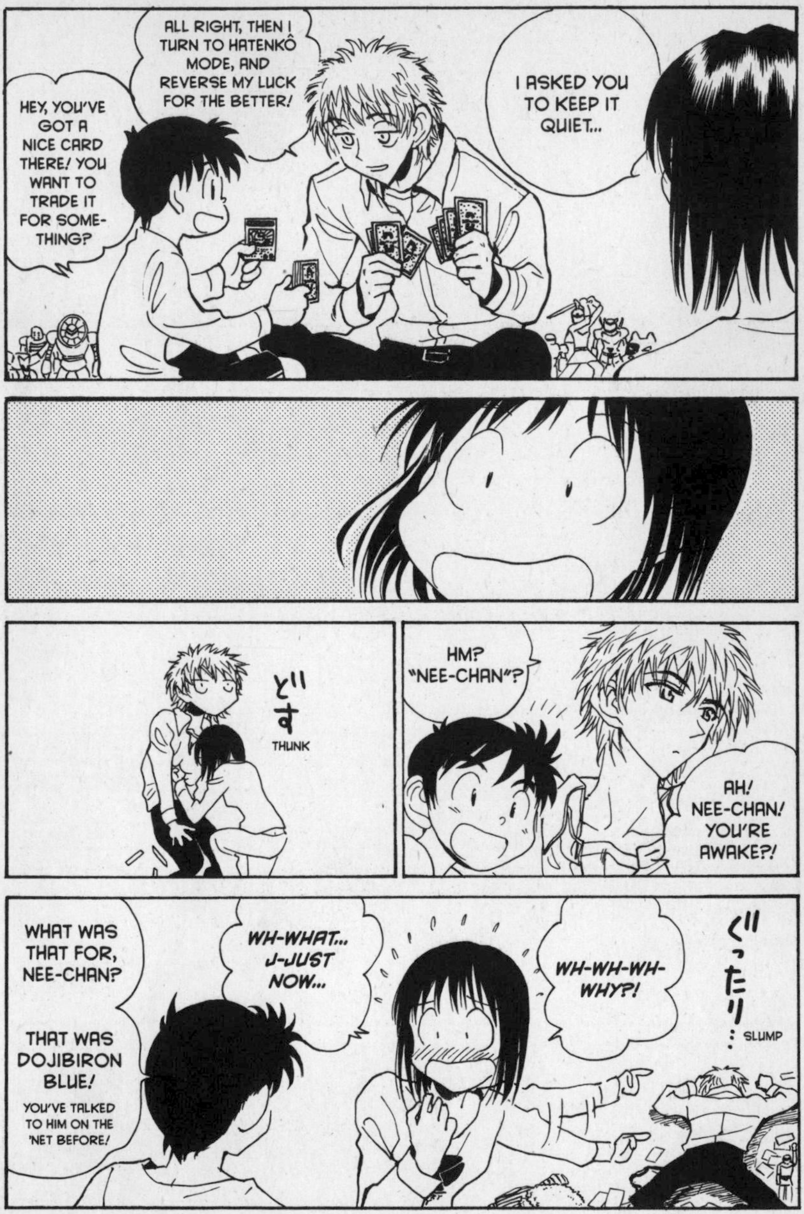
I ASKED YOU TO KEEP IT QUIET...
ALL RIGHT, THEN I TURN TO HATENKÔ MODE, AND REVERSE MY LUCK FOR THE BETTER!
HEY, YOU'VE GOT A NICE CARD THERE! YOU WANT TO TRADE IT FOR SOME-THING?
AH! NEE-CHAN! YOU'RE AWAKE?!
HM? "NEE-CHAN"?
どす
THUNK
ぐったり…
SLUMP
WH-WH-WH-WHY?!
WH-WHAT... J-JUST NOW...
WHAT WAS THAT FOR, NEE-CHAN?
THAT WAS DOJIBIRON BLUE!
YOU'VE TALKED TO HIM ON THE 'NET BEFORE!

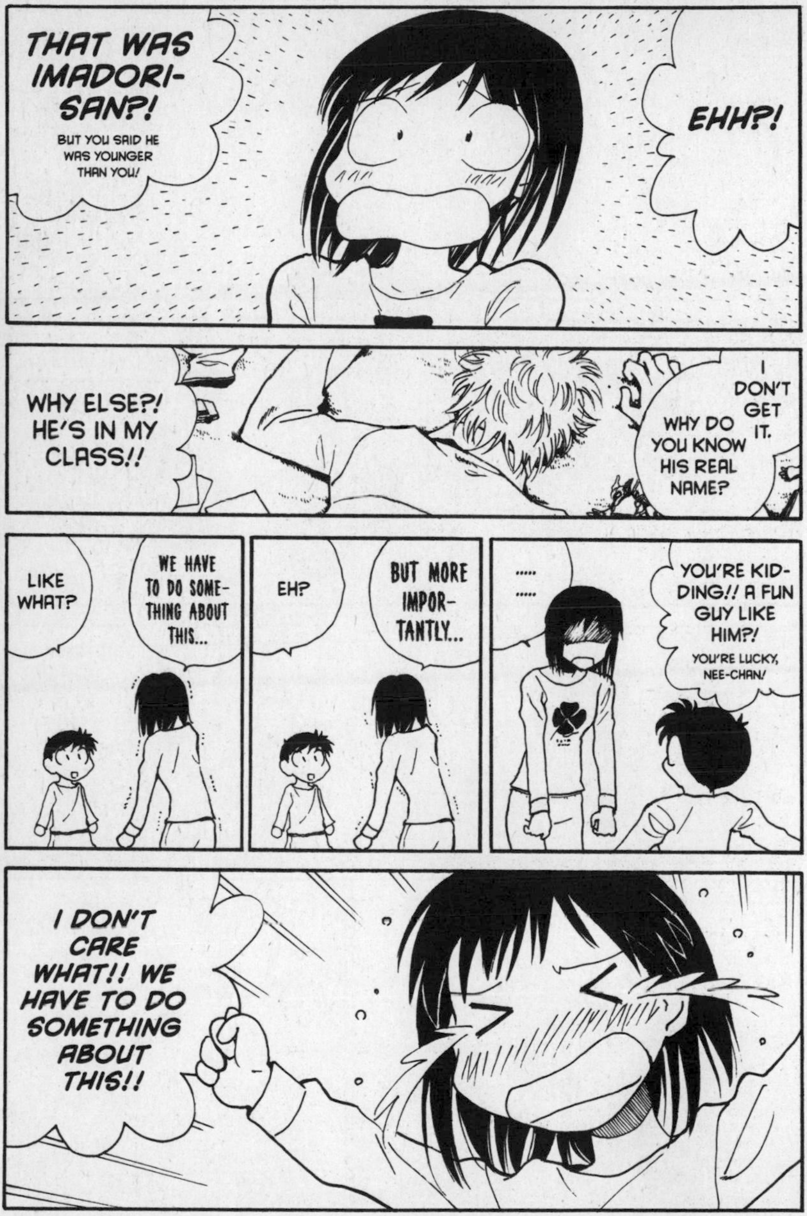
EHH?!
THAT WAS IMADORI-SAN?!
BUT YOU SAID HE WAS YOUNGER THAN YOU!
I DON'T GET IT.
WHY DO YOU KNOW HIS REAL NAME?
WHY ELSE?! HE'S IN MY CLASS!!
YOU'RE KIDDING!! A FUN GUY LIKE HIM?!
YOU'RE LUCKY, NEE-CHAN!
.....
.....
BUT MORE IMPORTANTLY...
EH?
WE HAVE TO DO SOMETHING ABOUT THIS...
LIKE WHAT?
I DON'T CARE WHAT!! WE HAVE TO DO SOMETHING ABOUT THIS!!

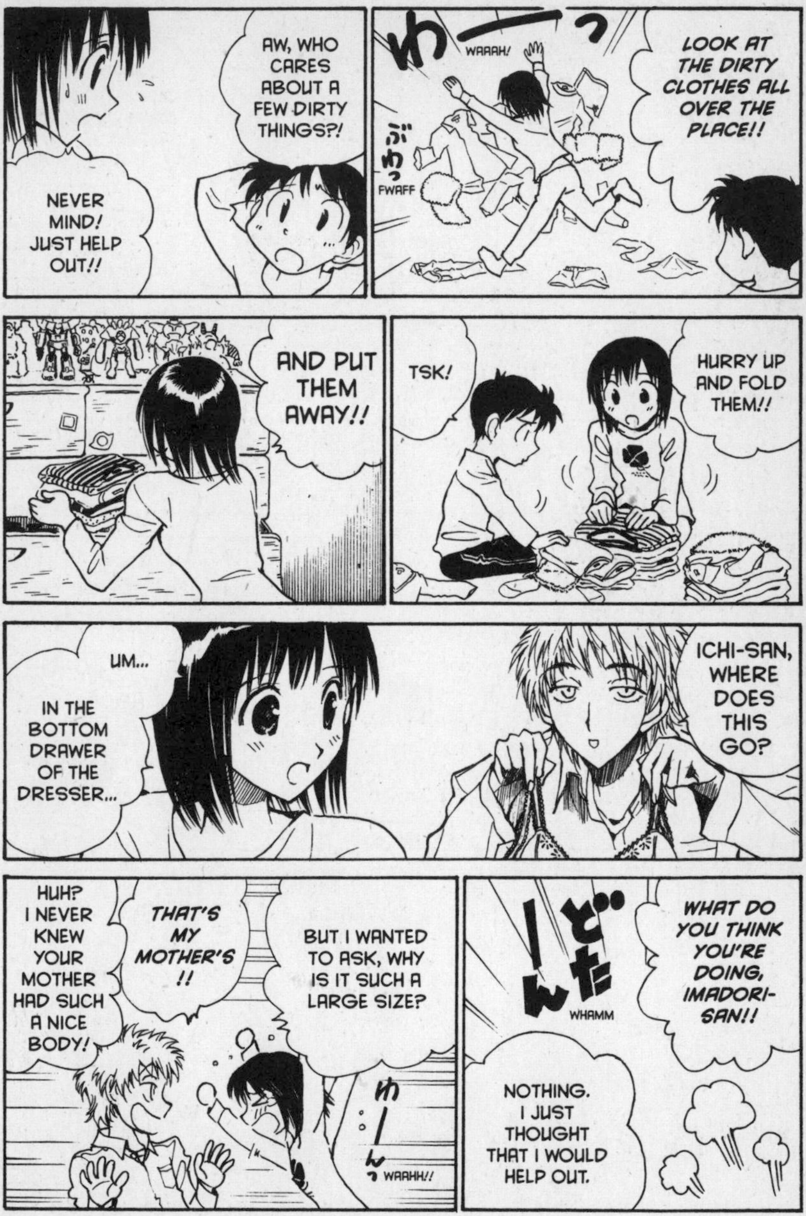
LOOK AT THE DIRTY CLOTHES ALL OVER THE PLACE!!
わーっ
WAAAH!
ぶわっ
FWAFF
AW, WHO CARES ABOUT A FEW DIRTY THINGS?!
NEVER MIND! JUST HELP OUT!!
HURRY UP AND FOLD THEM!!
TSK!
AND PUT THEM AWAY!!
ICHI-SAN, WHERE DOES THIS GO?
UM...
IN THE BOTTOM DRAWER OF THE DRESSER...
WHAT DO YOU THINK YOU'RE DOING, IMADORI-SAN!!
どたーん
WHAMM
NOTHING. I JUST THOUGHT THAT I WOULD HELP OUT.
BUT I WANTED TO ASK, WHY IS IT SUCH A LARGE SIZE?
THAT'S MY MOTHER'S!!
わーん
WAAHH!!
HUH? I NEVER KNEW YOUR MOTHER HAD SUCH A NICE BODY!

Too Late.

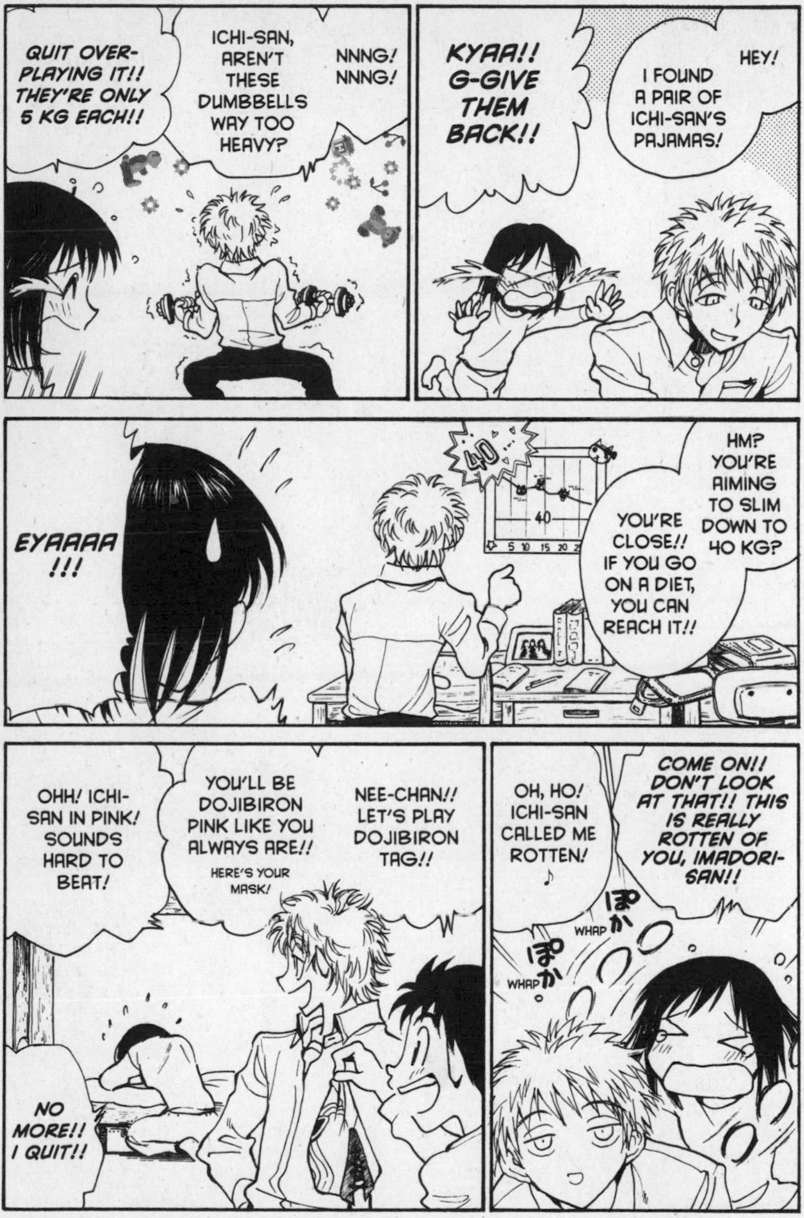

HEY!
I FOUND A PAIR OF ICHI-SAN'S PAJAMAS!
KYAA!! G-GIVE THEM BACK!!
NNNG! NNNG!
ICHI-SAN, AREN'T THESE DUMBBELLS WAY TOO HEAVY?
QUIT OVER-PLAYING IT!! THEY'RE ONLY 5 KG EACH!!
HM? YOU'RE AIMING TO SLIM DOWN TO 40 KG?
YOU'RE CLOSE!! IF YOU GO ON A DIET, YOU CAN REACH IT!!
40
EYAAAA!!!
COME ON!! DON'T LOOK AT THAT!! THIS IS REALLY ROTTEN OF YOU, IMADORI-SAN!!
OH, HO! ICHI-SAN CALLED ME ROTTEN! ♪
ぽか WHAP
ぽか WHAP
NEE-CHAN!! LET'S PLAY DOJIBIRON TAG!!
YOU'LL BE DOJIBIRON PINK LIKE YOU ALWAYS ARE!!
HERE'S YOUR MASK!
OHH! ICHI-SAN IN PINK! SOUNDS HARD TO BEAT!
NO MORE!! I QUIT!!

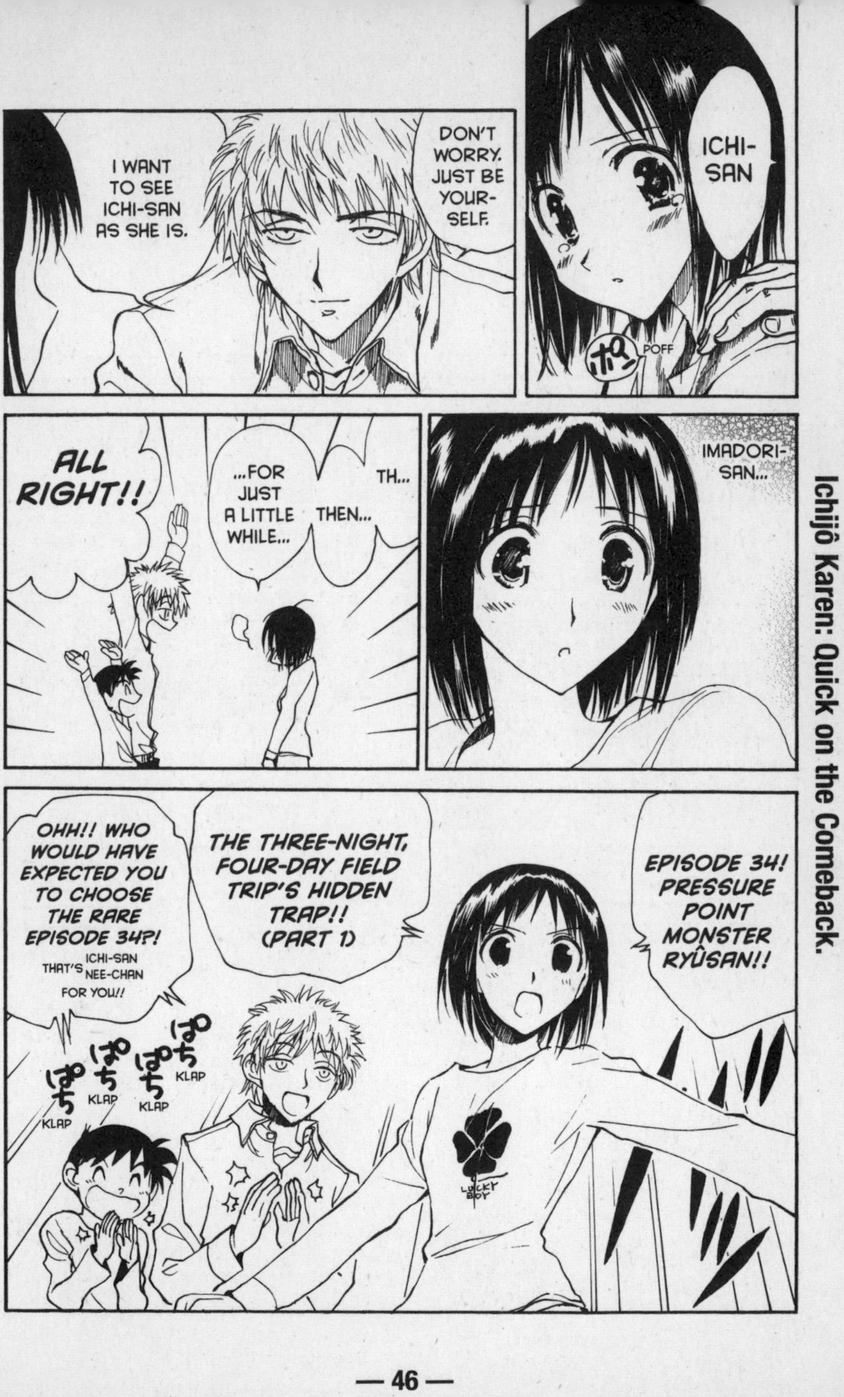
ICHI-SAN
ポン POFF
DON'T WORRY. JUST BE YOURSELF.
I WANT TO SEE ICHI-SAN AS SHE IS.
IMADORI-SAN...
TH... THEN...
...FOR JUST A LITTLE WHILE...
ALL RIGHT!!
EPISODE 34! PRESSURE POINT MONSTER RYÛSAN!!
THE THREE-NIGHT, FOUR-DAY FIELD TRIP'S HIDDEN TRAP!! (PART 1)
OHH!! WHO WOULD HAVE EXPECTED YOU TO CHOOSE THE RARE EPISODE 34?!
THAT'S ICHI-SAN NEE-CHAN FOR YOU!!
ぱち KLAP
ぱち KLAP
ぱち KLAP
ぱち KLAP
LUCKY BOY

Ichijô Karen: Quick on the Comeback.

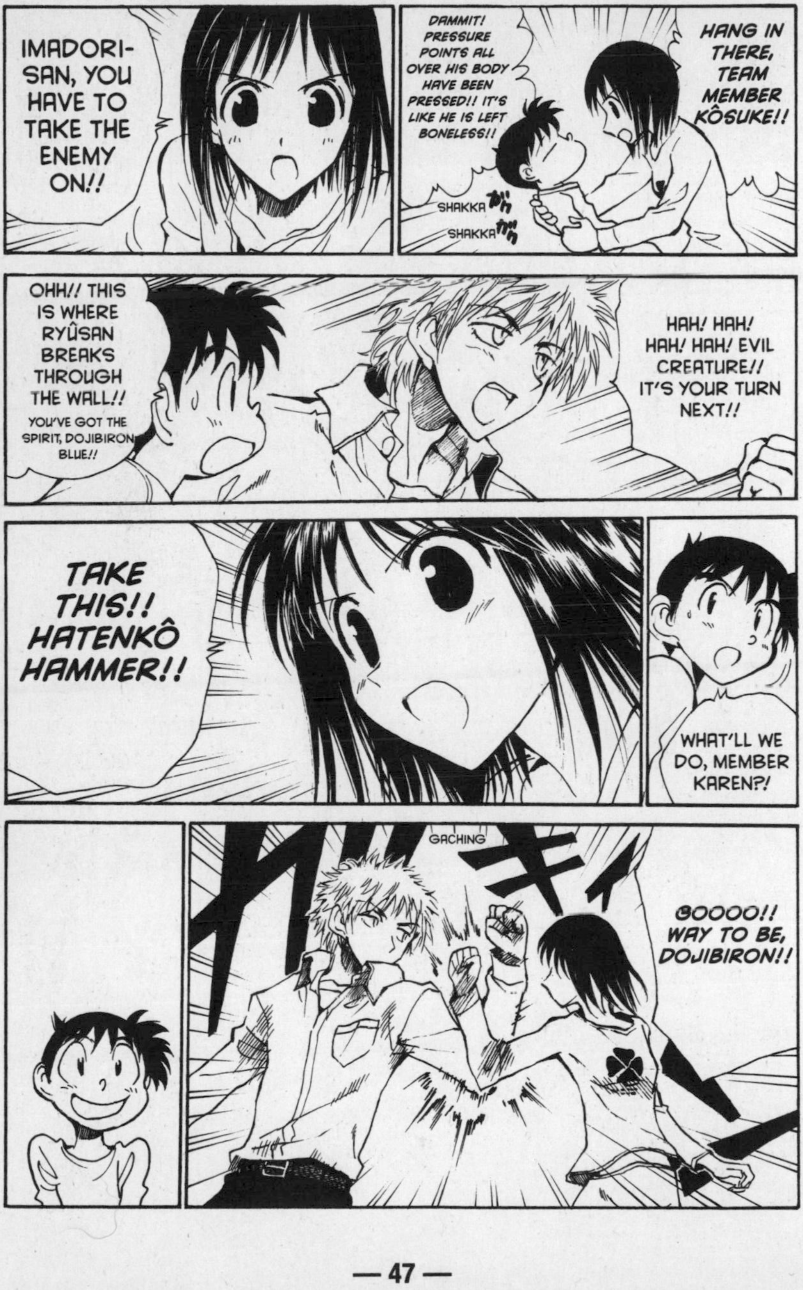
HANG IN THERE, TEAM MEMBER KÔSUKE!!
DAMMIT! PRESSURE POINTS ALL OVER HIS BODY HAVE BEEN PRESSED!! IT'S LIKE HE IS LEFT BONELESS!!
SHAKKA
SHAKKA
IMADORI-SAN, YOU HAVE TO TAKE THE ENEMY ON!!
HAH! HAH! HAH! HAH! EVIL CREATURE!! IT'S YOUR TURN NEXT!!
OHH!! THIS IS WHERE RYÛSAN BREAKS THROUGH THE WALL!!
YOU'VE GOT THE SPIRIT, DOJIBIRON BLUE!!
WHAT'LL WE DO, MEMBER KAREN?!
TAKE THIS!! HATENKÔ HAMMER!!
GACHING
GOOOO!! WAY TO BE, DOJIBIRON!!

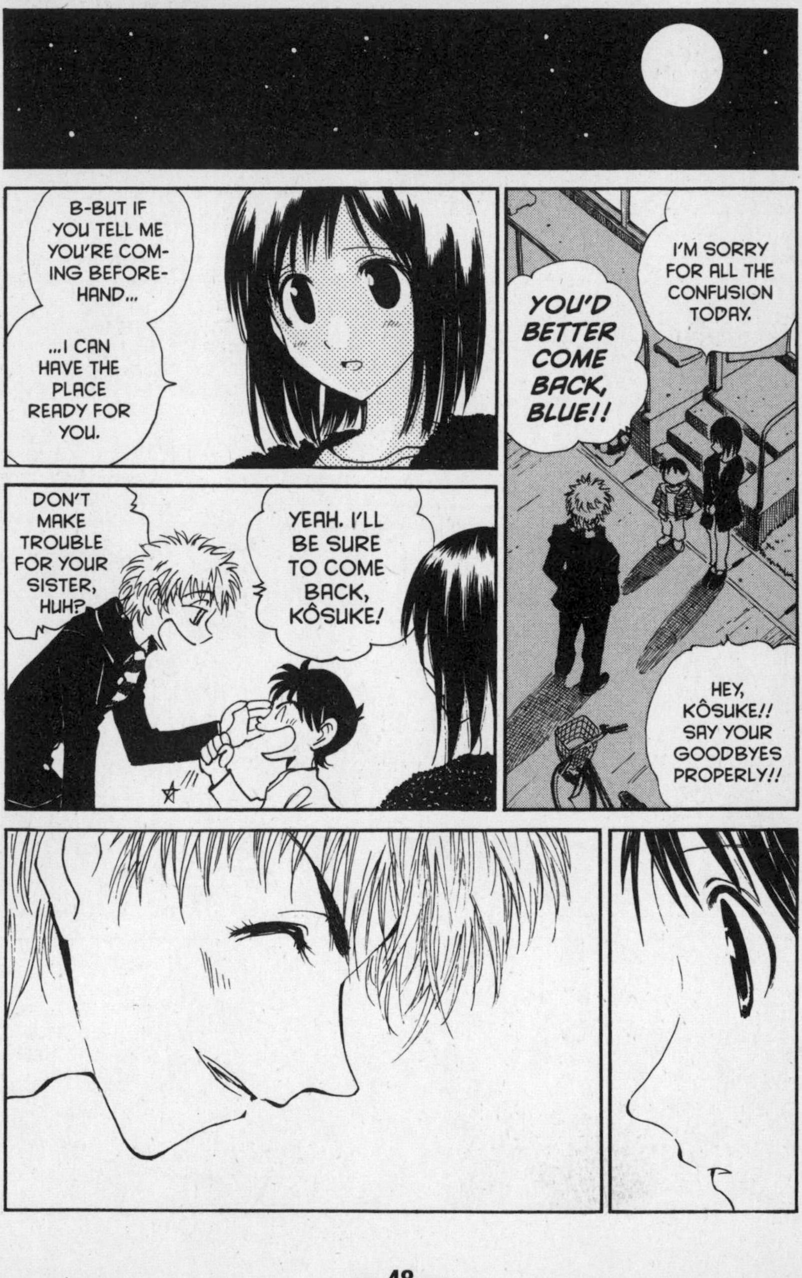
I'M SORRY FOR ALL THE CONFUSION TODAY.
YOU'D BETTER COME BACK, BLUE!!
HEY, KÔSUKE!! SAY YOUR GOODBYES PROPERLY!!
B-BUT IF YOU TELL ME YOU'RE COMING BEFOREHAND...
...I CAN HAVE THE PLACE READY FOR YOU.
YEAH. I'LL BE SURE TO COME BACK, KÔSUKE!
DON'T MAKE TROUBLE FOR YOUR SISTER, HUH?

And the Battle Ends...

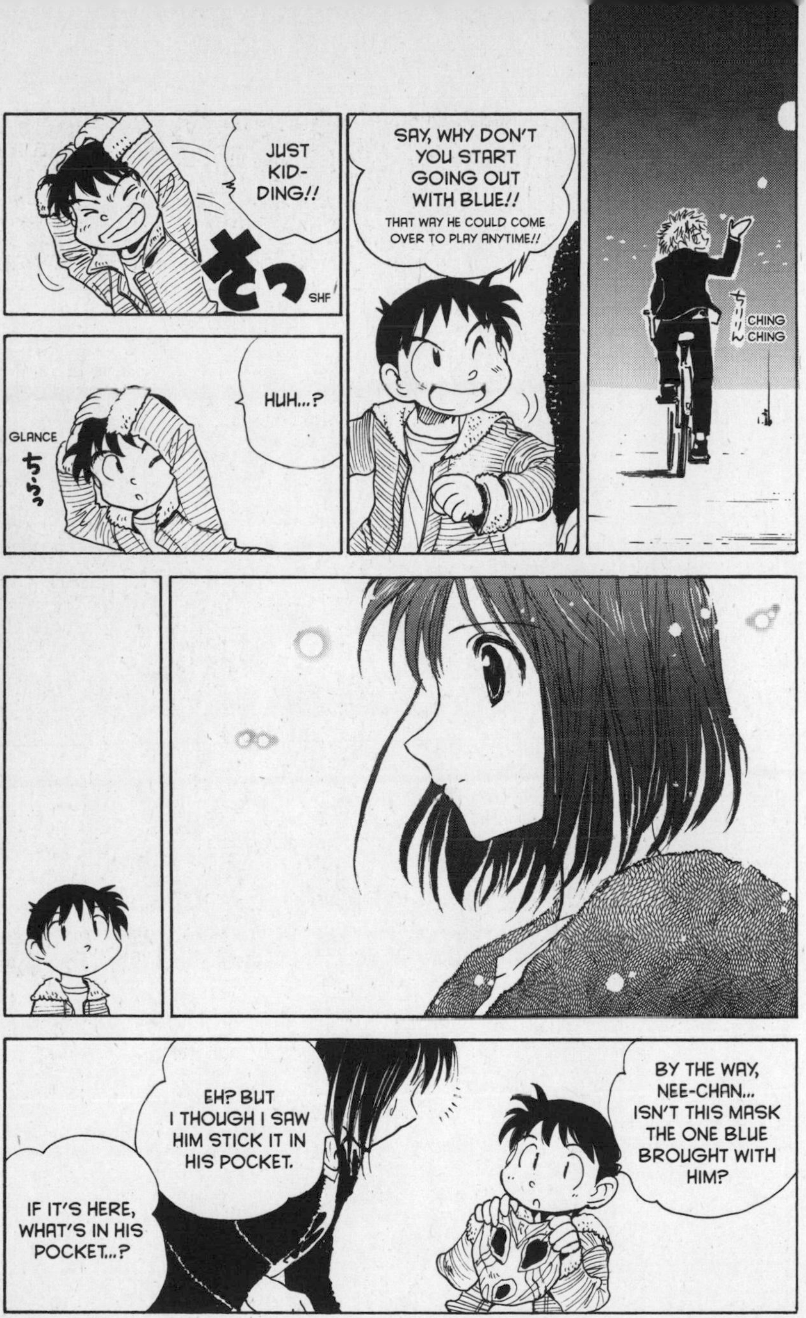
CHING CHING
SAY, WHY DON'T YOU START GOING OUT WITH BLUE!!
THAT WAY HE COULD COME OVER TO PLAY ANYTIME!!
JUST KID-DING!!
SHF
HUH...?
GLANCE
BY THE WAY, NEE-CHAN... ISN'T THIS MASK THE ONE BLUE BROUGHT WITH HIM?
EH? BUT I THOUGH I SAW HIM STICK IT IN HIS POCKET.
IF IT'S HERE, WHAT'S IN HIS POCKET...?

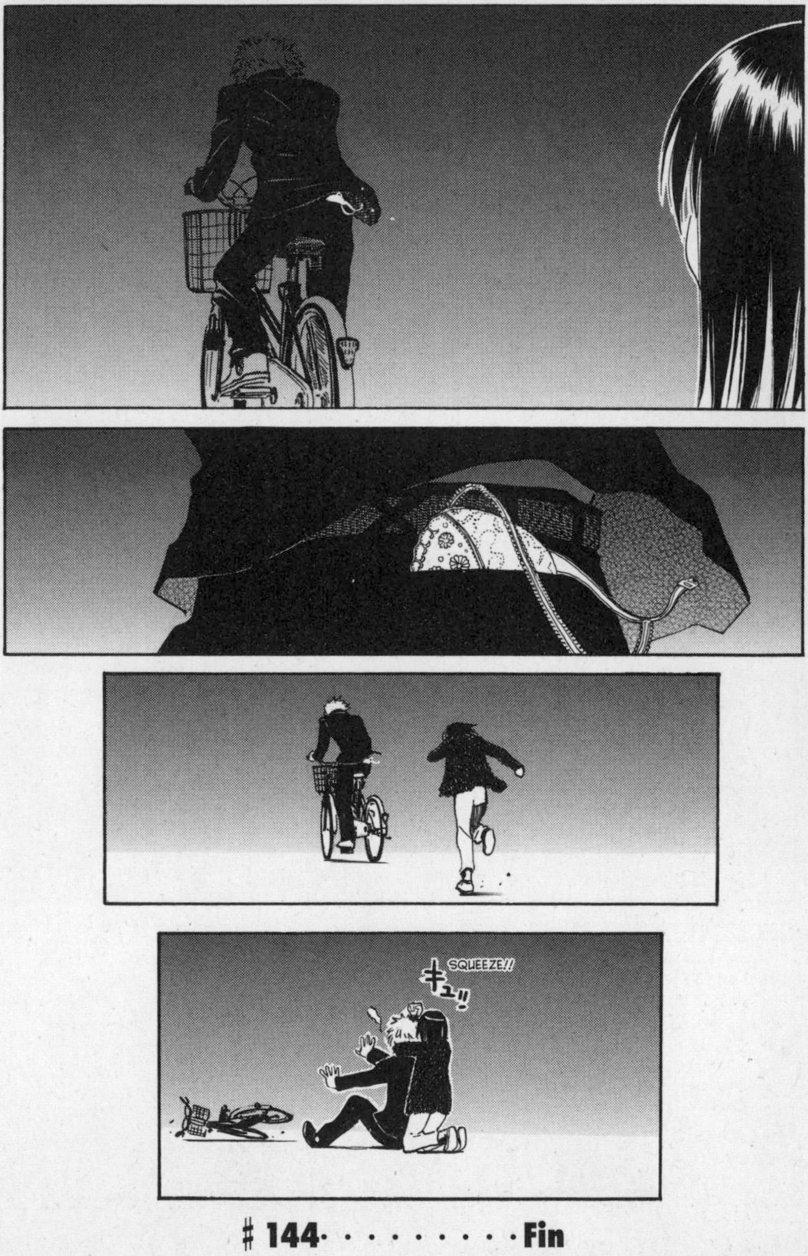
キュ!!
SQUEEZE!!

Cycling Off with Bra-vado!

144· · · · · · · · ·Fin

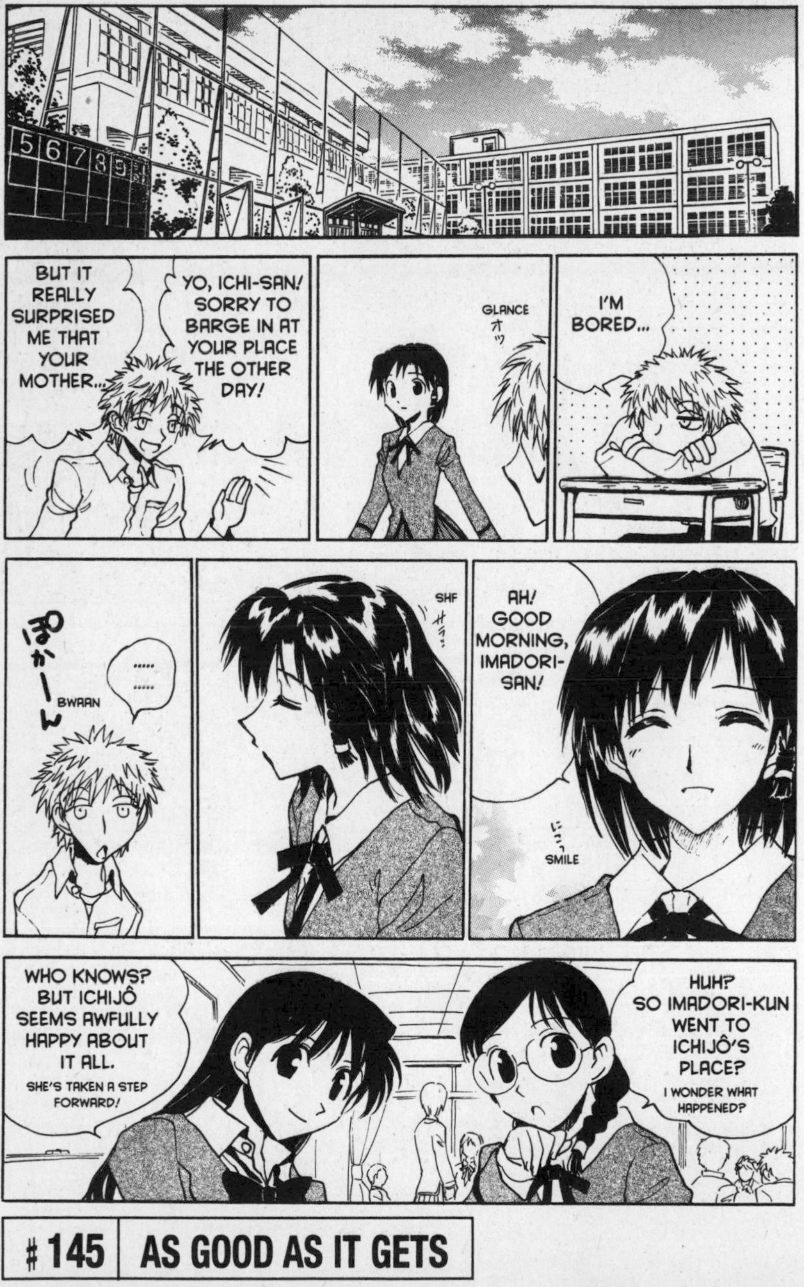
I'M BORED...
GLANCE
YO, ICHI-SAN! SORRY TO BARGE IN AT YOUR PLACE THE OTHER DAY!
BUT IT REALLY SURPRISED ME THAT YOUR MOTHER...
AH! GOOD MORNING, IMADORI-SAN!
にこっ
SMILE
SHF
......
......
ぽかーん
BWAAN
HUH? SO IMADORI-KUN WENT TO ICHIJÔ'S PLACE?
I WONDER WHAT HAPPENED?
WHO KNOWS? BUT ICHIJÔ SEEMS AWFULLY HAPPY ABOUT IT ALL.
SHE'S TAKEN A STEP FORWARD!

#145 AS GOOD AS IT GETS

Karasuma Ôji: At School After a Long Absence.

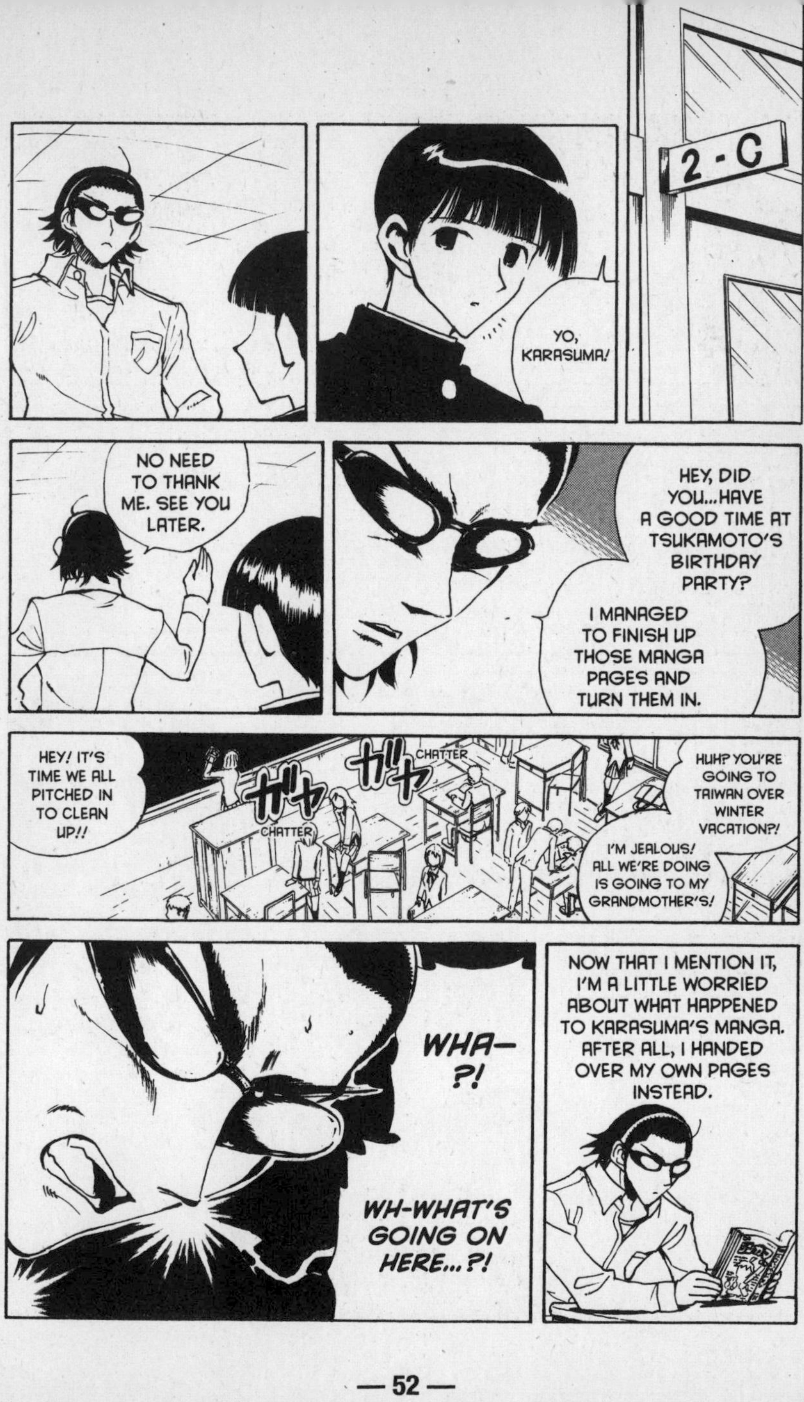

2-C
YO, KARASUMA!
HEY, DID YOU...HAVE A GOOD TIME AT TSUKAMOTO'S BIRTHDAY PARTY?
I MANAGED TO FINISH UP THOSE MANGA PAGES AND TURN THEM IN.
NO NEED TO THANK ME. SEE YOU LATER.
HUH? YOU'RE GOING TO TAIWAN OVER WINTER VACATION?!
I'M JEALOUS! ALL WE'RE DOING IS GOING TO MY GRANDMOTHER'S!
ガヤ CHATTER
ガヤ CHATTER
HEY! IT'S TIME WE ALL PITCHED IN TO CLEAN UP!!
NOW THAT I MENTION IT, I'M A LITTLE WORRIED ABOUT WHAT HAPPENED TO KARASUMA'S MANGA. AFTER ALL, I HANDED OVER MY OWN PAGES INSTEAD.
WHA—?!
WH-WHAT'S GOING ON HERE...?!

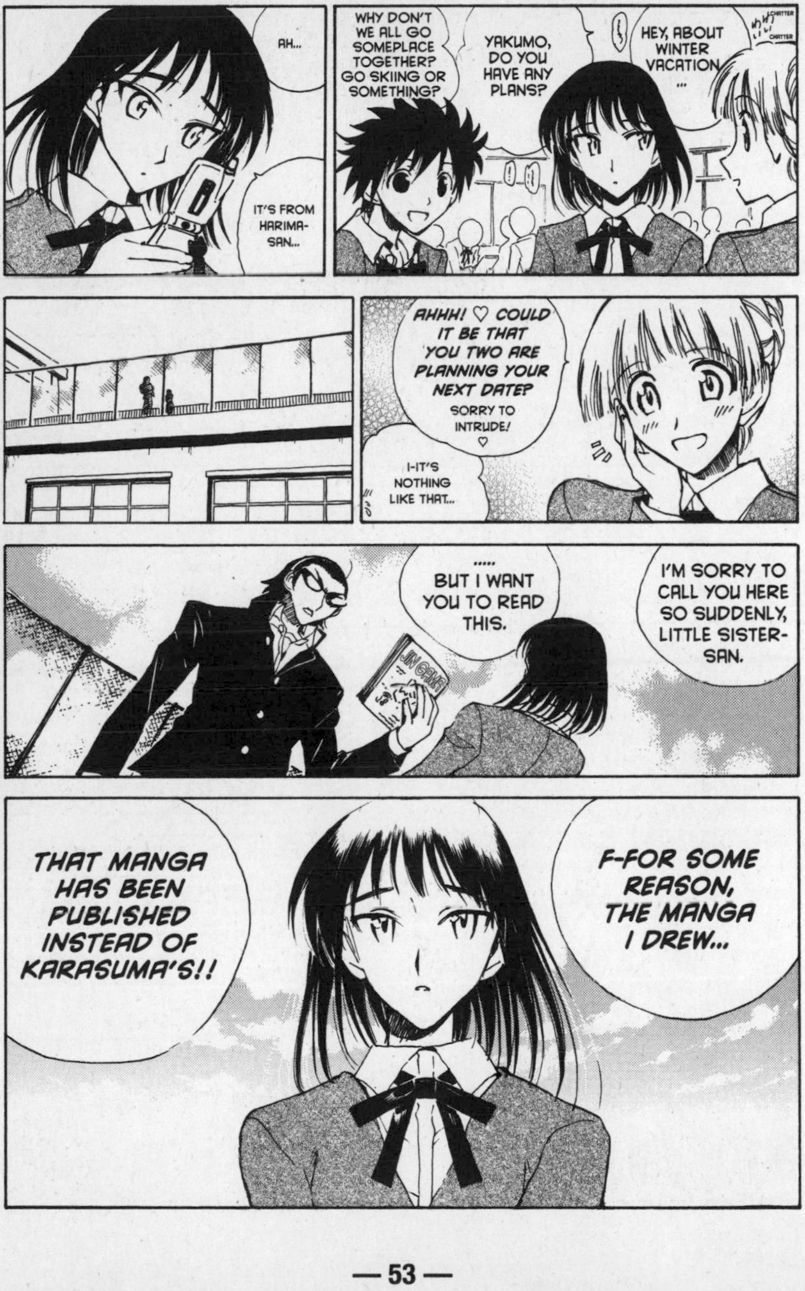
CHATTER
CHATTER
HEY, ABOUT WINTER VACATION ...
!
YAKUMO, DO YOU HAVE ANY PLANS?
WHY DON'T WE ALL GO SOMEPLACE TOGETHER? GO SKIING OR SOMETHING?
AH...
IT'S FROM HARIMA-SAN...
AHHH! ♡ COULD IT BE THAT YOU TWO ARE PLANNING YOUR NEXT DATE?
SORRY TO INTRUDE! ♡
I-IT'S NOTHING LIKE THAT...
I'M SORRY TO CALL YOU HERE SO SUDDENLY, LITTLE SISTER-SAN.
..... BUT I WANT YOU TO READ THIS.
F-FOR SOME REASON, THE MANGA I DREW...
THAT MANGA HAS BEEN PUBLISHED INSTEAD OF KARASUMA'S!!

Princess: Too Painfully Observant.

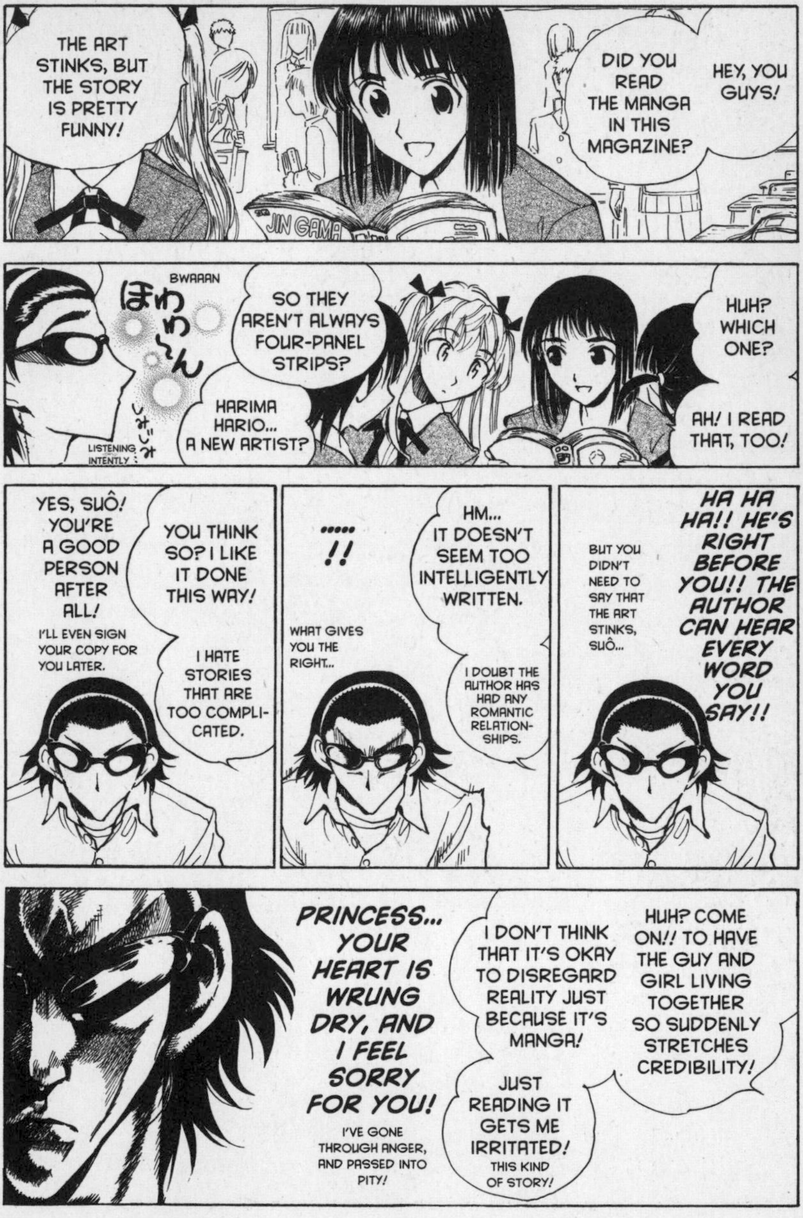
HEY, YOU GUYS!
DID YOU READ THE MANGA IN THIS MAGAZINE?
THE ART STINKS, BUT THE STORY IS PRETTY FUNNY!
JIN GAMA
HUH? WHICH ONE?
AH! I READ THAT, TOO!
SO THEY AREN'T ALWAYS FOUR-PANEL STRIPS?
HARIMA HARIO... A NEW ARTIST?
BWAAAN
ほわわ～ん
LISTENING INTENTLY
HA HA HA!! HE'S RIGHT BEFORE YOU!! THE AUTHOR CAN HEAR EVERY WORD YOU SAY!!
BUT YOU DIDN'T NEED TO SAY THAT THE ART STINKS, SUÔ...
HM... IT DOESN'T SEEM TOO INTELLIGENTLY WRITTEN.
I DOUBT THE AUTHOR HAS HAD ANY ROMANTIC RELATIONSHIPS.
......!!
WHAT GIVES YOU THE RIGHT...
YOU THINK SO? I LIKE IT DONE THIS WAY!
I HATE STORIES THAT ARE TOO COMPLICATED.
YES, SUÔ! YOU'RE A GOOD PERSON AFTER ALL!
I'LL EVEN SIGN YOUR COPY FOR YOU LATER.
HUH? COME ON!! TO HAVE THE GUY AND GIRL LIVING TOGETHER SO SUDDENLY STRETCHES CREDIBILITY!
I DON'T THINK THAT IT'S OKAY TO DISREGARD REALITY JUST BECAUSE IT'S MANGA!
JUST READING IT GETS ME IRRITATED! THIS KIND OF STORY!
PRINCESS... YOUR HEART IS WRUNG DRY, AND I FEEL SORRY FOR YOU!
I'VE GONE THROUGH ANGER, AND PASSED INTO PITY!

Harima Kenji: Has Lived for This Moment.

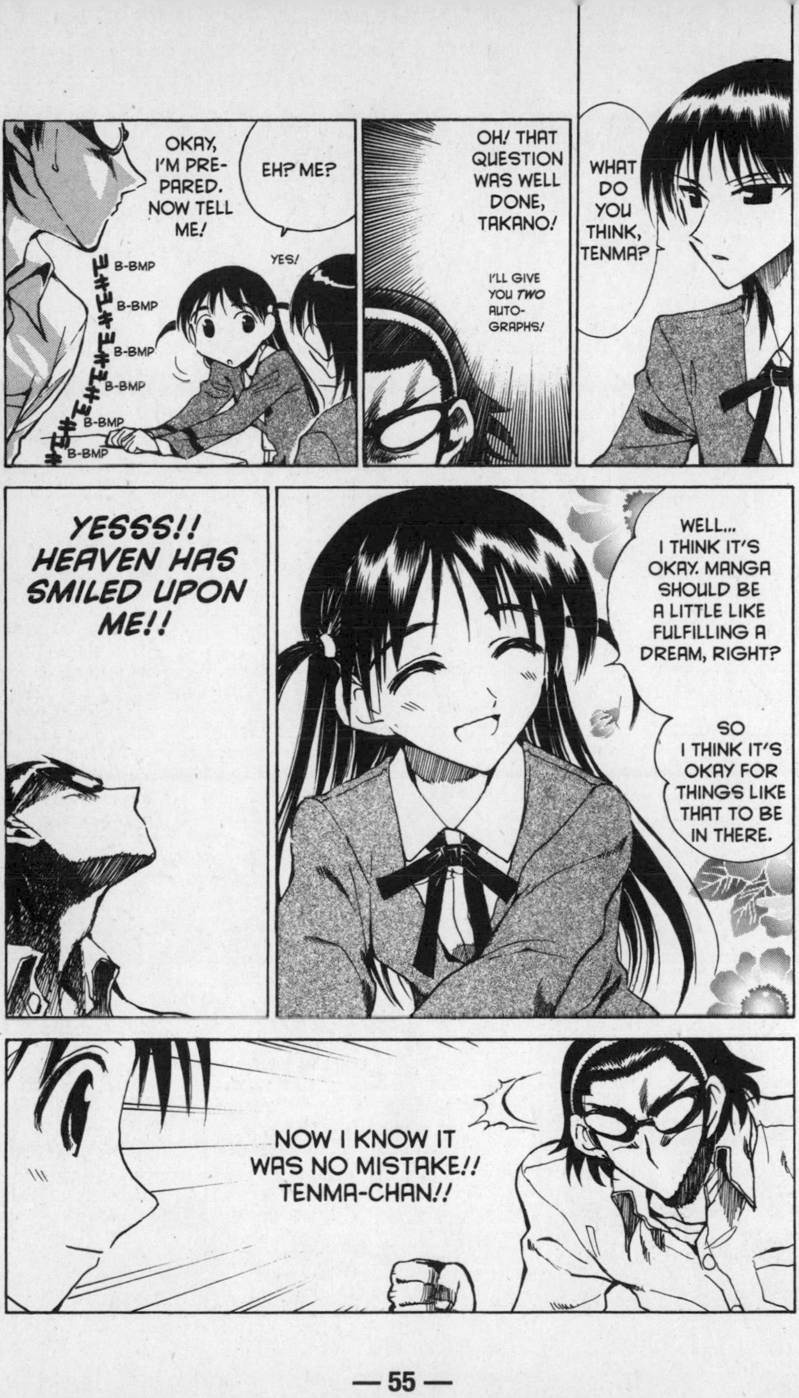
WHAT DO YOU THINK, TENMA?
OH! THAT QUESTION WAS WELL DONE, TAKANO!
I'LL GIVE YOU *TWO* AUTO-GRAPHS!
EH? ME?
YES!
OKAY, I'M PRE-PARED. NOW TELL ME!
B-BMP
B-BMP
B-BMP
B-BMP
B-BMP
B-BMP
WELL... I THINK IT'S OKAY. MANGA SHOULD BE A LITTLE LIKE FULFILLING A DREAM, RIGHT?
SO I THINK IT'S OKAY FOR THINGS LIKE THAT TO BE IN THERE.
YESSS!! HEAVEN HAS SMILED UPON ME!!
NOW I KNOW IT WAS NO MISTAKE!! TENMA-CHAN!!

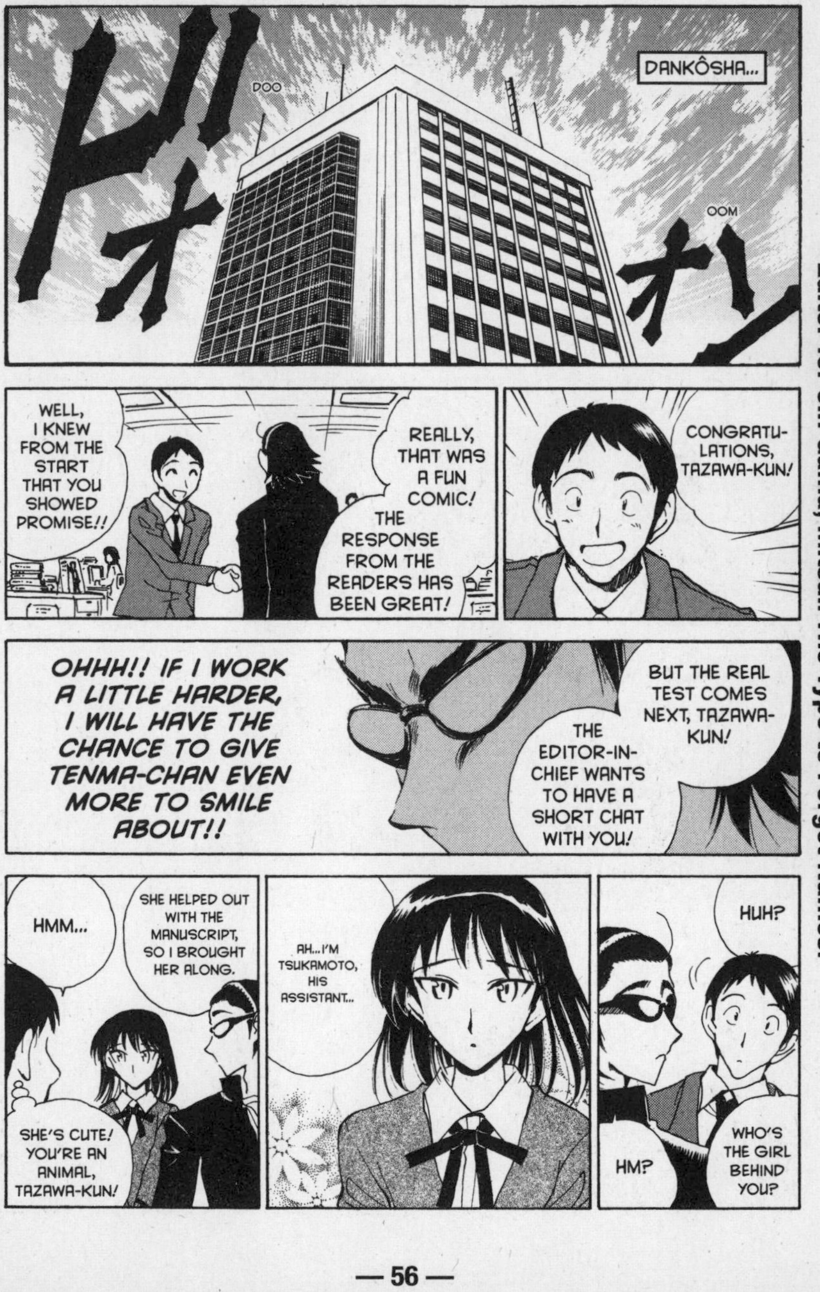
DANKÔSHA...
DOO
OOM
CONGRATULATIONS, TAZAWA-KUN!
REALLY, THAT WAS A FUN COMIC!
THE RESPONSE FROM THE READERS HAS BEEN GREAT!
WELL, I KNEW FROM THE START THAT YOU SHOWED PROMISE!!
BUT THE REAL TEST COMES NEXT, TAZAWA-KUN!
THE EDITOR-IN-CHIEF WANTS TO HAVE A SHORT CHAT WITH YOU!
OHHH!! IF I WORK A LITTLE HARDER, I WILL HAVE THE CHANCE TO GIVE TENMA-CHAN EVEN MORE TO SMILE ABOUT!!
HUH?
WHO'S THE GIRL BEHIND YOU?
HM?
AH...I'M TSUKAMOTO, HIS ASSISTANT...
SHE HELPED OUT WITH THE MANUSCRIPT, SO I BROUGHT HER ALONG.
HMM...
SHE'S CUTE! YOU'RE AN ANIMAL, TAZAWA-KUN!

Editor for Jin Gama, Mitsui: The Type to Forget Names.

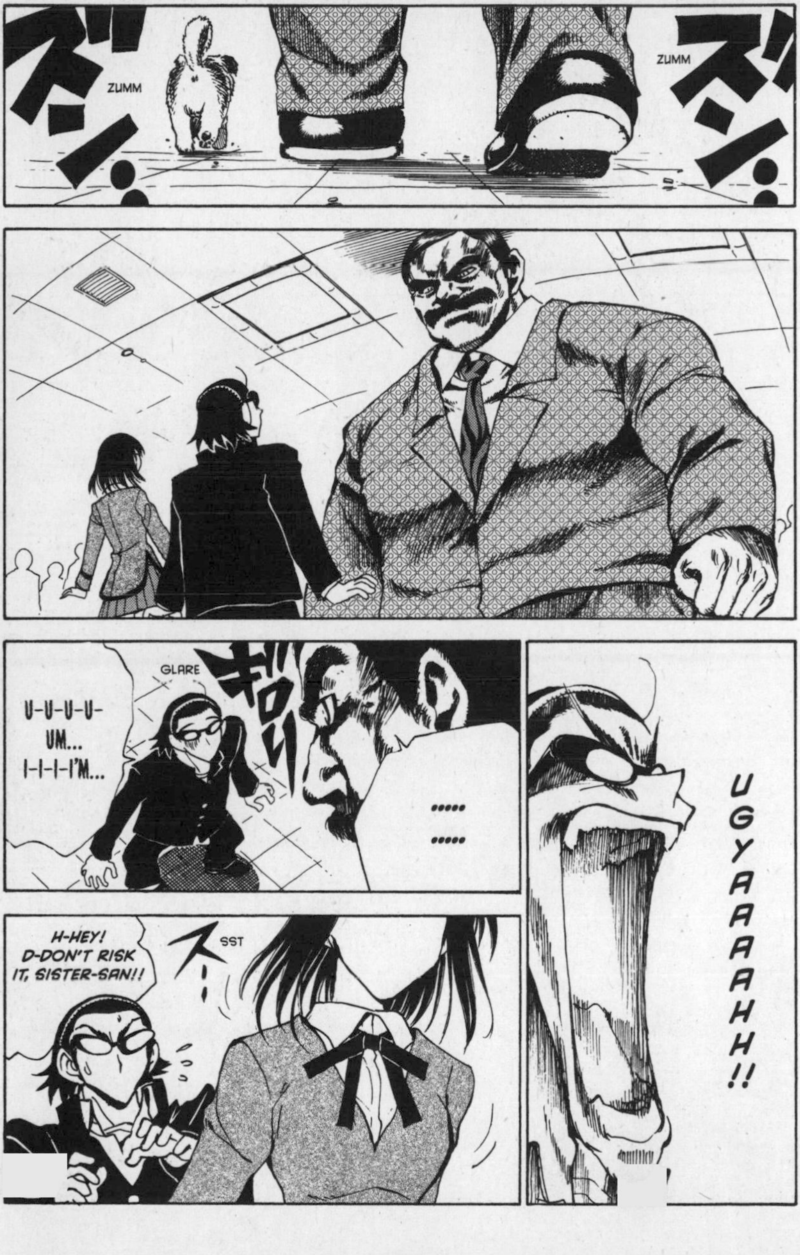
ZUMM
ZUMM
GLARE
U-U-U-U-UM... I-I-I-I'M...
.....
.....
UGYAAAAAHH!!
SST
H-HEY! D-DON'T RISK IT, SISTER-SAN!!

Jin Gama's Editor in Chief: Based on Nobody in Particular.

Editor in Chief: First Smile in 30 Years.

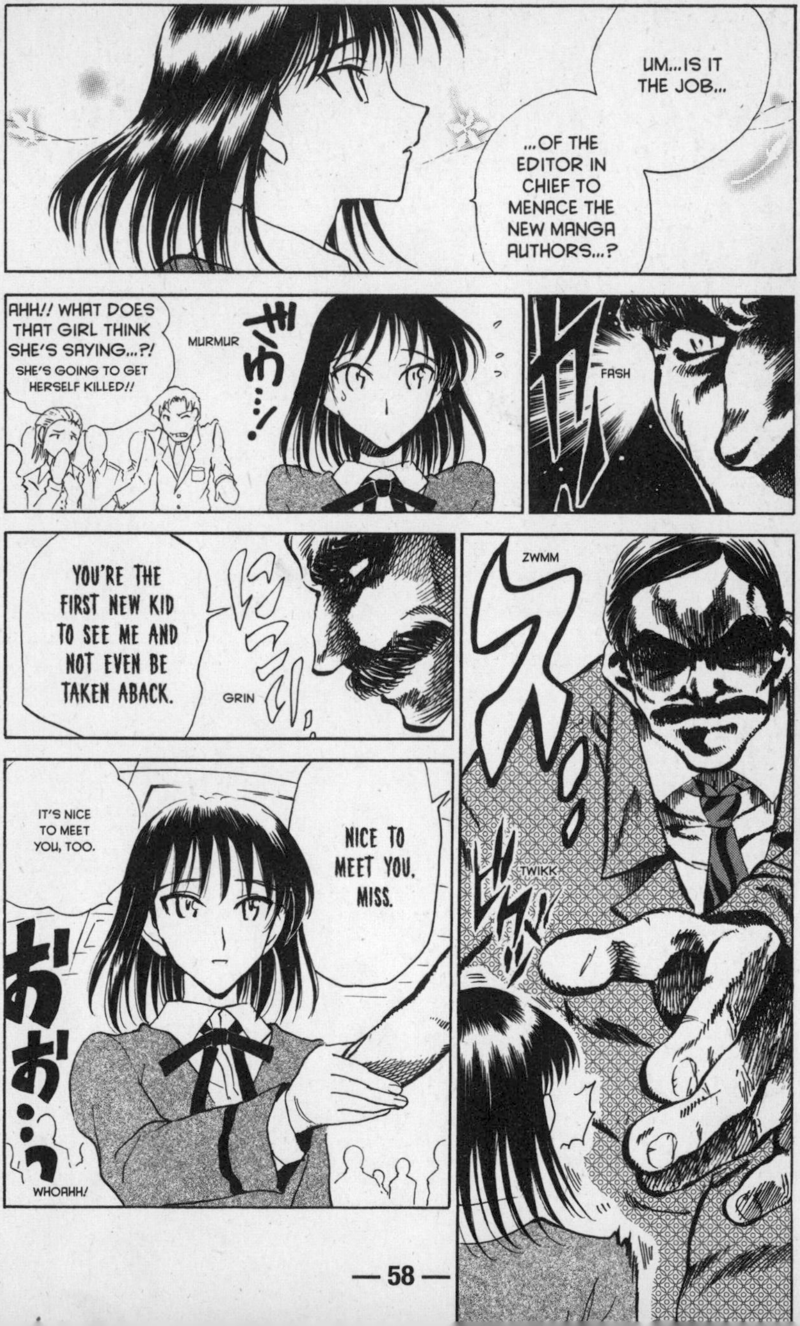
UM...IS IT THE JOB...
...OF THE EDITOR IN CHIEF TO MENACE THE NEW MANGA AUTHORS...?
FASH
MURMUR
AHH!! WHAT DOES THAT GIRL THINK SHE'S SAYING...?!
SHE'S GOING TO GET HERSELF KILLED!!
ZWMM
TWIKK
YOU'RE THE FIRST NEW KID TO SEE ME AND NOT EVEN BE TAKEN ABACK.
GRIN
NICE TO MEET YOU, MISS.
IT'S NICE TO MEET YOU, TOO.
WHOAHH!

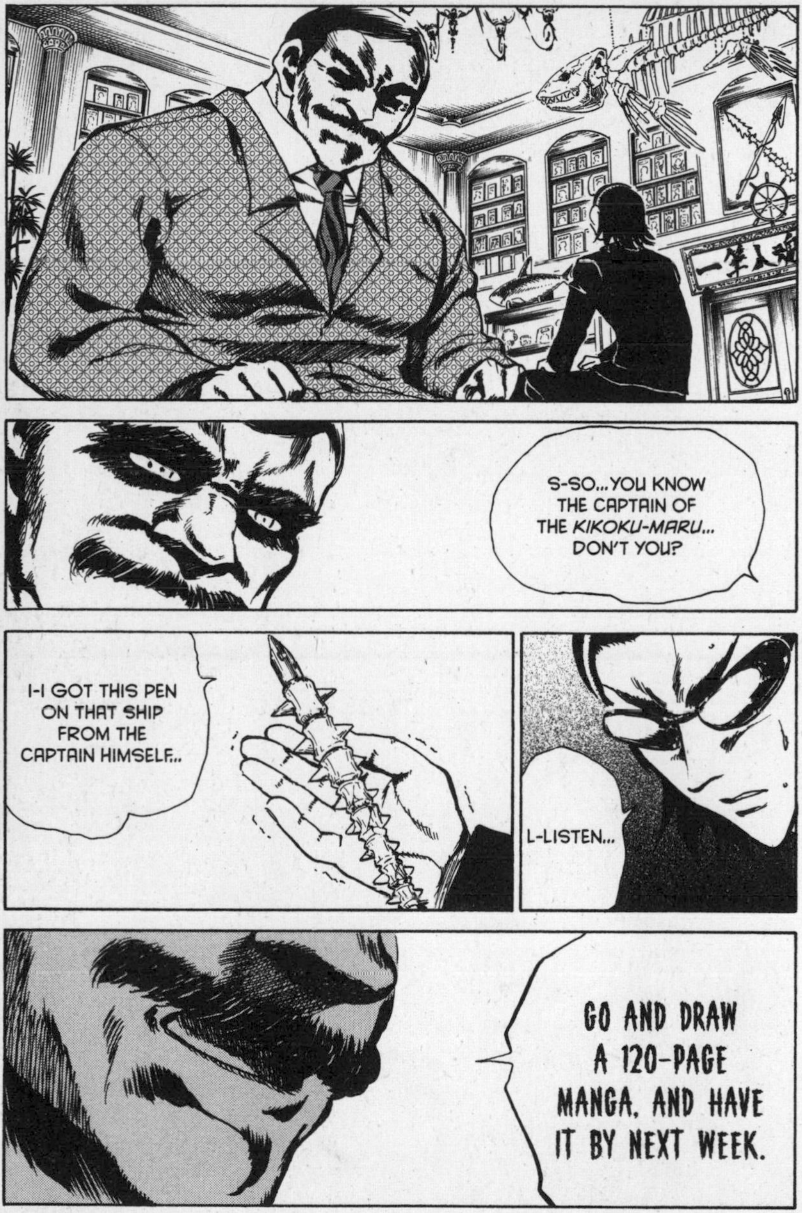
S-SO...YOU KNOW THE CAPTAIN OF THE *KIKOKU-MARU*... DON'T YOU?
L-LISTEN...
I-I GOT THIS PEN ON THAT SHIP FROM THE CAPTAIN HIMSELF...
GO AND DRAW A 120-PAGE MANGA, AND HAVE IT BY NEXT WEEK.

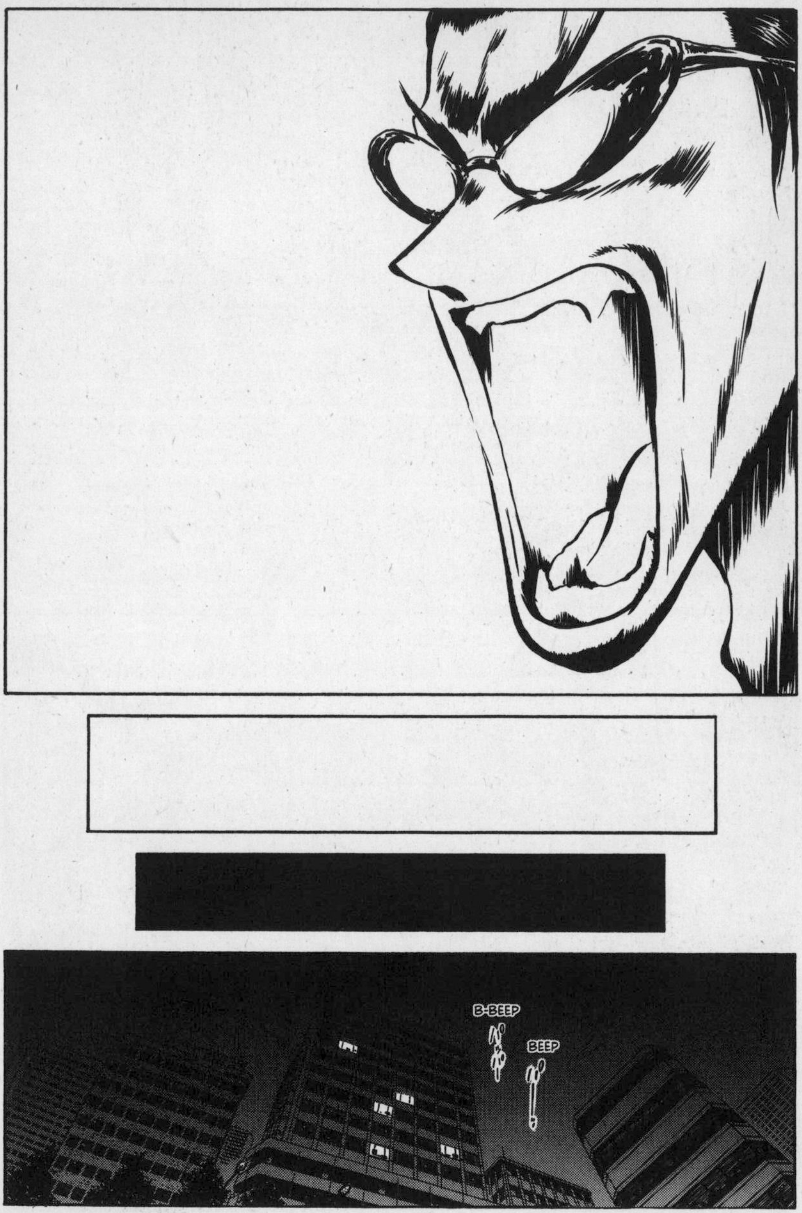
B-BEEP
BEEP

She Did Not Mince Words.

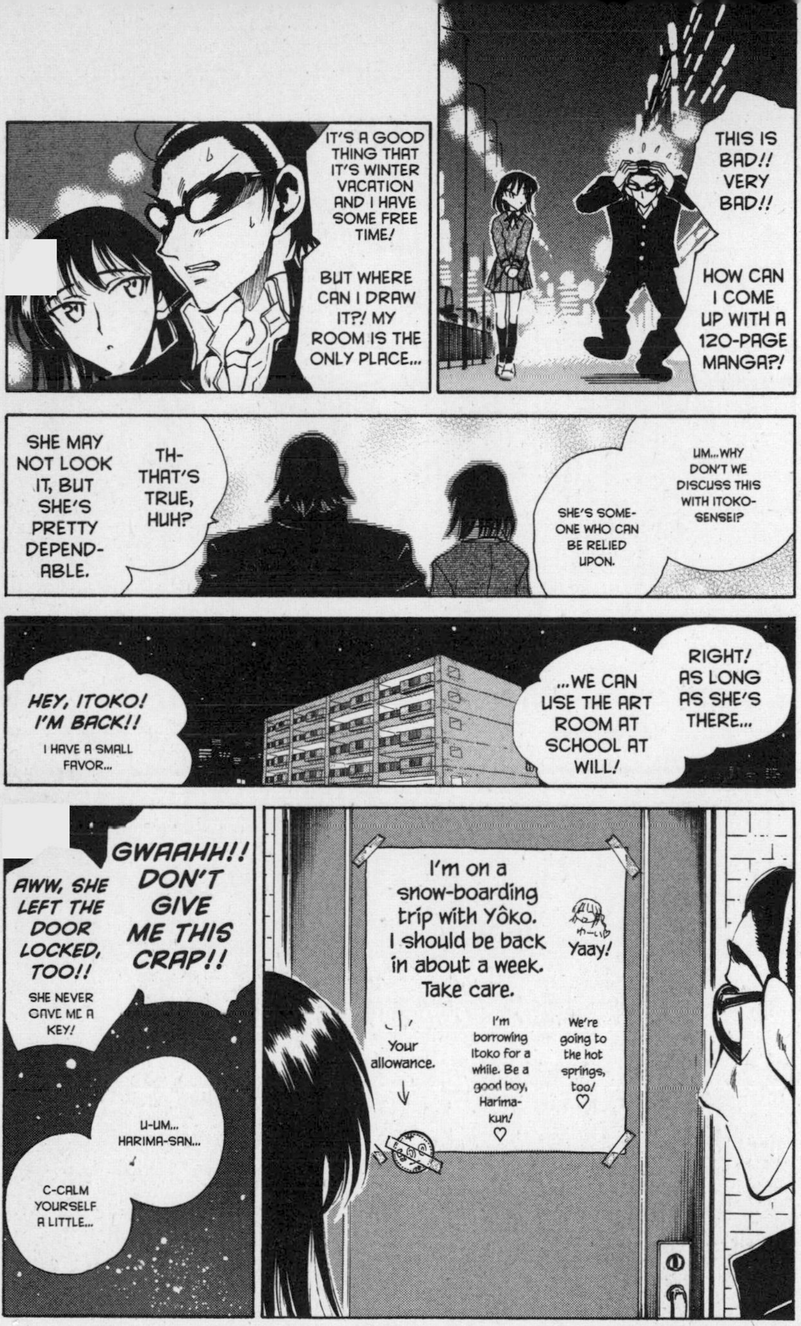
THIS IS BAD!! VERY BAD!!
HOW CAN I COME UP WITH A 120-PAGE MANGA?!
IT'S A GOOD THING THAT IT'S WINTER VACATION AND I HAVE SOME FREE TIME!
BUT WHERE CAN I DRAW IT?! MY ROOM IS THE ONLY PLACE...
UM...WHY DON'T WE DISCUSS THIS WITH ITOKO-SENSEI?
SHE'S SOMEONE WHO CAN BE RELIED UPON.
TH-THAT'S TRUE, HUH?
SHE MAY NOT LOOK IT, BUT SHE'S PRETTY DEPENDABLE.
RIGHT! AS LONG AS SHE'S THERE...
...WE CAN USE THE ART ROOM AT SCHOOL AT WILL!
HEY, ITOKO! I'M BACK!!
I HAVE A SMALL FAVOR...
I'm on a snow-boarding trip with Yôko. I should be back in about a week. Take care.
Yaay!
We're going to the hot springs, too! ♡
I'm borrowing Itoko for a while. Be a good boy, Harima-kun! ♡
Your allowance.
GWAAHH!! DON'T GIVE ME THIS CRAP!!
AWW, SHE LEFT THE DOOR LOCKED, TOO!!
SHE NEVER GAVE ME A KEY!
U-UM... HARIMA-SAN...
C-CALM YOURSELF A LITTLE...

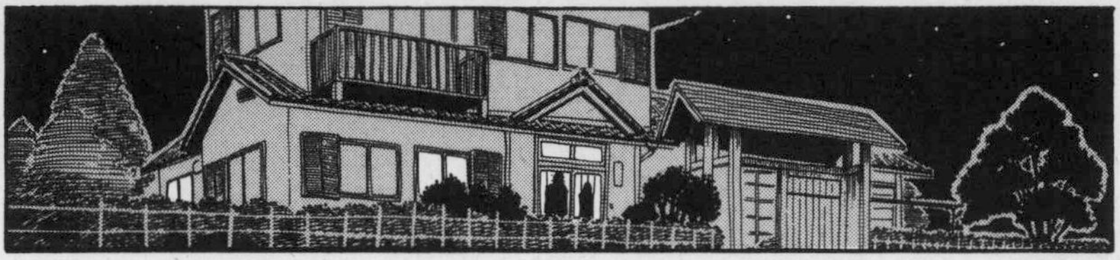

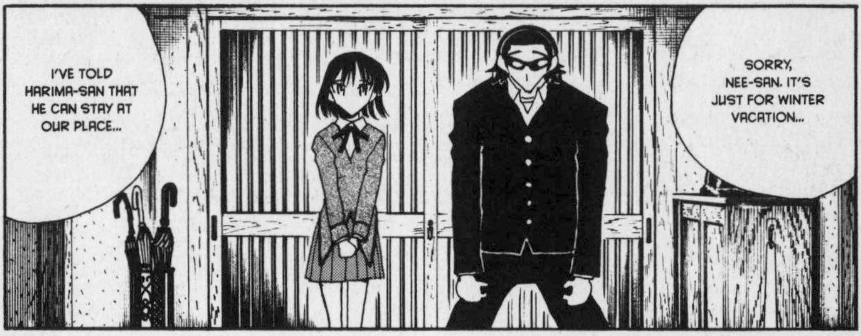
I'VE TOLD HARIMA-SAN THAT HE CAN STAY AT OUR PLACE...
SORRY, NEE-SAN. IT'S JUST FOR WINTER VACATION...

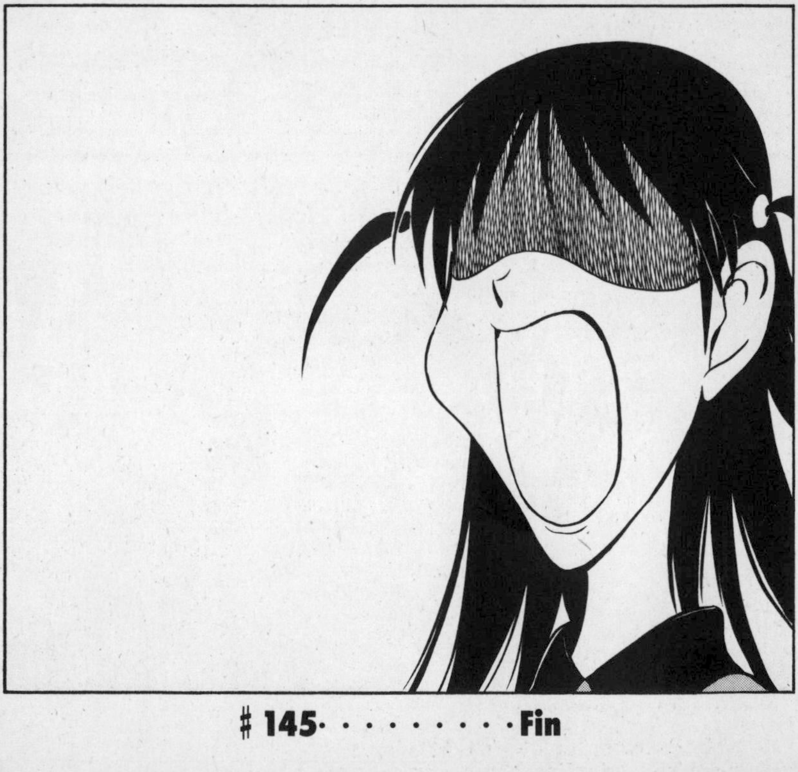

Well Done, Itoko! (Kenji)

145· · · · · · · · ·Fin

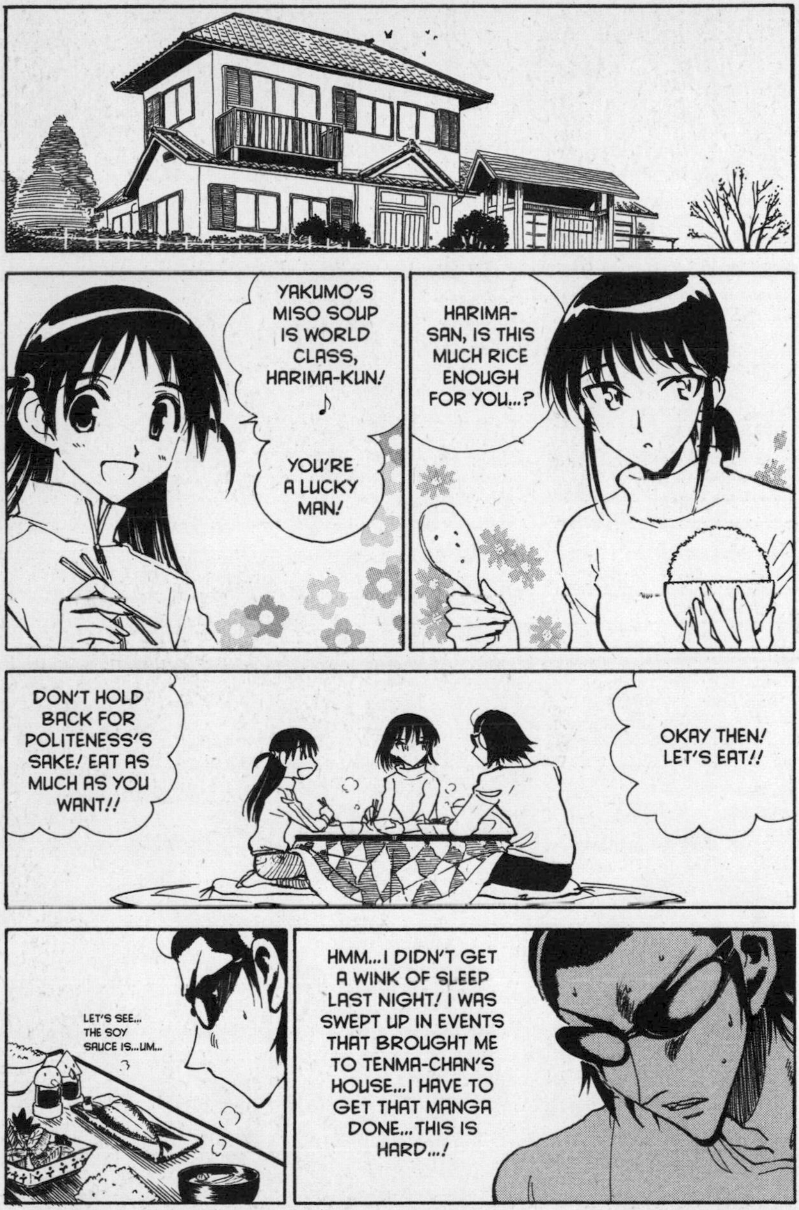
HARIMA-SAN, IS THIS MUCH RICE ENOUGH FOR YOU...?
YAKUMO'S MISO SOUP IS WORLD CLASS, HARIMA-KUN! ♪
YOU'RE A LUCKY MAN!
OKAY THEN! LET'S EAT!!
DON'T HOLD BACK FOR POLITENESS'S SAKE! EAT AS MUCH AS YOU WANT!!
HMM...I DIDN'T GET A WINK OF SLEEP LAST NIGHT! I WAS SWEPT UP IN EVENTS THAT BROUGHT ME TO TENMA-CHAN'S HOUSE...I HAVE TO GET THAT MANGA DONE...THIS IS HARD...!
LET'S SEE... THE SOY SAUCE IS...UM...

146 ONE HOUR WITH YOU

Harima: His Worries over His Manga Pages Have Flown to the Four Winds.

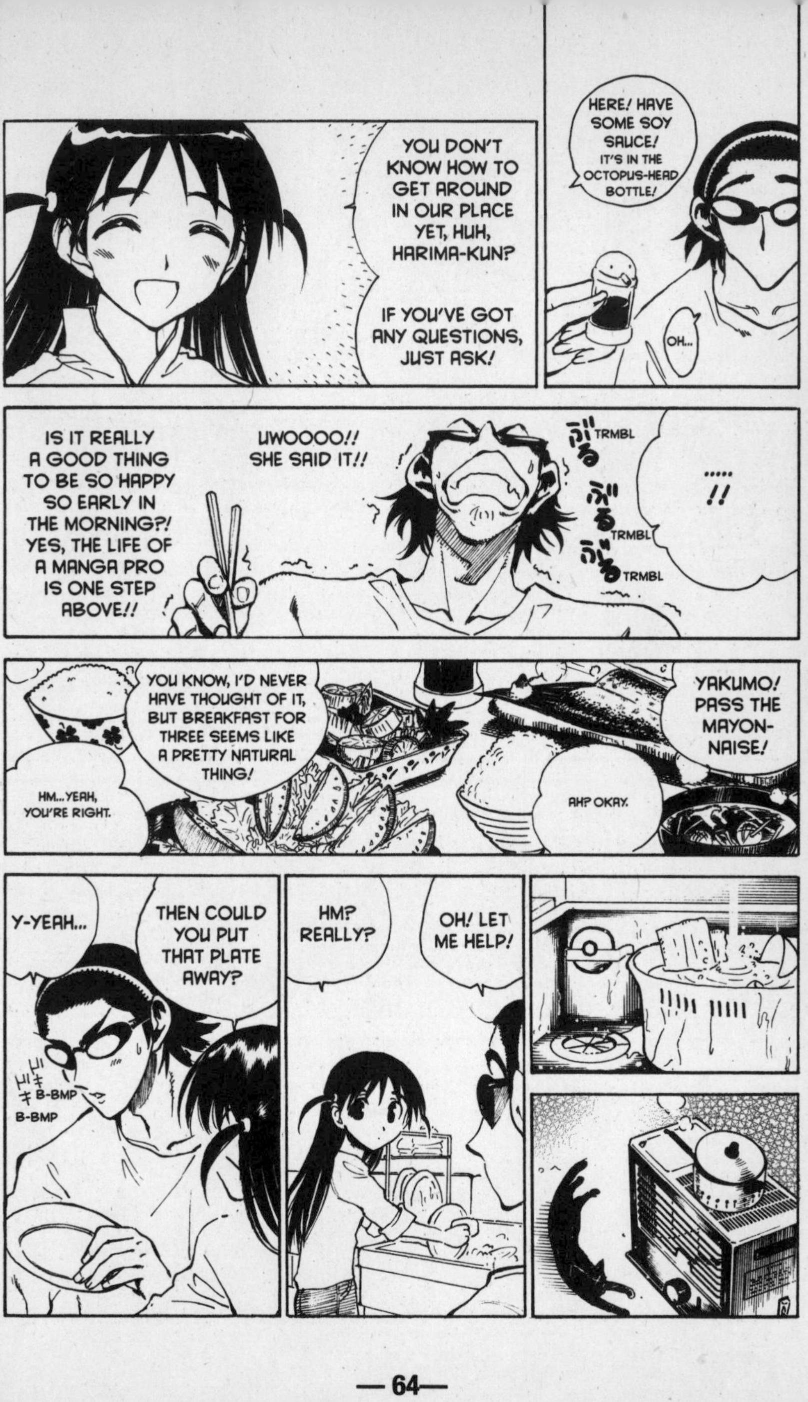
HERE! HAVE SOME SOY SAUCE! IT'S IN THE OCTOPUS-HEAD BOTTLE!
OH...
YOU DON'T KNOW HOW TO GET AROUND IN OUR PLACE YET, HUH, HARIMA-KUN?
IF YOU'VE GOT ANY QUESTIONS, JUST ASK!
.....!!
ぷる TRMBL
ぷる TRMBL
ぷる TRMBL
UWOOOO!! SHE SAID IT!!
IS IT REALLY A GOOD THING TO BE SO HAPPY SO EARLY IN THE MORNING?! YES, THE LIFE OF A MANGA PRO IS ONE STEP ABOVE!!
YAKUMO! PASS THE MAYON-NAISE!
AH? OKAY.
YOU KNOW, I'D NEVER HAVE THOUGHT OF IT, BUT BREAKFAST FOR THREE SEEMS LIKE A PRETTY NATURAL THING!
HM...YEAH, YOU'RE RIGHT.
OH! LET ME HELP!
HM? REALLY?
THEN COULD YOU PUT THAT PLATE AWAY?
Y-YEAH...
ドキ B-BMP
ドキ B-BMP

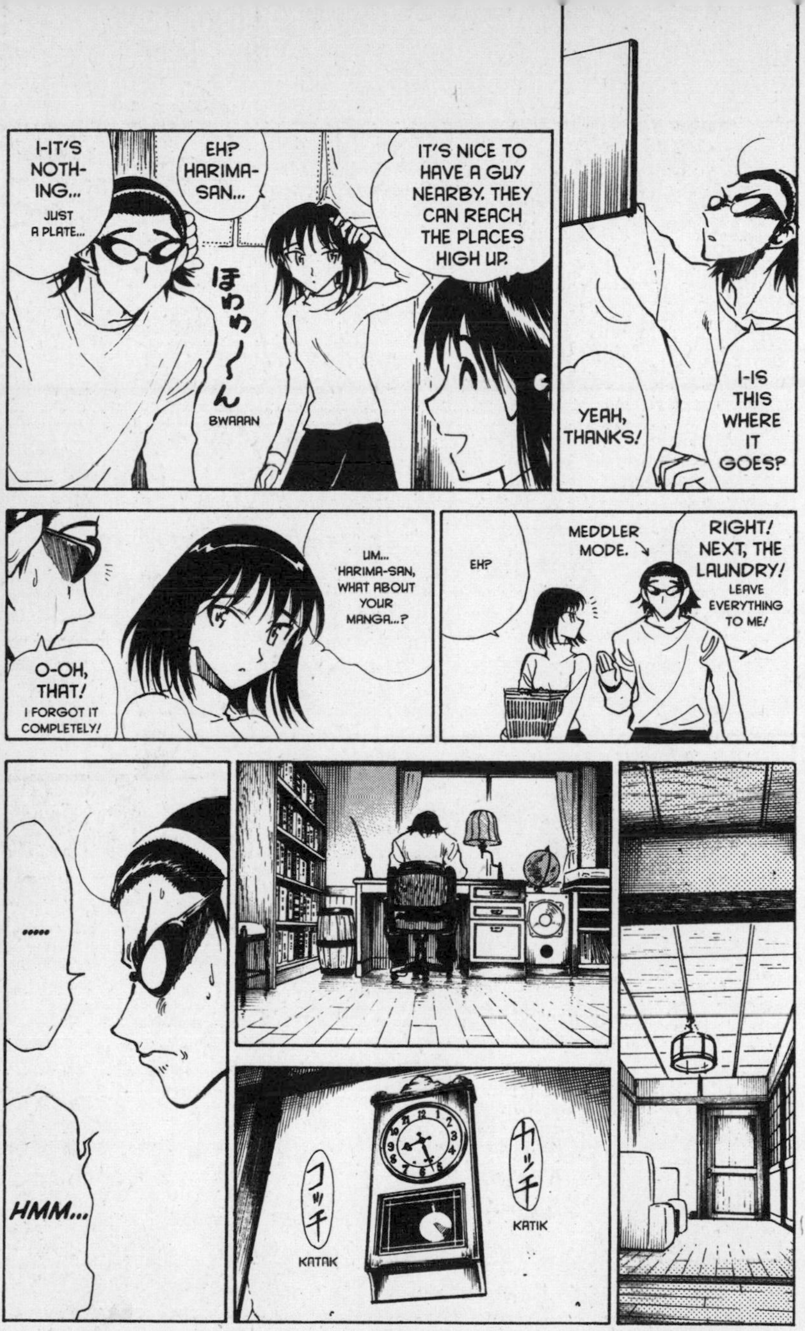
I-IS THIS WHERE IT GOES?
YEAH, THANKS!
IT'S NICE TO HAVE A GUY NEARBY. THEY CAN REACH THE PLACES HIGH UP.
EH? HARIMA-SAN...
ほわわ～ん
BWAAAN
I-IT'S NOTHING...
JUST A PLATE...
RIGHT! NEXT, THE LAUNDRY!
LEAVE EVERYTHING TO ME!
MEDDLER MODE.
EH?
UM... HARIMA-SAN, WHAT ABOUT YOUR MANGA...?
O-OH, THAT!
I FORGOT IT COMPLETELY!
カッチ
KATIK
コッチ
KATAK
......
HMM...

Harima: Drawing in the Study, Next Room Down the Hall.

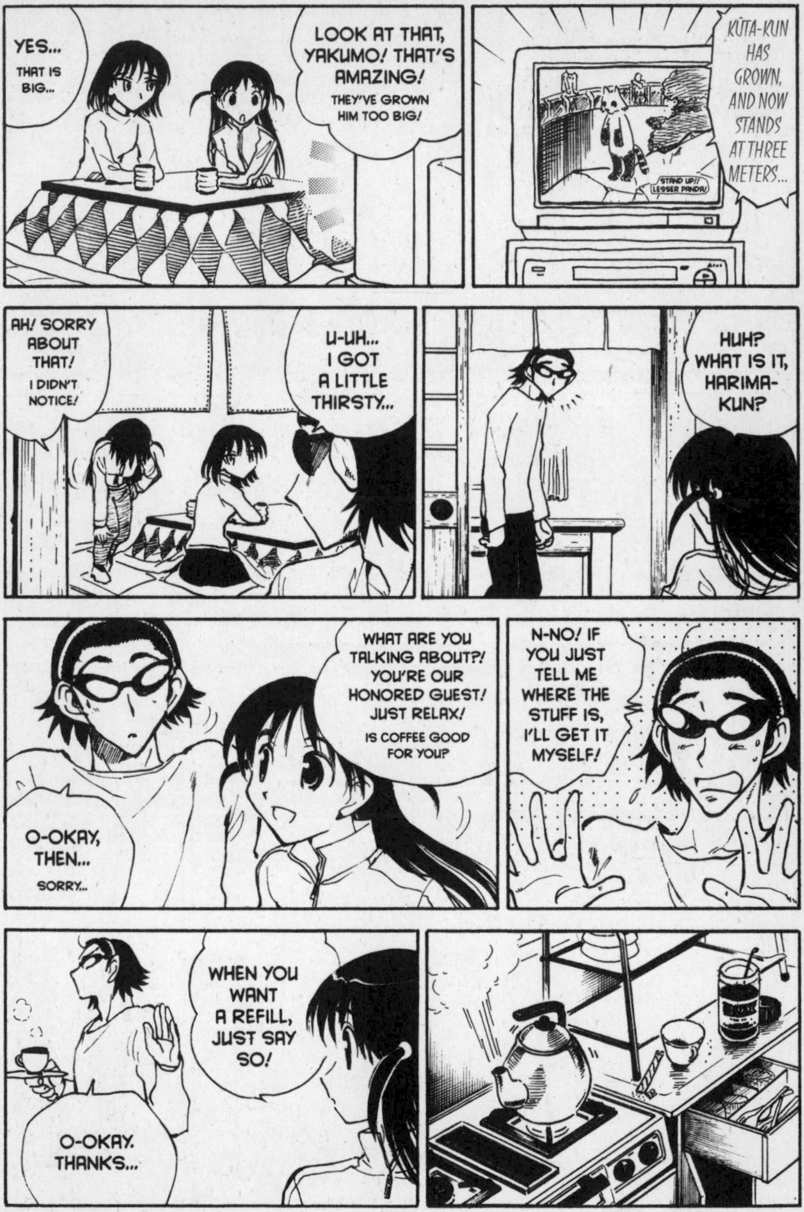

KŪTA-KUN HAS GROWN, AND NOW STANDS AT THREE METERS...
STAND UP!! LESSER PANDA!
LOOK AT THAT, YAKUMO! THAT'S AMAZING!
THEY'VE GROWN HIM TOO BIG!
YES... THAT IS BIG...
HUH? WHAT IS IT, HARIMA-KUN?
U-UH... I GOT A LITTLE THIRSTY...
AH! SORRY ABOUT THAT!
I DIDN'T NOTICE!
N-NO! IF YOU JUST TELL ME WHERE THE STUFF IS, I'LL GET IT MYSELF!
WHAT ARE YOU TALKING ABOUT?! YOU'RE OUR HONORED GUEST! JUST RELAX!
IS COFFEE GOOD FOR YOU?
O-OKAY, THEN...
SORRY...
WHEN YOU WANT A REFILL, JUST SAY SO!
O-OKAY. THANKS...

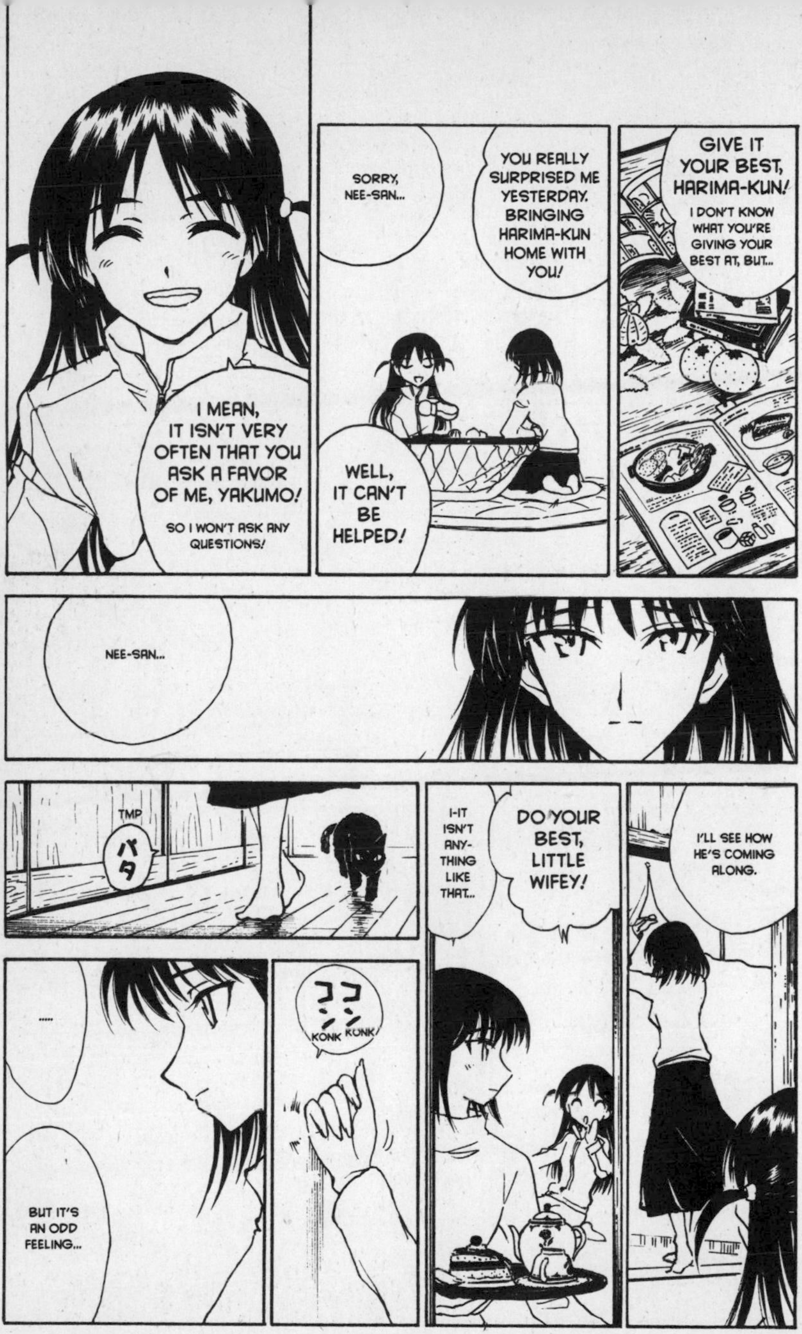
GIVE IT YOUR BEST, HARIMA-KUN!
I DON'T KNOW WHAT YOU'RE GIVING YOUR BEST AT, BUT...
YOU REALLY SURPRISED ME YESTERDAY. BRINGING HARIMA-KUN HOME WITH YOU!
SORRY, NEE-SAN...
WELL, IT CAN'T BE HELPED!
I MEAN, IT ISN'T VERY OFTEN THAT YOU ASK A FAVOR OF ME, YAKUMO!
SO I WON'T ASK ANY QUESTIONS!
NEE-SAN...
I'LL SEE HOW HE'S COMING ALONG.
DO YOUR BEST, LITTLE WIFEY!
I-IT ISN'T ANY-THING LIKE THAT...
パタ
TMP
コン コン
KONK KONK
.....
BUT IT'S AN ODD FEELING...

Tsukamoto Tenma: Sisterly...

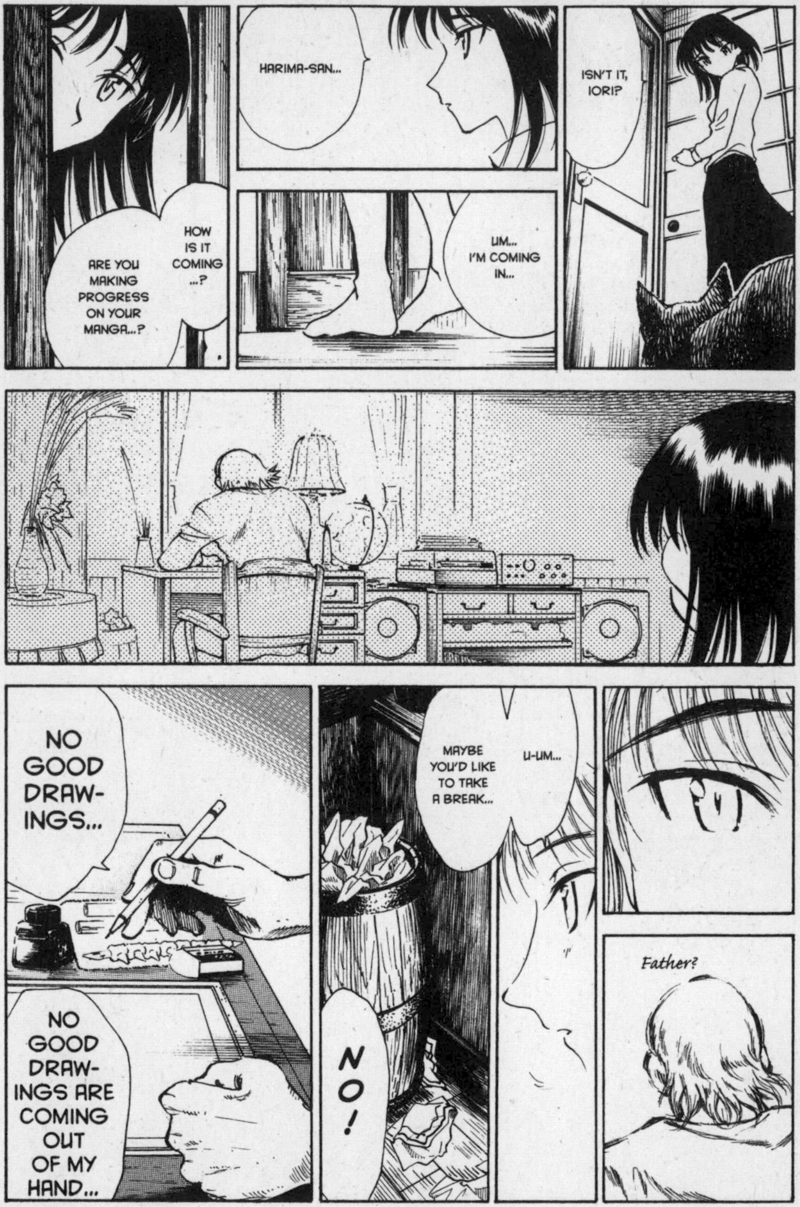
ISN'T IT, IORI?
HARIMA-SAN...
UM... I'M COMING IN...
HOW IS IT COMING ...?
ARE YOU MAKING PROGRESS ON YOUR MANGA...?
Father?
U-UM...
MAYBE YOU'D LIKE TO TAKE A BREAK...
NO!
NO GOOD DRAWINGS...
NO GOOD DRAWINGS ARE COMING OUT OF MY HAND...

Yakumo: Has Experience as a Model (Chapter 143).

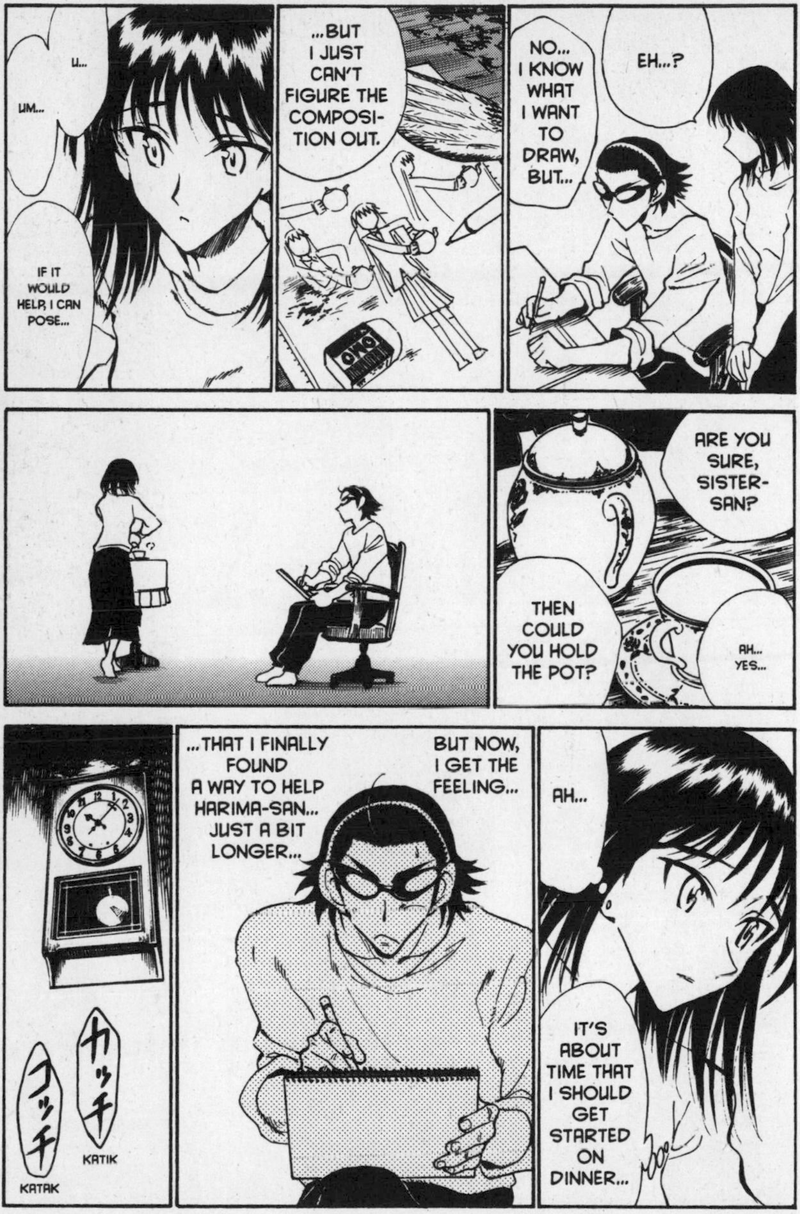
EH...?
NO... I KNOW WHAT I WANT TO DRAW, BUT...
...BUT I JUST CAN'T FIGURE THE COMPOSITION OUT.
U...
UM...
IF IT WOULD HELP, I CAN POSE...
ARE YOU SURE, SISTER-SAN?
AH... YES...
THEN COULD YOU HOLD THE POT?
AH...
IT'S ABOUT TIME THAT I SHOULD GET STARTED ON DINNER...
BUT NOW, I GET THE FEELING...
...THAT I FINALLY FOUND A WAY TO HELP HARIMA-SAN... JUST A BIT LONGER...
カッチ
KATIK
コッチ
KATAK

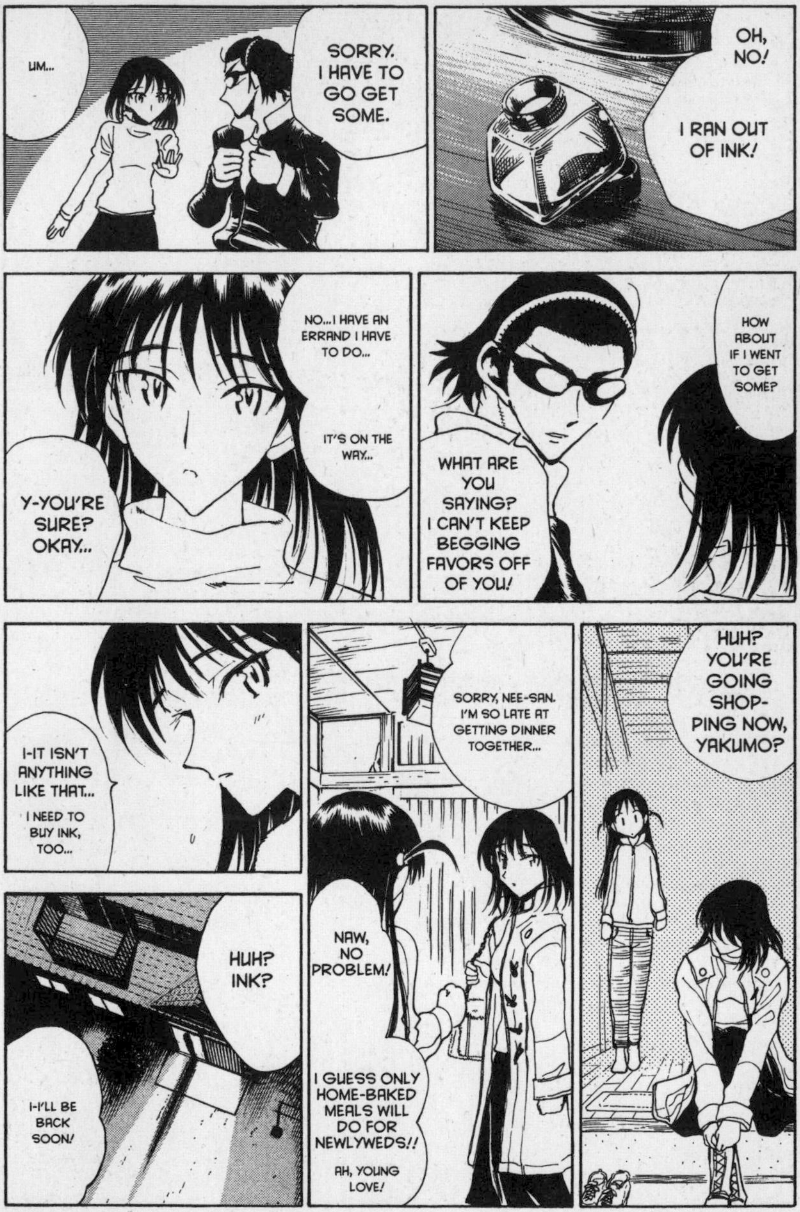
OH, NO!
I RAN OUT OF INK!
SORRY. I HAVE TO GO GET SOME.
UM...
HOW ABOUT IF I WENT TO GET SOME?
WHAT ARE YOU SAYING? I CAN'T KEEP BEGGING FAVORS OFF OF YOU!
NO...I HAVE AN ERRAND I HAVE TO DO...
IT'S ON THE WAY...
Y-YOU'RE SURE? OKAY...
HUH? YOU'RE GOING SHOP-PING NOW, YAKUMO?
SORRY, NEE-SAN. I'M SO LATE AT GETTING DINNER TOGETHER...
NAW, NO PROBLEM!
I GUESS ONLY HOME-BAKED MEALS WILL DO FOR NEWLYWEDS!!
AH, YOUNG LOVE!
I-IT ISN'T ANYTHING LIKE THAT...
I NEED TO BUY INK, TOO...
HUH? INK?
I-I'LL BE BACK SOON!

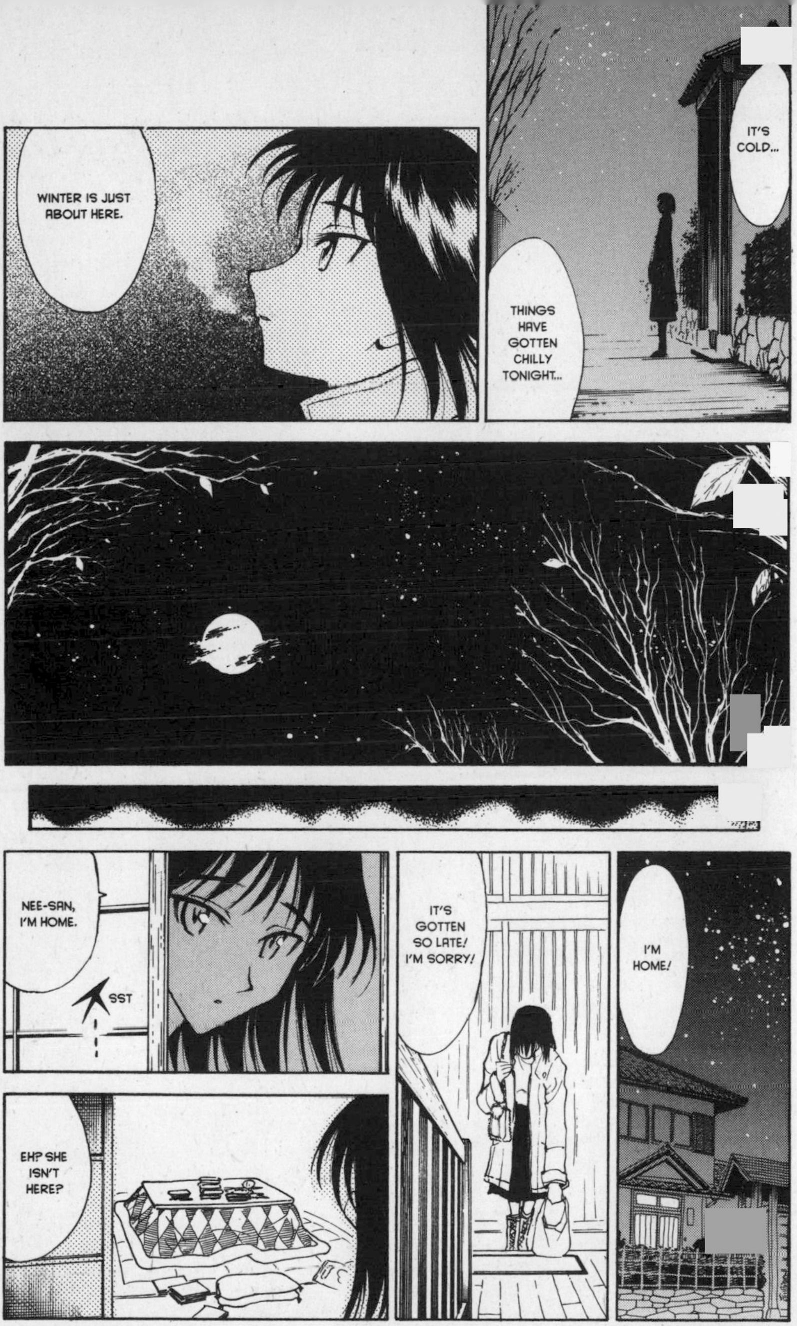
IT'S COLD...
THINGS HAVE GOTTEN CHILLY TONIGHT...
WINTER IS JUST ABOUT HERE.
I'M HOME!
IT'S GOTTEN SO LATE! I'M SORRY!
NEE-SAN, I'M HOME.
SST
EH? SHE ISN'T HERE?

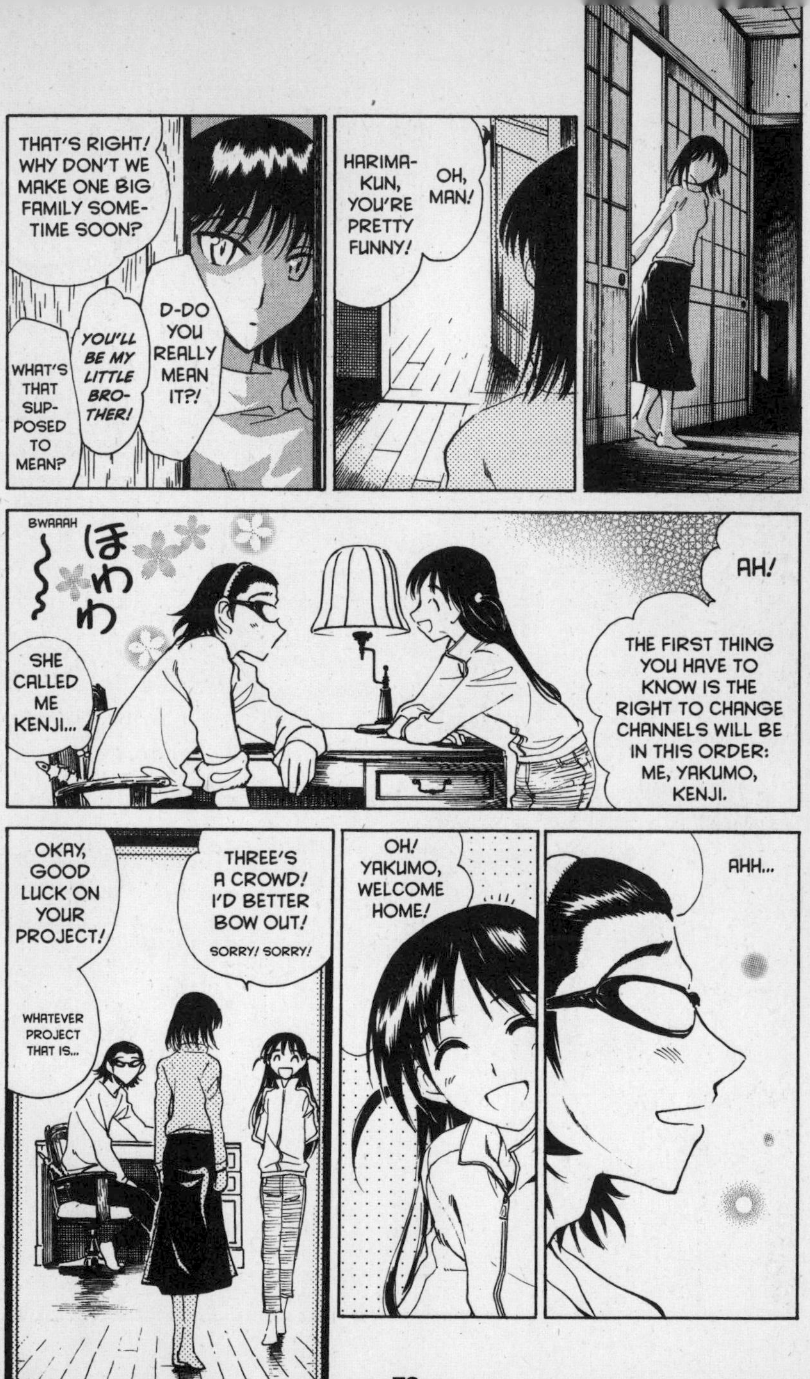
OH, MAN!
HARIMA-KUN, YOU'RE PRETTY FUNNY!
THAT'S RIGHT! WHY DON'T WE MAKE ONE BIG FAMILY SOMETIME SOON?
D-DO YOU REALLY MEAN IT?!
YOU'LL BE MY LITTLE BROTHER!
WHAT'S THAT SUPPOSED TO MEAN?
AH!
THE FIRST THING YOU HAVE TO KNOW IS THE RIGHT TO CHANGE CHANNELS WILL BE IN THIS ORDER: ME, YAKUMO, KENJI.
BWAAAH
ほわわ
SHE CALLED ME KENJI...
AHH...
OH! YAKUMO, WELCOME HOME!
THREE'S A CROWD! I'D BETTER BOW OUT!
SORRY! SORRY!
OKAY, GOOD LUCK ON YOUR PROJECT!
WHATEVER PROJECT THAT IS...

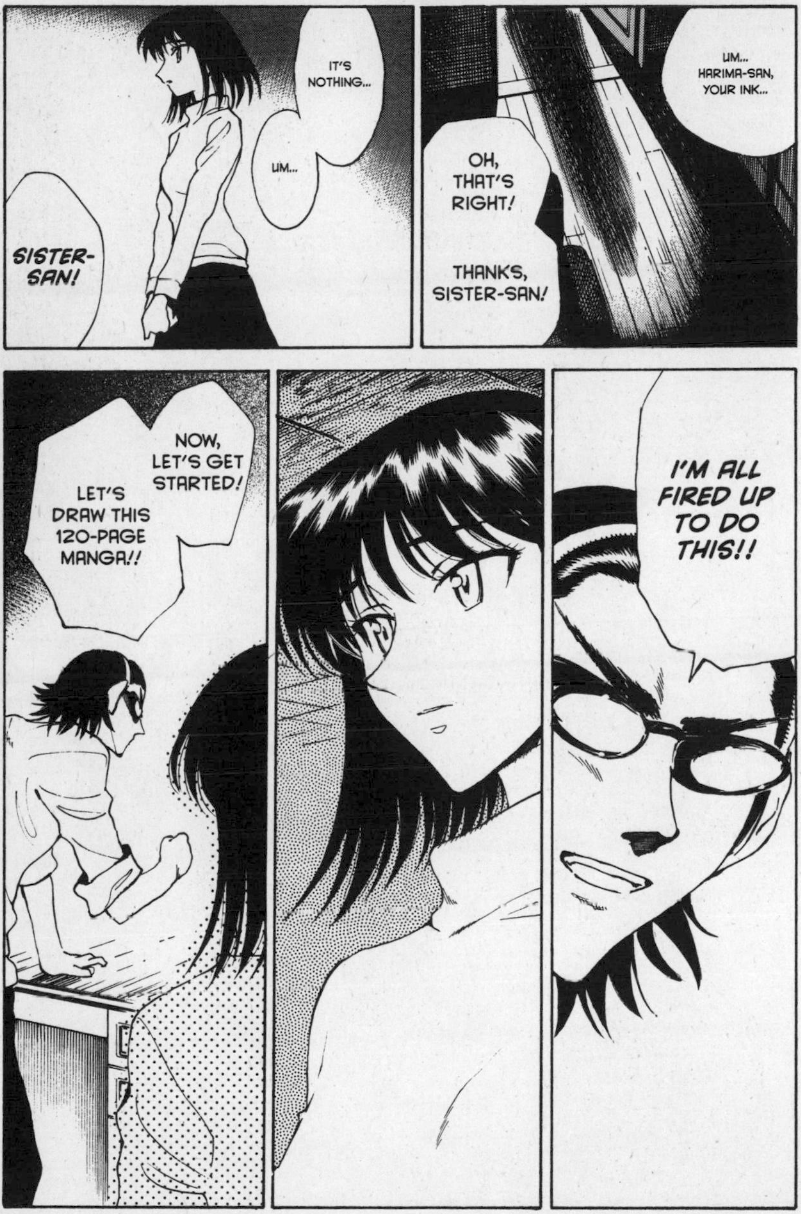
UM... HARIMA-SAN, YOUR INK...
OH, THAT'S RIGHT!
THANKS, SISTER-SAN!
IT'S NOTHING...
UM...
SISTER-SAN!
I'M ALL FIRED UP TO DO THIS!!
NOW, LET'S GET STARTED!
LET'S DRAW THIS 120-PAGE MANGA!!

It Was a Smile of Pure Joy...

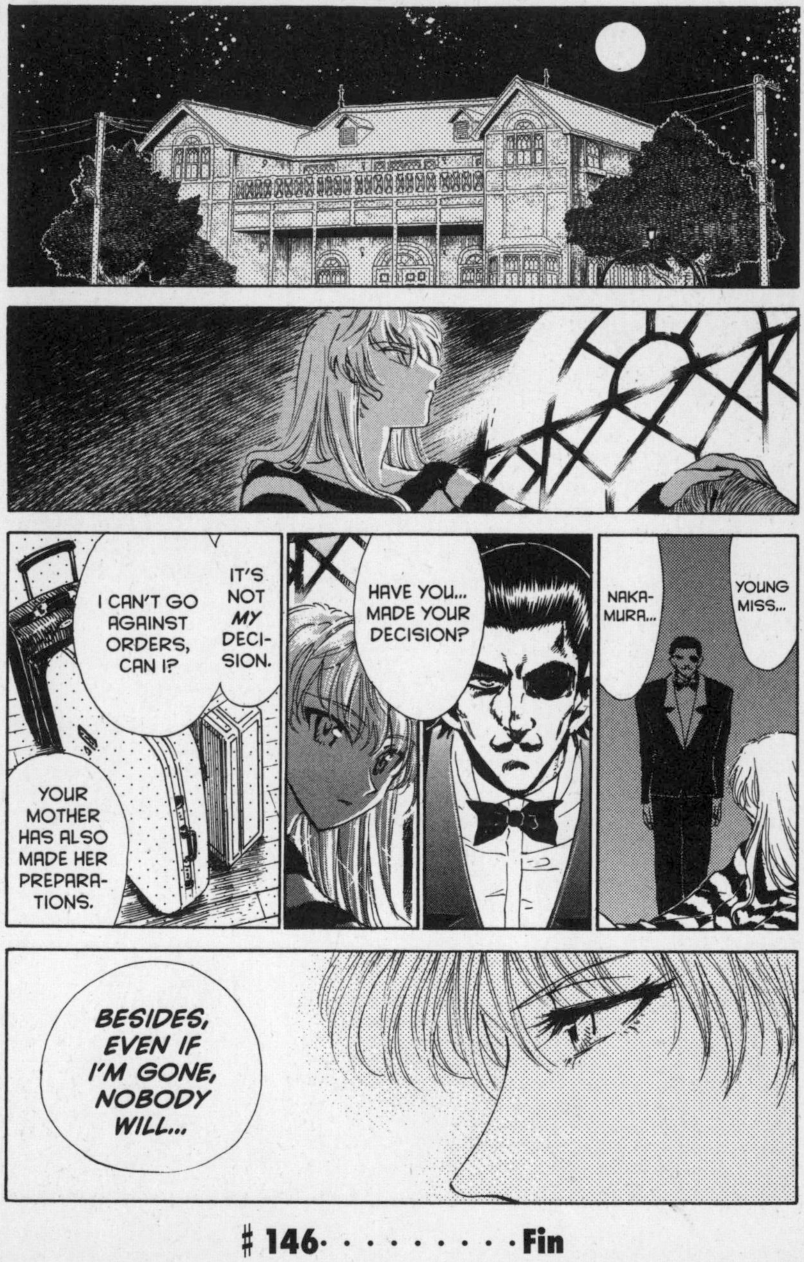
YOUNG MISS...
NAKAMURA...
HAVE YOU... MADE YOUR DECISION?
IT'S NOT *MY* DECISION.
I CAN'T GO AGAINST ORDERS, CAN I?
YOUR MOTHER HAS ALSO MADE HER PREPARATIONS.
BESIDES, EVEN IF I'M GONE, NOBODY WILL...

With Various Emotions in Play, the Winter Freeze Has Come to Yagami.

 # 146· · · · · · · · ·Fin

#147 TEST PILOT

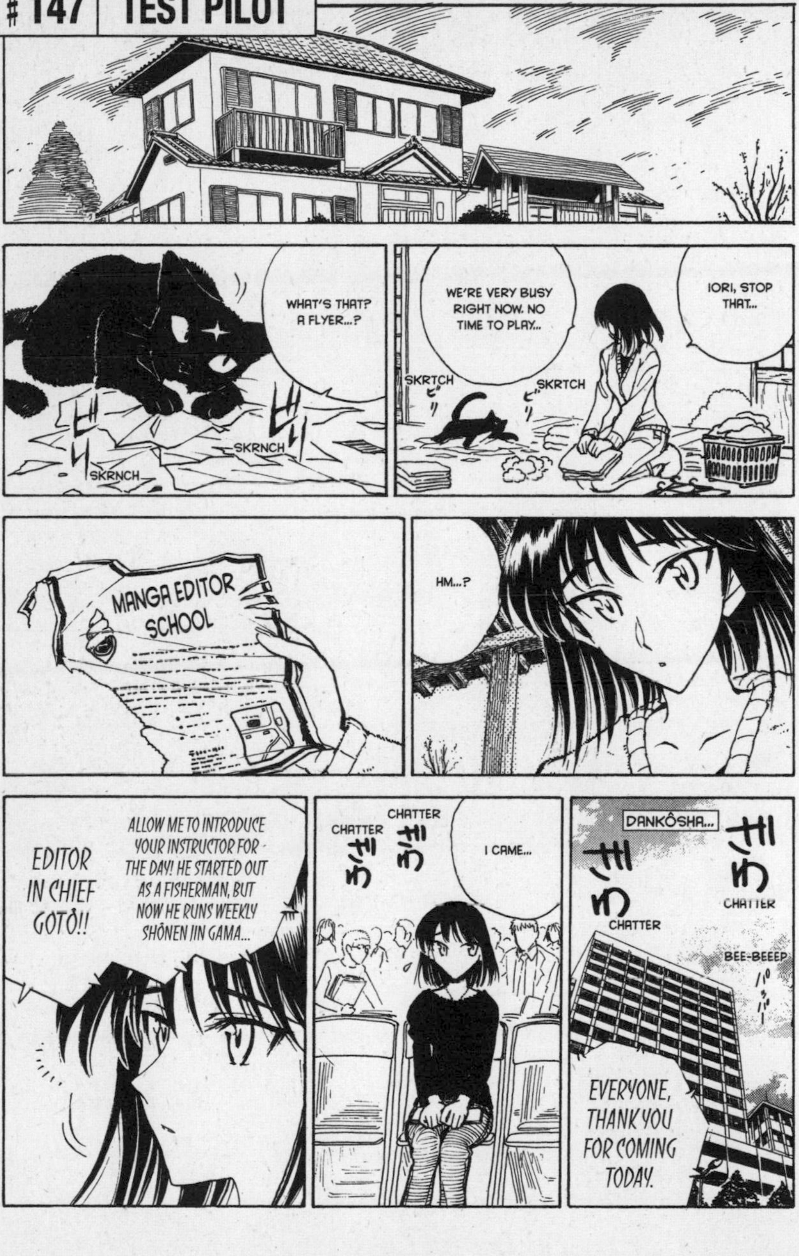
IORI, STOP THAT...
WE'RE VERY BUSY RIGHT NOW. NO TIME TO PLAY...
SKRTCH
SKRTCH
WHAT'S THAT? A FLYER...?
SKRNCH
SKRNCH
HM...?
MANGA EDITOR SCHOOL
DANKÔSHA...
CHATTER
CHATTER
BEE-BEEEP
EVERYONE, THANK YOU FOR COMING TODAY.
CHATTER
CHATTER
I CAME...
ALLOW ME TO INTRODUCE YOUR INSTRUCTOR FOR THE DAY! HE STARTED OUT AS A FISHERMAN, BUT NOW HE RUNS WEEKLY SHÔNEN JIN GAMA...
EDITOR IN CHIEF GOTÔ!!

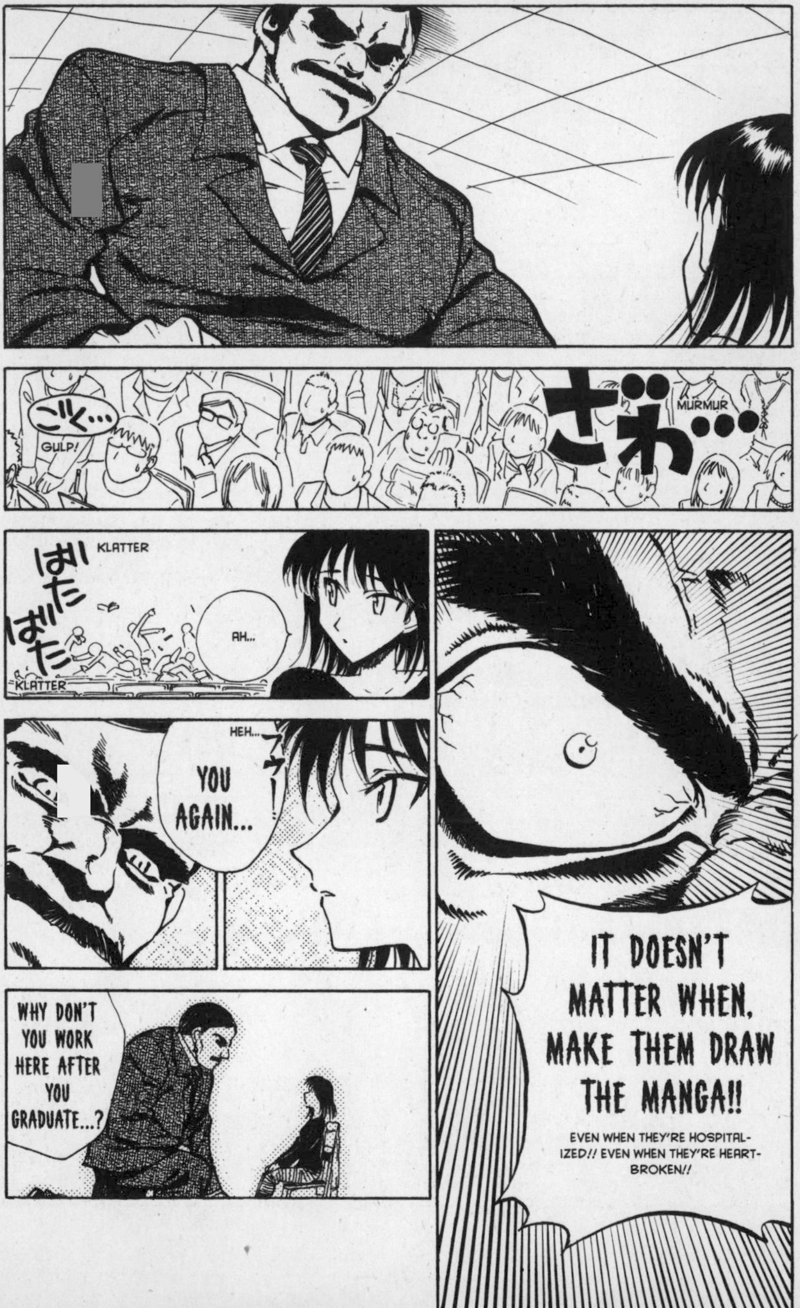
ざわ…
MURMUR
ごく…
GULP!
IT DOESN'T MATTER WHEN, MAKE THEM DRAW THE MANGA!!
EVEN WHEN THEY'RE HOSPITALIZED!! EVEN WHEN THEY'RE HEARTBROKEN!!
AH...
ばたばた
KLATTER
KLATTER
HEH...
YOU AGAIN...
WHY DON'T YOU WORK HERE AFTER YOU GRADUATE...?

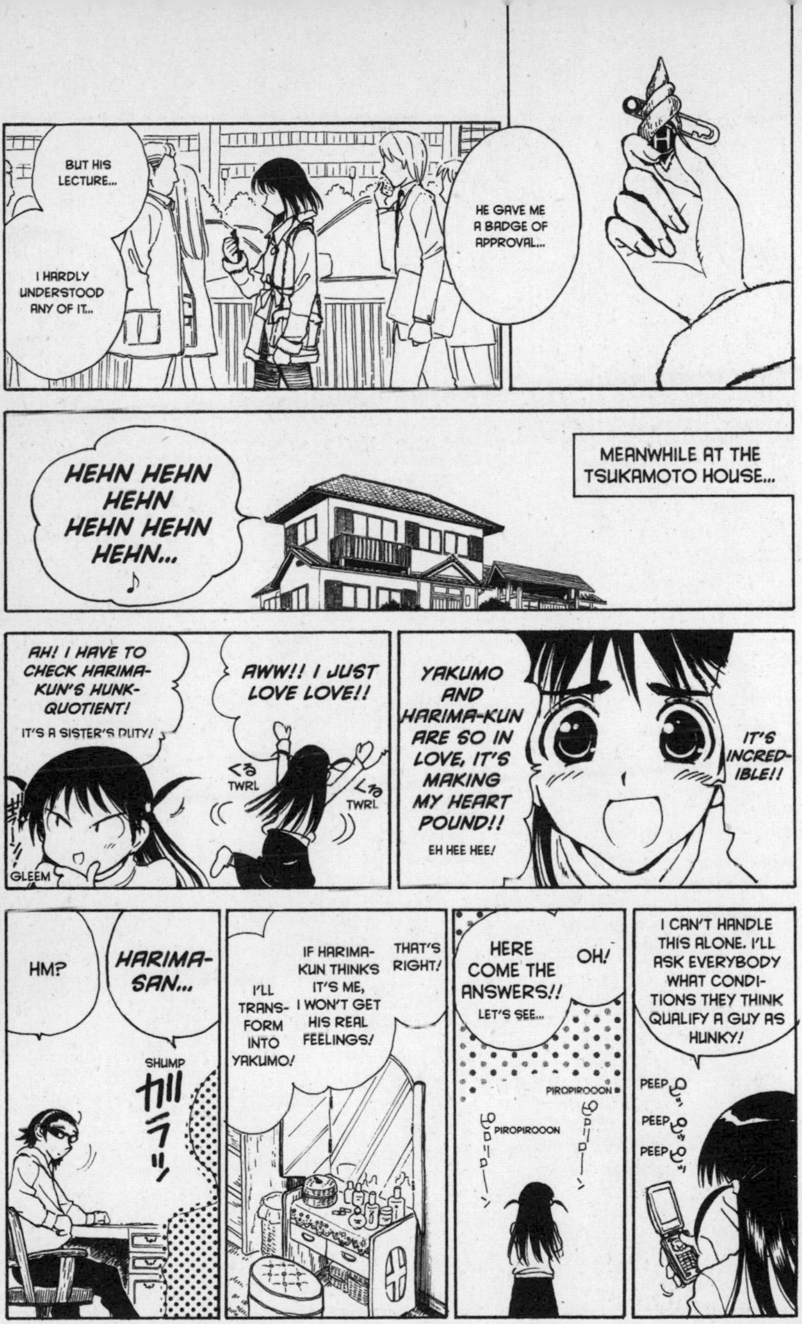
HE GAVE ME A BADGE OF APPROVAL...
BUT HIS LECTURE...
I HARDLY UNDERSTOOD ANY OF IT...
MEANWHILE AT THE TSUKAMOTO HOUSE...
HEHN HEHN HEHN HEHN HEHN HEHN... ♪
IT'S INCREDIBLE!!
YAKUMO AND HARIMA-KUN ARE SO IN LOVE, IT'S MAKING MY HEART POUND!!
EH HEE HEE!
AWW!! I JUST LOVE LOVE!!
くる TWRL
くる TWRL
AH! I HAVE TO CHECK HARIMA-KUN'S HUNK-QUOTIENT!
IT'S A SISTER'S DUTY!
GLEEM
I CAN'T HANDLE THIS ALONE. I'LL ASK EVERYBODY WHAT CONDITIONS THEY THINK QUALIFY A GUY AS HUNKY!
PEEP
PEEP
PEEP
OH!
HERE COME THE ANSWERS!!
LET'S SEE...
PIROPIROOON
PIROPIROOON
THAT'S RIGHT!
IF HARIMA-KUN THINKS IT'S ME, I WON'T GET HIS REAL FEELINGS!
I'LL TRANSFORM INTO YAKUMO!
HARIMA-SAN...
HM?
SHUMP

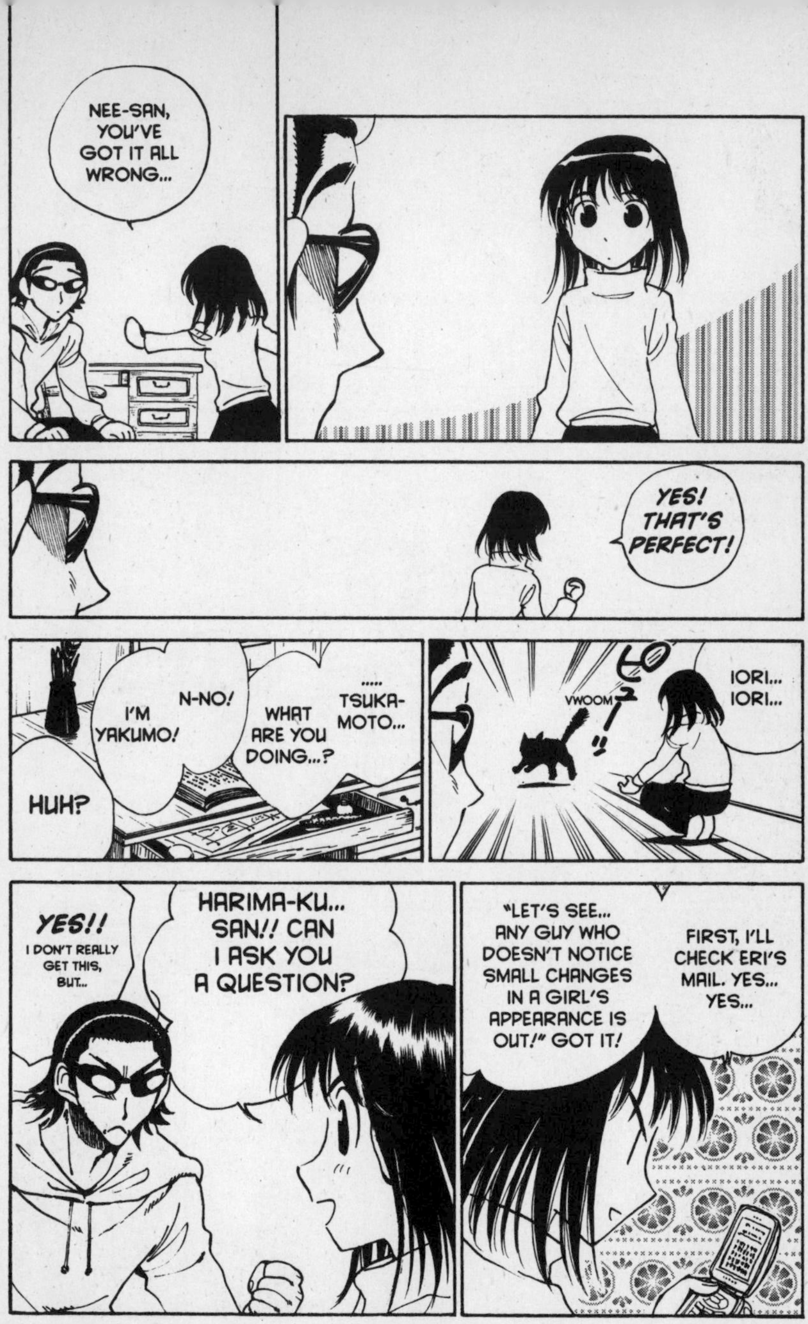
NEE-SAN, YOU'VE GOT IT ALL WRONG...
YES! THAT'S PERFECT!
IORI... IORI...
VWOOM
..... TSUKAMOTO... WHAT ARE YOU DOING...?
N-NO! I'M YAKUMO!
HUH?
FIRST, I'LL CHECK ERI'S MAIL. YES... YES...
"LET'S SEE... ANY GUY WHO DOESN'T NOTICE SMALL CHANGES IN A GIRL'S APPEARANCE IS OUT!" GOT IT!
HARIMA-KU... SAN!! CAN I ASK YOU A QUESTION?
YES!! I DON'T REALLY GET THIS, BUT...

Tsukamoto Tenma: Lots of Free Time.

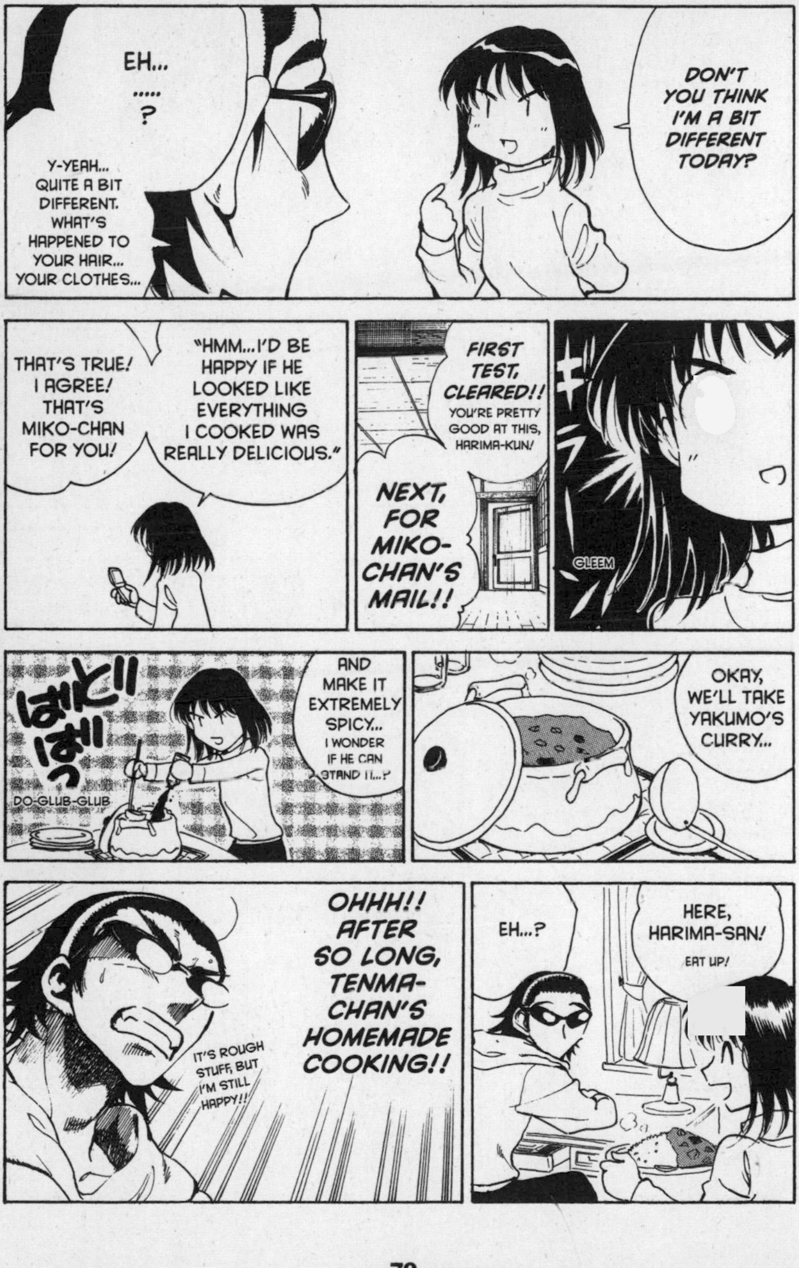
DON'T YOU THINK I'M A BIT DIFFERENT TODAY?
EH... ..... ?
Y-YEAH... QUITE A BIT DIFFERENT. WHAT'S HAPPENED TO YOUR HAIR... YOUR CLOTHES...
GLEEM
FIRST TEST, CLEARED!!
YOU'RE PRETTY GOOD AT THIS, HARIMA-KUN!
NEXT, FOR MIKO-CHAN'S MAIL!!
"HMM...I'D BE HAPPY IF HE LOOKED LIKE EVERYTHING I COOKED WAS REALLY DELICIOUS."
THAT'S TRUE! I AGREE! THAT'S MIKO-CHAN FOR YOU!
OKAY, WE'LL TAKE YAKUMO'S CURRY...
AND MAKE IT EXTREMELY SPICY...
I WONDER IF HE CAN STAND IT...?
DO-GLUB-GLUB
HERE, HARIMA-SAN!
EAT UP!
EH...?
OHHH!! AFTER SO LONG, TENMA-CHAN'S HOMEMADE COOKING!!
IT'S ROUGH STUFF, BUT I'M STILL HAPPY!!

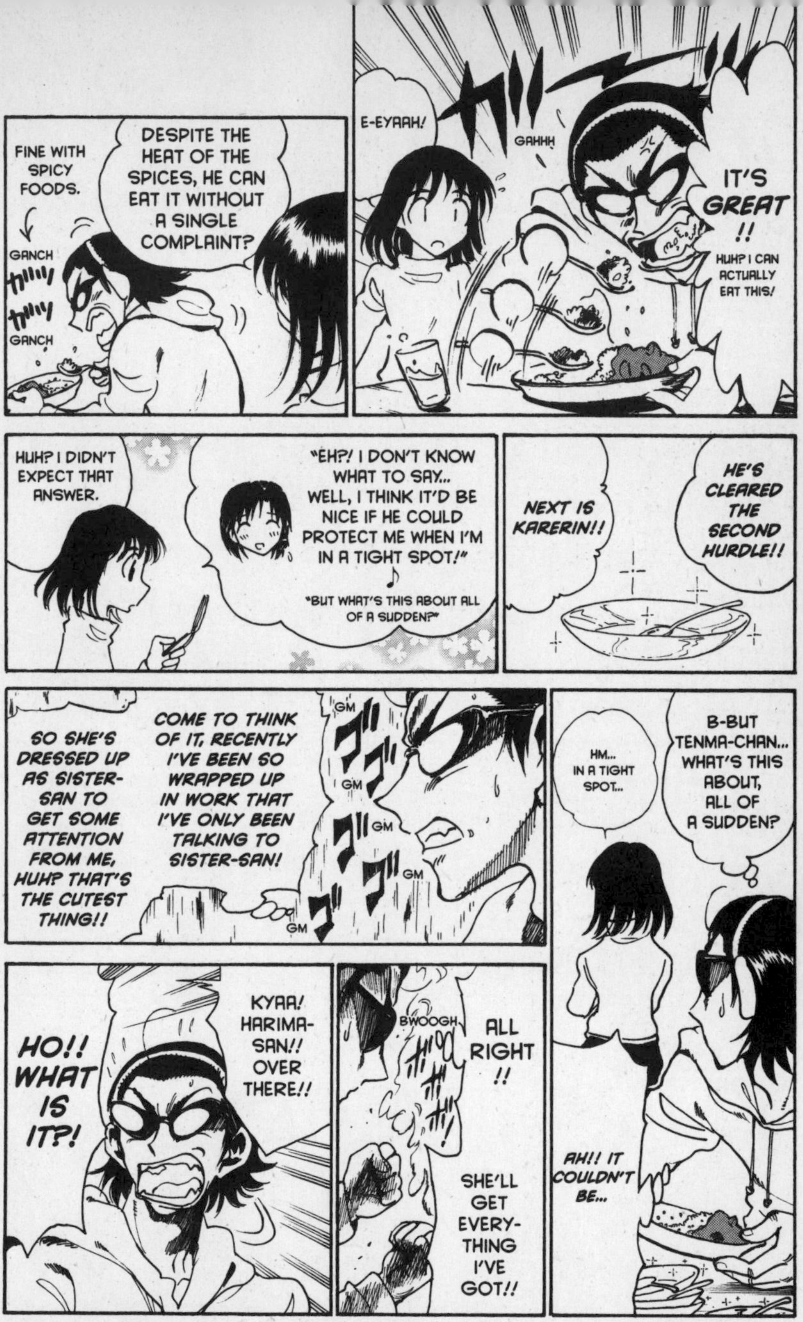

E-EYAAH!
GAHHH
IT'S GREAT!!
HUH? I CAN ACTUALLY EAT THIS!
DESPITE THE HEAT OF THE SPICES, HE CAN EAT IT WITHOUT A SINGLE COMPLAINT?
FINE WITH SPICY FOODS.
GANCH
GANCH
HE'S CLEARED THE SECOND HURDLE!!
NEXT IS KARERIN!!
"EH?! I DON'T KNOW WHAT TO SAY... WELL, I THINK IT'D BE NICE IF HE COULD PROTECT ME WHEN I'M IN A TIGHT SPOT!" ♪
"BUT WHAT'S THIS ABOUT ALL OF A SUDDEN?"
HUH? I DIDN'T EXPECT THAT ANSWER.
B-BUT TENMA-CHAN... WHAT'S THIS ABOUT, ALL OF A SUDDEN?
HM... IN A TIGHT SPOT...
AH!! IT COULDN'T BE...
GM
COME TO THINK OF IT, RECENTLY I'VE BEEN SO WRAPPED UP IN WORK THAT I'VE ONLY BEEN TALKING TO SISTER-SAN!
SO SHE'S DRESSED UP AS SISTER-SAN TO GET SOME ATTENTION FROM ME, HUH? THAT'S THE CUTEST THING!!
ALL RIGHT!!
BWOOGH
SHE'LL GET EVERYTHING I'VE GOT!!
KYAA! HARIMA-SAN!! OVER THERE!!
HO!! WHAT IS IT?!

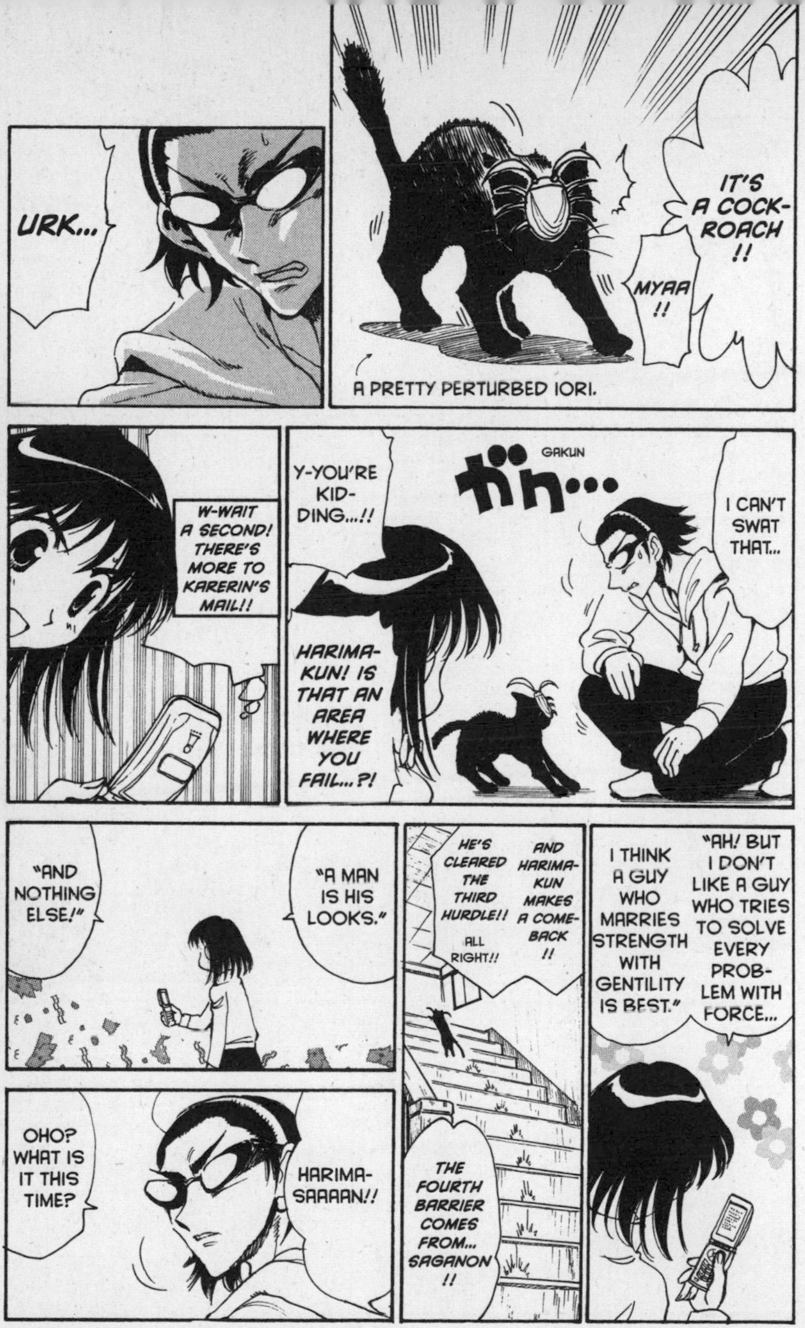
IT'S A COCKROACH!!
MYAA!!
A PRETTY PERTURBED IORI.
URK...
I CAN'T SWAT THAT...
GAKUN
Y-YOU'RE KIDDING...!!
HARIMA-KUN! IS THAT AN AREA WHERE YOU FAIL...?!
W-WAIT A SECOND! THERE'S MORE TO KARERIN'S MAIL!!
"AH! BUT I DON'T LIKE A GUY WHO TRIES TO SOLVE EVERY PROBLEM WITH FORCE...
I THINK A GUY WHO MARRIES STRENGTH WITH GENTILITY IS BEST."
AND HARIMA-KUN MAKES A COMEBACK!!
HE'S CLEARED THE THIRD HURDLE!!
ALL RIGHT!!
THE FOURTH BARRIER COMES FROM... SAGANON!!
"A MAN IS HIS LOOKS."
"AND NOTHING ELSE!"
HARIMA-SAAAAN!!
OHO? WHAT IS IT THIS TIME?

Saganon: Sagano Megumi, Heir to a Traditional Japanese Restaurant.

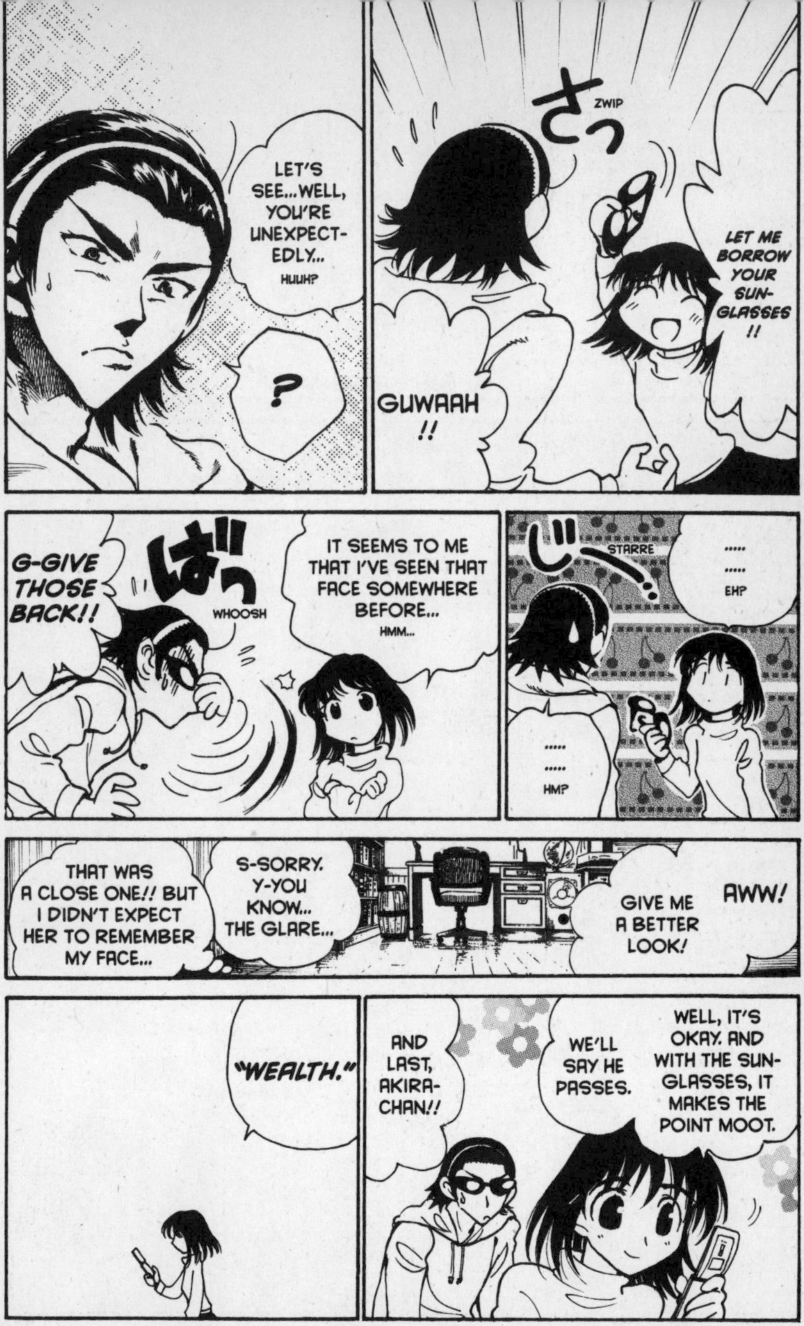
さっ
ZWIP
LET ME BORROW YOUR SUNGLASSES!!
GUWAAH!!
LET'S SEE...WELL, YOU'RE UNEXPECTEDLY...
HUUH?
?
じー
STARRE
.... EH?
.... HMP?
IT SEEMS TO ME THAT I'VE SEEN THAT FACE SOMEWHERE BEFORE...
HMM...
ばっ
WHOOSH
G-GIVE THOSE BACK!!
AWW!
GIVE ME A BETTER LOOK!
S-SORRY. Y-YOU KNOW... THE GLARE...
THAT WAS A CLOSE ONE!! BUT I DIDN'T EXPECT HER TO REMEMBER MY FACE...
WELL, IT'S OKAY. AND WITH THE SUNGLASSES, IT MAKES THE POINT MOOT.
WE'LL SAY HE PASSES.
AND LAST, AKIRA-CHAN!!
"WEALTH."

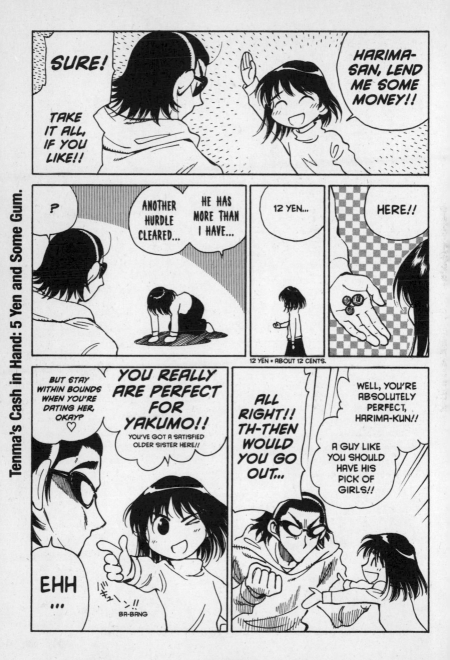

HARIMA-SAN, LEND ME SOME MONEY!!
SURE!
TAKE IT ALL, IF YOU LIKE!!
HERE!!
12 YEN...
HE HAS MORE THAN I HAVE...
ANOTHER HURDLE CLEARED...
?
12 YEN = ABOUT 12 CENTS.
WELL, YOU'RE ABSOLUTELY PERFECT, HARIMA-KUN!!
A GUY LIKE YOU SHOULD HAVE HIS PICK OF GIRLS!!
ALL RIGHT!! TH-THEN WOULD YOU GO OUT...
YOU REALLY ARE PERFECT FOR YAKUMO!!
YOU'VE GOT A SATISFIED OLDER SISTER HERE!!
BUT STAY WITHIN BOUNDS WHEN YOU'RE DATING HER, OKAY? ♡
BA-BANG
EHH ...

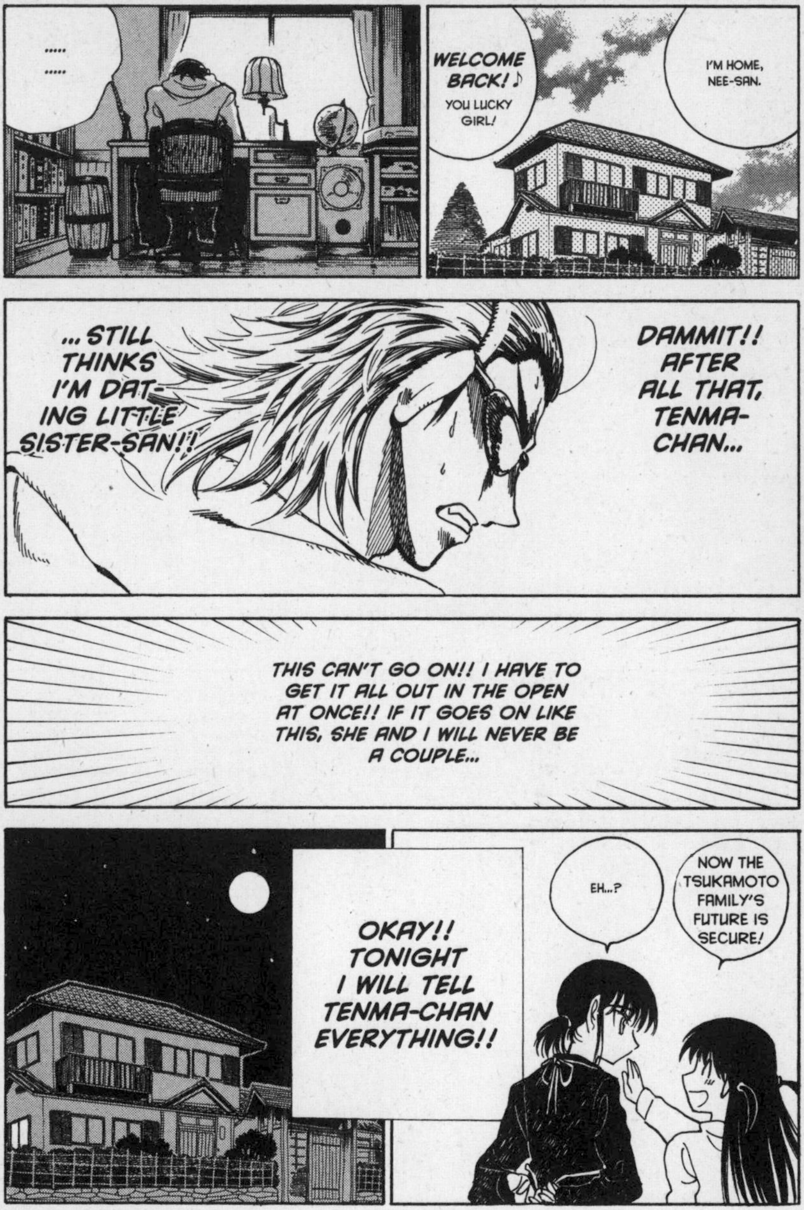
I'M HOME, NEE-SAN.
WELCOME BACK! ♪
YOU LUCKY GIRL!
......
......
DAMMIT!! AFTER ALL THAT, TENMA-CHAN...
...STILL THINKS I'M DATING LITTLE SISTER-SAN!!
THIS CAN'T GO ON!! I HAVE TO GET IT ALL OUT IN THE OPEN AT ONCE!! IF IT GOES ON LIKE THIS, SHE AND I WILL NEVER BE A COUPLE...
NOW THE TSUKAMOTO FAMILY'S FUTURE IS SECURE!
EH...?
OKAY!! TONIGHT I WILL TELL TENMA-CHAN EVERYTHING!!

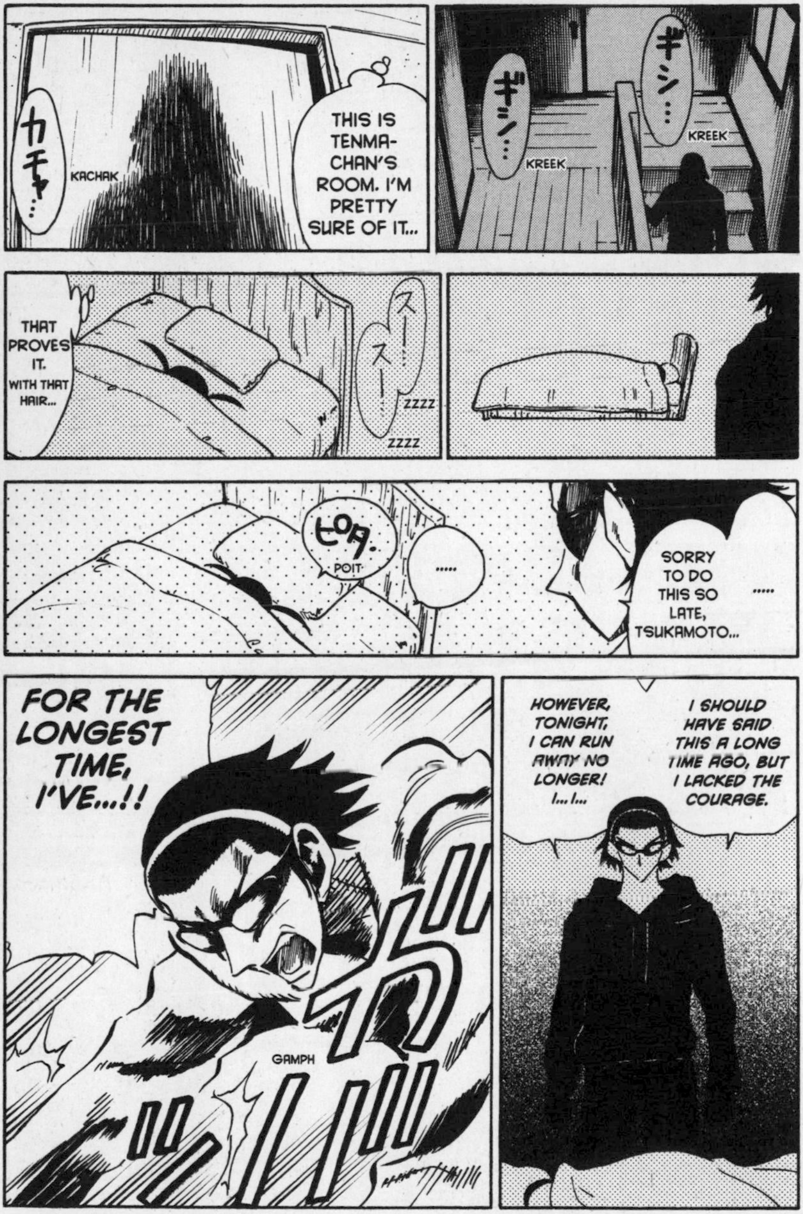
ギシ…
KREEK
ギシ…
KREEK
THIS IS TENMA-CHAN'S ROOM. I'M PRETTY SURE OF IT...
カチャ…
KACHAK
スー…
スー…
ZZZZ
ZZZZ
THAT PROVES IT. WITH THAT HAIR...
.....
SORRY TO DO THIS SO LATE, TSUKAMOTO...
.....
ピタ.
POIT
I SHOULD HAVE SAID THIS A LONG TIME AGO, BUT I LACKED THE COURAGE.
HOWEVER, TONIGHT, I CAN RUN AWAY NO LONGER! I... I...
FOR THE LONGEST TIME, I'VE...!!
GAMPH

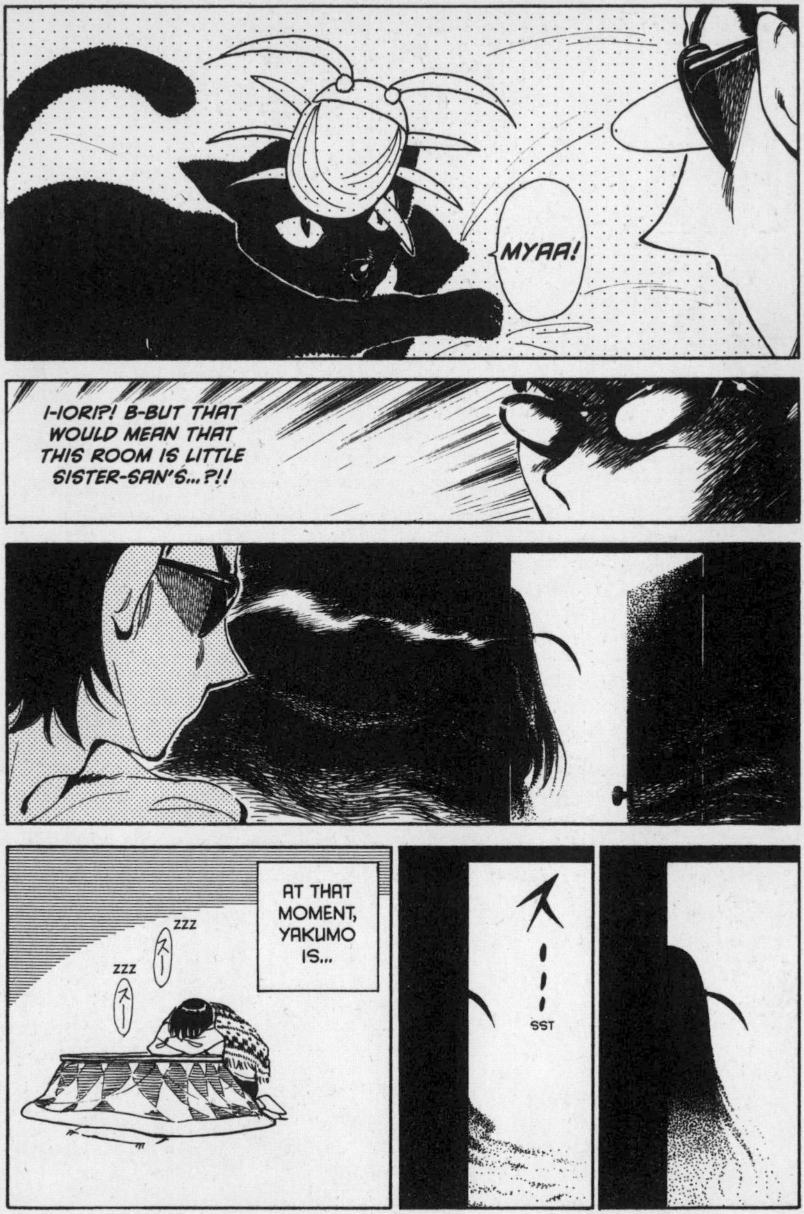
MYAA!
I-IORI?! B-BUT THAT WOULD MEAN THAT THIS ROOM IS LITTLE SISTER-SAN'S...?!!
ス…
SST
AT THAT MOMENT, YAKUMO IS...
スー
ZZZ
スー
ZZZ

We Dub Thee: Cockroach Hair.

147 · · · · · · · · Fin

#148 SANS TOIT NI LOI

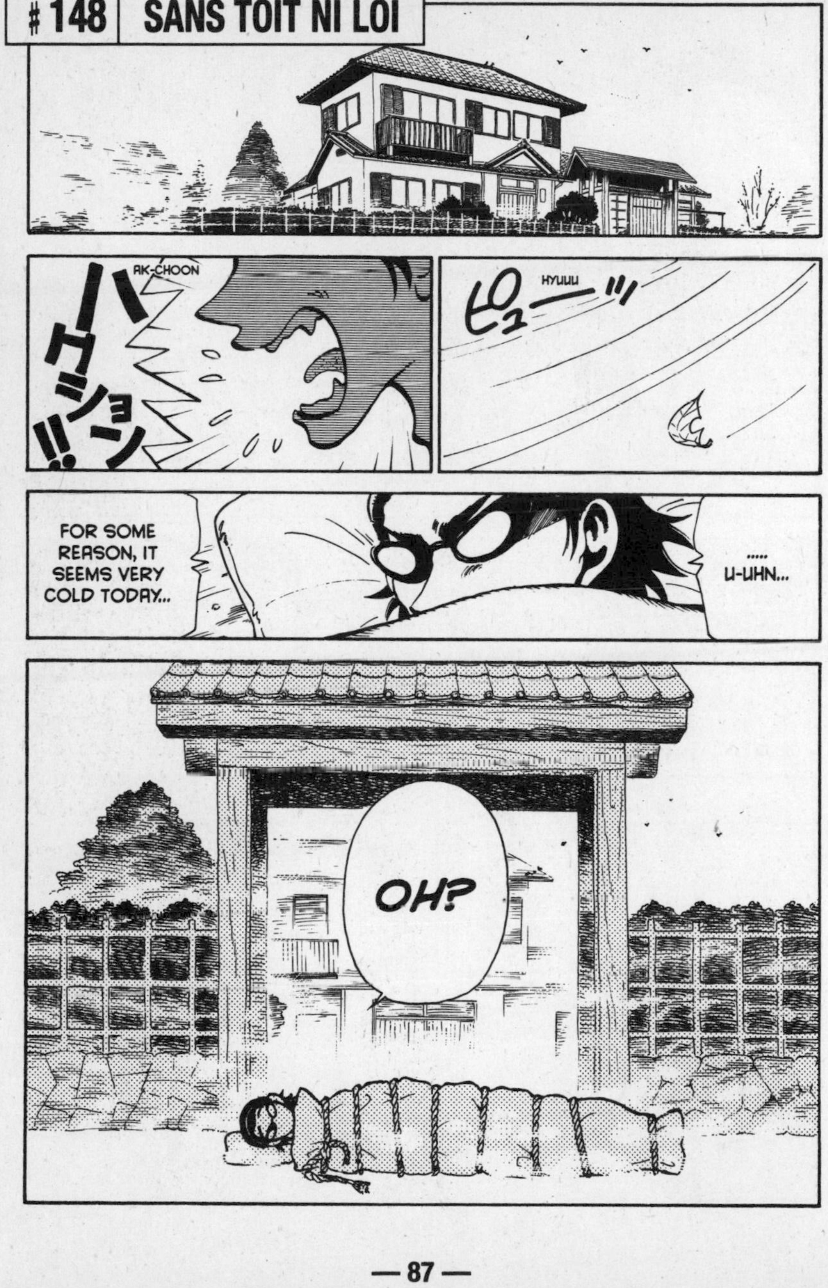
ピューーッ
HYUUU
ハクショーン!!
AK-CHOON
..... U-UHN...
FOR SOME REASON, IT SEEMS VERY COLD TODAY...
OH?

Last Night: Harima Took Decisive Action Toward Confessing His Love for Tenma.

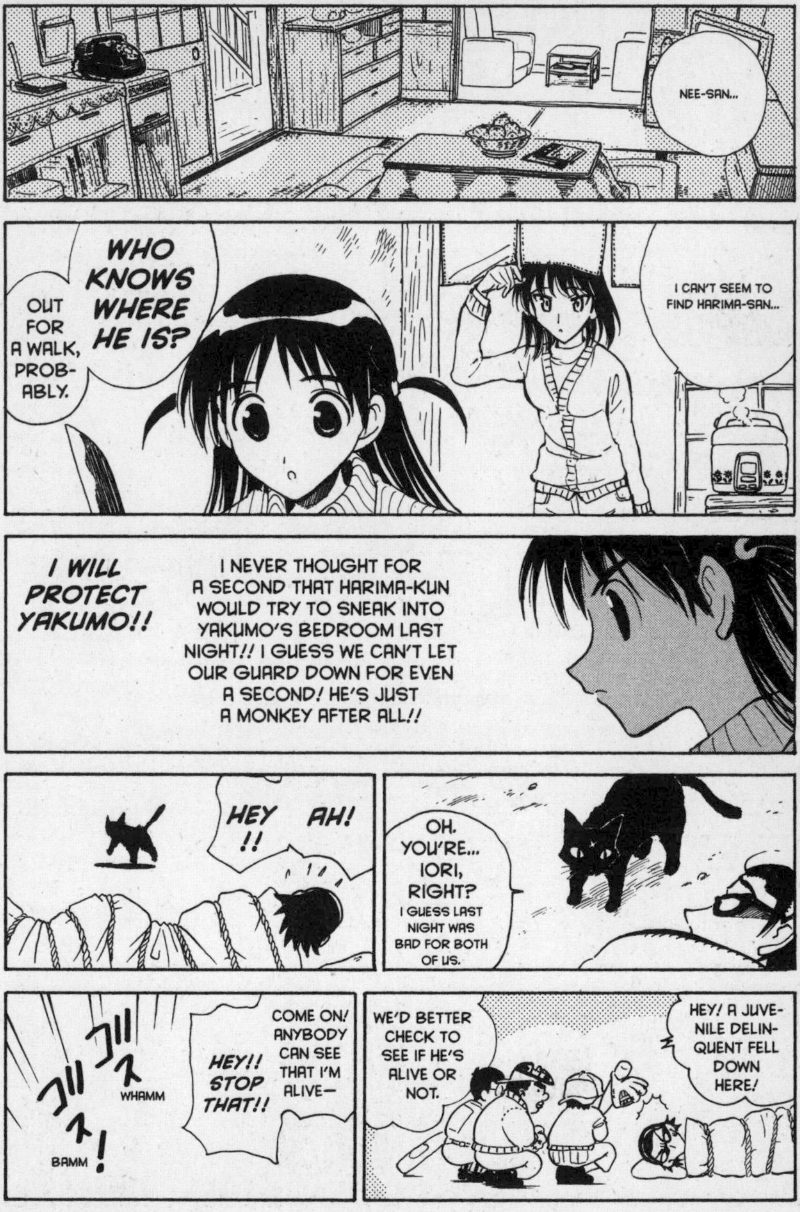
NEE-SAN...
I CAN'T SEEM TO FIND HARIMA-SAN...
WHO KNOWS WHERE HE IS?
OUT FOR A WALK, PROBABLY.
I NEVER THOUGHT FOR A SECOND THAT HARIMA-KUN WOULD TRY TO SNEAK INTO YAKUMO'S BEDROOM LAST NIGHT!! I GUESS WE CAN'T LET OUR GUARD DOWN FOR EVEN A SECOND! HE'S JUST A MONKEY AFTER ALL!!
I WILL PROTECT YAKUMO!!
OH. YOU'RE... IORI, RIGHT?
I GUESS LAST NIGHT WAS BAD FOR BOTH OF US.
AH!
HEY!!
HEY! A JUVENILE DELINQUENT FELL DOWN HERE!
WE'D BETTER CHECK TO SEE IF HE'S ALIVE OR NOT.
COME ON! ANYBODY CAN SEE THAT I'M ALIVE—
HEY!! STOP THAT!!
WHAMM
BAMM

However, He Entered Yakumo's Bedroom by Mistake. Just So You Know.

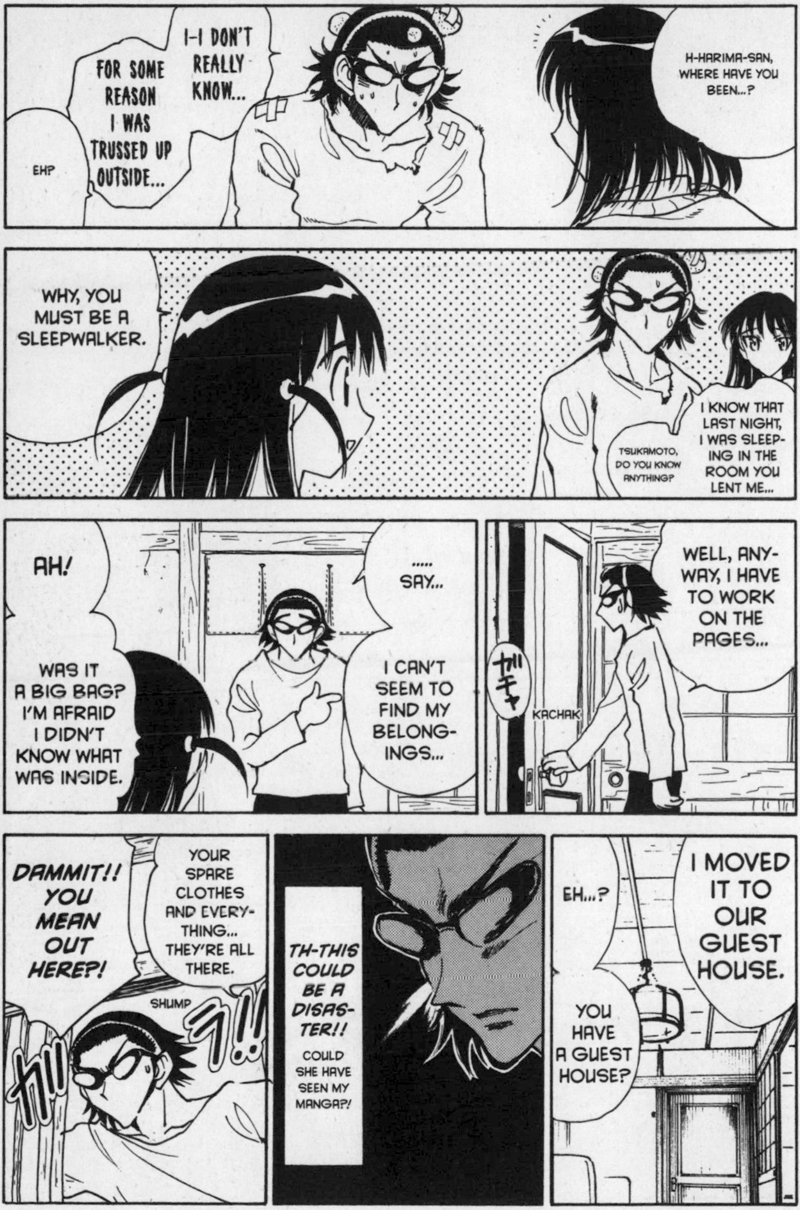

H-HARIMA-SAN, WHERE HAVE YOU BEEN...?
I-I DON'T REALLY KNOW...
FOR SOME REASON I WAS TRUSSED UP OUTSIDE...
EH?
I KNOW THAT LAST NIGHT, I WAS SLEEPING IN THE ROOM YOU LENT ME...
TSUKAMOTO, DO YOU KNOW ANYTHING?
WHY, YOU MUST BE A SLEEPWALKER.
WELL, ANYWAY, I HAVE TO WORK ON THE PAGES...
ガチャ
KACHAK
..... SAY...
I CAN'T SEEM TO FIND MY BELONGINGS...
AH!
WAS IT A BIG BAG? I'M AFRAID I DIDN'T KNOW WHAT WAS INSIDE.
I MOVED IT TO OUR GUEST HOUSE.
EH...?
YOU HAVE A GUEST HOUSE?
TH-THIS COULD BE A DISASTER!!
COULD SHE HAVE SEEN MY MANGA?!
YOUR SPARE CLOTHES AND EVERYTHING... THEY'RE ALL THERE.
DAMMIT!! YOU MEAN OUT HERE?!
SHUMP

(Note) Tenma Is Also a Modern High School Student.

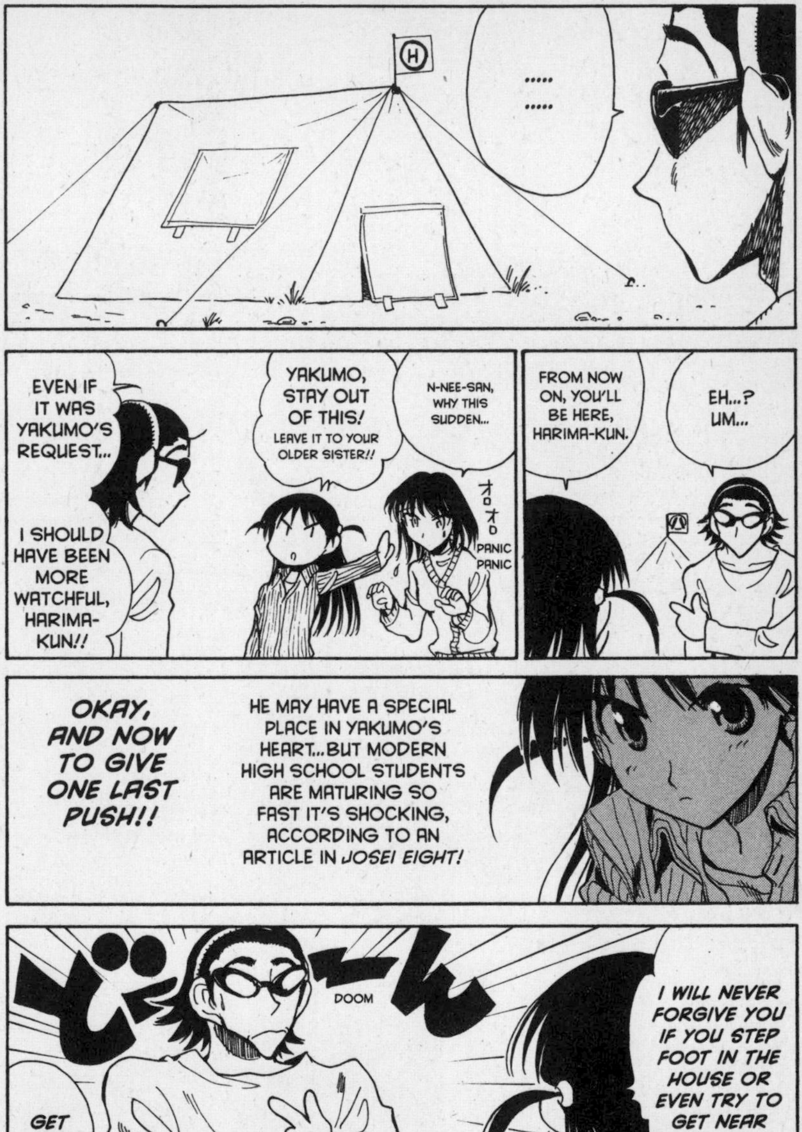
......
......
EH...? UM...
FROM NOW ON, YOU'LL BE HERE, HARIMA-KUN.
N-NEE-SAN, WHY THIS SUDDEN...
オロオロ
PANIC PANIC
YAKUMO, STAY OUT OF THIS! LEAVE IT TO YOUR OLDER SISTER!!
EVEN IF IT WAS YAKUMO'S REQUEST...
I SHOULD HAVE BEEN MORE WATCHFUL, HARIMA-KUN!!
HE MAY HAVE A SPECIAL PLACE IN YAKUMO'S HEART...BUT MODERN HIGH SCHOOL STUDENTS ARE MATURING SO FAST IT'S SHOCKING, ACCORDING TO AN ARTICLE IN *JOSEI EIGHT*!
OKAY, AND NOW TO GIVE ONE LAST PUSH!!
I WILL NEVER FORGIVE YOU IF YOU STEP FOOT IN THE HOUSE OR EVEN TRY TO GET NEAR YAKUMO!!
DOOM
GET ME?!

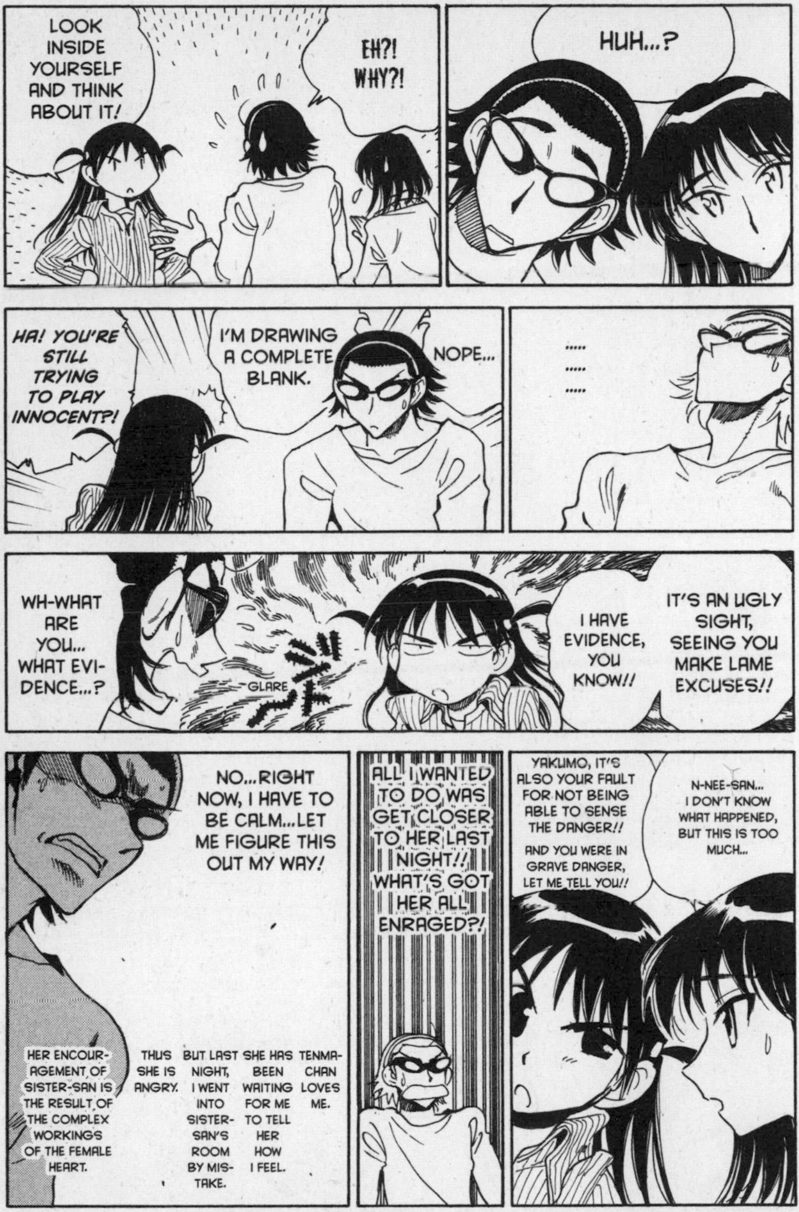
HUH...?
EH?! WHY?!
LOOK INSIDE YOURSELF AND THINK ABOUT IT!
......
......
......
NOPE...
I'M DRAWING A COMPLETE BLANK.
HA! YOU'RE STILL TRYING TO PLAY INNOCENT?!
IT'S AN UGLY SIGHT, SEEING YOU MAKE LAME EXCUSES!!
I HAVE EVIDENCE, YOU KNOW!!
GLARE
WH-WHAT ARE YOU... WHAT EVIDENCE...?
N-NEE-SAN... I DON'T KNOW WHAT HAPPENED, BUT THIS IS TOO MUCH...
YAKUMO, IT'S ALSO YOUR FAULT FOR NOT BEING ABLE TO SENSE THE DANGER!!
AND YOU WERE IN GRAVE DANGER, LET ME TELL YOU!!
ALL I WANTED TO DO WAS GET CLOSER TO HER LAST NIGHT!! WHAT'S GOT HER ALL ENRAGED?!
NO...RIGHT NOW, I HAVE TO BE CALM...LET ME FIGURE THIS OUT MY WAY!
TENMA-CHAN LOVES ME.
SHE HAS BEEN WAITING FOR ME TO TELL HER HOW I FEEL.
BUT LAST NIGHT, I WENT INTO SISTER-SAN'S ROOM BY MISTAKE.
THUS SHE IS ANGRY.
HER ENCOURAGEMENT OF SISTER-SAN IS THE RESULT OF THE COMPLEX WORKINGS OF THE FEMALE HEART.

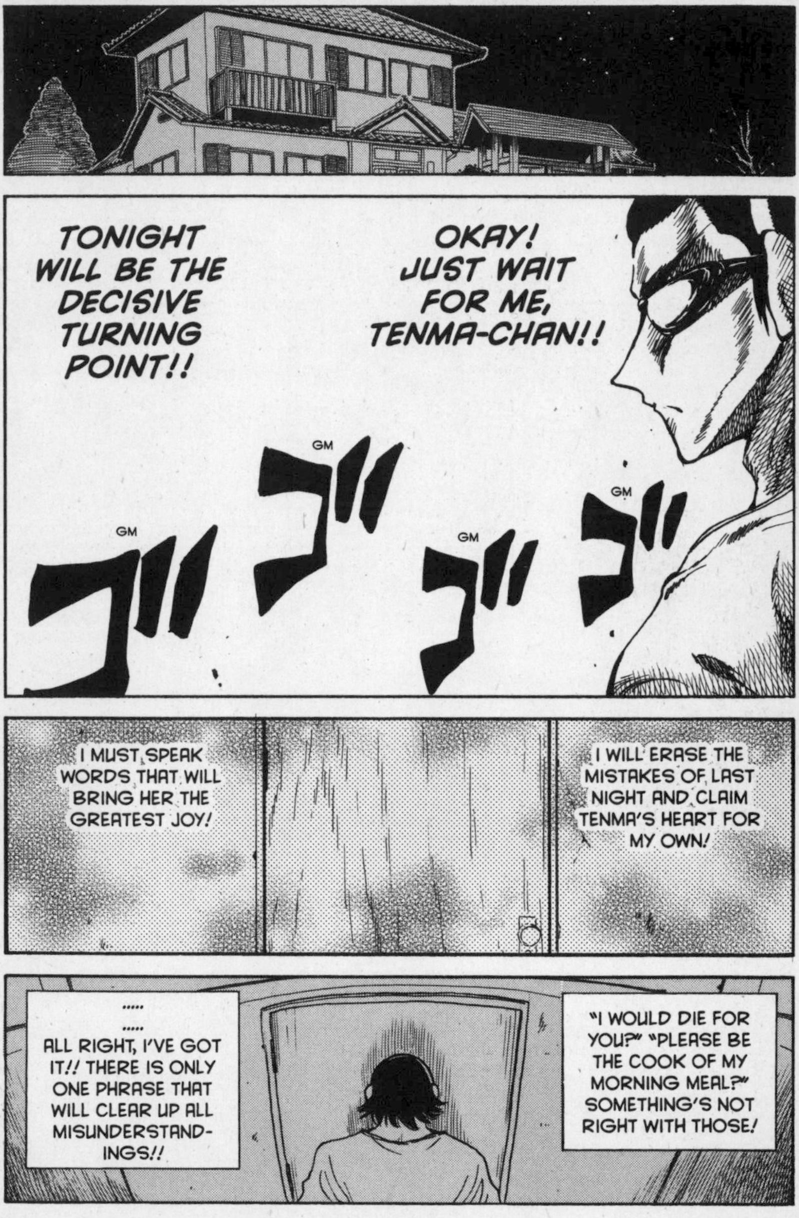
OKAY! JUST WAIT FOR ME, TENMA-CHAN!!
TONIGHT WILL BE THE DECISIVE TURNING POINT!!
GM
GM
GM
GM
I WILL ERASE THE MISTAKES OF LAST NIGHT AND CLAIM TENMA'S HEART FOR MY OWN!
I MUST SPEAK WORDS THAT WILL BRING HER THE GREATEST JOY!
"I WOULD DIE FOR YOU?" "PLEASE BE THE COOK OF MY MORNING MEAL?" SOMETHING'S NOT RIGHT WITH THOSE!
.... ALL RIGHT, I'VE GOT IT!! THERE IS ONLY ONE PHRASE THAT WILL CLEAR UP ALL MISUNDERSTAND-INGS!!

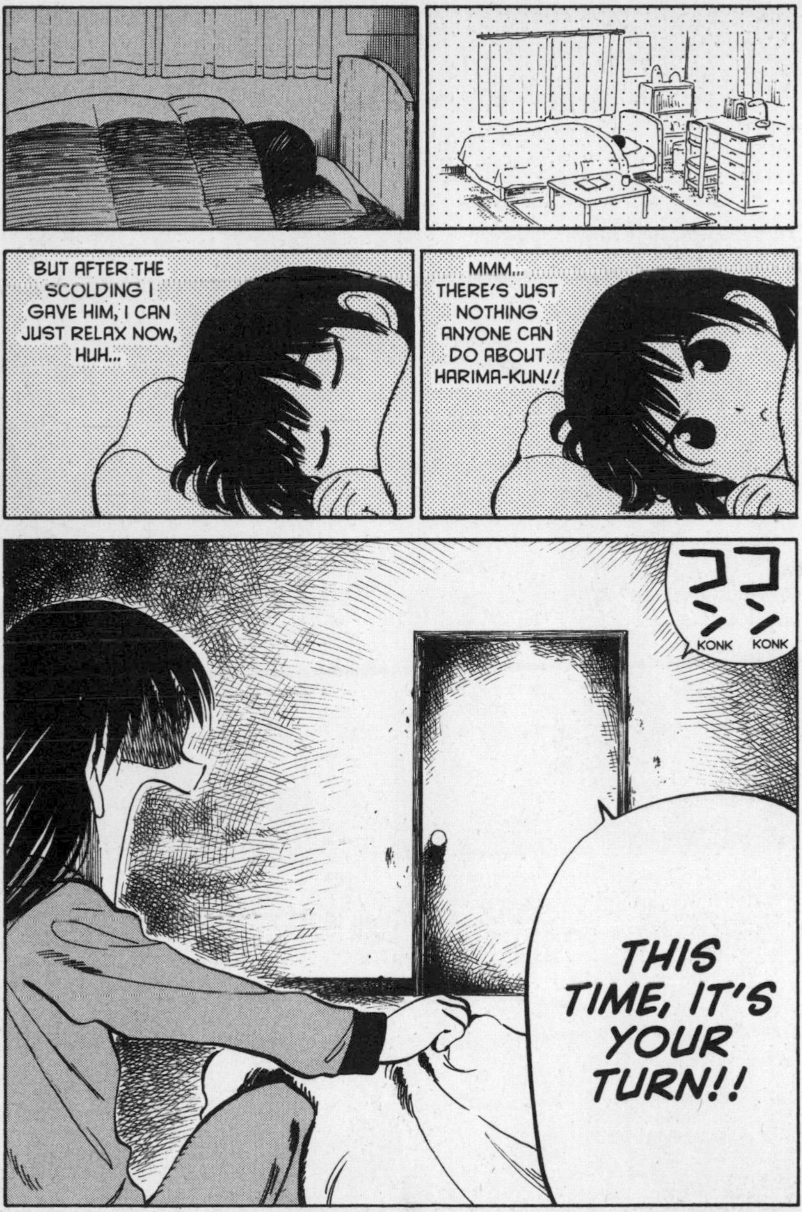
MMM... THERE'S JUST NOTHING ANYONE CAN DO ABOUT HARIMA-KUN!!
BUT AFTER THE SCOLDING I GAVE HIM, I CAN JUST RELAX NOW, HUH...
ココンッ
KONK KONK
THIS TIME, IT'S YOUR TURN!!

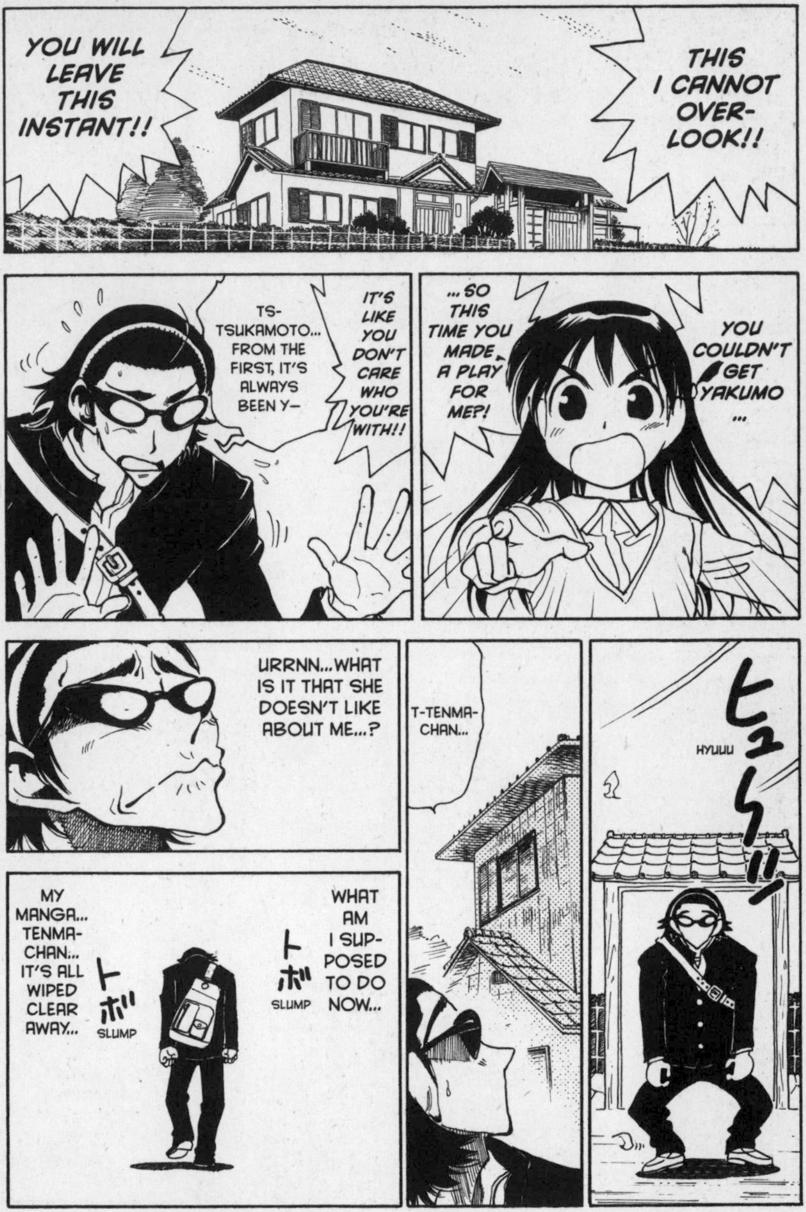
THIS I CANNOT OVER-LOOK!!
YOU WILL LEAVE THIS INSTANT!!
YOU COULDN'T GET YAKUMO ...
...SO THIS TIME YOU MADE A PLAY FOR ME?!
IT'S LIKE YOU DON'T CARE WHO YOU'RE WITH!!
TS-TSUKAMOTO... FROM THE FIRST, IT'S ALWAYS BEEN Y—
ヒュ~ゥ
HYUUU
T-TENMA-CHAN...
URRNN...WHAT IS IT THAT SHE DOESN'T LIKE ABOUT ME...?
WHAT AM I SUP-POSED TO DO NOW...
トボ
SLUMP
MY MANGA... TENMA-CHAN... IT'S ALL WIPED CLEAR AWAY...
トボ
SLUMP

Harima's Life as a Lodger: Over After Two Days.

At Least in the Part Exaggerated by Harima.

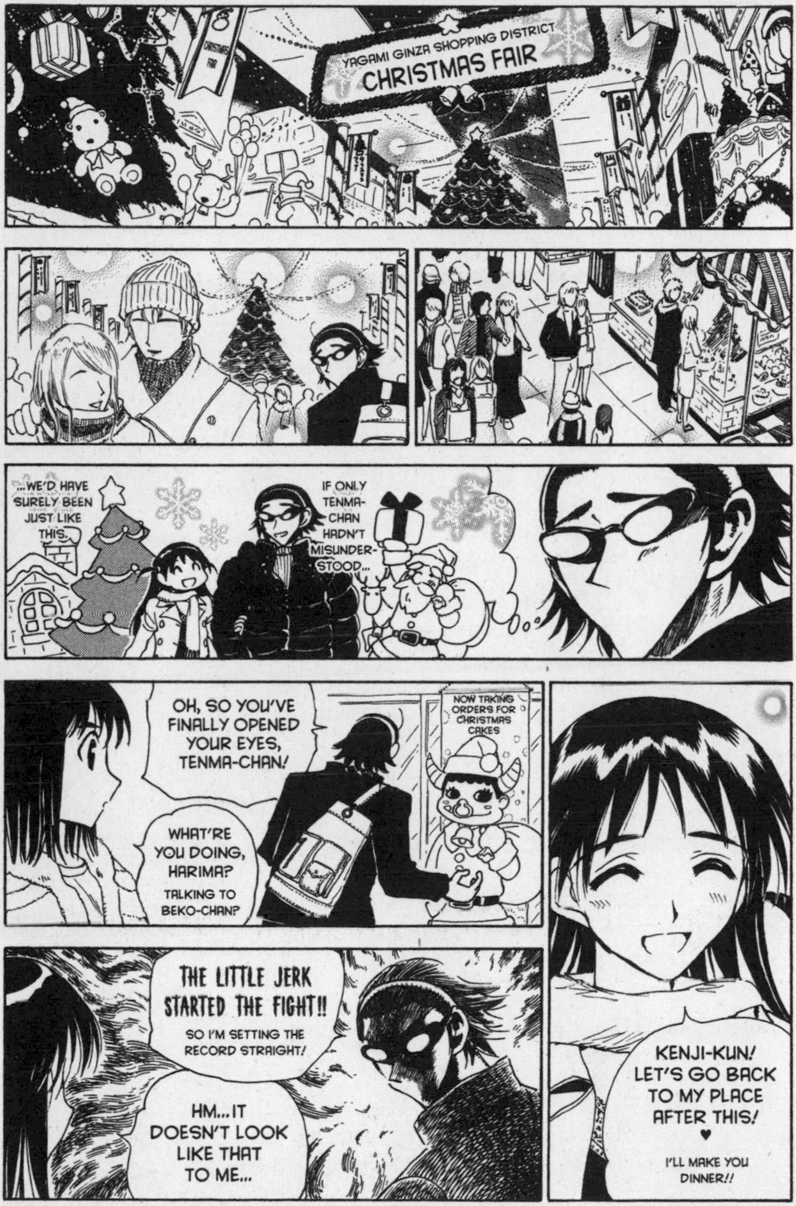

YAGAMI GINZA SHOPPING DISTRICT
CHRISTMAS FAIR
CHRISTMAS FAIR
IF ONLY TENMA-CHAN HADN'T MISUNDERSTOOD...
...WE'D HAVE SURELY BEEN JUST LIKE THIS.
KENJI-KUN! LET'S GO BACK TO MY PLACE AFTER THIS! ♥
I'LL MAKE YOU DINNER!!
NOW TAKING ORDERS FOR CHRISTMAS CAKES
OH, SO YOU'VE FINALLY OPENED YOUR EYES, TENMA-CHAN!
WHAT'RE YOU DOING, HARIMA?
TALKING TO BEKO-CHAN?
THE LITTLE JERK STARTED THE FIGHT!!
SO I'M SETTING THE RECORD STRAIGHT!
HM...IT DOESN'T LOOK LIKE THAT TO ME...

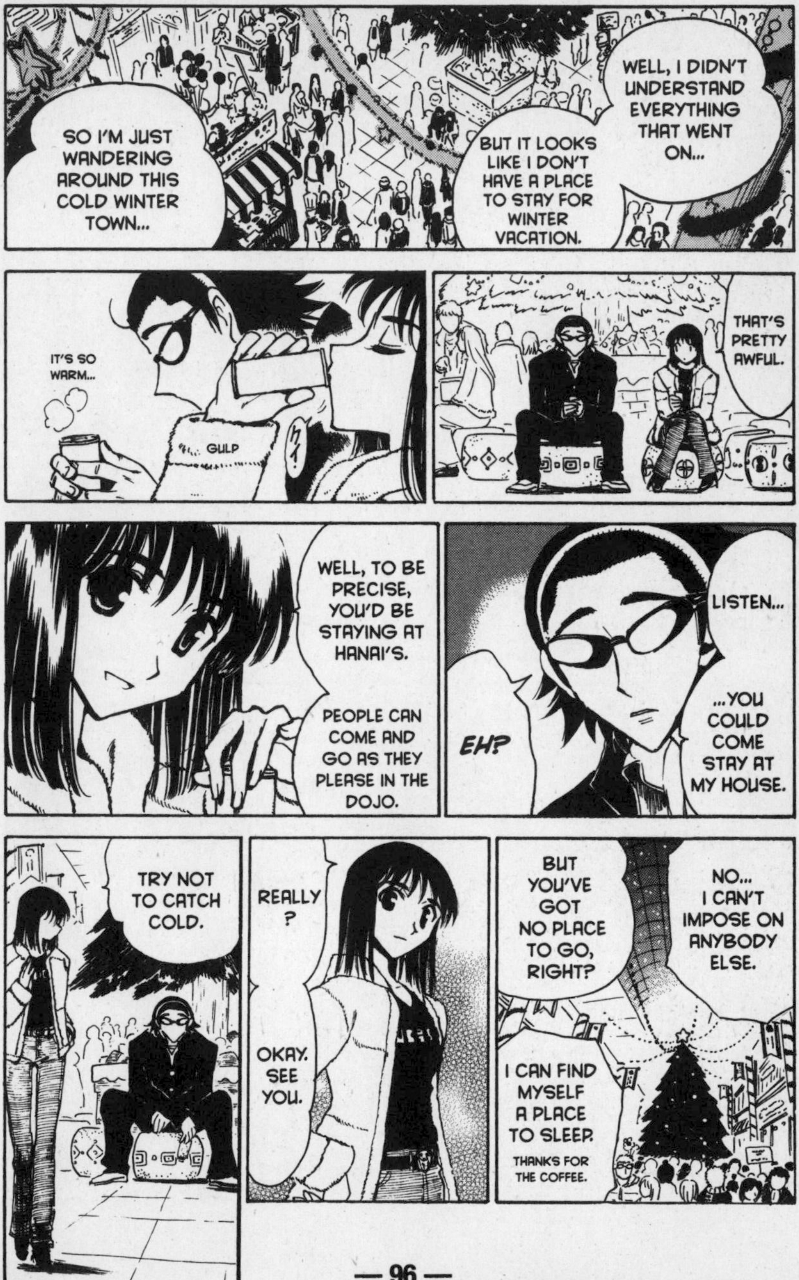
WELL, I DIDN'T UNDERSTAND EVERYTHING THAT WENT ON...
BUT IT LOOKS LIKE I DON'T HAVE A PLACE TO STAY FOR WINTER VACATION.
SO I'M JUST WANDERING AROUND THIS COLD WINTER TOWN...
THAT'S PRETTY AWFUL.
IT'S SO WARM...
GULP
LISTEN...
...YOU COULD COME STAY AT MY HOUSE.
EH?
WELL, TO BE PRECISE, YOU'D BE STAYING AT HANAI'S.
PEOPLE CAN COME AND GO AS THEY PLEASE IN THE DOJO.
NO... I CAN'T IMPOSE ON ANYBODY ELSE.
BUT YOU'VE GOT NO PLACE TO GO, RIGHT?
I CAN FIND MYSELF A PLACE TO SLEEP.
THANKS FOR THE COFFEE.
REALLY?
OKAY. SEE YOU.
TRY NOT TO CATCH COLD.

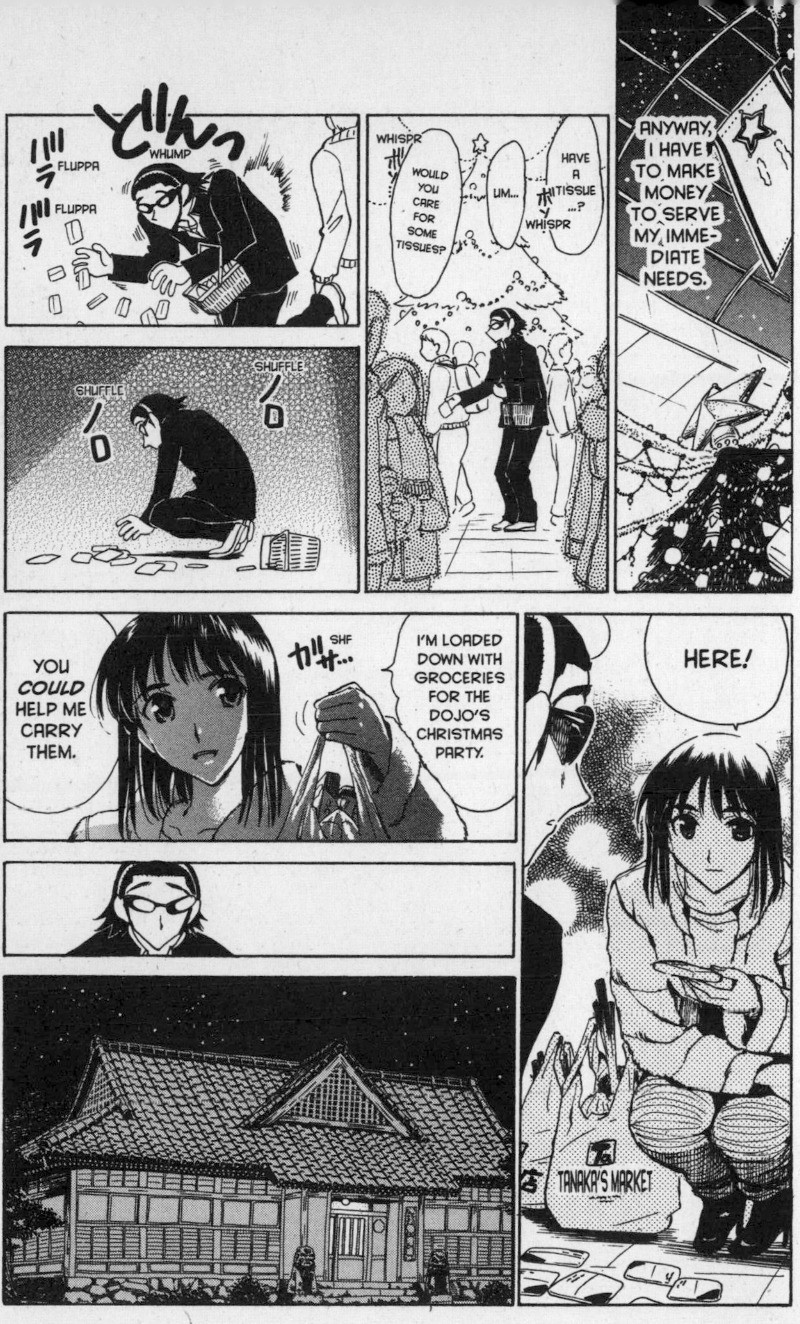
ANYWAY, I HAVE TO MAKE MONEY TO SERVE MY IMMEDIATE NEEDS.
HAVE A TISSUE ...?
WHISPR
UM...
WOULD YOU CARE FOR SOME TISSUES?
WHISPR
WHUMP
FLUPPA
FLUPPA
SHUFFLE
SHUFFLE
HERE!
I'M LOADED DOWN WITH GROCERIES FOR THE DOJO'S CHRISTMAS PARTY.
SHF
YOU *COULD* HELP ME CARRY THEM.
TANAKA'S MARKET

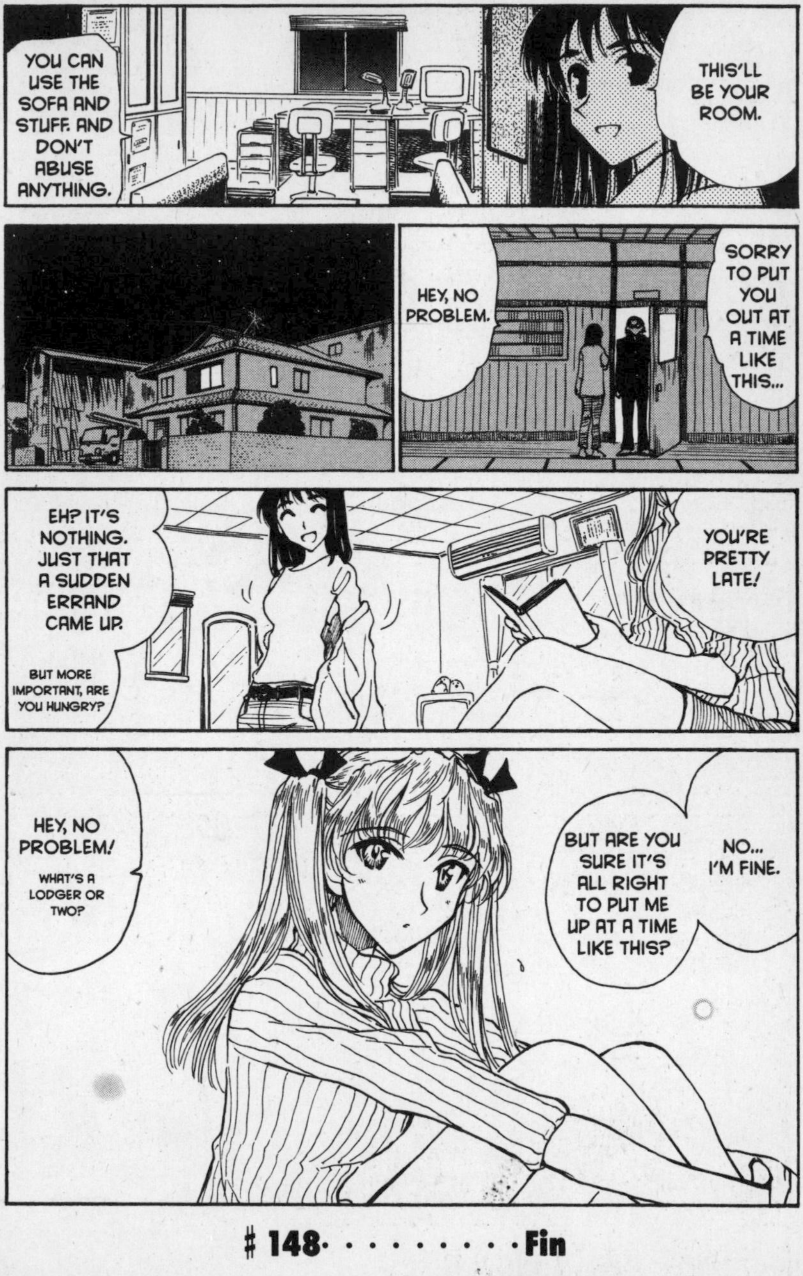
THIS'LL BE YOUR ROOM.
YOU CAN USE THE SOFA AND STUFF. AND DON'T ABUSE ANYTHING.
SORRY TO PUT YOU OUT AT A TIME LIKE THIS...
HEY, NO PROBLEM.
YOU'RE PRETTY LATE!
EH? IT'S NOTHING. JUST THAT A SUDDEN ERRAND CAME UP.
BUT MORE IMPORTANT, ARE YOU HUNGRY?
NO... I'M FINE.
BUT ARE YOU SURE IT'S ALL RIGHT TO PUT ME UP AT A TIME LIKE THIS?
HEY, NO PROBLEM!
WHAT'S A LODGER OR TWO?

Harima's Life as a Lodger: The Start of the Unexpected Sequel?!

 # 148· · · · · · · ·Fin

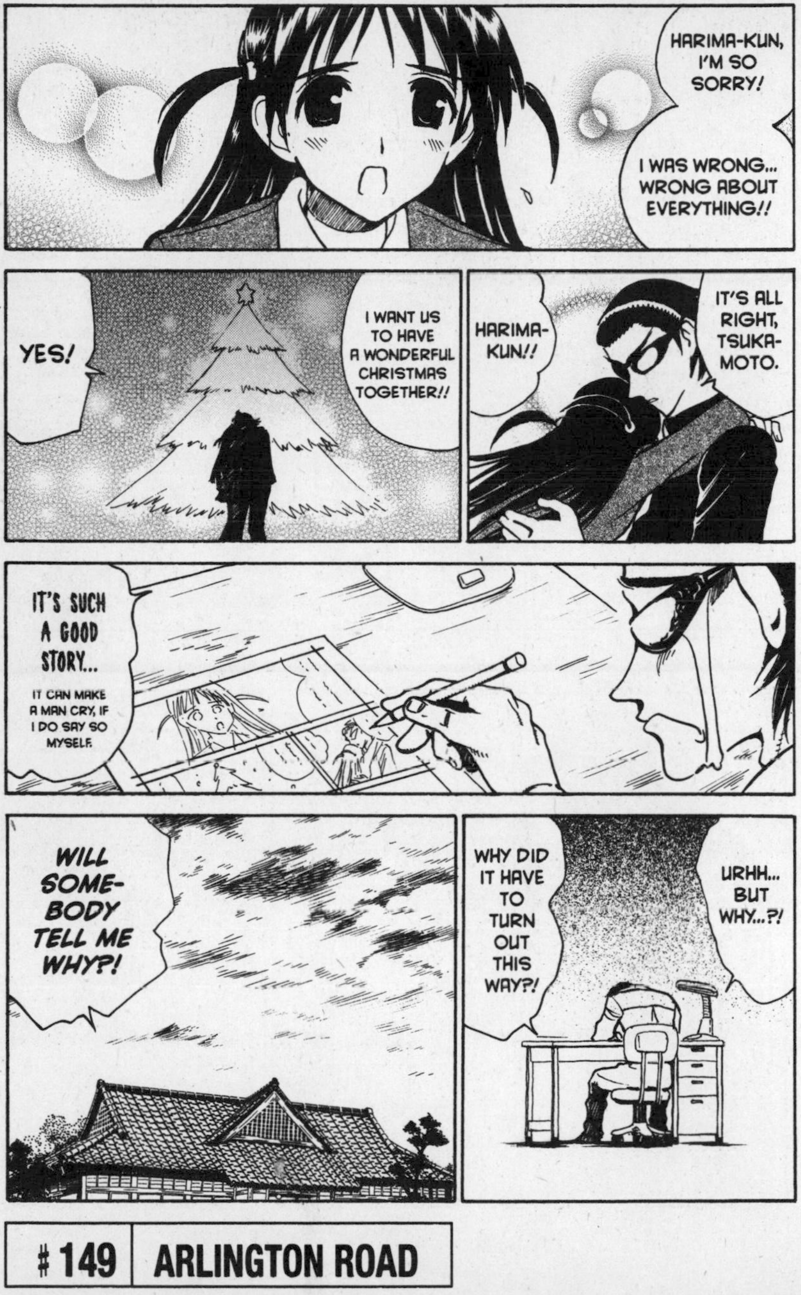
HARIMA-KUN, I'M SO SORRY!
I WAS WRONG... WRONG ABOUT EVERYTHING!!
IT'S ALL RIGHT, TSUKA-MOTO.
HARIMA-KUN!!
I WANT US TO HAVE A WONDERFUL CHRISTMAS TOGETHER!!
YES!
IT'S SUCH A GOOD STORY...
IT CAN MAKE A MAN CRY, IF I DO SAY SO MYSELF.
URHH... BUT WHY...?!
WHY DID IT HAVE TO TURN OUT THIS WAY?!
WILL SOMEBODY TELL ME WHY?!

#149 ARLINGTON ROAD

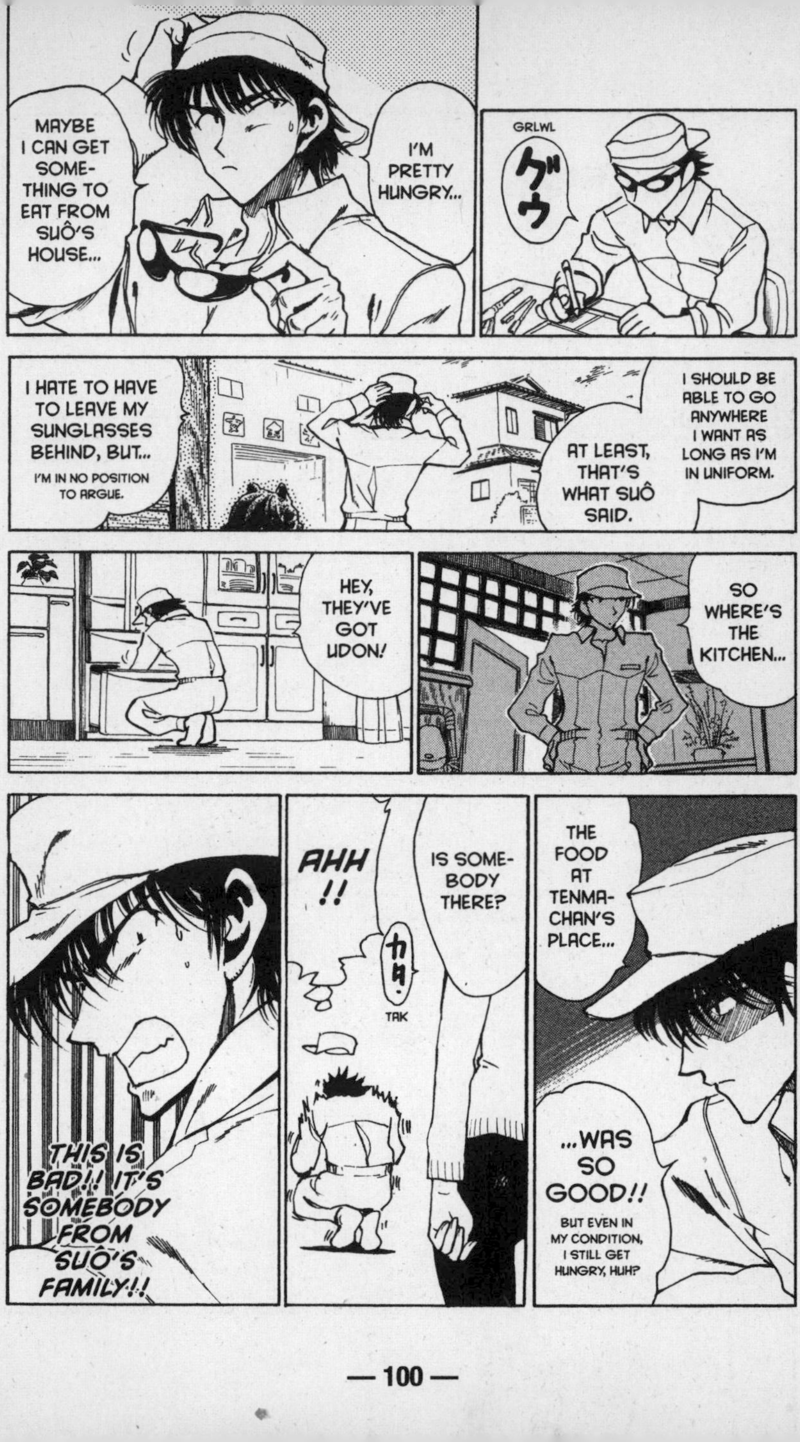
GRLWL
グゥ
I'M PRETTY HUNGRY...
MAYBE I CAN GET SOME-THING TO EAT FROM SUÔ'S HOUSE...
I SHOULD BE ABLE TO GO ANYWHERE I WANT AS LONG AS I'M IN UNIFORM.
AT LEAST, THAT'S WHAT SUÔ SAID.
I HATE TO HAVE TO LEAVE MY SUNGLASSES BEHIND, BUT...
I'M IN NO POSITION TO ARGUE.
SO WHERE'S THE KITCHEN...
HEY, THEY'VE GOT UDON!
THE FOOD AT TENMA-CHAN'S PLACE...
...WAS SO GOOD!!
BUT EVEN IN MY CONDITION, I STILL GET HUNGRY, HUH?
IS SOME-BODY THERE?
AHH !!
カタ
TAK
THIS IS BAD!! IT'S SOMEBODY FROM SUÔ'S FAMILY!!

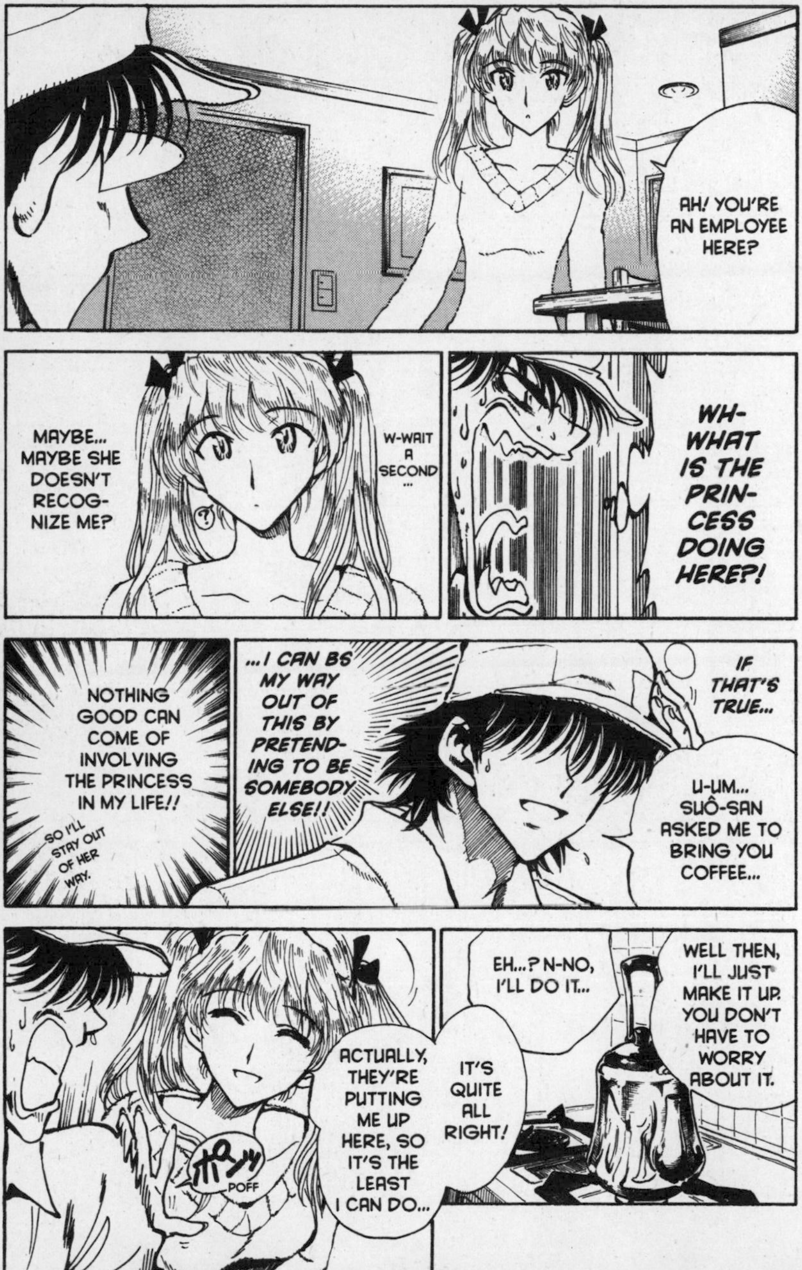
AH! YOU'RE AN EMPLOYEE HERE?
WH-WHAT IS THE PRINCESS DOING HERE?!
W-WAIT A SECOND ...
MAYBE... MAYBE SHE DOESN'T RECOGNIZE ME?
IF THAT'S TRUE...
...I CAN BS MY WAY OUT OF THIS BY PRETENDING TO BE SOMEBODY ELSE!!
U-UM... SUÔ-SAN ASKED ME TO BRING YOU COFFEE...
NOTHING GOOD CAN COME OF INVOLVING THE PRINCESS IN MY LIFE!!
SO I'LL STAY OUT OF HER WAY.
WELL THEN, I'LL JUST MAKE IT UP. YOU DON'T HAVE TO WORRY ABOUT IT.
EH...? N-NO, I'LL DO IT...
IT'S QUITE ALL RIGHT!
ACTUALLY, THEY'RE PUTTING ME UP HERE, SO IT'S THE LEAST I CAN DO...
ポンッ
POFF

Oddly, He Hasn't Been Found Out Yet.

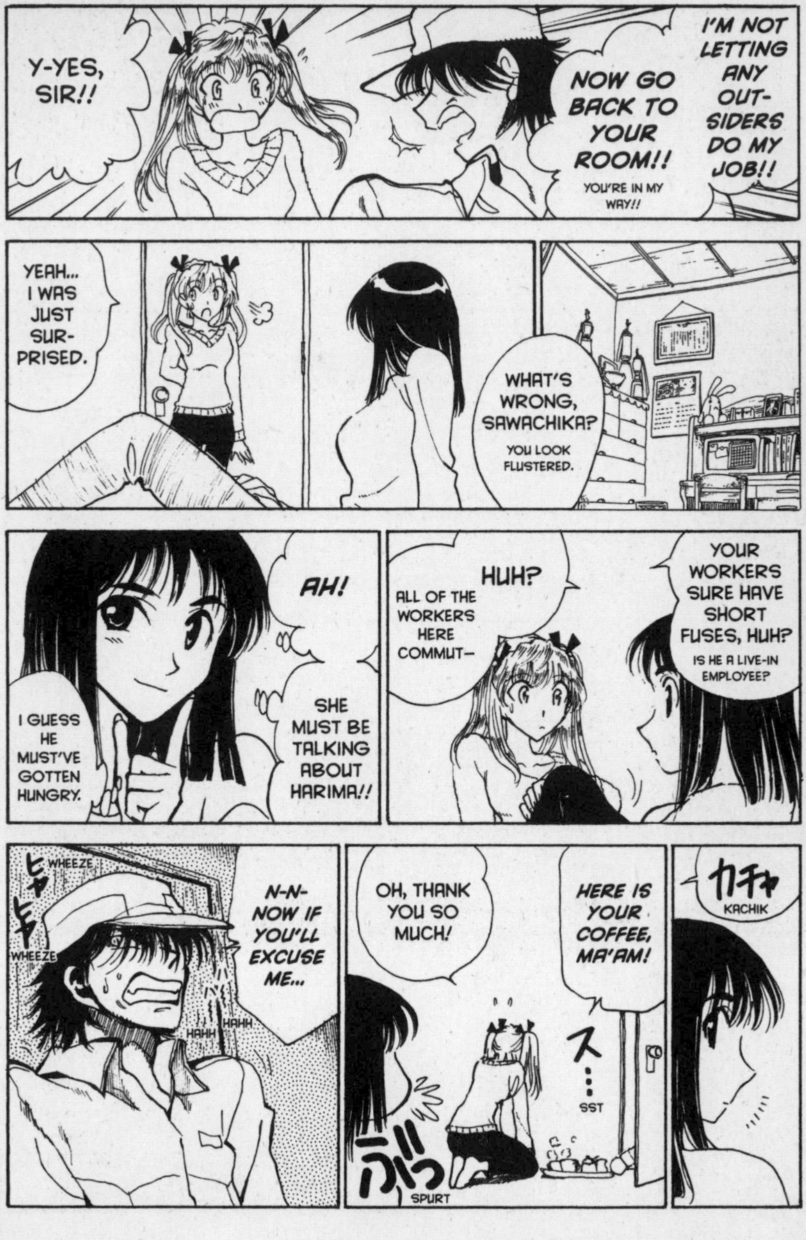
I'M NOT LETTING ANY OUT-SIDERS DO MY JOB!!
NOW GO BACK TO YOUR ROOM!!
YOU'RE IN MY WAY!!
Y-YES, SIR!!
WHAT'S WRONG, SAWACHIKA?
YOU LOOK FLUSTERED.
YEAH... I WAS JUST SUR-PRISED.
YOUR WORKERS SURE HAVE SHORT FUSES, HUH?
IS HE A LIVE-IN EMPLOYEE?
HUH?
ALL OF THE WORKERS HERE COMMUT—
AH!
SHE MUST BE TALKING ABOUT HARIMA!!
I GUESS HE MUST'VE GOTTEN HUNGRY.
カチャ
KACHIK
HERE IS YOUR COFFEE, MA'AM!
OH, THANK YOU SO MUCH!
ス…
SST
ぶっ
SPURT
N-N-NOW IF YOU'LL EXCUSE ME...
WHEEZE
WHEEZE
HAHH
HAHH

The Roll: Mikoto's Ruse.

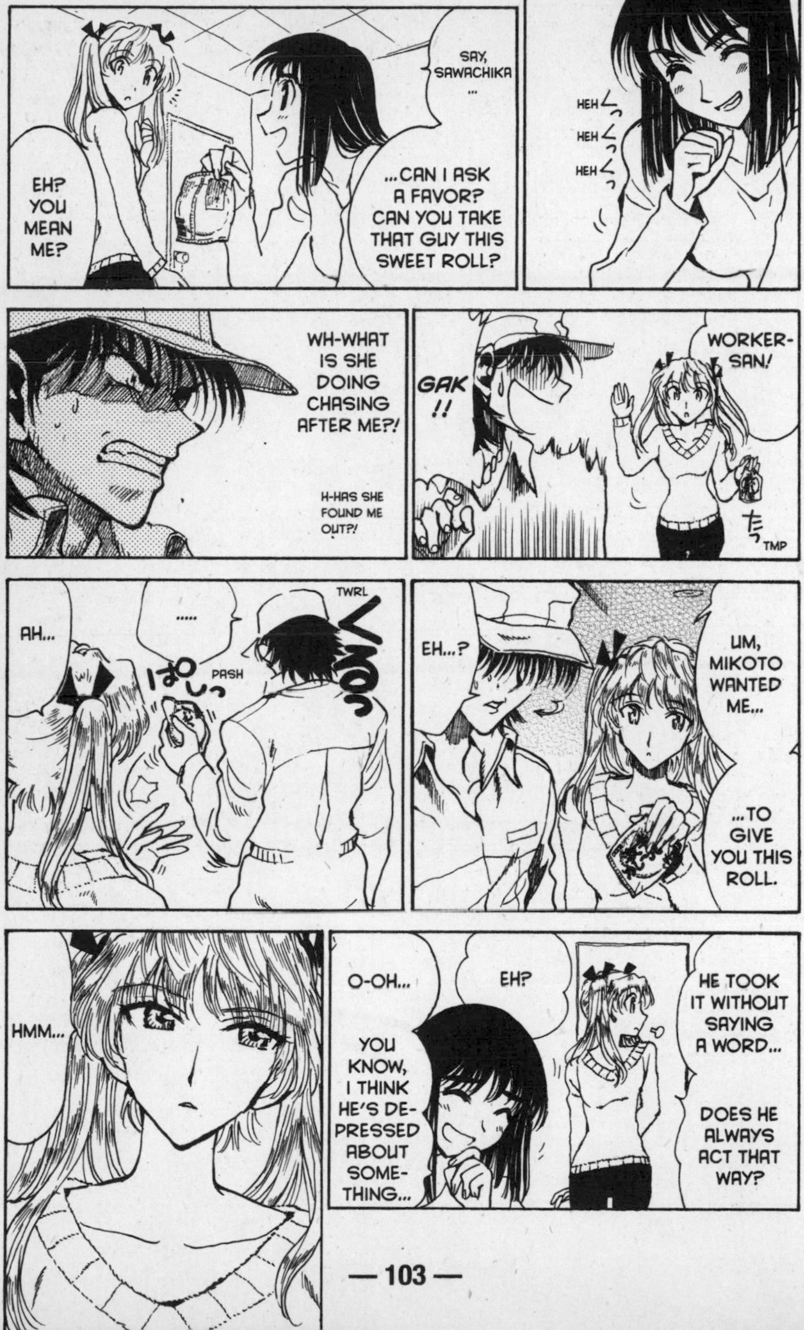
HEH
HEH
HEH
SAY, SAWACHIKA ...
...CAN I ASK A FAVOR? CAN YOU TAKE THAT GUY THIS SWEET ROLL?
EH? YOU MEAN ME?
WORKER-SAN!
TMP
GAK !!
WH-WHAT IS SHE DOING CHASING AFTER ME?!
H-HAS SHE FOUND ME OUT?!
UM, MIKOTO WANTED ME...
...TO GIVE YOU THIS ROLL.
EH...?
TWRL
.....
PASH
AH...
HE TOOK IT WITHOUT SAYING A WORD...
DOES HE ALWAYS ACT THAT WAY?
EH?
O-OH...
YOU KNOW, I THINK HE'S DE-PRESSED ABOUT SOME-THING...
HMM...

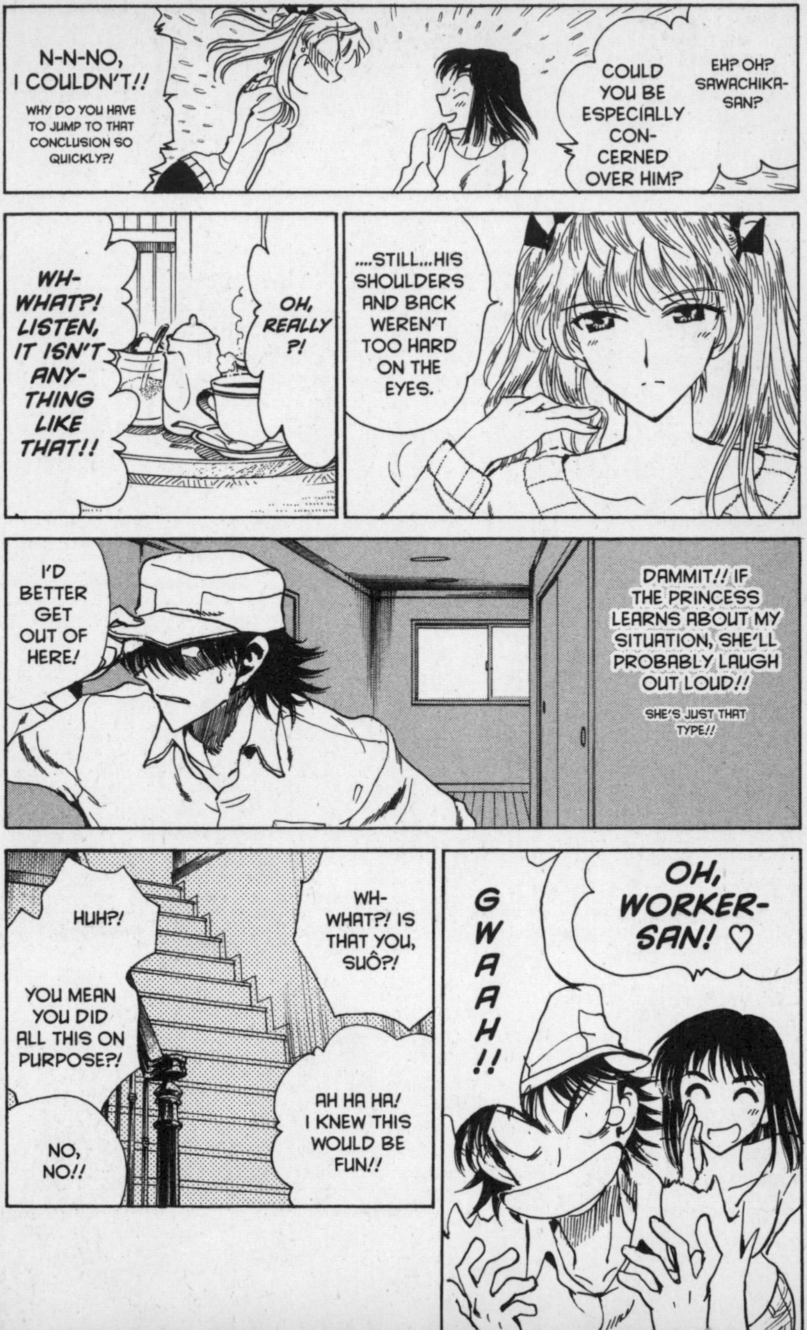
EH? OH? SAWACHIKA-SAN?
COULD YOU BE ESPECIALLY CON-CERNED OVER HIM?
N-N-NO, I COULDN'T!!
WHY DO YOU HAVE TO JUMP TO THAT CONCLUSION SO QUICKLY?!
....STILL...HIS SHOULDERS AND BACK WEREN'T TOO HARD ON THE EYES.
OH, REALLY?!
WH-WHAT?! LISTEN, IT ISN'T ANY-THING LIKE THAT!!
DAMMIT!! IF THE PRINCESS LEARNS ABOUT MY SITUATION, SHE'LL PROBABLY LAUGH OUT LOUD!!
SHE'S JUST THAT TYPE!!
I'D BETTER GET OUT OF HERE!
OH, WORKER-SAN! ♡
GWAAAH!!
WH-WHAT?! IS THAT YOU, SUÔ?!
HUH?!
YOU MEAN YOU DID ALL THIS ON PURPOSE?!
AH HA HA! I KNEW THIS WOULD BE FUN!!
NO, NO!!

Suô Mikoto: Greater Part — Enjoying This. Lesser Part — Nice Person.

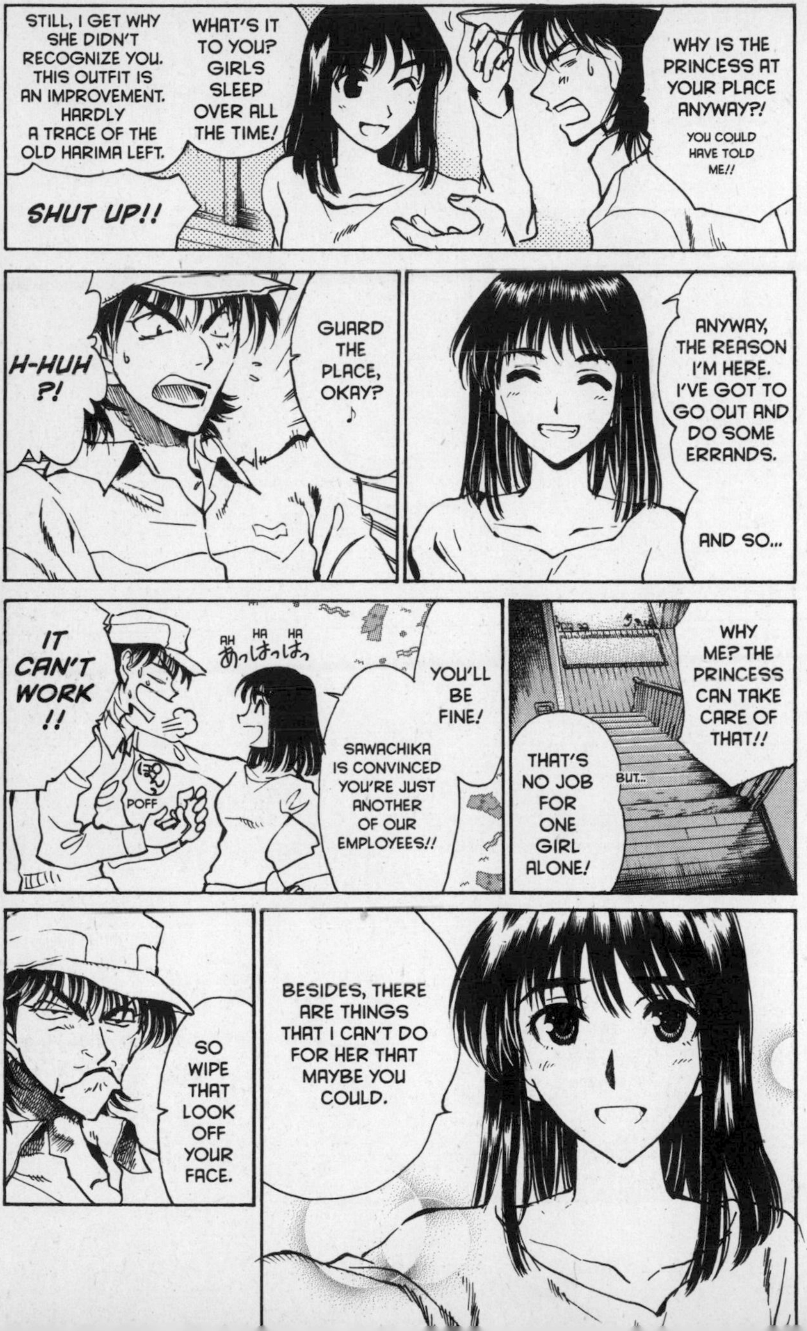
WHY IS THE PRINCESS AT YOUR PLACE ANYWAY?!
YOU COULD HAVE TOLD ME!!
WHAT'S IT TO YOU? GIRLS SLEEP OVER ALL THE TIME!
STILL, I GET WHY SHE DIDN'T RECOGNIZE YOU. THIS OUTFIT IS AN IMPROVEMENT. HARDLY A TRACE OF THE OLD HARIMA LEFT.
SHUT UP!!
ANYWAY, THE REASON I'M HERE. I'VE GOT TO GO OUT AND DO SOME ERRANDS.
AND SO...
GUARD THE PLACE, OKAY? ♪
H-HUH ?!
WHY ME? THE PRINCESS CAN TAKE CARE OF THAT!!
BUT...
THAT'S NO JOB FOR ONE GIRL ALONE!
YOU'LL BE FINE!
SAWACHIKA IS CONVINCED YOU'RE JUST ANOTHER OF OUR EMPLOYEES!!
AH HA HA
あっはっはっ
IT CAN'T WORK !!
POFF
BESIDES, THERE ARE THINGS THAT I CAN'T DO FOR HER THAT MAYBE YOU COULD.
SO WIPE THAT LOOK OFF YOUR FACE.

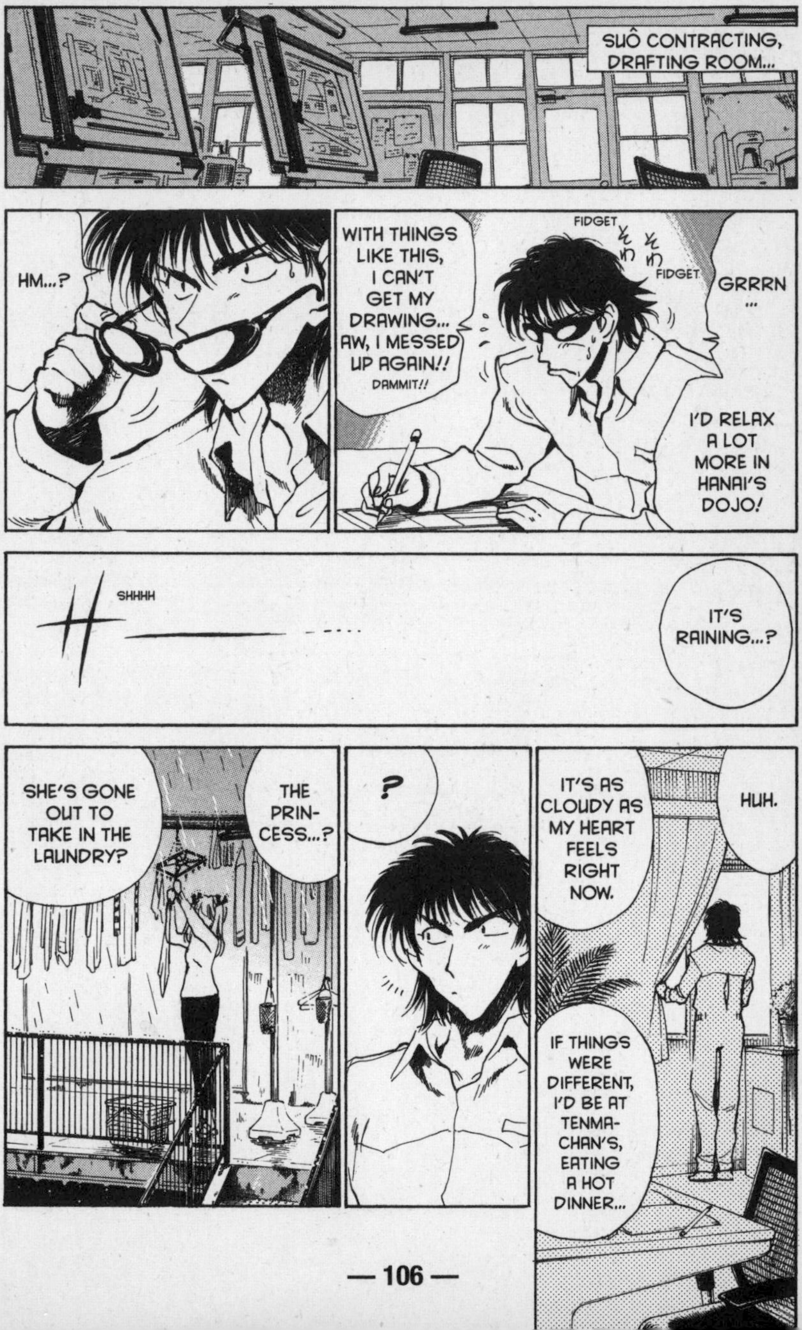
SUÔ CONTRACTING, DRAFTING ROOM...
GRRRN ...
FIDGET
FIDGET
WITH THINGS LIKE THIS, I CAN'T GET MY DRAWING... AW, I MESSED UP AGAIN!!
DAMMIT!!
I'D RELAX A LOT MORE IN HANAI'S DOJO!
HM...?
IT'S RAINING...?
SHHHH
HUH.
IT'S AS CLOUDY AS MY HEART FEELS RIGHT NOW.
IF THINGS WERE DIFFERENT, I'D BE AT TENMA-CHAN'S, EATING A HOT DINNER...
?
THE PRIN-CESS...?
SHE'S GONE OUT TO TAKE IN THE LAUNDRY?

Currently Drawing a 120-page Manga. Just So You Know.

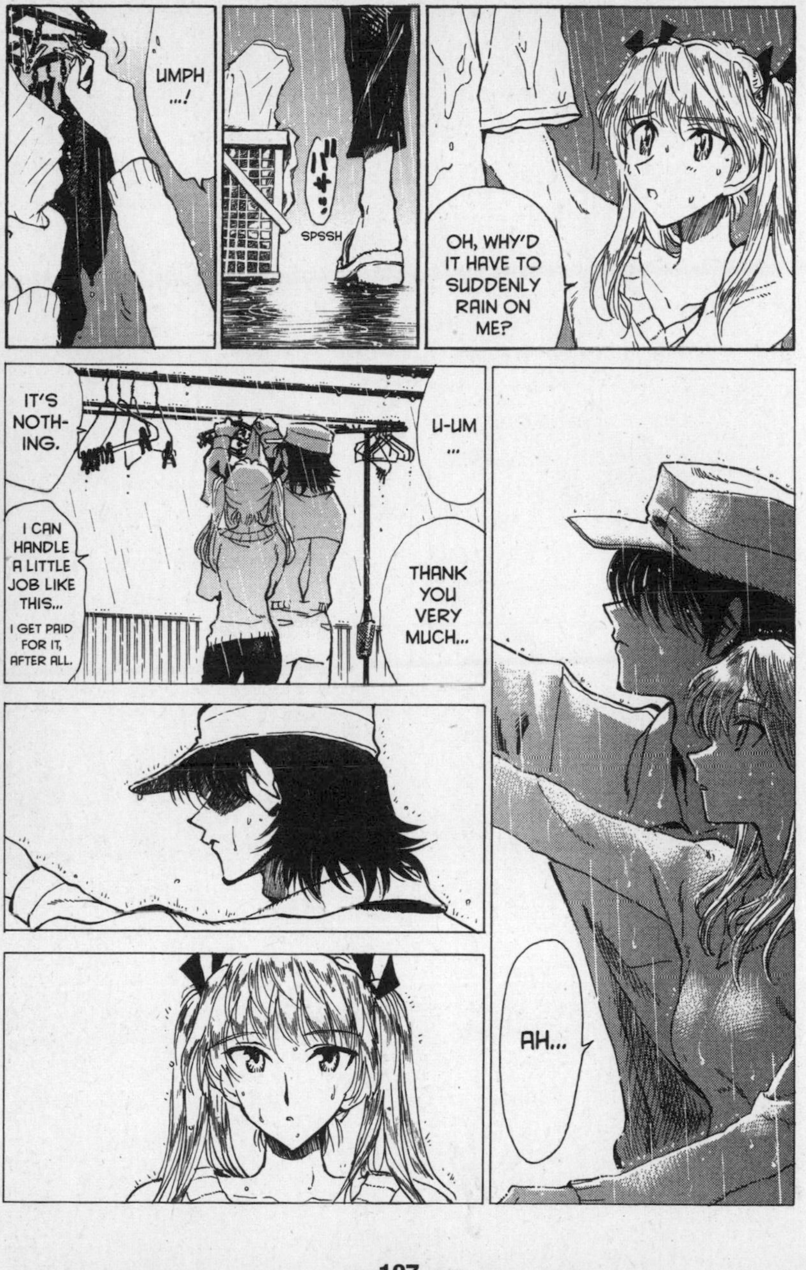
OH, WHY'D IT HAVE TO SUDDENLY RAIN ON ME?
バサッ
SPSSH
UMPH ...!
AH...
U-UM ...
THANK YOU VERY MUCH...
IT'S NOTHING.
I CAN HANDLE A LITTLE JOB LIKE THIS...
I GET PAID FOR IT, AFTER ALL.

Late Night at Hanai's Dojo.

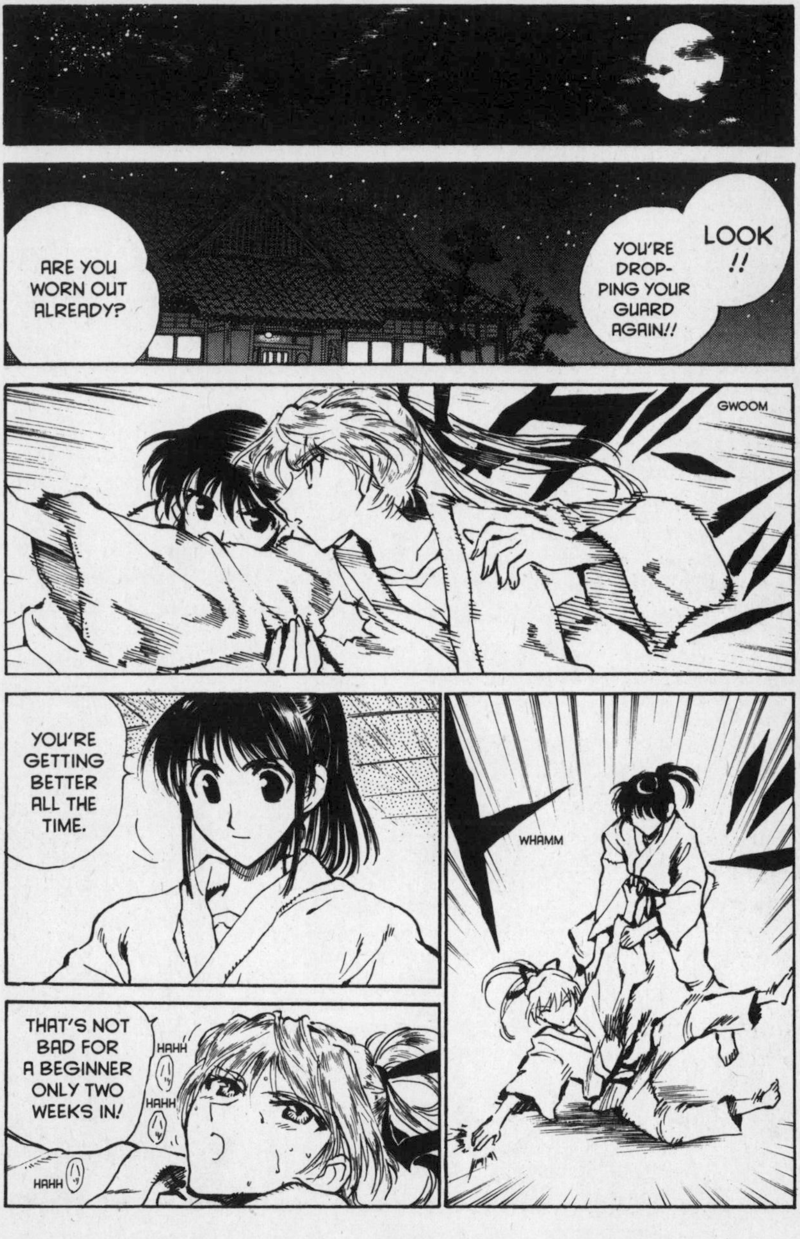
LOOK!!
YOU'RE DROP-PING YOUR GUARD AGAIN!!
ARE YOU WORN OUT ALREADY?
GWOOM
WHAMM
YOU'RE GETTING BETTER ALL THE TIME.
HAHH
HAHH
THAT'S NOT BAD FOR A BEGINNER ONLY TWO WEEKS IN!
HAHH

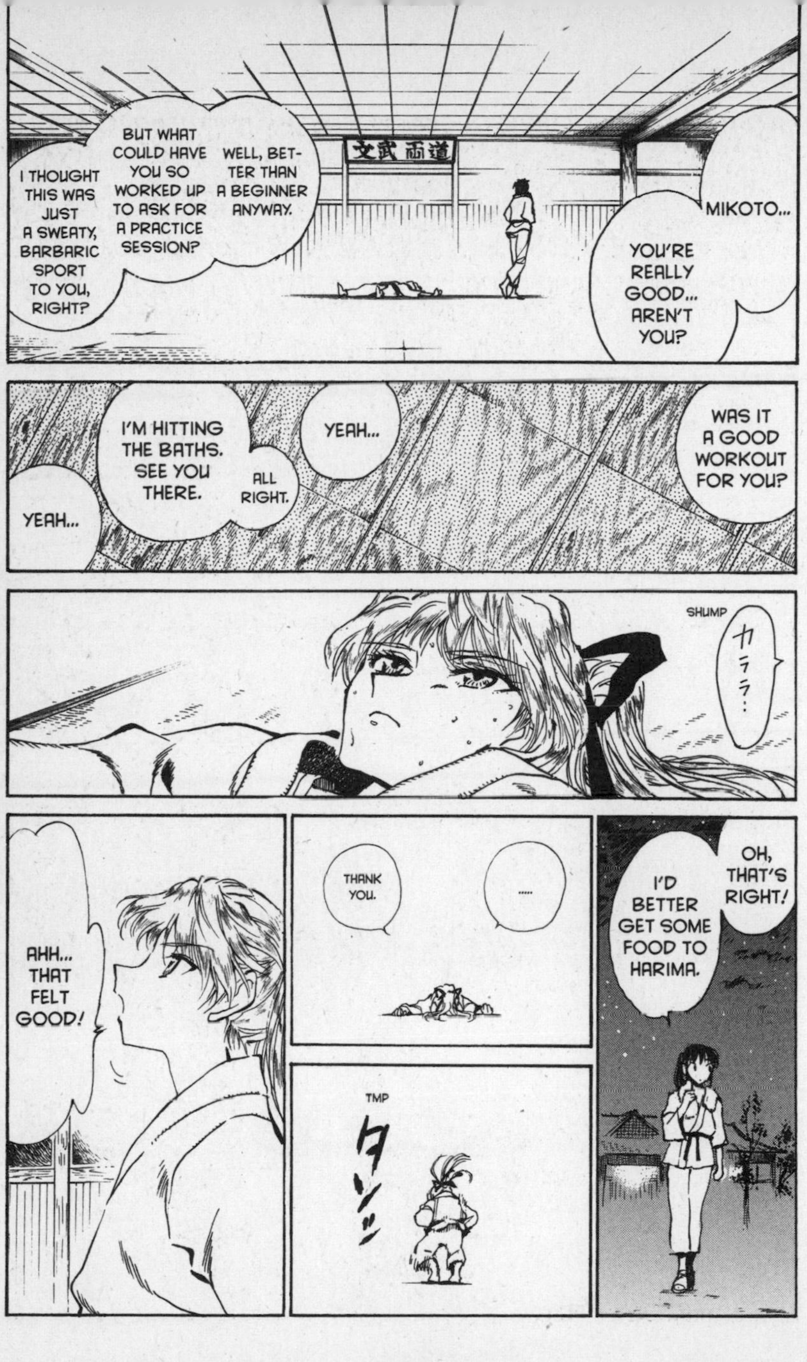
MIKOTO...
YOU'RE REALLY GOOD... AREN'T YOU?
WELL, BET-TER THAN A BEGINNER ANYWAY.
BUT WHAT COULD HAVE YOU SO WORKED UP TO ASK FOR A PRACTICE SESSION?
I THOUGHT THIS WAS JUST A SWEATY, BARBARIC SPORT TO YOU, RIGHT?
WAS IT A GOOD WORKOUT FOR YOU?
YEAH...
ALL RIGHT.
I'M HITTING THE BATHS. SEE YOU THERE.
YEAH...
SHUMP
カララ…
OH, THAT'S RIGHT!
I'D BETTER GET SOME FOOD TO HARIMA.
.....
THANK YOU.
TMP
タンッ
AHH... THAT FELT GOOD!

It Isn't Mikoto. Just So You Know.

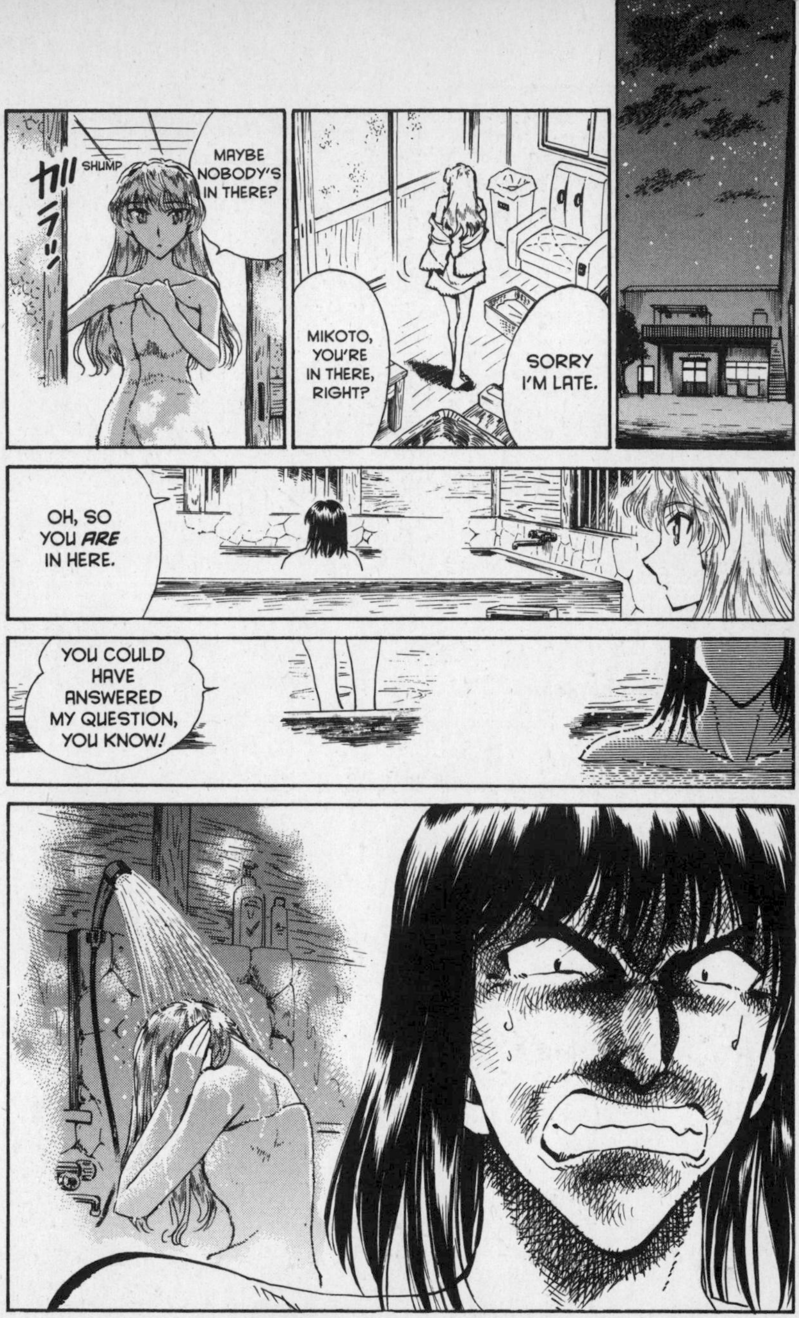
SORRY I'M LATE.
MIKOTO, YOU'RE IN THERE, RIGHT?
SHUMP
MAYBE NOBODY'S IN THERE?
OH, SO YOU *ARE* IN HERE.
YOU COULD HAVE ANSWERED MY QUESTION, YOU KNOW!

 # 149· · · · · · · · ·Fin

#150 LEGAL EAGLES

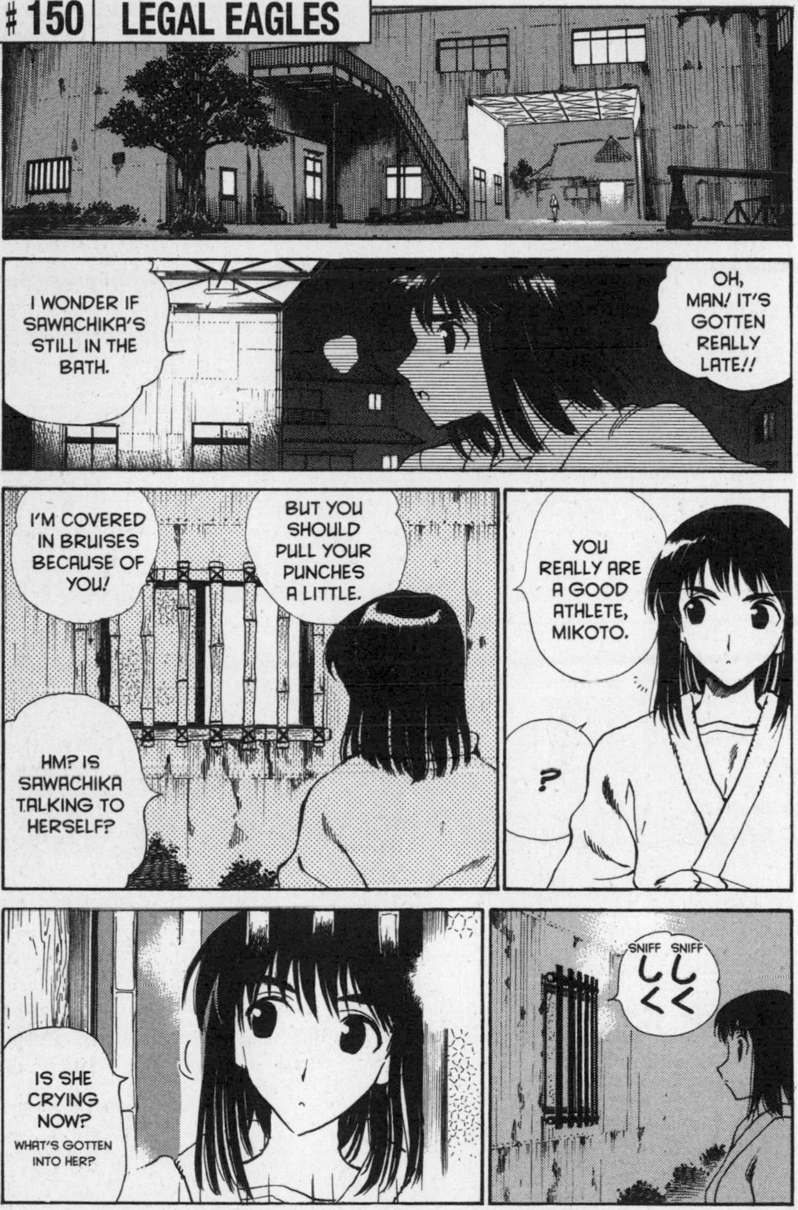
OH, MAN! IT'S GOTTEN REALLY LATE!!
I WONDER IF SAWACHIKA'S STILL IN THE BATH.
YOU REALLY ARE A GOOD ATHLETE, MIKOTO.
?
BUT YOU SHOULD PULL YOUR PUNCHES A LITTLE.
I'M COVERED IN BRUISES BECAUSE OF YOU!
HM? IS SAWACHIKA TALKING TO HERSELF?
SNIFF SNIFF
しくしく
IS SHE CRYING NOW?
WHAT'S GOTTEN INTO HER?

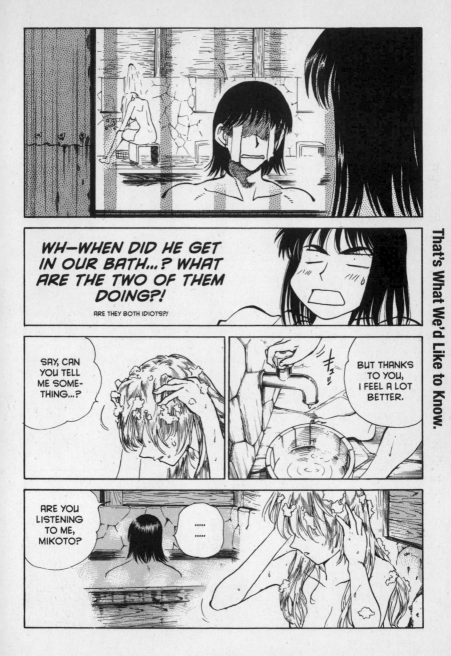

WH—WHEN DID HE GET IN OUR BATH...? WHAT ARE THE TWO OF THEM DOING?!
ARE THEY BOTH IDIOTS?!
BUT THANKS TO YOU, I FEEL A LOT BETTER.
SAY, CAN YOU TELL ME SOMETHING...?
....
ARE YOU LISTENING TO ME, MIKOTO?

It Isn't the Sound of a Jet Engine. Just So You Know.

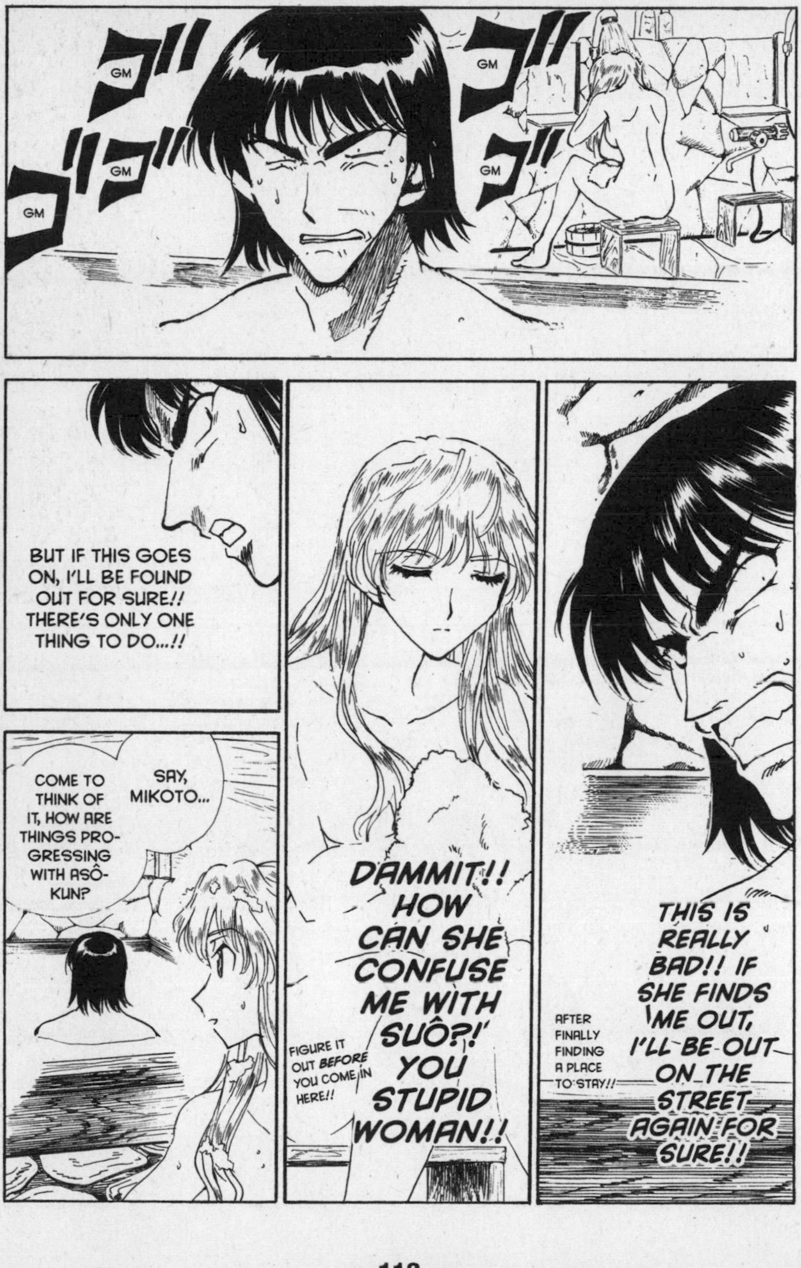
GM
GM
GM
GM
GM
THIS IS REALLY BAD!! IF SHE FINDS ME OUT, I'LL BE OUT ON THE STREET AGAIN FOR SURE!!
AFTER FINALLY FINDING A PLACE TO STAY!!
DAMMIT!! HOW CAN SHE CONFUSE ME WITH SUÔ?!' YOU STUPID WOMAN!!
FIGURE IT OUT *BEFORE* YOU COME IN HERE!!
BUT IF THIS GOES ON, I'LL BE FOUND OUT FOR SURE!! THERE'S ONLY ONE THING TO DO...!!
SAY, MIKOTO...
COME TO THINK OF IT, HOW ARE THINGS PRO-GRESSING WITH ASÔ-KUN?

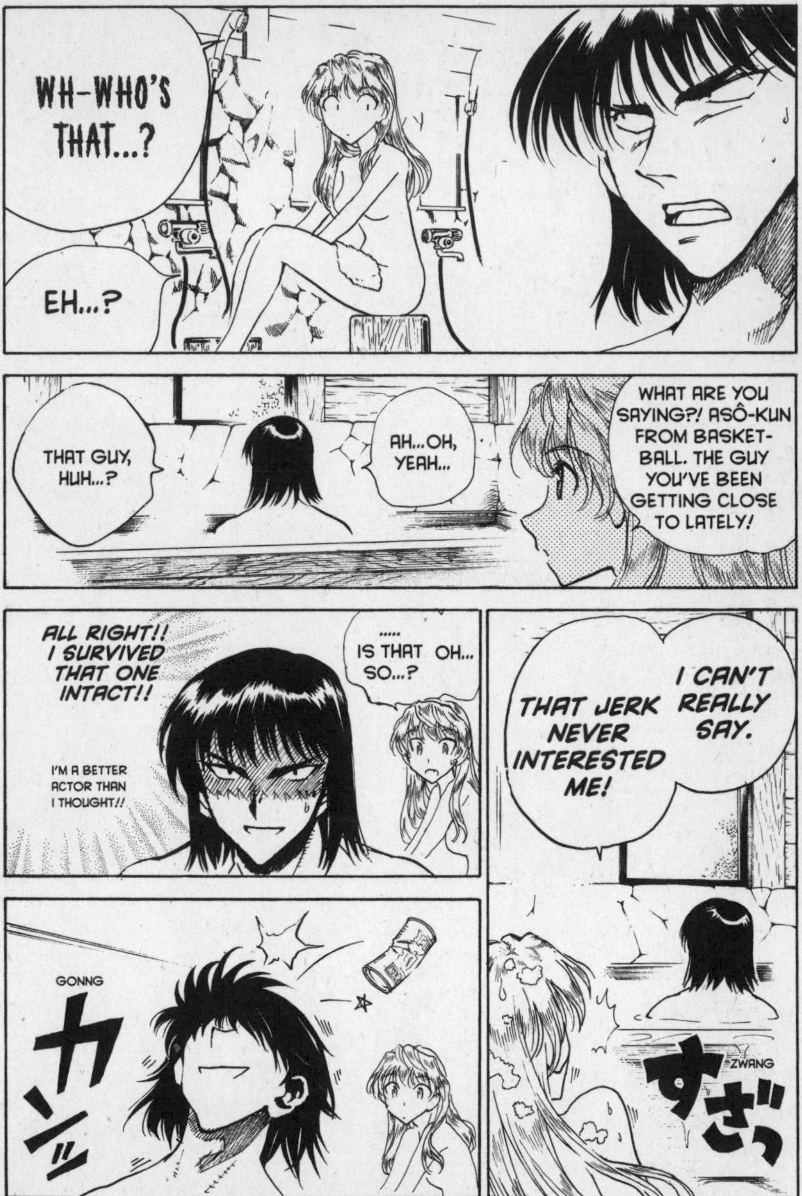
WH-WHO'S THAT...?
EH...?
WHAT ARE YOU SAYING?! ASÔ-KUN FROM BASKET-BALL. THE GUY YOU'VE BEEN GETTING CLOSE TO LATELY!
AH...OH, YEAH...
THAT GUY, HUH...?
I CAN'T REALLY SAY.
THAT JERK NEVER INTERESTED ME!
ZWANG
すざっ
OH...
..... IS THAT SO...?
ALL RIGHT!! I SURVIVED THAT ONE INTACT!!
I'M A BETTER ACTOR THAN I THOUGHT!!
GONNG
カンッ

Harima Kenji: Promoted from Suô's Worker to Suô Mikoto Herself.

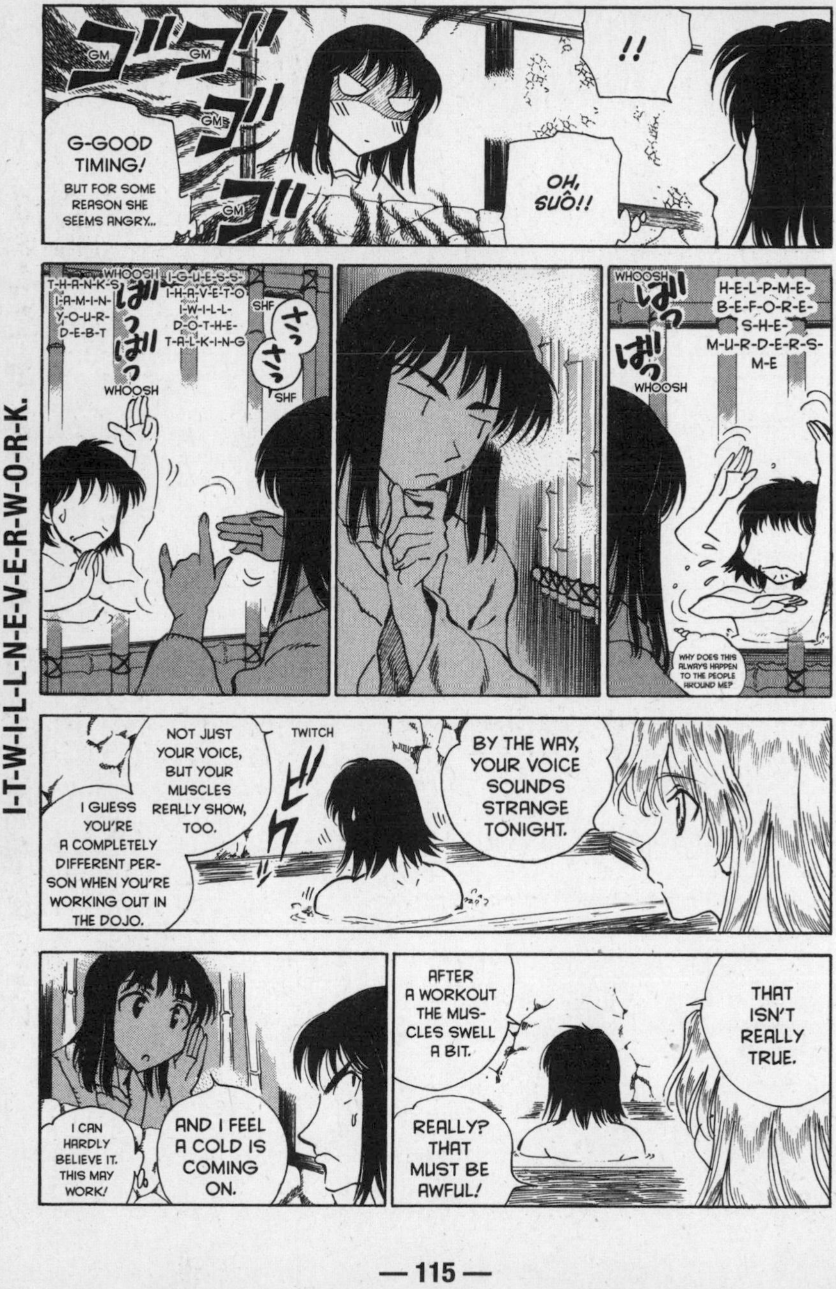

!!
OH, SUÔ!!
ゴゴゴゴ
GM GM GM GM
G-GOOD TIMING!
BUT FOR SOME REASON SHE SEEMS ANGRY...
WHOOSH
ばっ ばっ
H-E-L-P-M-E-B-E-F-O-R-E-S-H-E-M-U-R-D-E-R-S-M-E
WHOOSH
WHY DOES THIS ALWAYS HAPPEN TO THE PEOPLE AROUND ME?
さっ さっ
SHF
I-G-U-E-S-S-I-H-A-V-E-T-O-I-W-I-L-L-D-O-T-H-E-T-A-L-K-I-N-G
WHOOSH
ばっ ばっ
T-H-A-N-K-S-I-A-M-I-N-Y-O-U-R-D-E-B-T
WHOOSH
SHF
BY THE WAY, YOUR VOICE SOUNDS STRANGE TONIGHT.
TWITCH
NOT JUST YOUR VOICE, BUT YOUR MUSCLES REALLY SHOW, TOO.
I GUESS YOU'RE A COMPLETELY DIFFERENT PERSON WHEN YOU'RE WORKING OUT IN THE DOJO.
THAT ISN'T REALLY TRUE.
AFTER A WORKOUT THE MUSCLES SWELL A BIT.
REALLY? THAT MUST BE AWFUL!
AND I FEEL A COLD IS COMING ON.
I CAN HARDLY BELIEVE IT. THIS MAY WORK!
I-T-W-I-L-L-N-E-V-E-R-W-O-R-K.

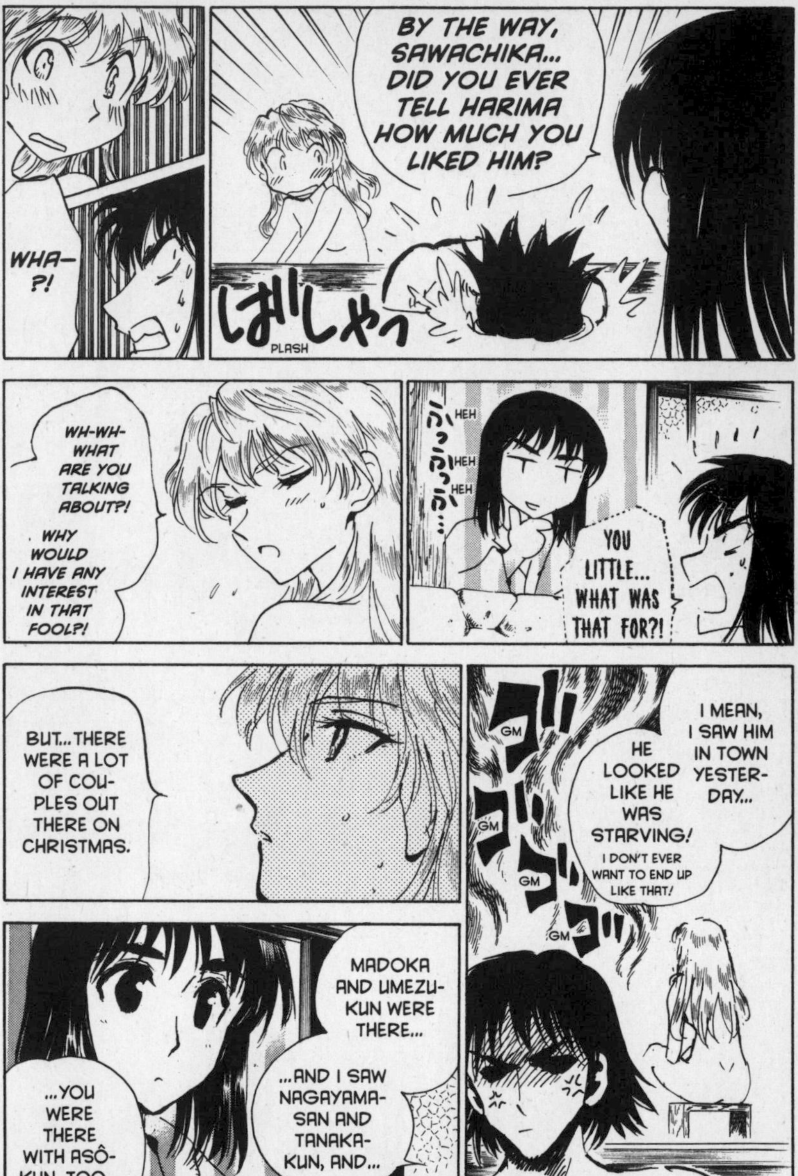
BY THE WAY, SAWACHIKA... DID YOU EVER TELL HARIMA HOW MUCH YOU LIKED HIM?
ぱしゃっ
PLASH
WHA—?!
ふっふっふ…
HEH
HEH
HEH
YOU LITTLE... WHAT WAS THAT FOR?!
WH-WH-WHAT ARE YOU TALKING ABOUT?!
WHY WOULD I HAVE ANY INTEREST IN THAT FOOL?!
GM
GM
GM
GM
I MEAN, I SAW HIM IN TOWN YESTER-DAY...
HE LOOKED LIKE HE WAS STARVING!
I DON'T EVER WANT TO END UP LIKE THAT!
BUT...THERE WERE A LOT OF COU-PLES OUT THERE ON CHRISTMAS.
MADOKA AND UMEZU-KUN WERE THERE...
...AND I SAW NAGAYAMA-SAN AND TANAKA-KUN, AND...
...YOU WERE THERE WITH ASÔ-KUN, TOO...

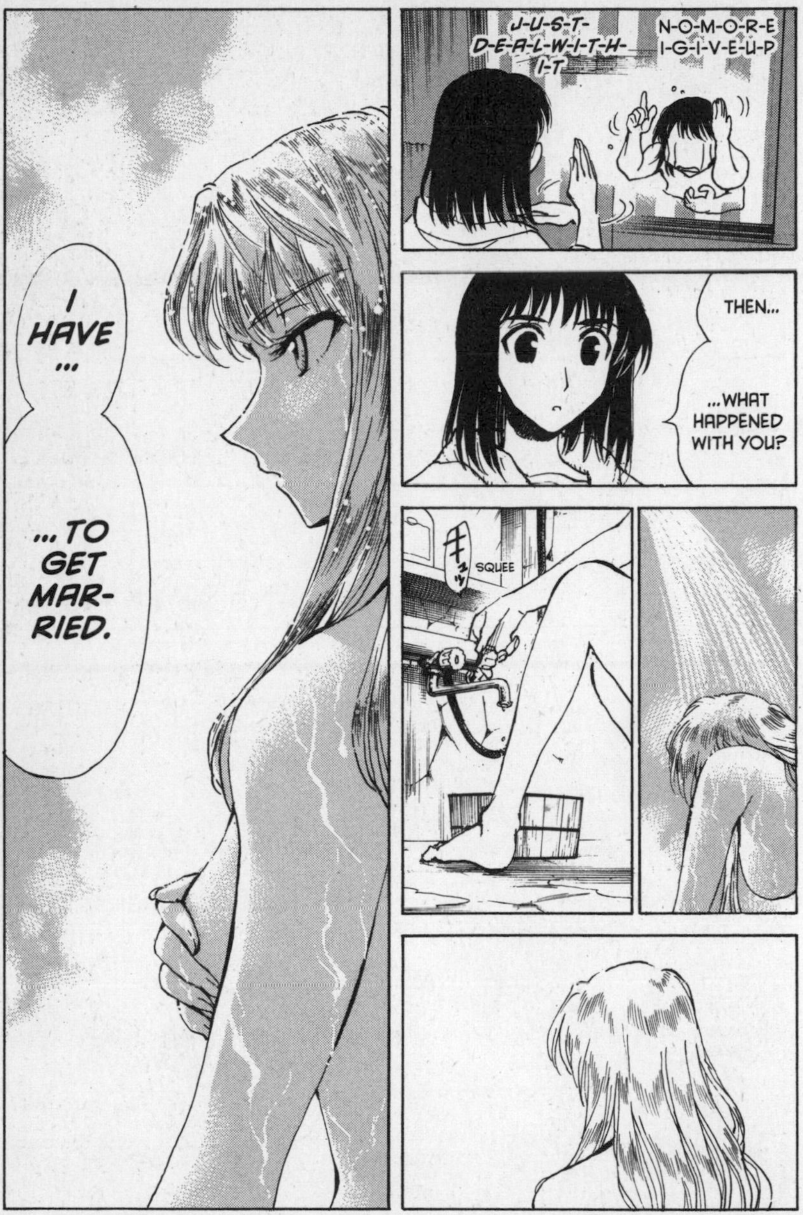
N-O-M-O-R-E I-G-I-V-E-U-P
J-U-S-T-D-E-A-L-W-I-T-H-I-T
THEN...
...WHAT HAPPENED WITH YOU?
キュッ
SQUEE
I HAVE...
...TO GET MARRIED.

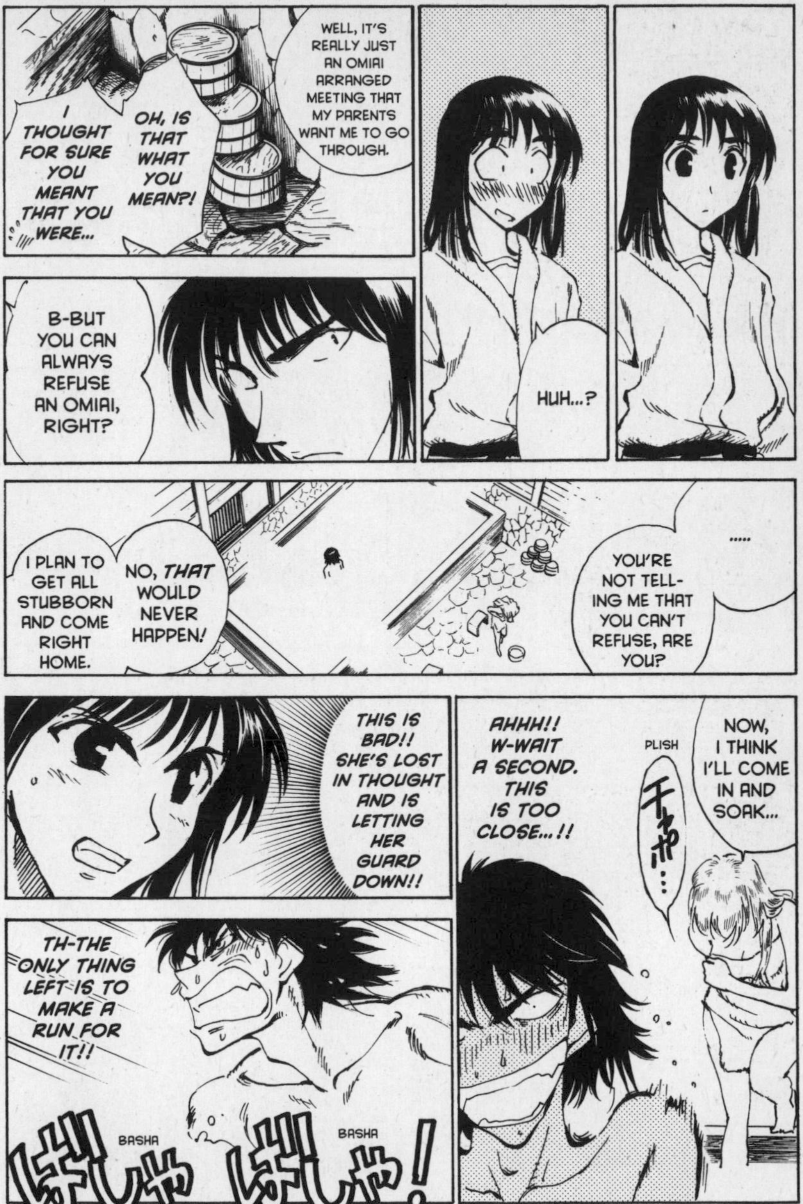
HUH...?
WELL, IT'S REALLY JUST AN OMIAI ARRANGED MEETING THAT MY PARENTS WANT ME TO GO THROUGH.
OH, IS THAT WHAT YOU MEAN?!
I THOUGHT FOR SURE YOU MEANT THAT YOU WERE...
B-BUT YOU CAN ALWAYS REFUSE AN OMIAI, RIGHT?
.....
YOU'RE NOT TELLING ME THAT YOU CAN'T REFUSE, ARE YOU?
NO, THAT WOULD NEVER HAPPEN!
I PLAN TO GET ALL STUBBORN AND COME RIGHT HOME.
NOW, I THINK I'LL COME IN AND SOAK...
PLISH
チャポ...
AHHH!! W-WAIT A SECOND. THIS IS TOO CLOSE...!!
THIS IS BAD!! SHE'S LOST IN THOUGHT AND IS LETTING HER GUARD DOWN!!
TH-THE ONLY THING LEFT IS TO MAKE A RUN FOR IT!!
BASHA BASHA
ばしゃ ばしゃ!

A Gas Explosion in the Bath.

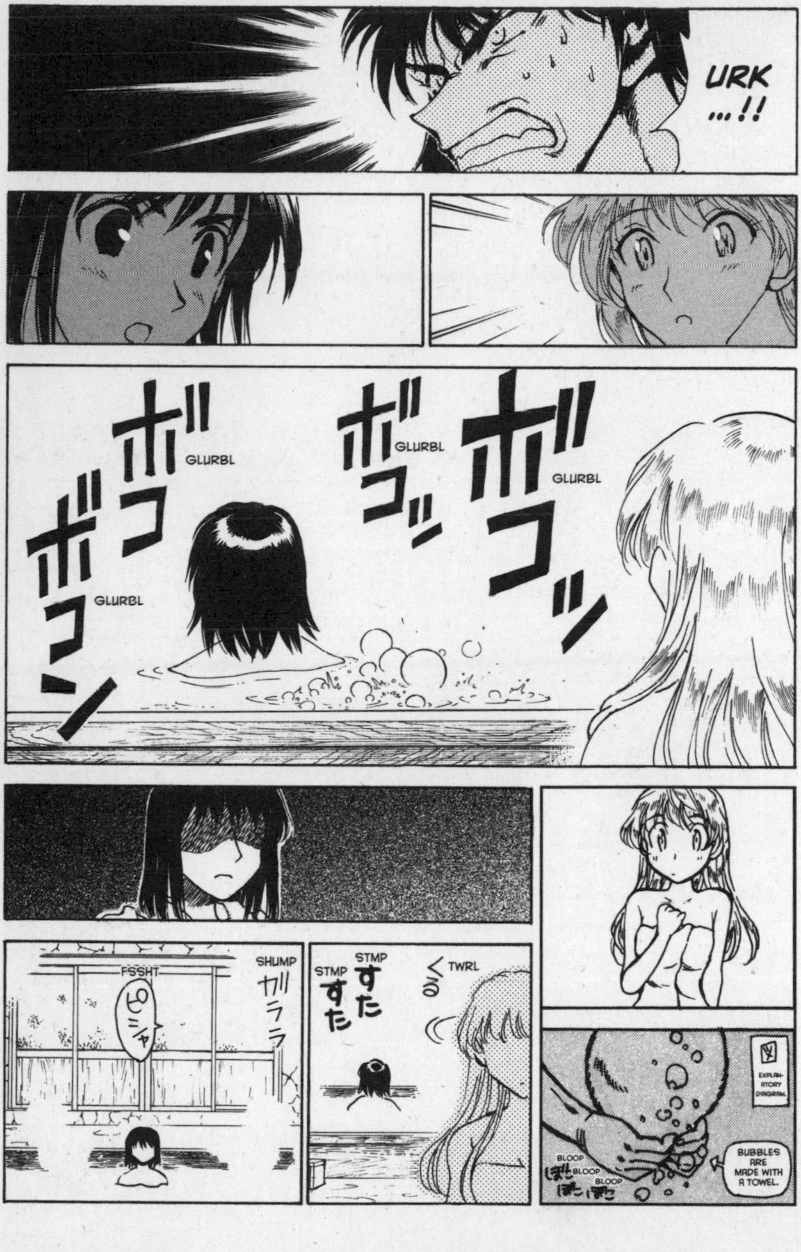
URK ...!!
ボコッ
GLURBL
ボコッ
GLURBL
ボコ
GLURBL
ボコン
GLURBL
EXPLANATORY DIAGRAM
BUBBLES ARE MADE WITH A TOWEL.
BLOOP BLOOP BLOOP
ぽこぽこぽこ
くる
TWRL
すた すた
STMP STMP
SHUMP
カラララ
FSSHT
ピシャ

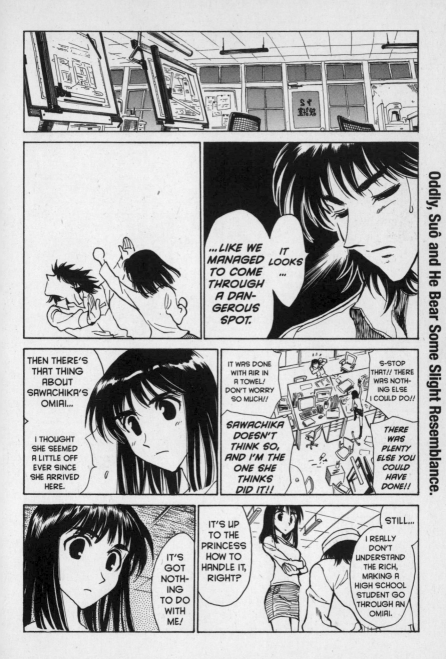

IT LOOKS...
...LIKE WE MANAGED TO COME THROUGH A DANGEROUS SPOT.
S-STOP THAT!! THERE WAS NOTHING ELSE I COULD DO!!
IT WAS DONE WITH AIR IN A TOWEL! DON'T WORRY SO MUCH!!
THERE WAS PLENTY ELSE YOU COULD HAVE DONE!!
SAWACHIKA DOESN'T THINK SO, AND I'M THE ONE SHE THINKS DID IT!!
THEN THERE'S THAT THING ABOUT SAWACHIKA'S OMIAI...
I THOUGHT SHE SEEMED A LITTLE OFF EVER SINCE SHE ARRIVED HERE.
STILL...
I REALLY DON'T UNDERSTAND THE RICH, MAKING A HIGH SCHOOL STUDENT GO THROUGH AN OMIAI.
IT'S UP TO THE PRINCESS HOW TO HANDLE IT, RIGHT?
IT'S GOT NOTHING TO DO WITH ME!

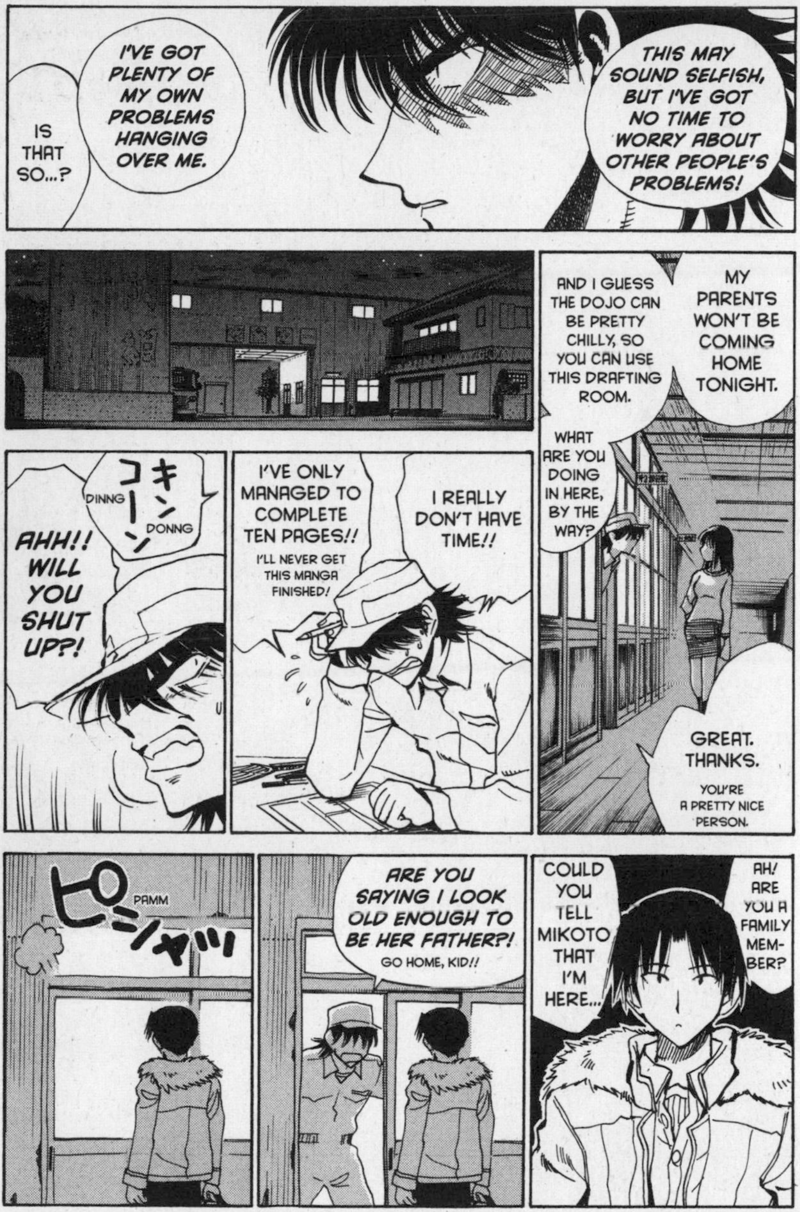
THIS MAY SOUND SELFISH, BUT I'VE GOT NO TIME TO WORRY ABOUT OTHER PEOPLE'S PROBLEMS!
I'VE GOT PLENTY OF MY OWN PROBLEMS HANGING OVER ME.
IS THAT SO...?
MY PARENTS WON'T BE COMING HOME TONIGHT.
AND I GUESS THE DOJO CAN BE PRETTY CHILLY, SO YOU CAN USE THIS DRAFTING ROOM.
WHAT ARE YOU DOING IN HERE, BY THE WAY?
GREAT. THANKS.
YOU'RE A PRETTY NICE PERSON.
I REALLY DON'T HAVE TIME!!
I'VE ONLY MANAGED TO COMPLETE TEN PAGES!!
I'LL NEVER GET THIS MANGA FINISHED!
キンコーン
DINNG DONNG
AHH!! WILL YOU SHUT UP?!
AH! ARE YOU A FAMILY MEMBER?
COULD YOU TELL MIKOTO THAT I'M HERE...
ARE YOU SAYING I LOOK OLD ENOUGH TO BE HER FATHER?!
GO HOME, KID!!
ピシャッ
PAMM

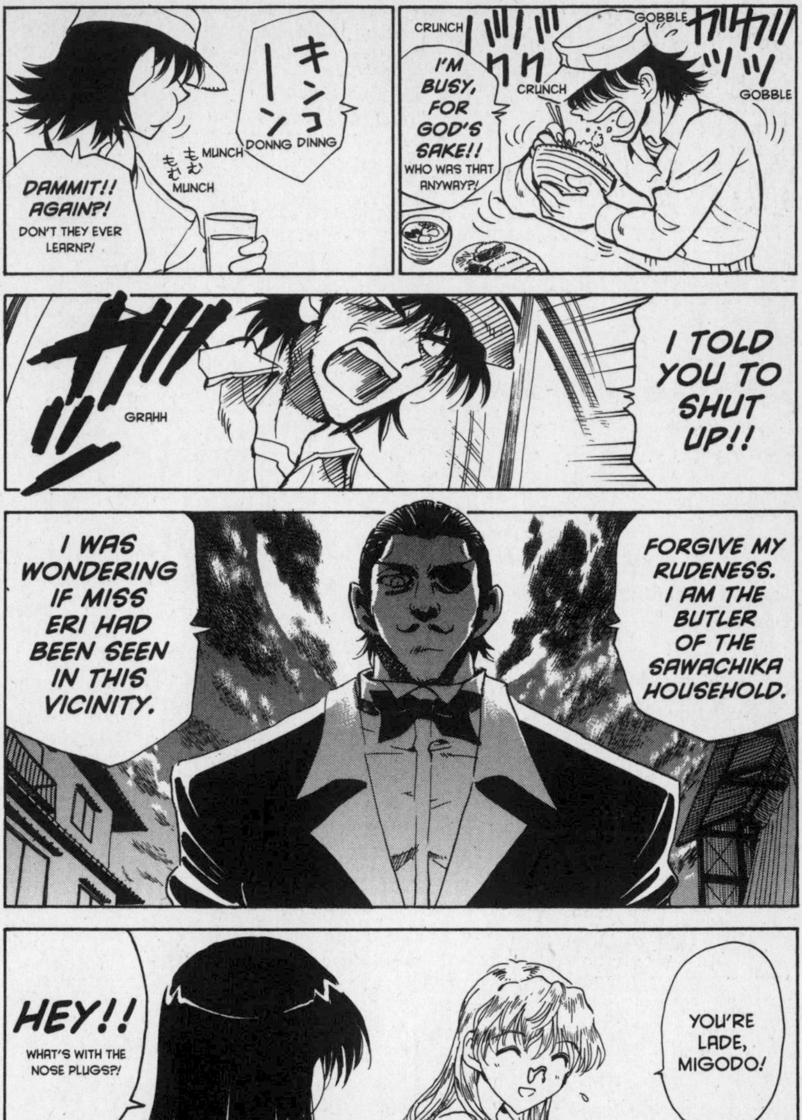
CRUNCH
GOBBLE
ガツガツ
バリバリ
I'M BUSY, FOR GOD'S SAKE!!
WHO WAS THAT ANYWAY?!
CRUNCH
GOBBLE
キンコーン
DONNG DINNG
もむもむ
MUNCH
MUNCH
DAMMIT!! AGAIN?!
DON'T THEY EVER LEARN?!
I TOLD YOU TO SHUT UP!!
GRAHH
FORGIVE MY RUDENESS. I AM THE BUTLER OF THE SAWACHIKA HOUSEHOLD.
I WAS WONDERING IF MISS ERI HAD BEEN SEEN IN THIS VICINITY.
YOU'RE LADE, MIGODO!
HEY!!
WHAT'S WITH THE NOSE PLUGS?!

Now Make Friends and Play Nice.

 # 150· · · · · · · ·Fin

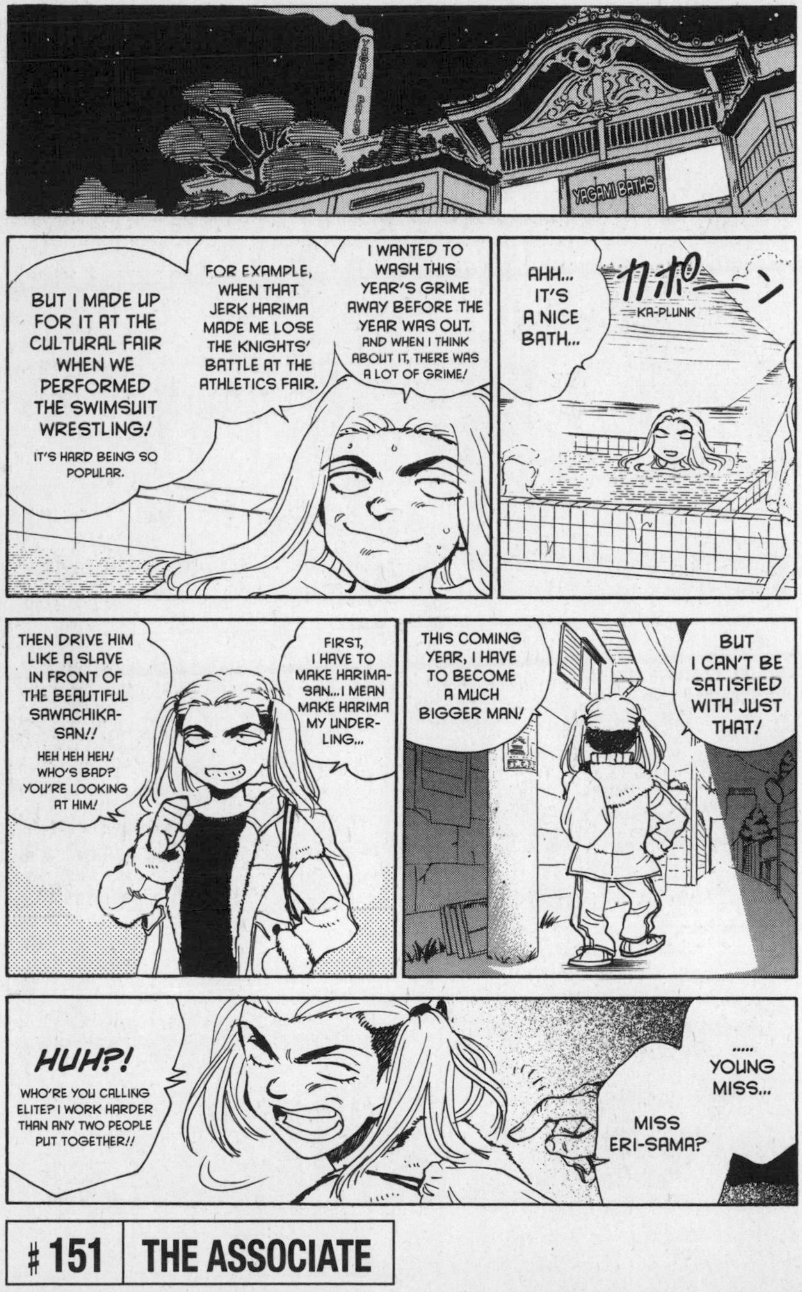
YAGAMI BATHS
AHH... IT'S A NICE BATH...
カポーン
KA-PLUNK
I WANTED TO WASH THIS YEAR'S GRIME AWAY BEFORE THE YEAR WAS OUT.
AND WHEN I THINK ABOUT IT, THERE WAS A LOT OF GRIME!
FOR EXAMPLE, WHEN THAT JERK HARIMA MADE ME LOSE THE KNIGHTS' BATTLE AT THE ATHLETICS FAIR.
BUT I MADE UP FOR IT AT THE CULTURAL FAIR WHEN WE PERFORMED THE SWIMSUIT WRESTLING!
IT'S HARD BEING SO POPULAR.
BUT I CAN'T BE SATISFIED WITH JUST THAT!
THIS COMING YEAR, I HAVE TO BECOME A MUCH BIGGER MAN!
FIRST, I HAVE TO MAKE HARIMA-SAN...I MEAN MAKE HARIMA MY UNDER-LING...
THEN DRIVE HIM LIKE A SLAVE IN FRONT OF THE BEAUTIFUL SAWACHIKA-SAN!!
HEH HEH HEH! WHO'S BAD? YOU'RE LOOKING AT HIM!
..... YOUNG MISS...
MISS ERI-SAMA?
HUH?!
WHO'RE YOU CALLING ELITE? I WORK HARDER THAN ANY TWO PEOPLE PUT TOGETHER!!

#151 THE ASSOCIATE

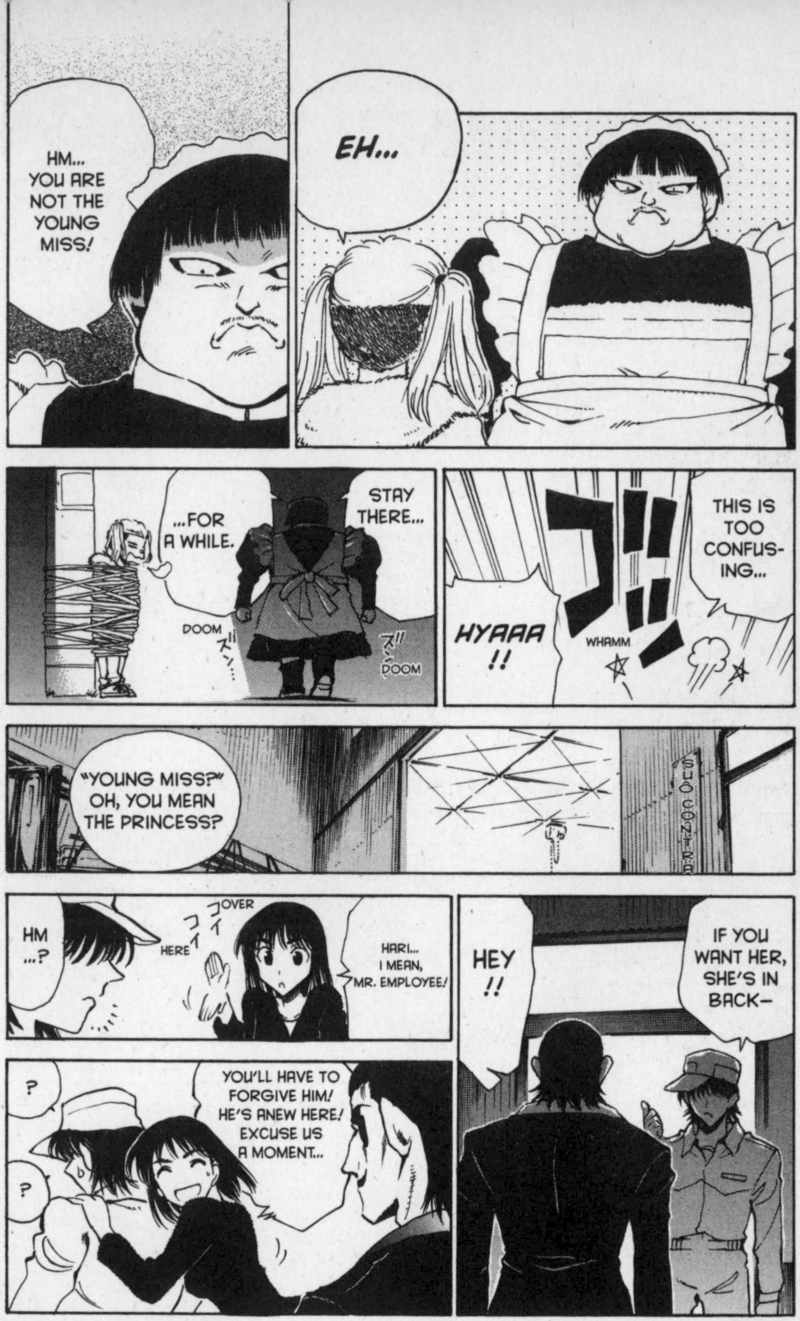
EH...
HM... YOU ARE NOT THE YOUNG MISS!
THIS IS TOO CONFUSING...
WHAMM
HYAAA!!
STAY THERE...
...FOR A WHILE.
DOOM
DOOM
SUO CONTRA
"YOUNG MISS?" OH, YOU MEAN THE PRINCESS?
IF YOU WANT HER, SHE'S IN BACK—
HEY!!
HARI... I MEAN, MR. EMPLOYEE!
OVER HERE
HM ...?
YOU'LL HAVE TO FORGIVE HIM! HE'S ANEW HERE! EXCUSE US A MOMENT...
?
?

Yoshidayama Jirô's Ambitions for 2005: Ended.

She Knew, and Was Prepared.

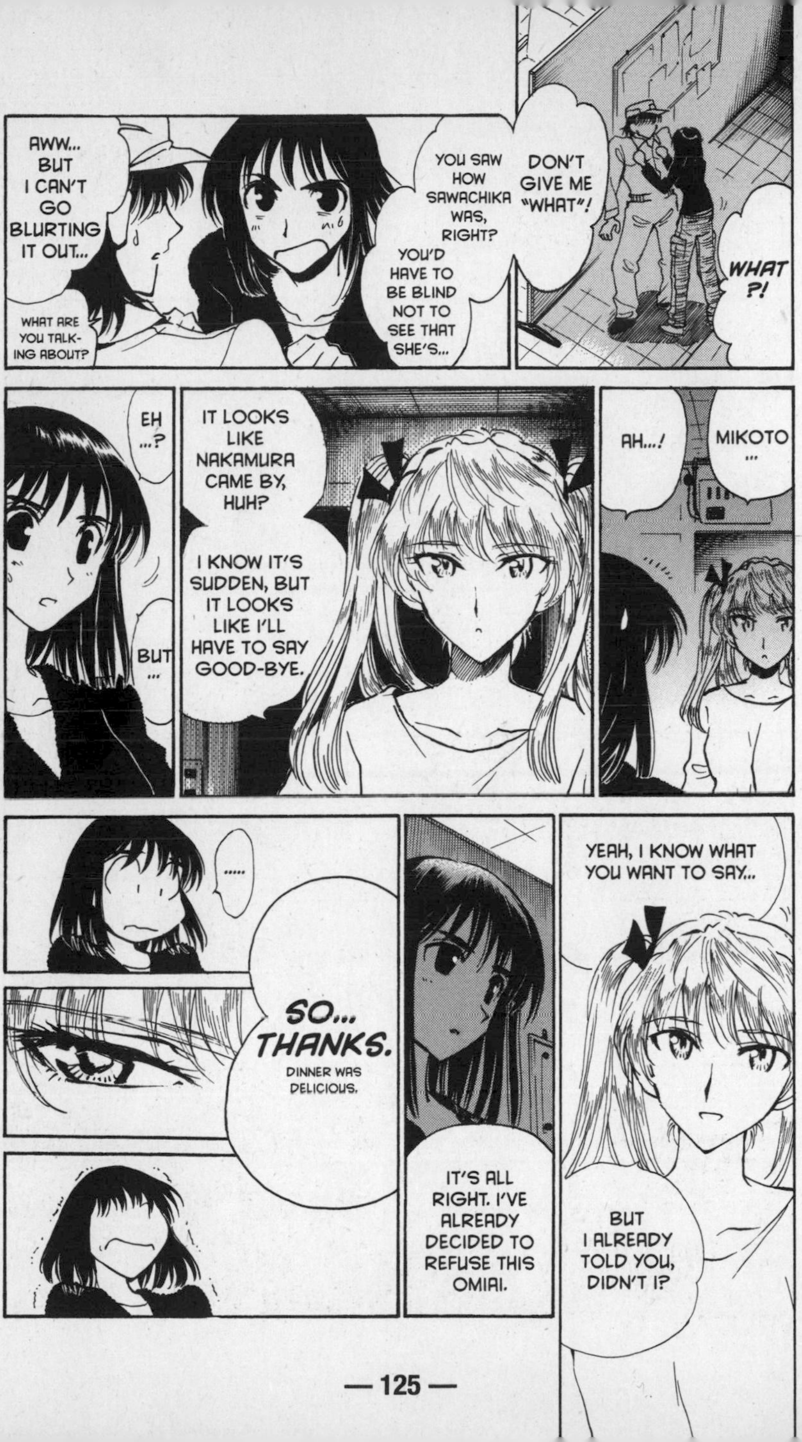
WHAT ?!
DON'T GIVE ME "WHAT"!
YOU SAW HOW SAWACHIKA WAS, RIGHT?
YOU'D HAVE TO BE BLIND NOT TO SEE THAT SHE'S...
AWW... BUT I CAN'T GO BLURTING IT OUT...
WHAT ARE YOU TALKING ABOUT?
MIKOTO ...
AH...!
IT LOOKS LIKE NAKAMURA CAME BY, HUH?
I KNOW IT'S SUDDEN, BUT IT LOOKS LIKE I'LL HAVE TO SAY GOOD-BYE.
EH ...?
BUT ...
YEAH, I KNOW WHAT YOU WANT TO SAY...
BUT I ALREADY TOLD YOU, DIDN'T I?
IT'S ALL RIGHT. I'VE ALREADY DECIDED TO REFUSE THIS OMIAI.
.....
SO... THANKS.
DINNER WAS DELICIOUS.

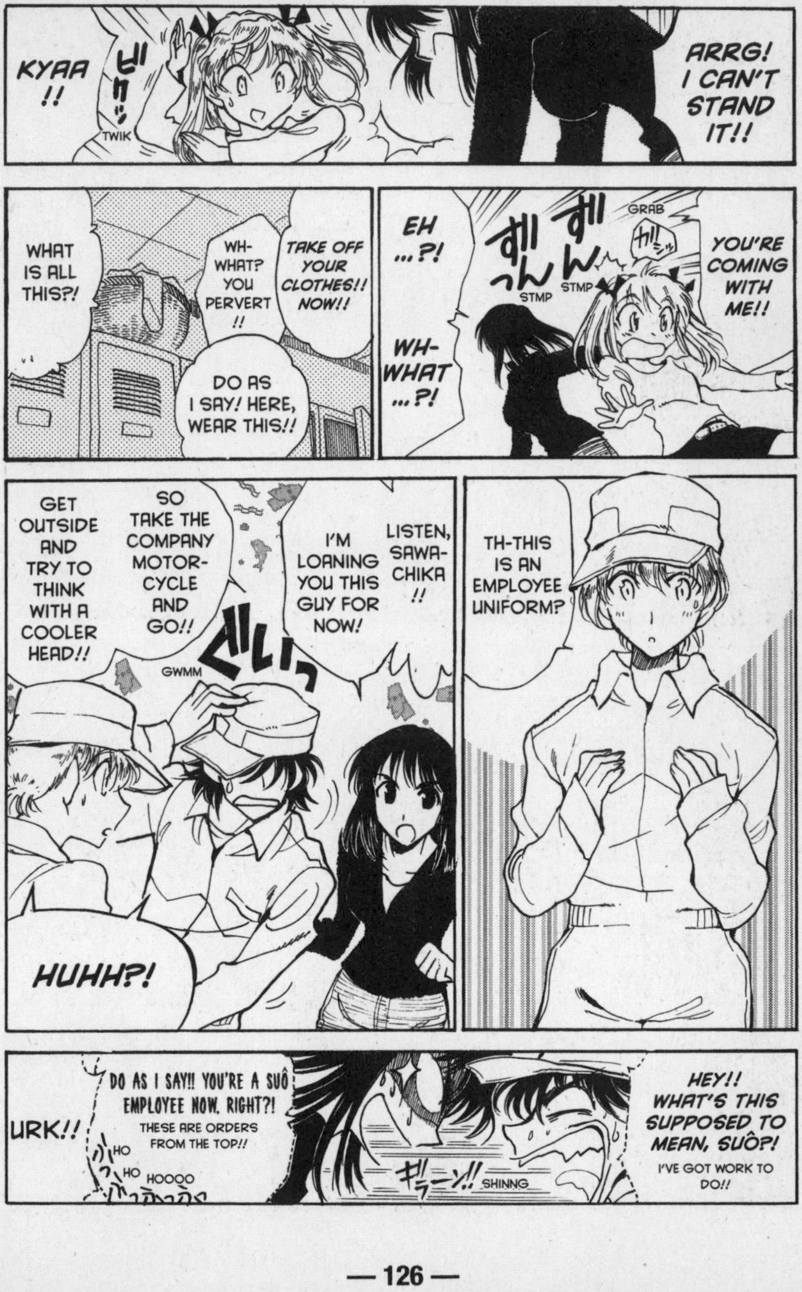
ARRG! I CAN'T STAND IT!!
KYAA!!
TWIK
YOU'RE COMING WITH ME!!
GRAB
STMP
STMP
EH ...?!
WH-WHAT ...?!
TAKE OFF YOUR CLOTHES!! NOW!!
WH-WHAT? YOU PERVERT!!
WHAT IS ALL THIS?!
DO AS I SAY! HERE, WEAR THIS!!
TH-THIS IS AN EMPLOYEE UNIFORM?
LISTEN, SAWA-CHIKA!!
I'M LOANING YOU THIS GUY FOR NOW!
SO TAKE THE COMPANY MOTOR-CYCLE AND GO!!
GET OUTSIDE AND TRY TO THINK WITH A COOLER HEAD!!
GWMM
HUHH?!
HEY!! WHAT'S THIS SUPPOSED TO MEAN, SUÔ?!
I'VE GOT WORK TO DO!!
SHINNG
DO AS I SAY!! YOU'RE A SUÔ EMPLOYEE NOW, RIGHT?!
THESE ARE ORDERS FROM THE TOP!!
HO
HO
HOOOO
URK!!

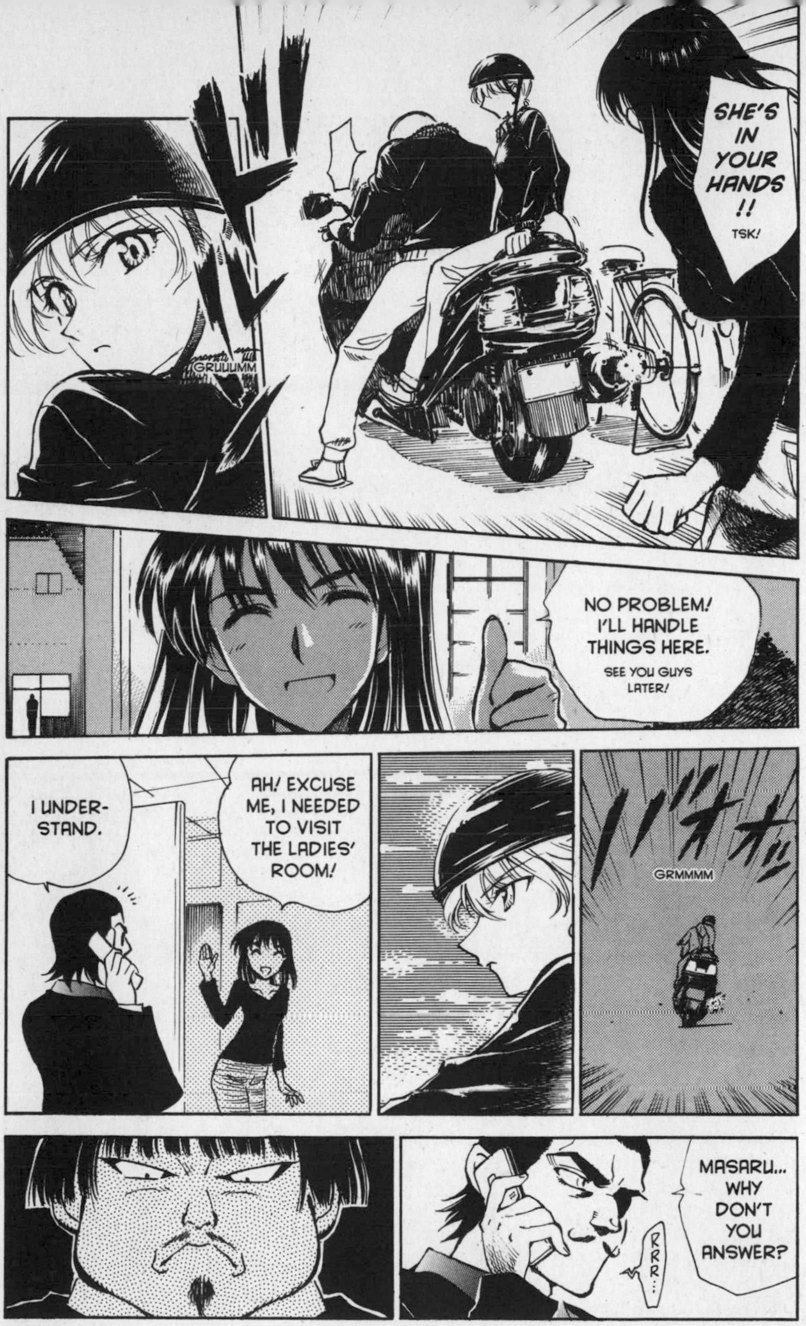
SHE'S IN YOUR HANDS !!
TSK!
GRUUUMM
NO PROBLEM! I'LL HANDLE THINGS HERE.
SEE YOU GUYS LATER!
GRMMMM
AH! EXCUSE ME, I NEEDED TO VISIT THE LADIES' ROOM!
I UNDER-STAND.
MASARU... WHY DON'T YOU ANSWER?
RRR...

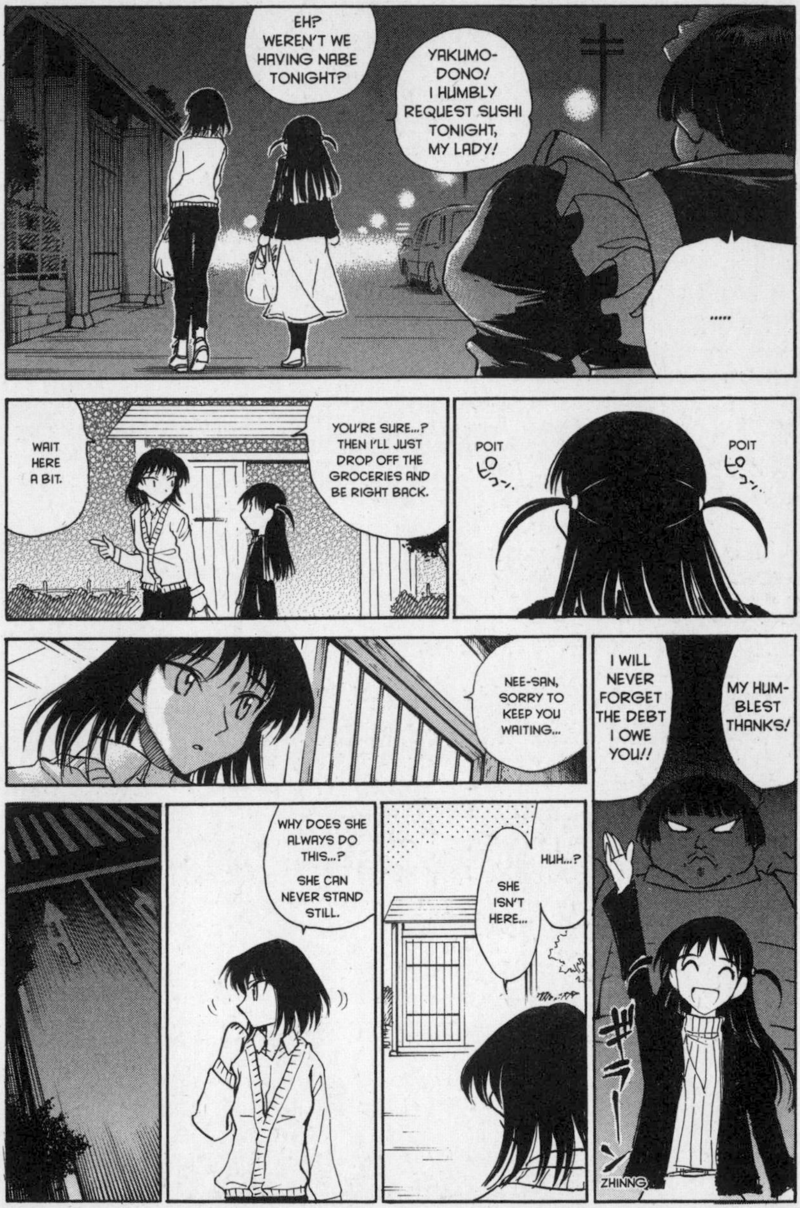
.....
YAKUMO-DONO! I HUMBLY REQUEST SUSHI TONIGHT, MY LADY!
EH? WEREN'T WE HAVING NABE TONIGHT?
POIT
POIT
YOU'RE SURE...? THEN I'LL JUST DROP OFF THE GROCERIES AND BE RIGHT BACK.
WAIT HERE A BIT.
MY HUM-BLEST THANKS!
I WILL NEVER FORGET THE DEBT I OWE YOU!!
ZHINNG
NEE-SAN, SORRY TO KEEP YOU WAITING...
HUH...?
SHE ISN'T HERE...
WHY DOES SHE ALWAYS DO THIS...?
SHE CAN NEVER STAND STILL.

Tsukamoto Tenma: Loves the Samurai Dramas.

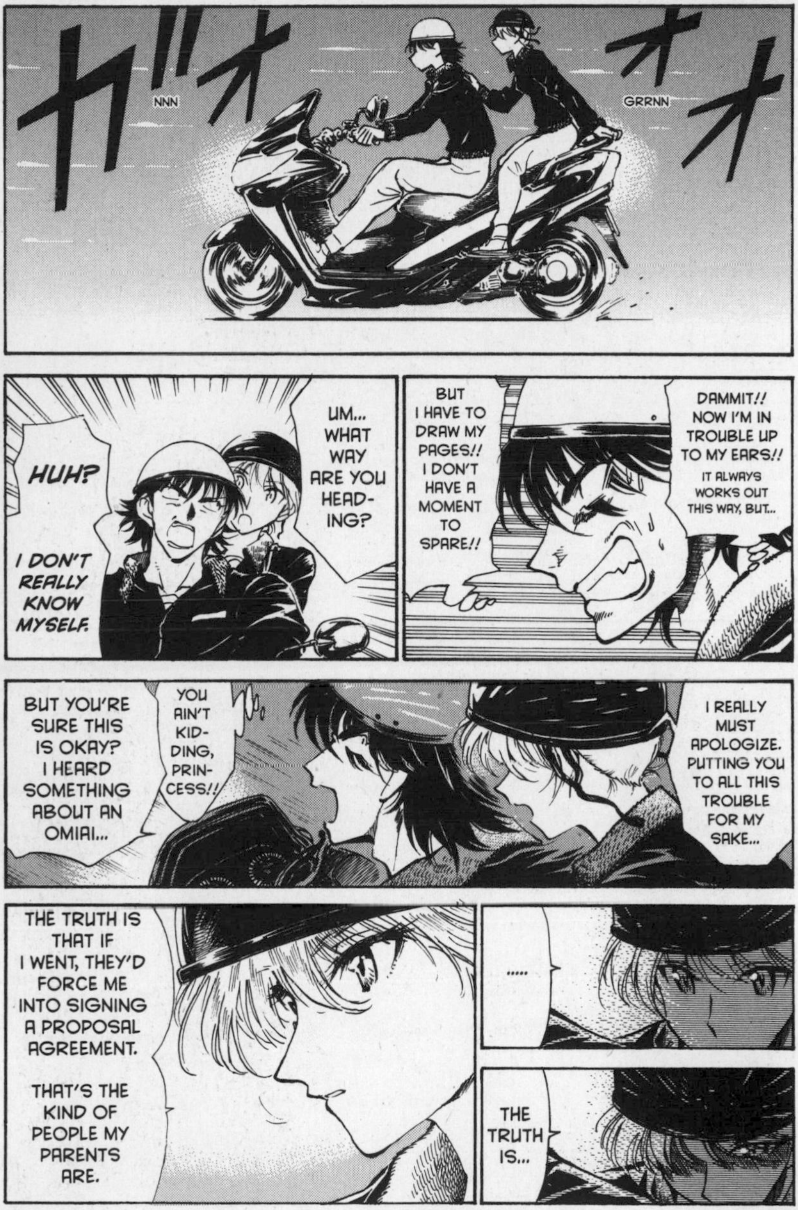
ガオ
NNN
オオ
GRRNN
DAMMIT!! NOW I'M IN TROUBLE UP TO MY EARS!!
IT ALWAYS WORKS OUT THIS WAY, BUT...
BUT I HAVE TO DRAW MY PAGES!! I DON'T HAVE A MOMENT TO SPARE!!
UM... WHAT WAY ARE YOU HEADING?
HUH?
I DON'T REALLY KNOW MYSELF.
I REALLY MUST APOLOGIZE. PUTTING YOU TO ALL THIS TROUBLE FOR MY SAKE...
YOU AIN'T KIDDING, PRINCESS!!
BUT YOU'RE SURE THIS IS OKAY? I HEARD SOMETHING ABOUT AN OMIAI...
.....
THE TRUTH IS...
THE TRUTH IS THAT IF I WENT, THEY'D FORCE ME INTO SIGNING A PROPOSAL AGREEMENT.
THAT'S THE KIND OF PEOPLE MY PARENTS ARE.

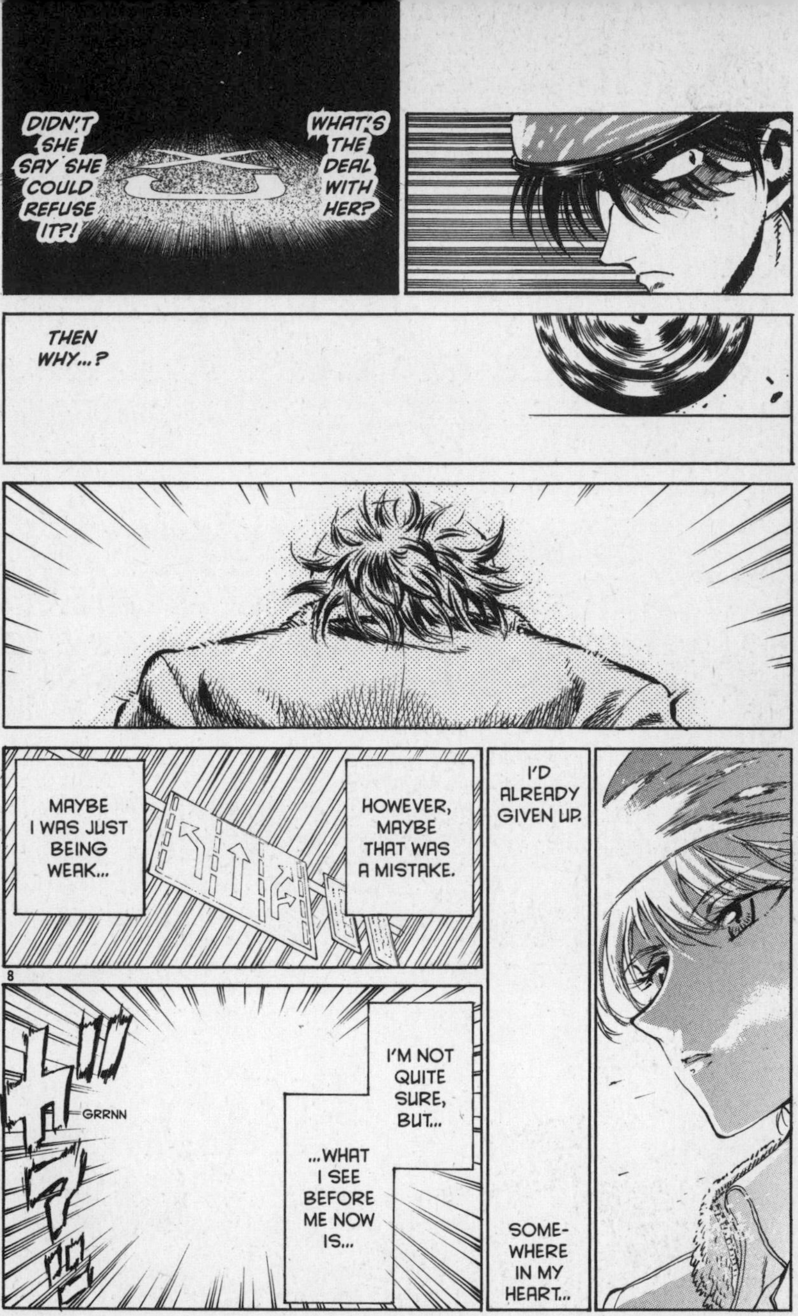
WHAT'S THE DEAL WITH HER?
DIDN'T SHE SAY SHE COULD REFUSE IT?!
THEN WHY...?
I'D ALREADY GIVEN UP.
SOME-WHERE IN MY HEART...
HOWEVER, MAYBE THAT WAS A MISTAKE.
MAYBE I WAS JUST BEING WEAK...
8
I'M NOT QUITE SURE, BUT...
...WHAT I SEE BEFORE ME NOW IS...
GRRNN

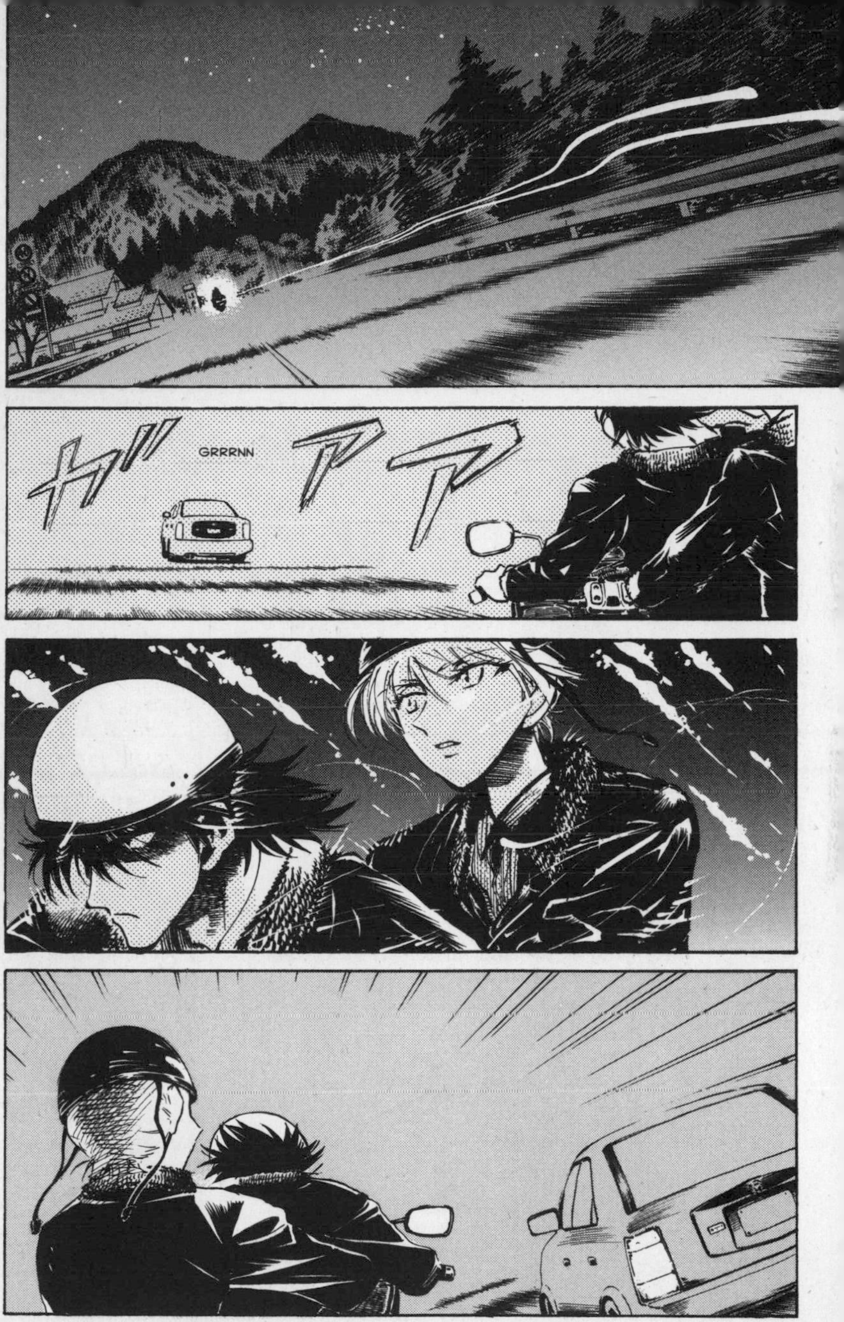
ガァァ
GRRRNN

Before Their Eyes: Masaru and Tenma.

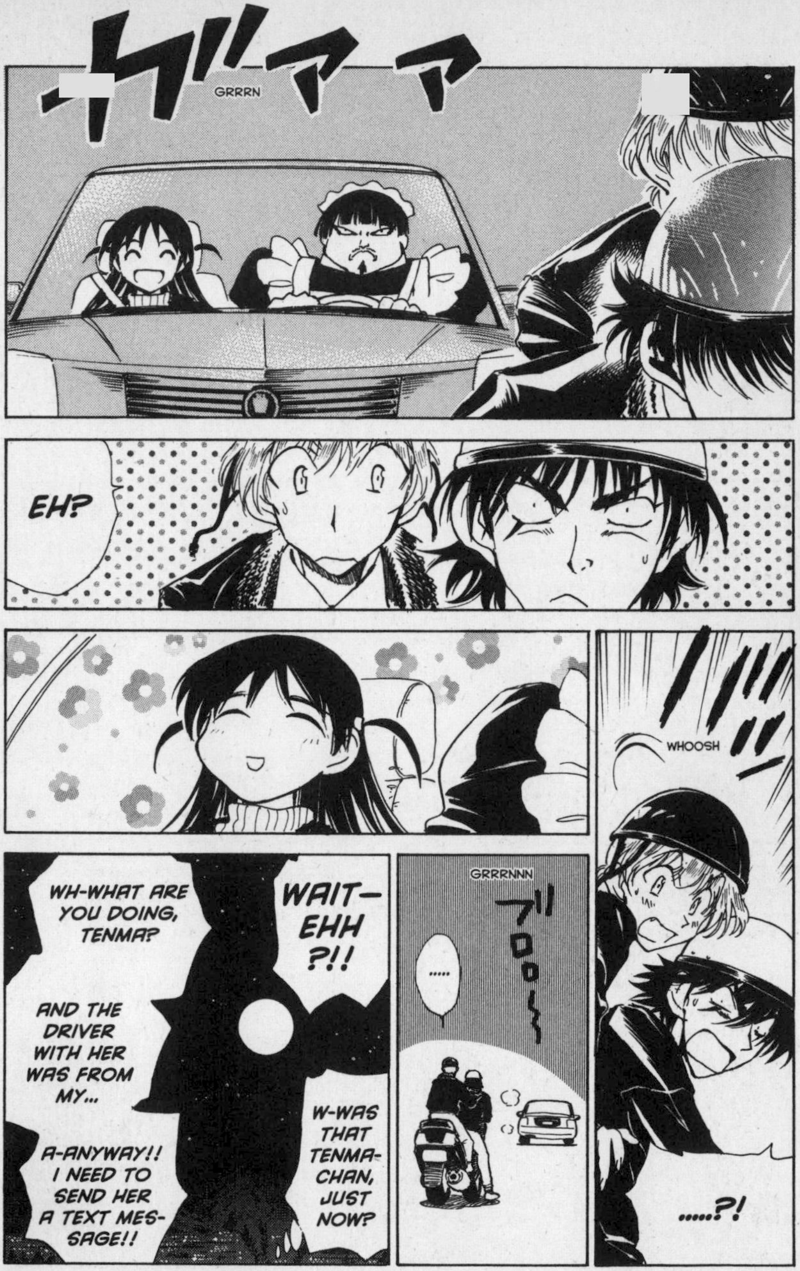
GRRRN
EH?
WHOOSH
.....?!
GRRRNNN
.....
W-WAS THAT TENMA-CHAN, JUST NOW?
WAIT— EHH ?!!
WH-WHAT ARE YOU DOING, TENMA?
AND THE DRIVER WITH HER WAS FROM MY...
A-ANYWAY!! I NEED TO SEND HER A TEXT MES-SAGE!!

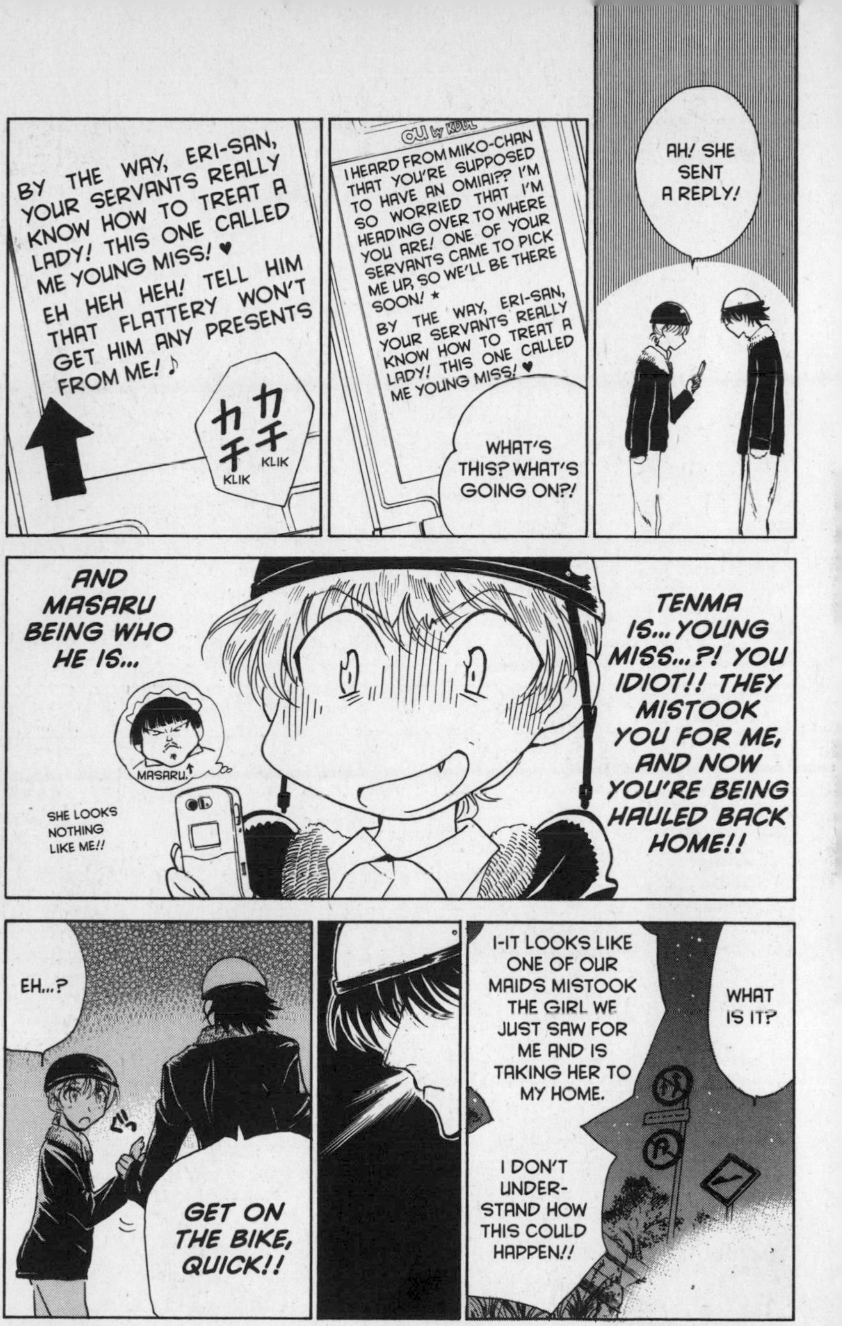
AH! SHE SENT A REPLY!
OU by KDDI
I HEARD FROM MIKO-CHAN THAT YOU'RE SUPPOSED TO HAVE AN OMIAI?? I'M SO WORRIED THAT I'M HEADING OVER TO WHERE YOU ARE! ONE OF YOUR SERVANTS CAME TO PICK ME UP, SO WE'LL BE THERE SOON! ★
BY THE WAY, ERI-SAN, YOUR SERVANTS REALLY KNOW HOW TO TREAT A LADY! THIS ONE CALLED ME YOUNG MISS! ♥
WHAT'S THIS? WHAT'S GOING ON?!
BY THE WAY, ERI-SAN, YOUR SERVANTS REALLY KNOW HOW TO TREAT A LADY! THIS ONE CALLED ME YOUNG MISS! ♥
EH HEH HEH! TELL HIM THAT FLATTERY WON'T GET HIM ANY PRESENTS FROM ME! ♪
カチ カチ
KLIK KLIK
TENMA IS... YOUNG MISS...?! YOU IDIOT!! THEY MISTOOK YOU FOR ME, AND NOW YOU'RE BEING HAULED BACK HOME!!
AND MASARU BEING WHO HE IS...
MASARU.
SHE LOOKS NOTHING LIKE ME!!
WHAT IS IT?
I-IT LOOKS LIKE ONE OF OUR MAIDS MISTOOK THE GIRL WE JUST SAW FOR ME AND IS TAKING HER TO MY HOME.
I DON'T UNDER-STAND HOW THIS COULD HAPPEN!!
EH...?
GET ON THE BIKE, QUICK!!

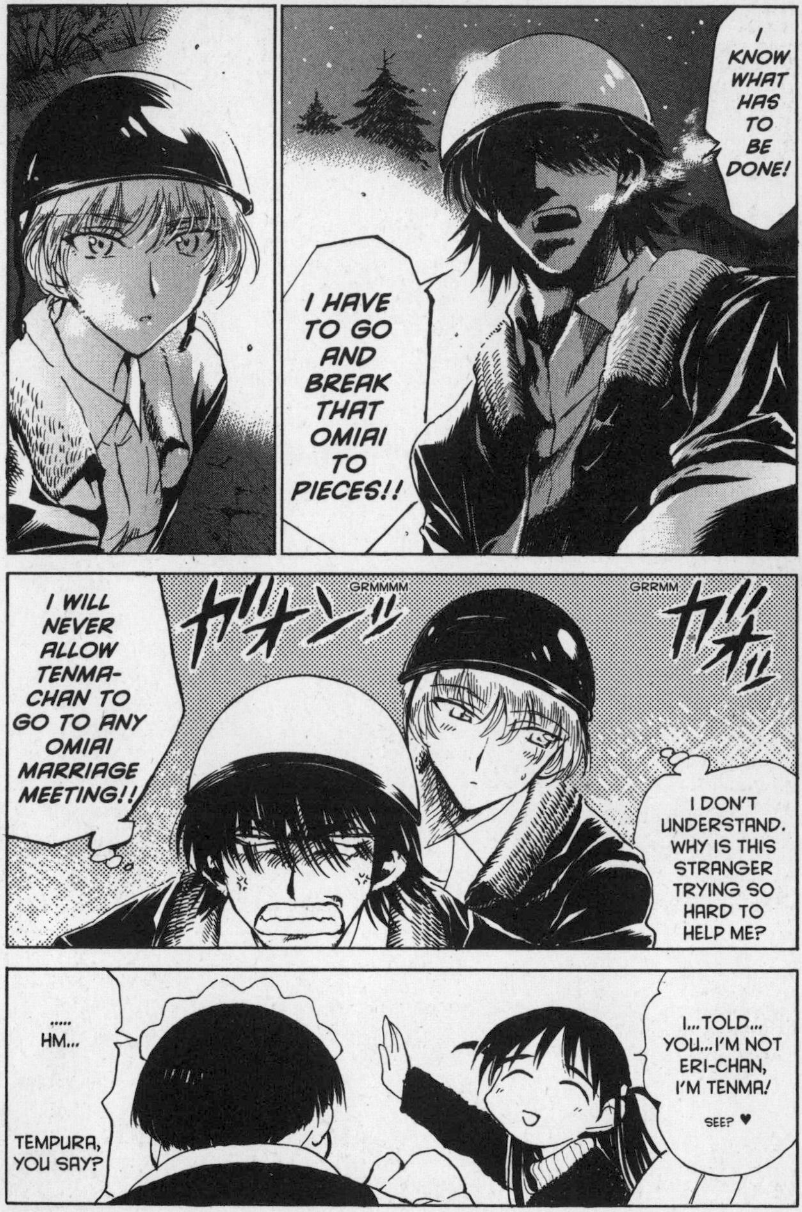

Nee-san, the Sushi... (Yakumo)

151· · · · · · · · ·Fin

152 CHARLIE AND LOUISE

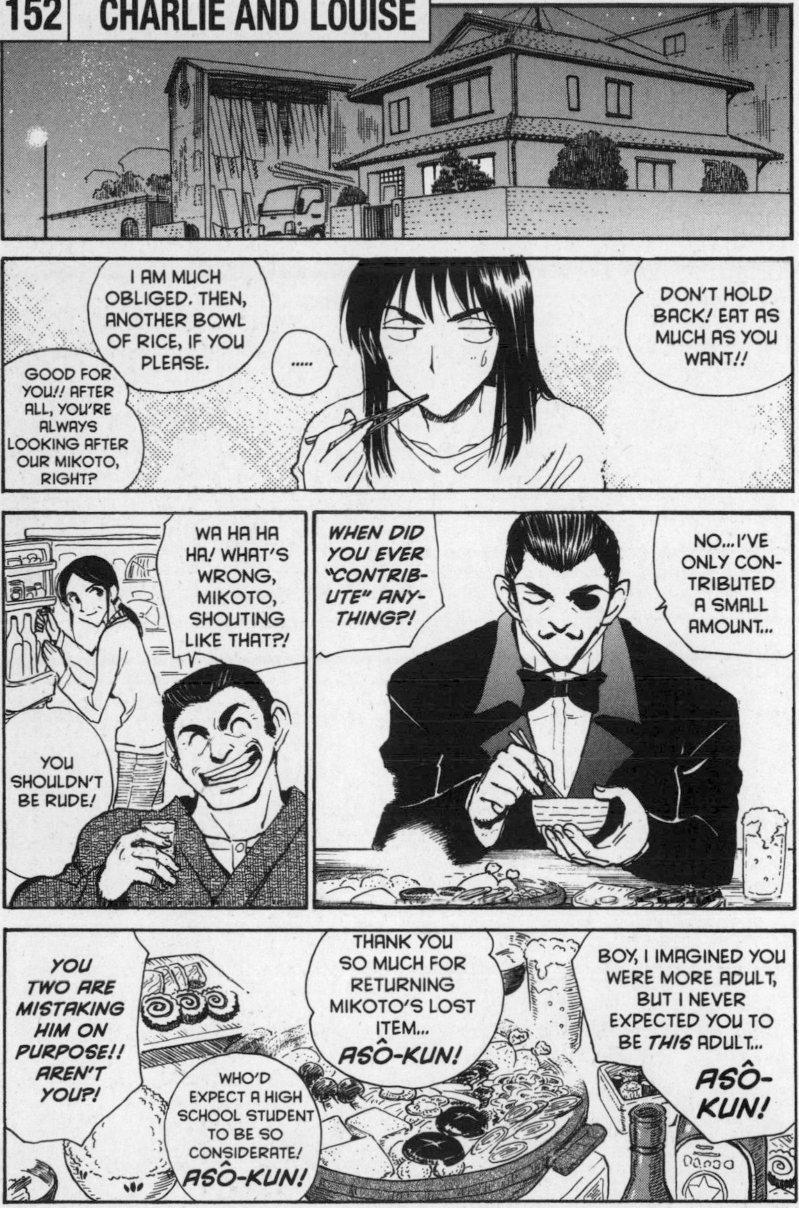
DON'T HOLD BACK! EAT AS MUCH AS YOU WANT!!
.....
I AM MUCH OBLIGED. THEN, ANOTHER BOWL OF RICE, IF YOU PLEASE.
GOOD FOR YOU!! AFTER ALL, YOU'RE ALWAYS LOOKING AFTER OUR MIKOTO, RIGHT?
NO...I'VE ONLY CONTRIBUTED A SMALL AMOUNT...
WHEN DID YOU EVER "CONTRIBUTE" ANYTHING?!
WA HA HA HA! WHAT'S WRONG, MIKOTO, SHOUTING LIKE THAT?!
YOU SHOULDN'T BE RUDE!
BOY, I IMAGINED YOU WERE MORE ADULT, BUT I NEVER EXPECTED YOU TO BE *THIS* ADULT... *ASÔ-KUN!*
THANK YOU SO MUCH FOR RETURNING MIKOTO'S LOST ITEM... *ASÔ-KUN!*
WHO'D EXPECT A HIGH SCHOOL STUDENT TO BE SO CONSIDERATE! *ASÔ-KUN!*
YOU TWO ARE MISTAKING HIM ON PURPOSE!! AREN'T YOU?!

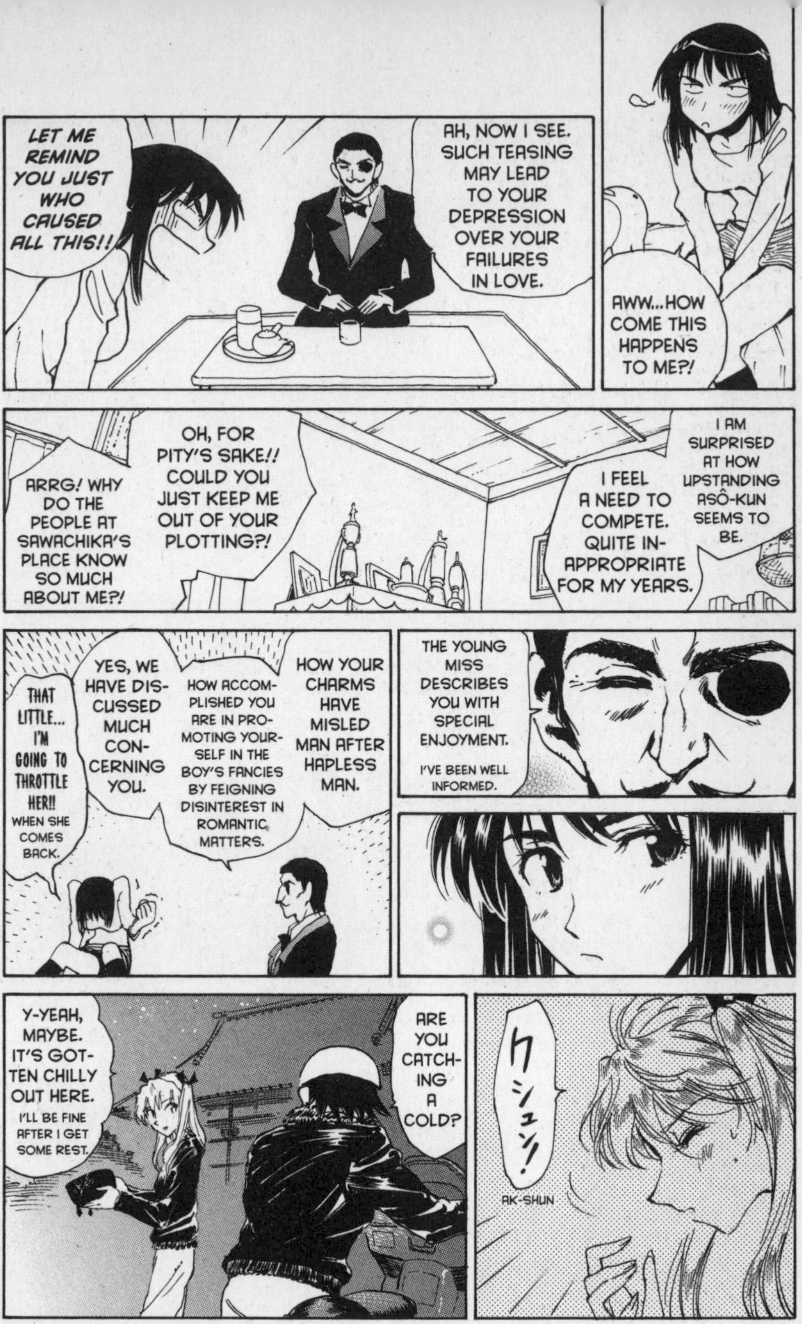
AWW...HOW COME THIS HAPPENS TO ME?!
AH, NOW I SEE. SUCH TEASING MAY LEAD TO YOUR DEPRESSION OVER YOUR FAILURES IN LOVE.
LET ME REMIND YOU JUST WHO CAUSED ALL THIS!!
I AM SURPRISED AT HOW UPSTANDING ASÔ-KUN SEEMS TO BE.
I FEEL A NEED TO COMPETE. QUITE INAPPROPRIATE FOR MY YEARS.
OH, FOR PITY'S SAKE!! COULD YOU JUST KEEP ME OUT OF YOUR PLOTTING?!
ARRG! WHY DO THE PEOPLE AT SAWACHIKA'S PLACE KNOW SO MUCH ABOUT ME?!
THE YOUNG MISS DESCRIBES YOU WITH SPECIAL ENJOYMENT.
I'VE BEEN WELL INFORMED.
HOW YOUR CHARMS HAVE MISLED MAN AFTER HAPLESS MAN.
HOW ACCOMPLISHED YOU ARE IN PROMOTING YOURSELF IN THE BOY'S FANCIES BY FEIGNING DISINTEREST IN ROMANTIC MATTERS.
YES, WE HAVE DISCUSSED MUCH CONCERNING YOU.
THAT LITTLE... I'M GOING TO THROTTLE HER!!
WHEN SHE COMES BACK.
クシュン!
AK-SHUN
ARE YOU CATCHING A COLD?
Y-YEAH, MAYBE. IT'S GOTTEN CHILLY OUT HERE.
I'LL BE FINE AFTER I GET SOME REST.

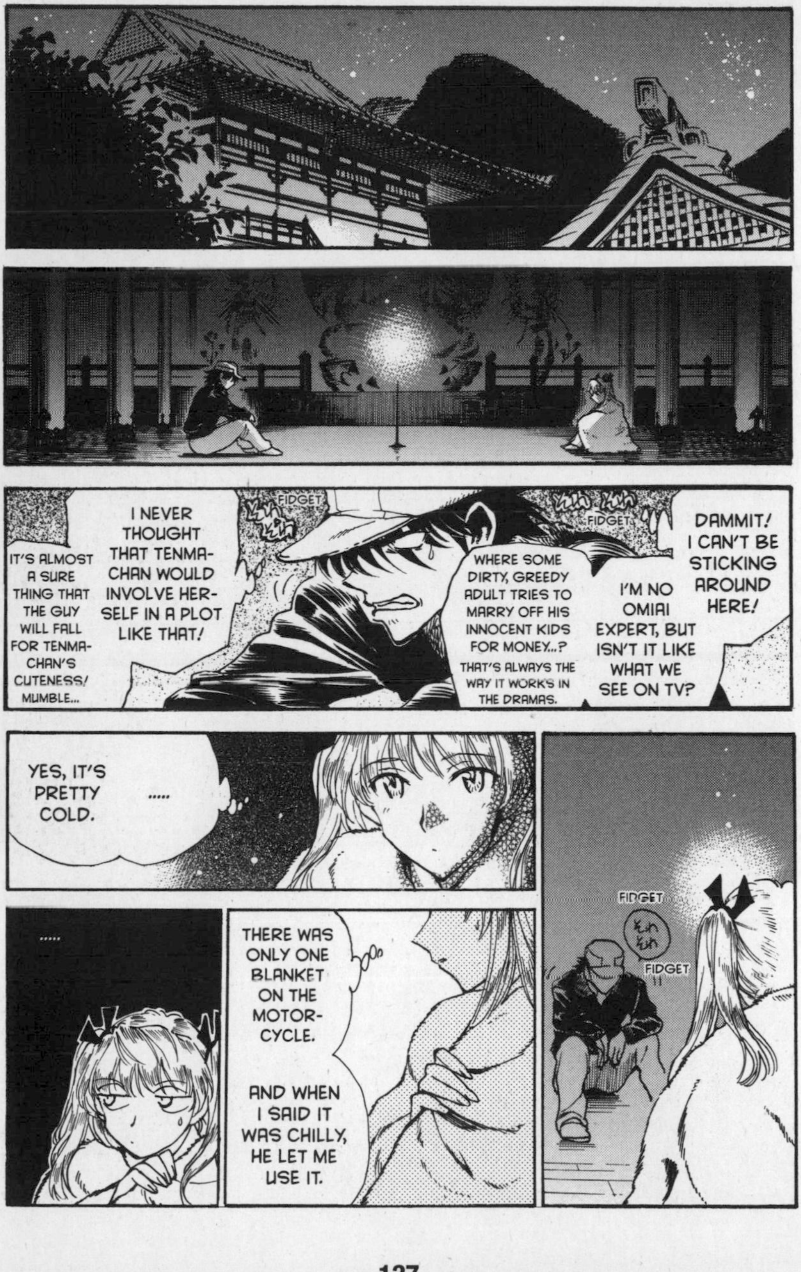
DAMMIT! I CAN'T BE STICKING AROUND HERE!
FIDGET
I'M NO OMIAI EXPERT, BUT ISN'T IT LIKE WHAT WE SEE ON TV?
WHERE SOME DIRTY, GREEDY ADULT TRIES TO MARRY OFF HIS INNOCENT KIDS FOR MONEY...?
THAT'S ALWAYS THE WAY IT WORKS IN THE DRAMAS.
FIDGET
I NEVER THOUGHT THAT TENMA-CHAN WOULD INVOLVE HER-SELF IN A PLOT LIKE THAT!
IT'S ALMOST A SURE THING THAT THE GUY WILL FALL FOR TENMA-CHAN'S CUTENESS! MUMBLE...
FIDGET
FIDGET
.....
YES, IT'S PRETTY COLD.
THERE WAS ONLY ONE BLANKET ON THE MOTOR-CYCLE.
AND WHEN I SAID IT WAS CHILLY, HE LET ME USE IT.
.....

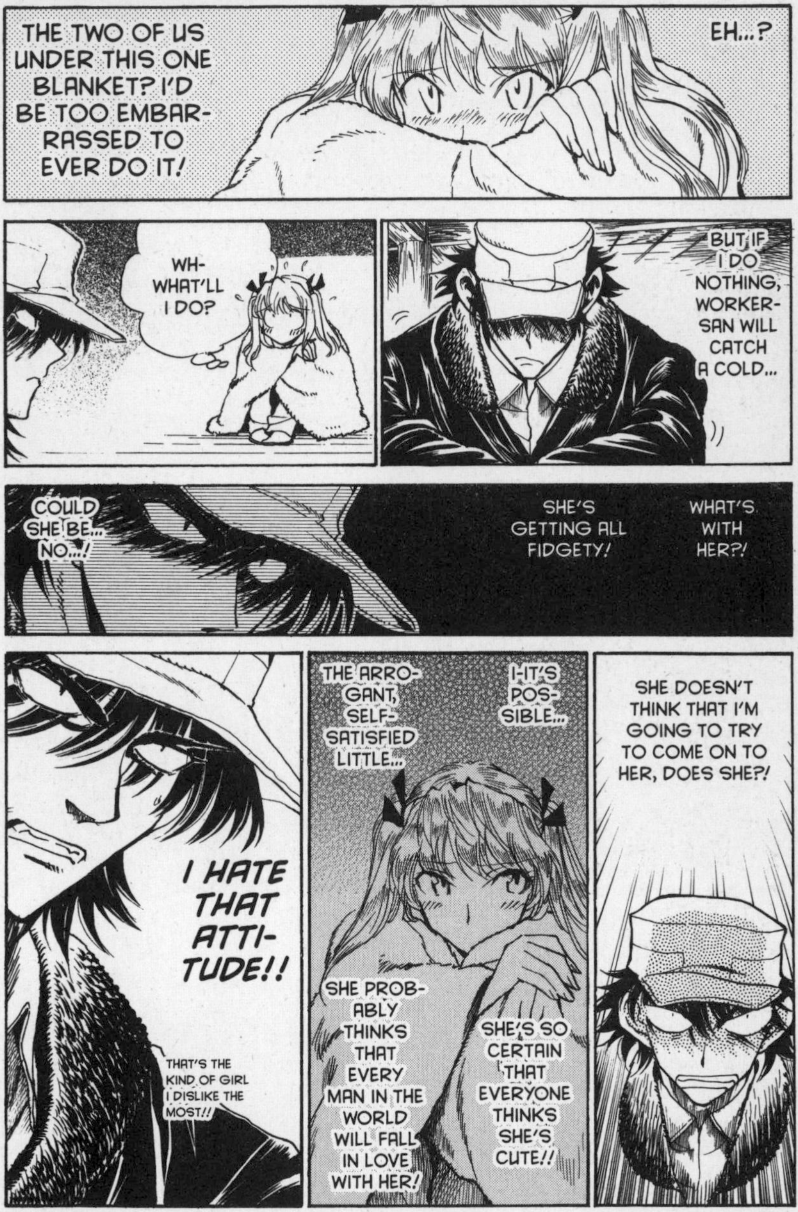
EH...?
THE TWO OF US UNDER THIS ONE BLANKET? I'D BE TOO EMBARRASSED TO EVER DO IT!
BUT IF I DO NOTHING, WORKER-SAN WILL CATCH A COLD...
WH-WHAT'LL I DO?
WHAT'S WITH HER?!
SHE'S GETTING ALL FIDGETY!
COULD SHE BE... NO...!
SHE DOESN'T THINK THAT I'M GOING TO TRY TO COME ON TO HER, DOES SHE?!
I-IT'S POSSIBLE...
THE ARROGANT, SELF-SATISFIED LITTLE...
SHE'S SO CERTAIN THAT EVERYONE THINKS SHE'S CUTE!!
SHE PROBABLY THINKS THAT EVERY MAN IN THE WORLD WILL FALL IN LOVE WITH HER!
I HATE THAT ATTITUDE!!
THAT'S THE KIND OF GIRL I DISLIKE THE MOST!!

And Presently Pursuing Tenma (Mistaken for Sawachika).

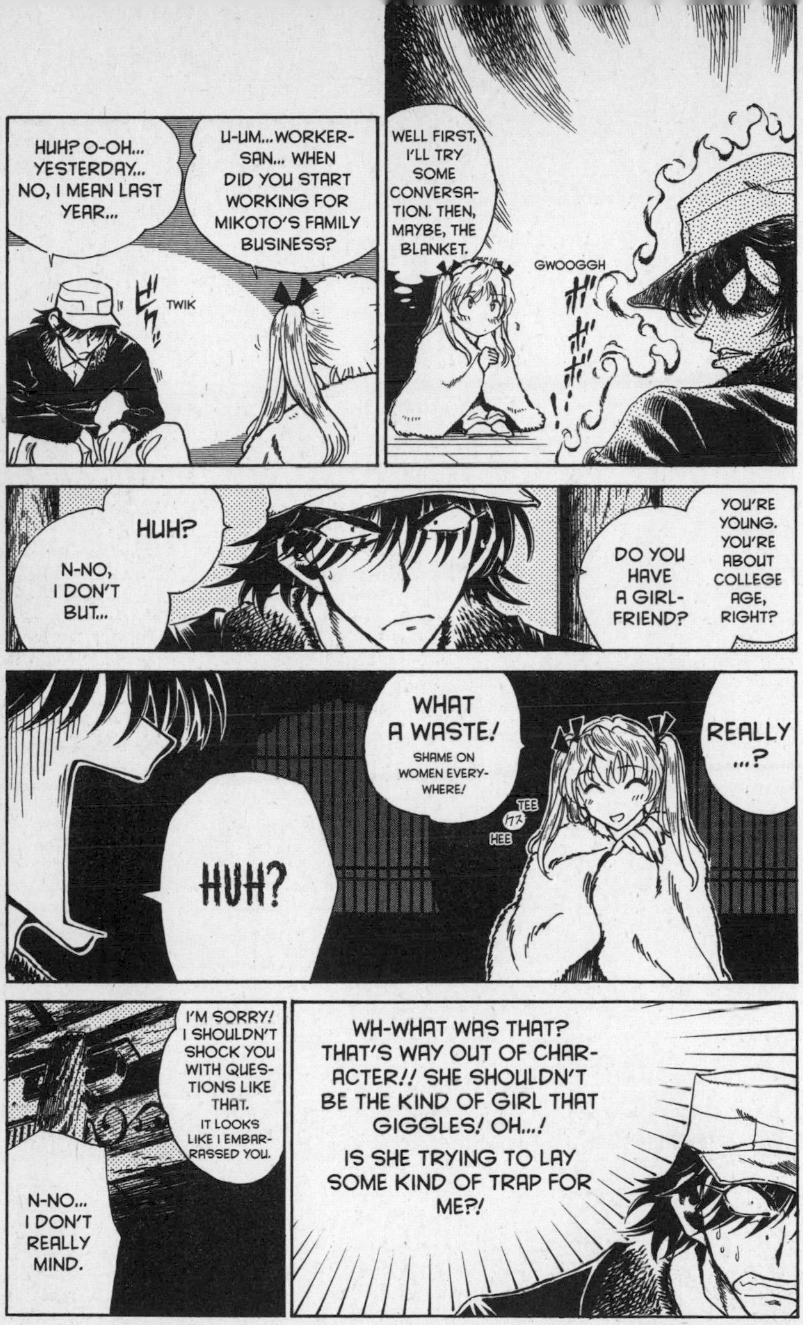

WELL FIRST, I'LL TRY SOME CONVERSA-TION. THEN, MAYBE, THE BLANKET.
GWOOOGGH
U-UM...WORKER-SAN... WHEN DID YOU START WORKING FOR MIKOTO'S FAMILY BUSINESS?
HUH? O-OH... YESTERDAY... NO, I MEAN LAST YEAR...
TWIK
YOU'RE YOUNG. YOU'RE ABOUT COLLEGE AGE, RIGHT?
DO YOU HAVE A GIRL-FRIEND?
HUH?
N-NO, I DON'T BUT...
REALLY ...?
WHAT A WASTE!
SHAME ON WOMEN EVERY-WHERE!
TEE HEE
HUH?
WH-WHAT WAS THAT? THAT'S WAY OUT OF CHAR-ACTER!! SHE SHOULDN'T BE THE KIND OF GIRL THAT GIGGLES! OH...!
IS SHE TRYING TO LAY SOME KIND OF TRAP FOR ME?!
I'M SORRY! I SHOULDN'T SHOCK YOU WITH QUES-TIONS LIKE THAT.
IT LOOKS LIKE I EMBAR-RASSED YOU.
N-NO... I DON'T REALLY MIND.

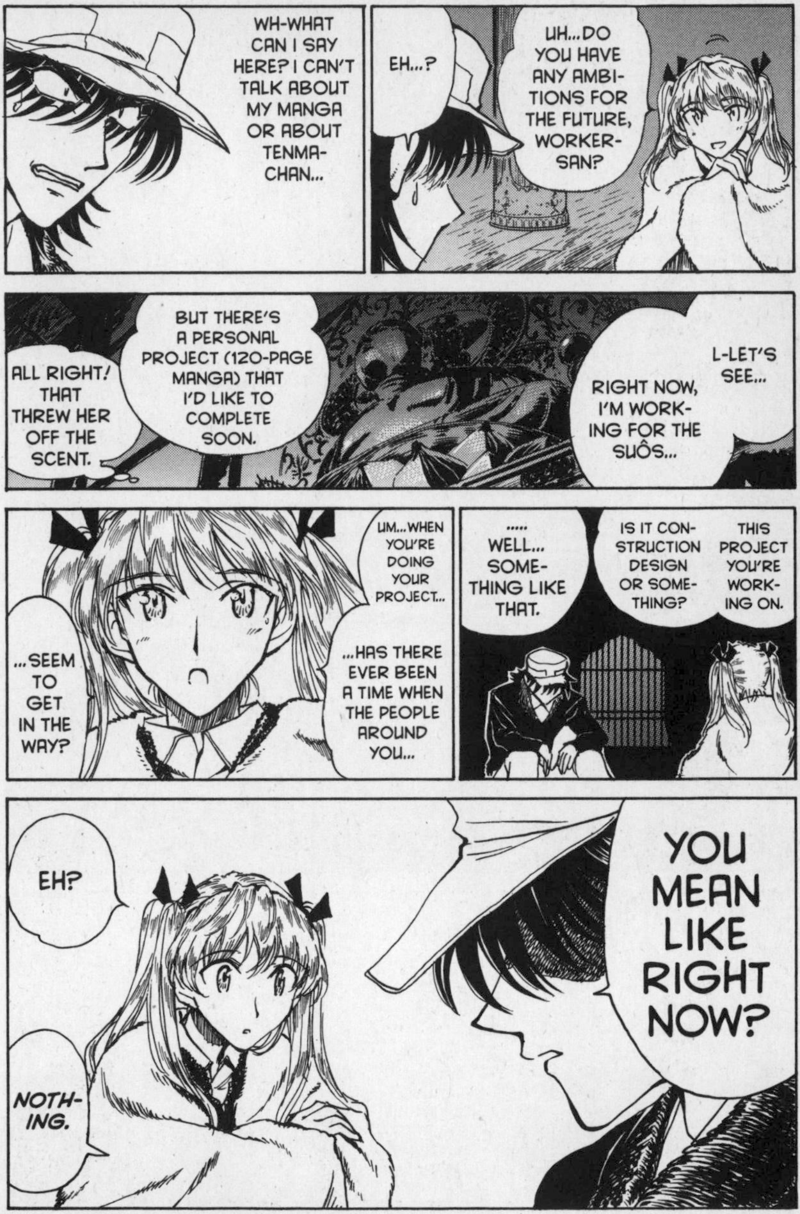
UH...DO YOU HAVE ANY AMBITIONS FOR THE FUTURE, WORKER-SAN?
EH...?
WH-WHAT CAN I SAY HERE? I CAN'T TALK ABOUT MY MANGA OR ABOUT TENMA-CHAN...
L-LET'S SEE...
RIGHT NOW, I'M WORKING FOR THE SUÔS...
BUT THERE'S A PERSONAL PROJECT (120-PAGE MANGA) THAT I'D LIKE TO COMPLETE SOON.
ALL RIGHT! THAT THREW HER OFF THE SCENT.
THIS PROJECT YOU'RE WORKING ON.
IS IT CONSTRUCTION DESIGN OR SOMETHING?
.....
WELL... SOMETHING LIKE THAT.
UM...WHEN YOU'RE DOING YOUR PROJECT...
...HAS THERE EVER BEEN A TIME WHEN THE PEOPLE AROUND YOU...
...SEEM TO GET IN THE WAY?
YOU MEAN LIKE RIGHT NOW?
EH?
NOTHING.

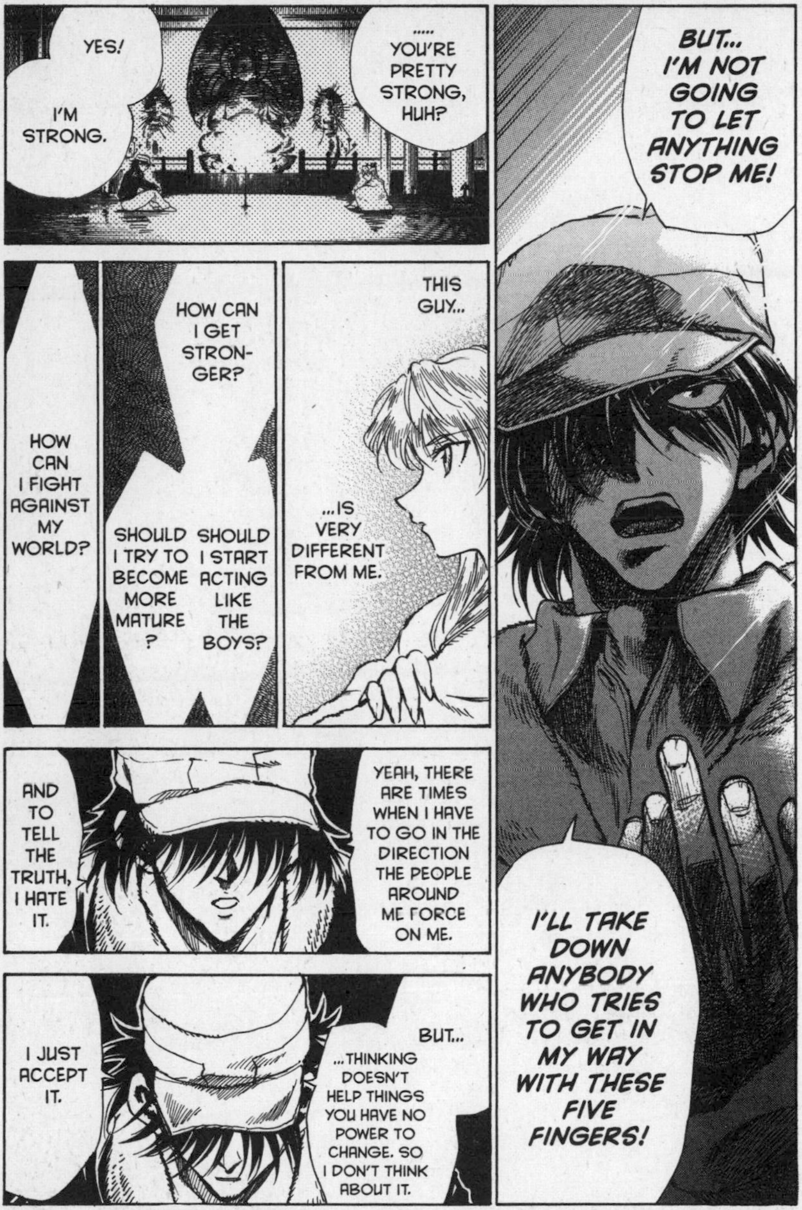
BUT... I'M NOT GOING TO LET ANYTHING STOP ME!
I'LL TAKE DOWN ANYBODY WHO TRIES TO GET IN MY WAY WITH THESE FIVE FINGERS!
..... YOU'RE PRETTY STRONG, HUH?
YES!
I'M STRONG.
THIS GUY...
...IS VERY DIFFERENT FROM ME.
HOW CAN I GET STRONGER?
SHOULD I START ACTING LIKE THE BOYS?
SHOULD I TRY TO BECOME MORE MATURE?
HOW CAN I FIGHT AGAINST MY WORLD?
YEAH, THERE ARE TIMES WHEN I HAVE TO GO IN THE DIRECTION THE PEOPLE AROUND ME FORCE ON ME.
AND TO TELL THE TRUTH, I HATE IT.
BUT...
...THINKING DOESN'T HELP THINGS YOU HAVE NO POWER TO CHANGE. SO I DON'T THINK ABOUT IT.
I JUST ACCEPT IT.

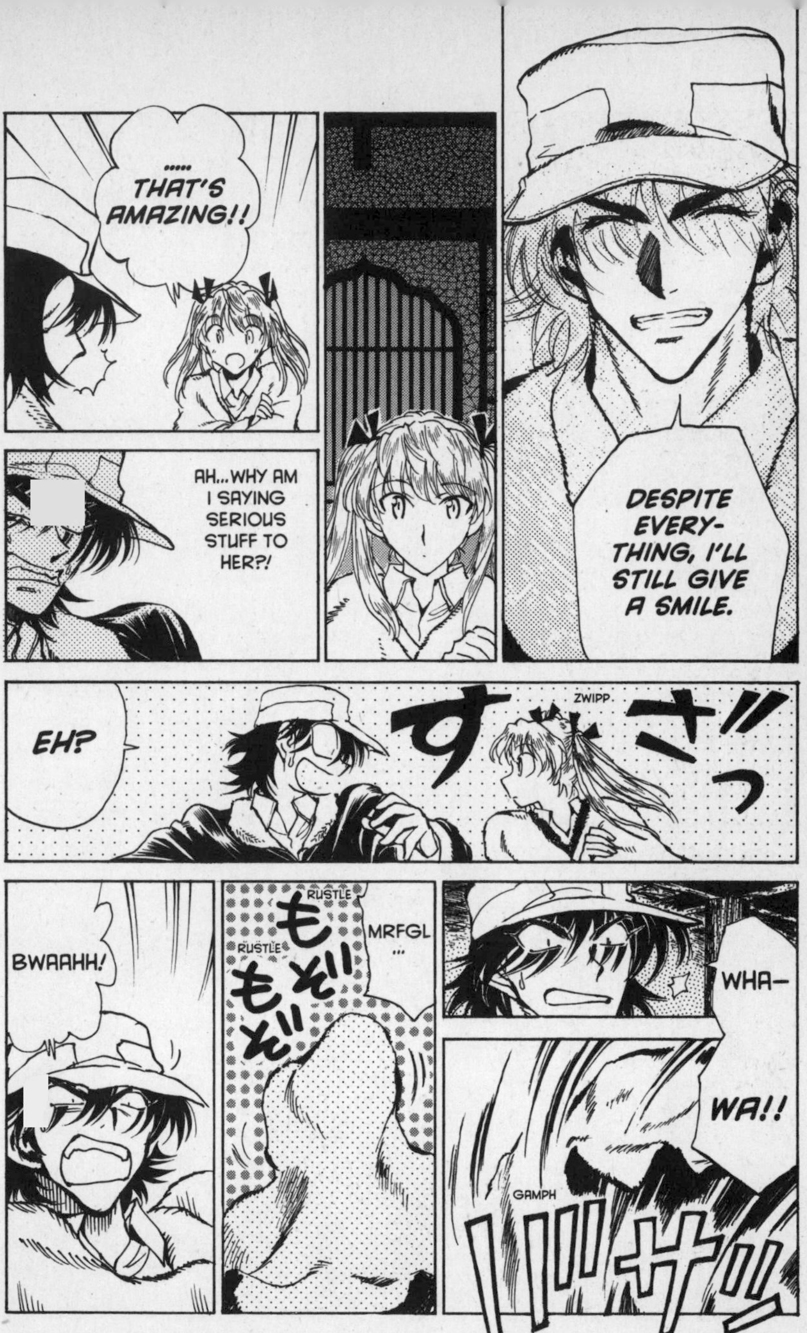
DESPITE EVERY-THING, I'LL STILL GIVE A SMILE.
...... THAT'S AMAZING!!
AH...WHY AM I SAYING SERIOUS STUFF TO HER?!
ZWIPP
さっ
す
EH?
WHA-
WA!!
GAMPH
MRFGL ...
RUSTLE
もぞ
RUSTLE
もぞ
BWAAHH!

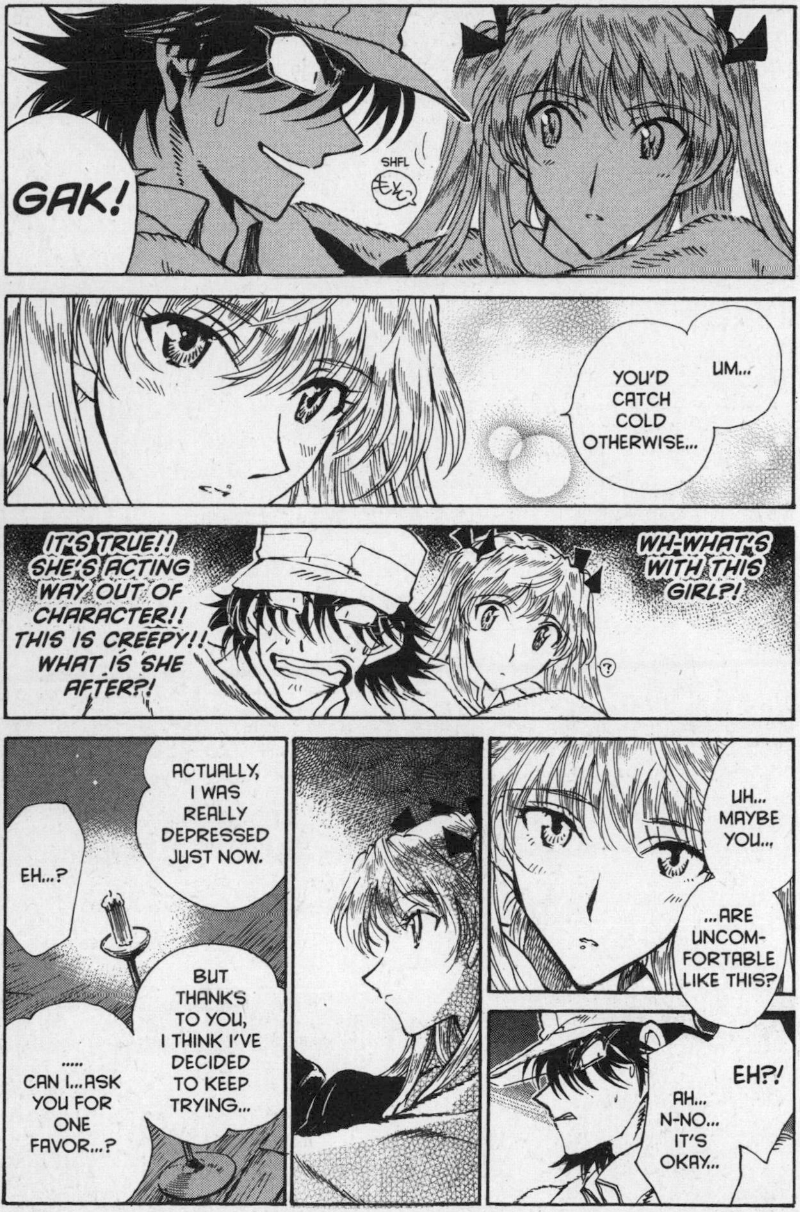
SHFL
GAK!
UM...
YOU'D CATCH COLD OTHERWISE...
WH-WHAT'S WITH THIS GIRL?!
IT'S TRUE!! SHE'S ACTING WAY OUT OF CHARACTER!! THIS IS CREEPY!! WHAT IS SHE AFTER?!
UH... MAYBE YOU...,
...ARE UNCOM-FORTABLE LIKE THIS?
EH?!
AH... N-NO... IT'S OKAY...
ACTUALLY, I WAS REALLY DEPRESSED JUST NOW.
EH...?
BUT THANKS TO YOU, I THINK I'VE DECIDED TO KEEP TRYING...
..... CAN I...ASK YOU FOR ONE FAVOR...?

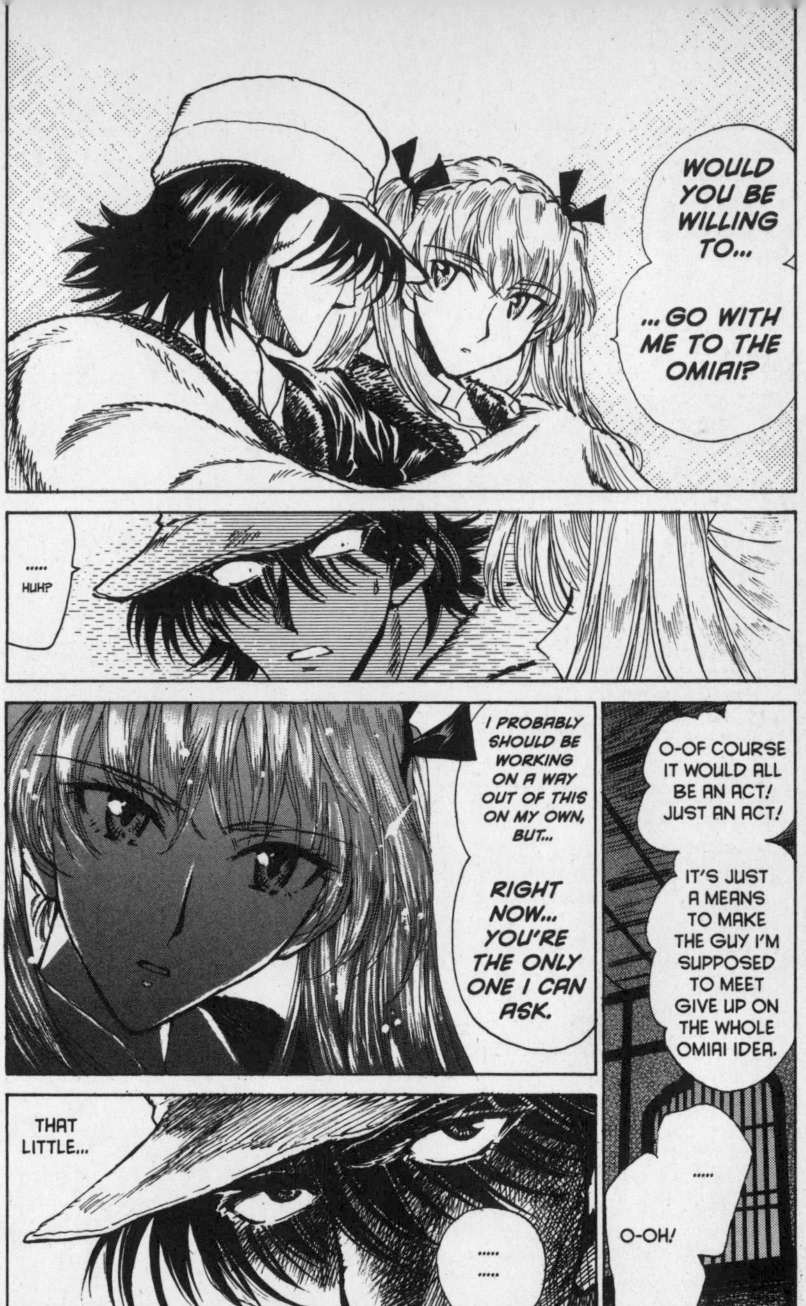
WOULD YOU BE WILLING TO...
...GO WITH ME TO THE OMIAI?
..... HUH?
O-OF COURSE IT WOULD ALL BE AN ACT! JUST AN ACT!
IT'S JUST A MEANS TO MAKE THE GUY I'M SUPPOSED TO MEET GIVE UP ON THE WHOLE OMIAI IDEA.
.....
O-OH!
I PROBABLY SHOULD BE WORKING ON A WAY OUT OF THIS ON MY OWN, BUT...
RIGHT NOW... YOU'RE THE ONLY ONE I CAN ASK.
....
THAT LITTLE...

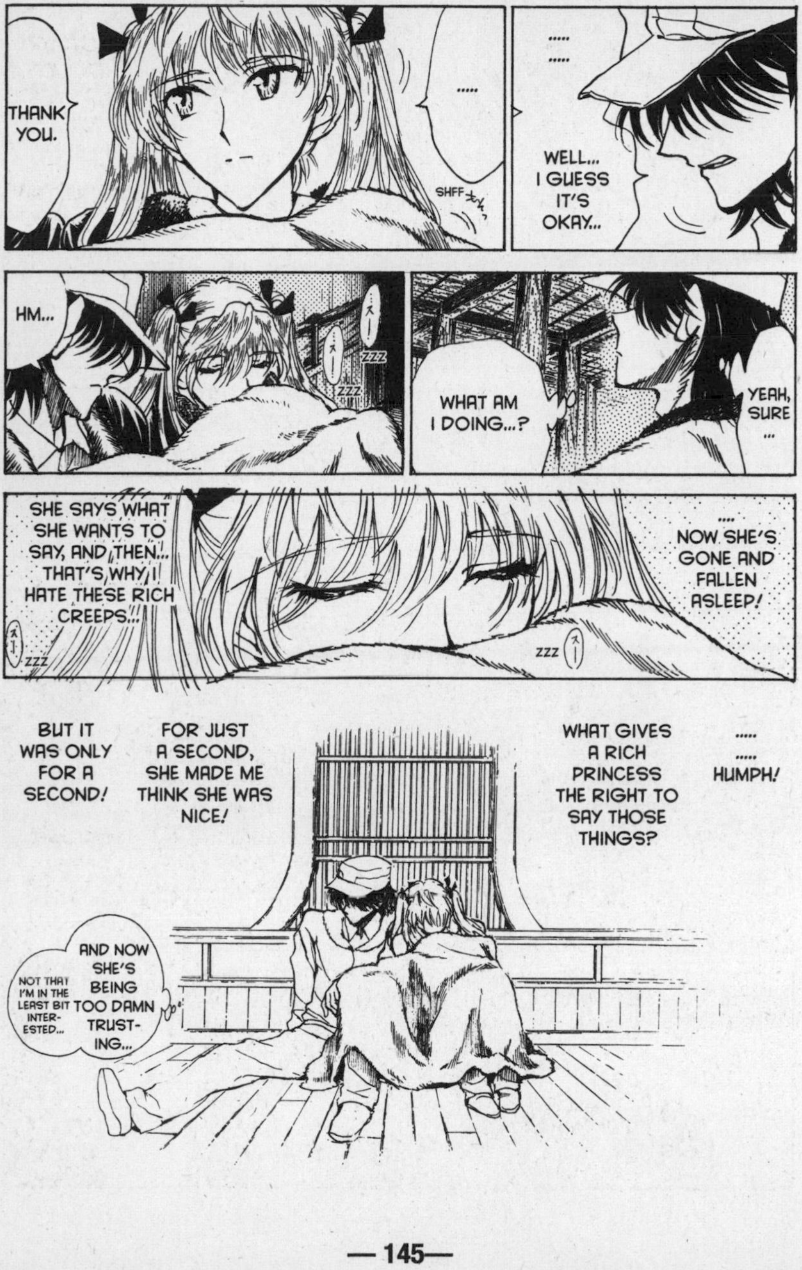
.....
.....
WELL... I GUESS IT'S OKAY...
.....
SHFF
THANK YOU.
YEAH, SURE ...
WHAT AM I DOING...?
...スー
...スー
ZZZ
ZZZ
HM...
.... NOW SHE'S GONE AND FALLEN ASLEEP!
スー
ZZZ
SHE SAYS WHAT SHE WANTS TO SAY, AND THEN... THAT'S WHY I HATE THESE RICH CREEPS...
スー
ZZZ
.....
.....
HUMPH!
WHAT GIVES A RICH PRINCESS THE RIGHT TO SAY THOSE THINGS?
FOR JUST A SECOND, SHE MADE ME THINK SHE WAS NICE!
BUT IT WAS ONLY FOR A SECOND!
AND NOW SHE'S BEING TOO DAMN TRUST-ING...
NOT THAT I'M IN THE LEAST BIT INTER-ESTED...

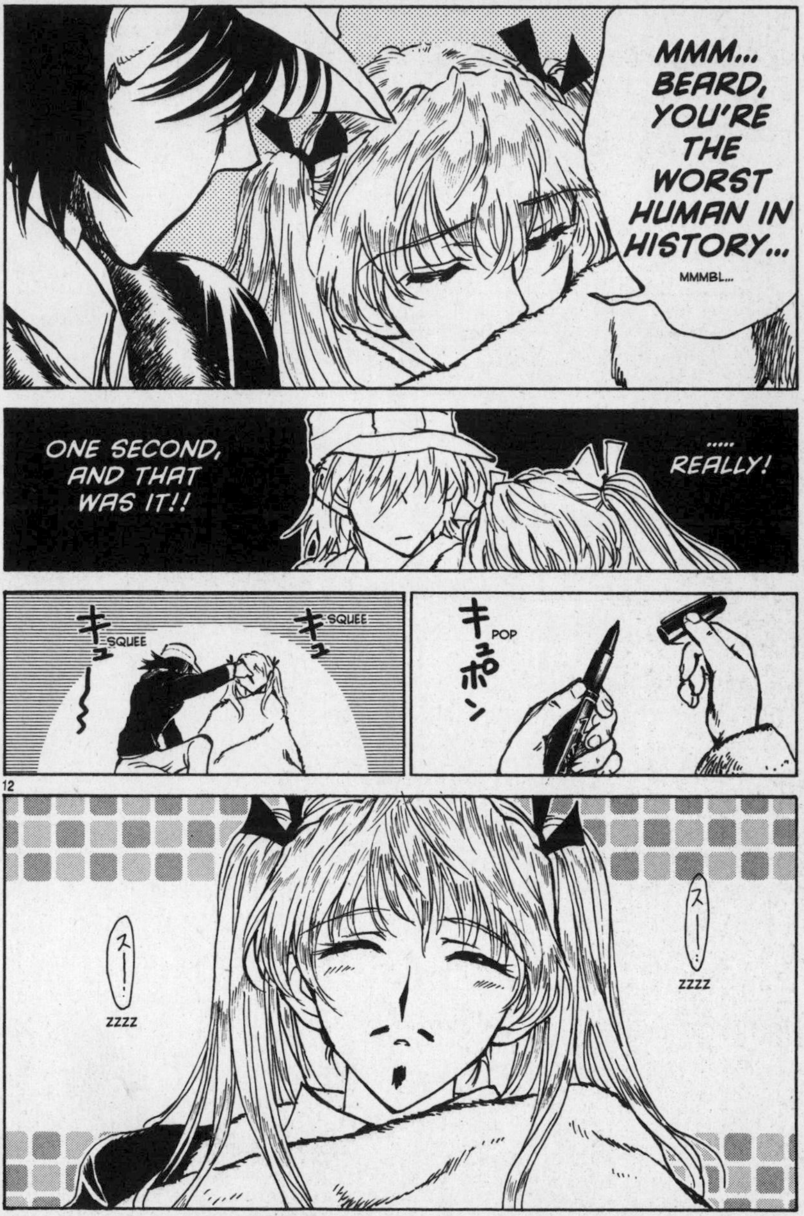
MMM... BEARD, YOU'RE THE WORST HUMAN IN HISTORY...
MMMBL...
..... REALLY!
ONE SECOND, AND THAT WAS IT!!
キュポン
POP
キュ
SQUEE
キュー~
SQUEE
スー!
ZZZZ
スー!
ZZZZ

Two Beards Together Make a Pair.

 # 152· · · · · · · · ·Fin

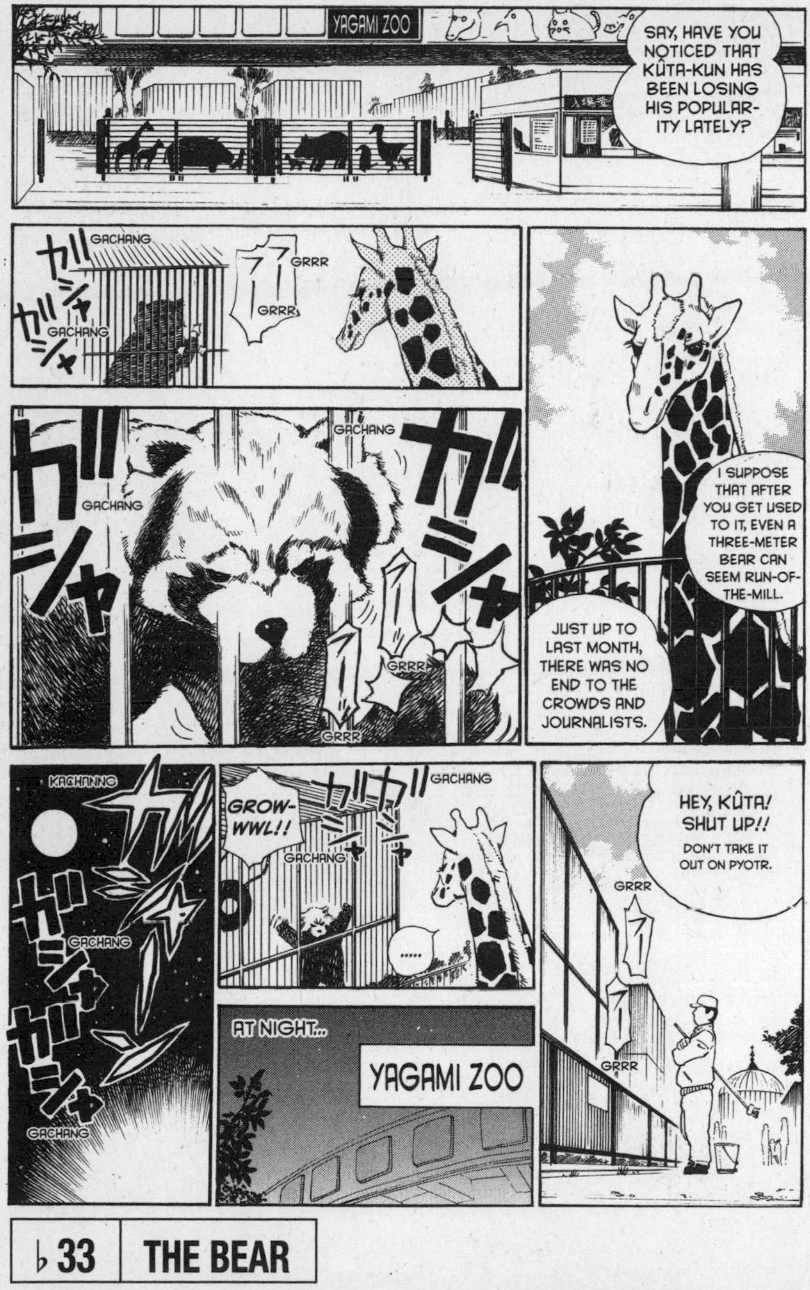
YAGAMI ZOO
SAY, HAVE YOU NOTICED THAT KÛTA-KUN HAS BEEN LOSING HIS POPULAR-ITY LATELY?
I SUPPOSE THAT AFTER YOU GET USED TO IT, EVEN A THREE-METER BEAR CAN SEEM RUN-OF-THE-MILL.
JUST UP TO LAST MONTH, THERE WAS NO END TO THE CROWDS AND JOURNALISTS.
GRRR
GRRR
GACHANG
GACHANG
GACHANG
GACHANG
GRRR
GRRR
HEY, KÛTA! SHUT UP!!
DON'T TAKE IT OUT ON PYOTR.
GRRR
GRRR
GACHANG
GROW-WWL!!
GACHANG
......
AT NIGHT...
YAGAMI ZOO
KACHANNG
GACHANG
GACHANG

♭33 THE BEAR

Hanai Haruki: Starts His Complete Misunderstanding.

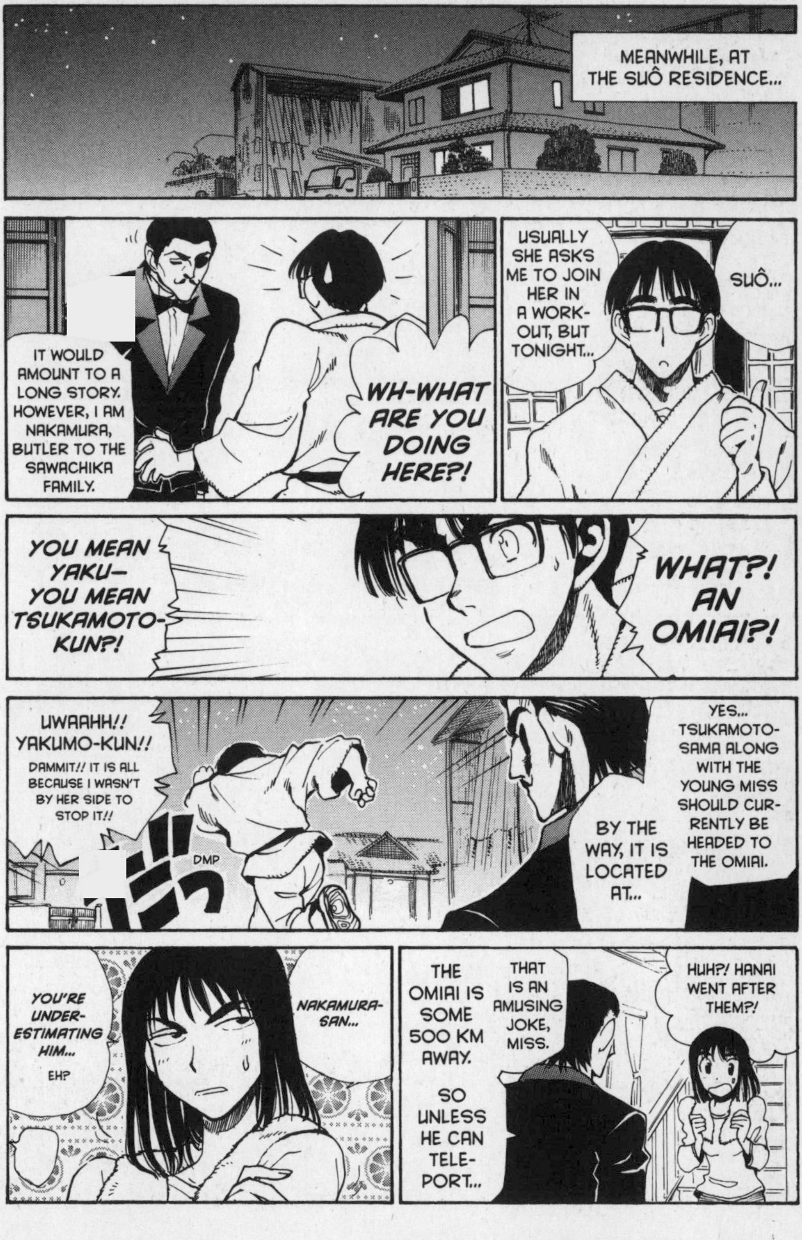
MEANWHILE, AT THE SUÔ RESIDENCE...
SUÔ...
USUALLY SHE ASKS ME TO JOIN HER IN A WORK-OUT, BUT TONIGHT...
WH-WHAT ARE YOU DOING HERE?!
IT WOULD AMOUNT TO A LONG STORY. HOWEVER, I AM NAKAMURA, BUTLER TO THE SAWACHIKA FAMILY.
WHAT?! AN OMIAI?!
YOU MEAN YAKU— YOU MEAN TSUKAMOTO-KUN?!
YES... TSUKAMOTO-SAMA ALONG WITH THE YOUNG MISS SHOULD CURRENTLY BE HEADED TO THE OMIAI.
BY THE WAY, IT IS LOCATED AT...
UWAAHH!! YAKUMO-KUN!!
DAMMIT!! IT IS ALL BECAUSE I WASN'T BY HER SIDE TO STOP IT!!
DMP
HUH?! HANAI WENT AFTER THEM?!
THAT IS AN AMUSING JOKE, MISS.
THE OMIAI IS SOME 500 KM AWAY.
SO UNLESS HE CAN TELEPORT...
NAKAMURA-SAN...
YOU'RE UNDER-ESTIMATING HIM...
EH?

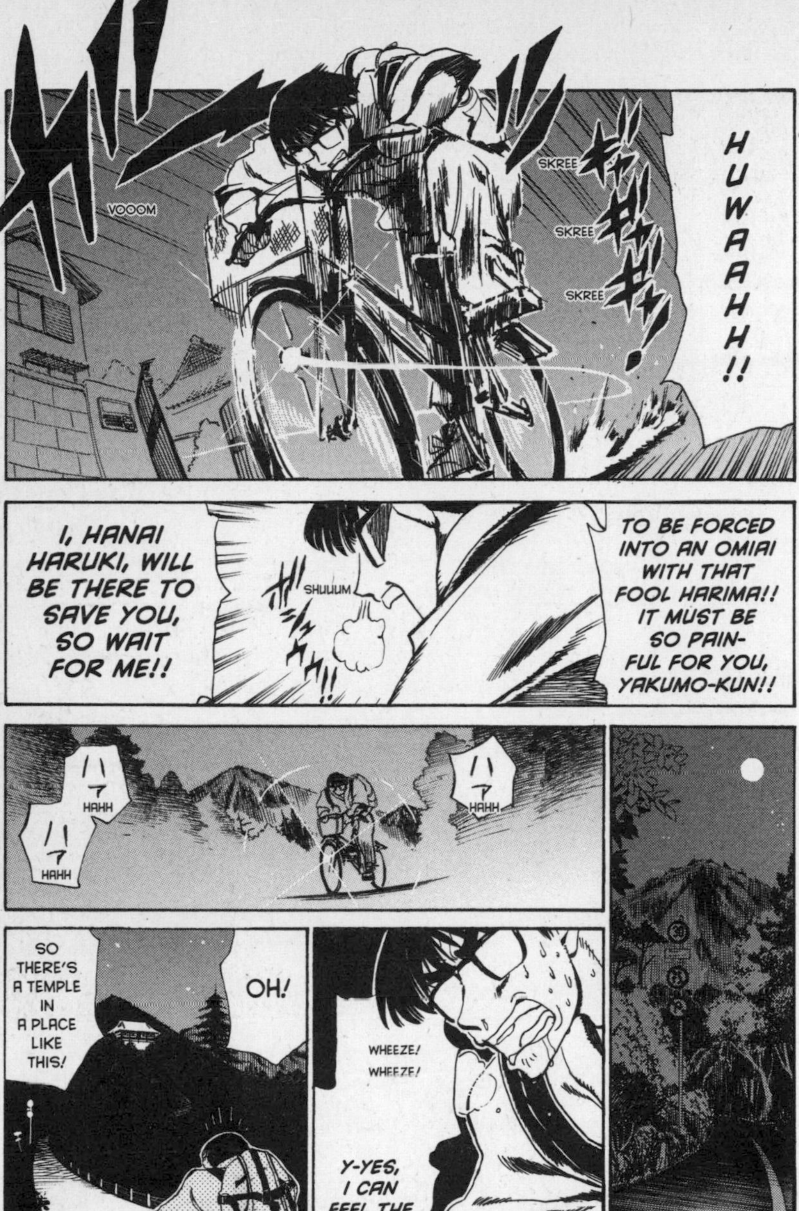
HUWAAAHH!!
SKREE
SKREE
SKREE
VOOOM
TO BE FORCED INTO AN OMIAI WITH THAT FOOL HARIMA!! IT MUST BE SO PAIN-FUL FOR YOU, YAKUMO-KUN!!
SHUUUM
I, HANAI HARUKI, WILL BE THERE TO SAVE YOU, SO WAIT FOR ME!!
ハァ HAHH
ハァ HAHH
ハァ HAHH
WHEEZE! WHEEZE!
Y-YES, I CAN FEEL THE PAIN...
OH!
SO THERE'S A TEMPLE IN A PLACE LIKE THIS!

Hanai: Would Bike a Thousand Miles.

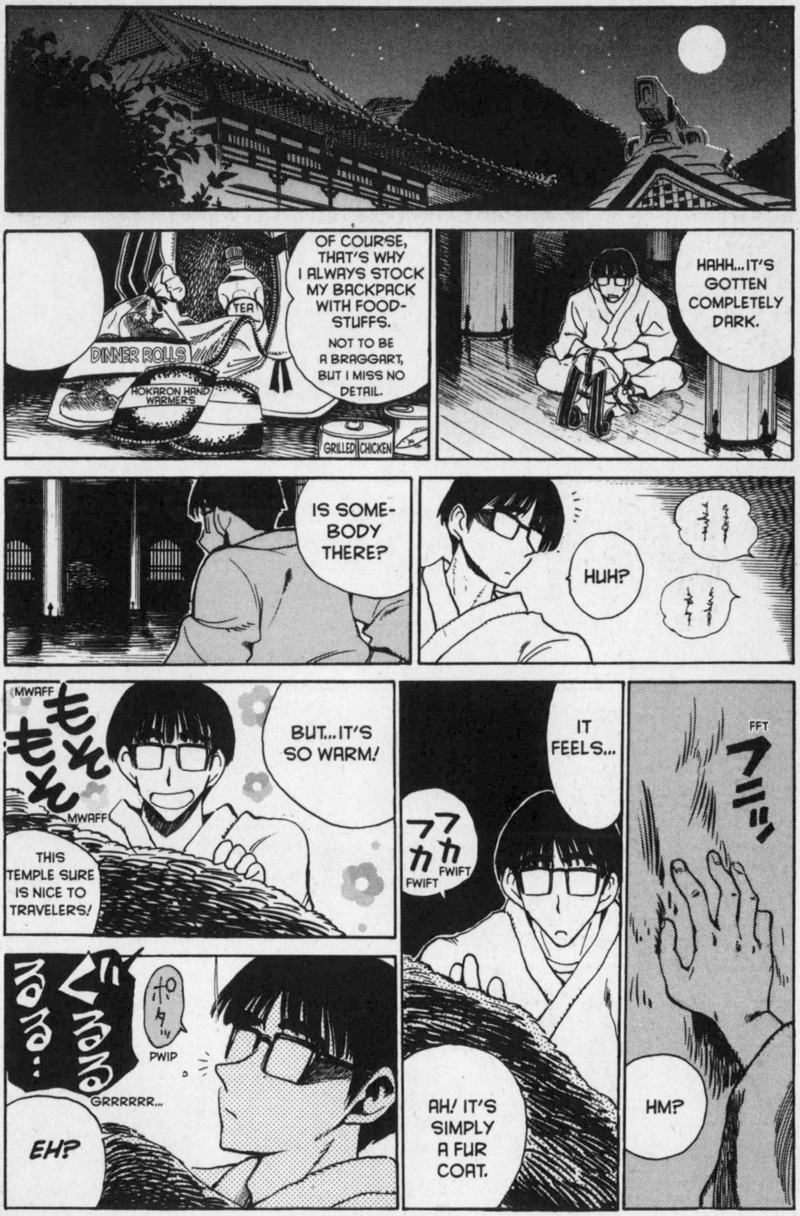
HAHH...IT'S GOTTEN COMPLETELY DARK.
OF COURSE, THAT'S WHY I ALWAYS STOCK MY BACKPACK WITH FOOD-STUFFS.
NOT TO BE A BRAGGART, BUT I MISS NO DETAIL.
TEA
DINNER ROLLS
HOKARON HAND WARMERS
GRILLED CHICKEN
HUH?
IS SOME-BODY THERE?
フニッ
FFT
HM?
IT FEELS...
フカフカ
FWIFT
FWIFT
AH! IT'S SIMPLY A FUR COAT.
もそもそ
MWAFF
MWAFF
BUT...IT'S SO WARM!
THIS TEMPLE SURE IS NICE TO TRAVELERS!
ポタッ
PWIP
ぐるるる..
GRRRRRR...
EH?

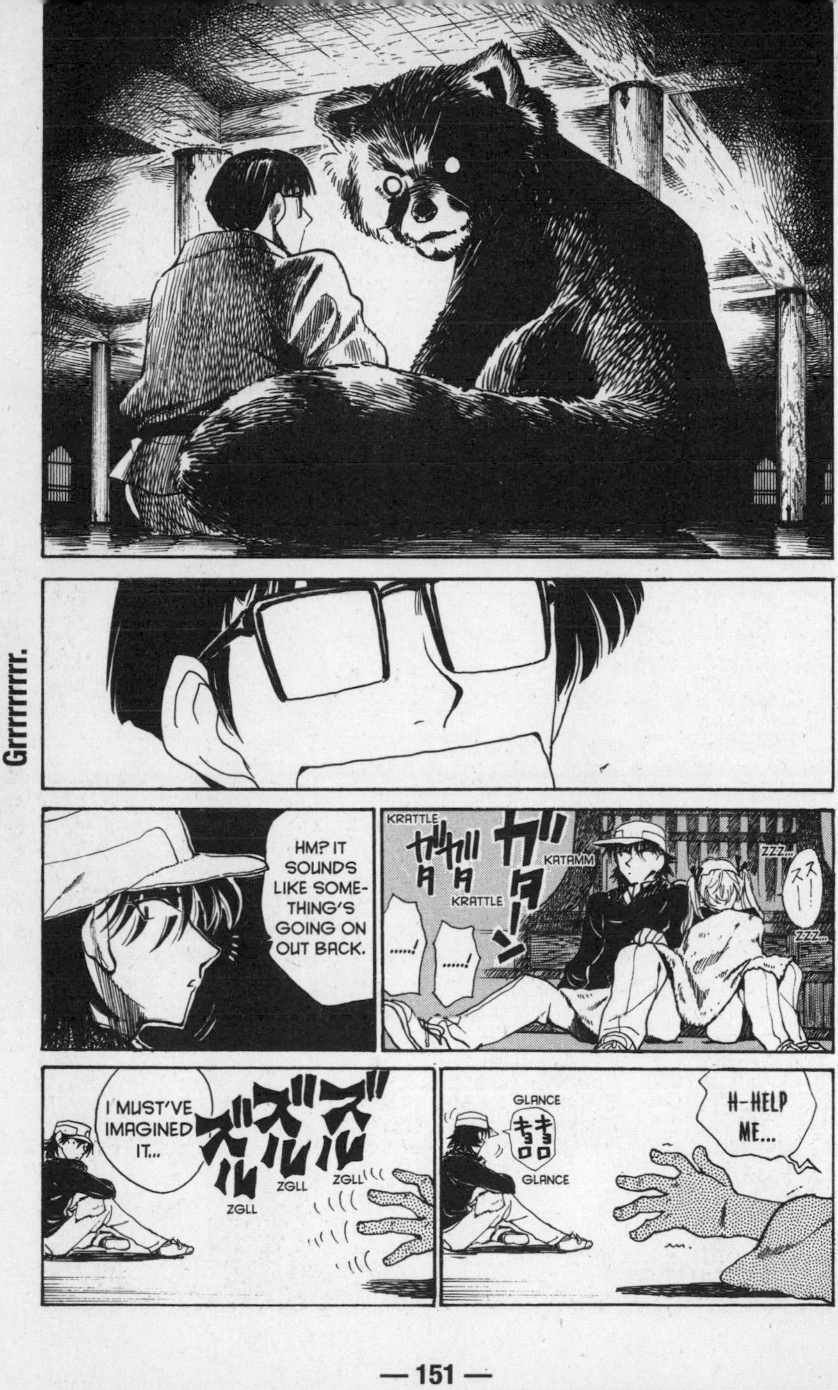
Grrrrrrrr.
KRATTLE
KRATTLE
KATAMM
ZZZ...
ZZZ...
......!
......!
HM? IT SOUNDS LIKE SOME-THING'S GOING ON OUT BACK.
GLANCE
GLANCE
H-HELP ME...
I MUST'VE IMAGINED IT...
ZGLL
ZGLL
ZGLL

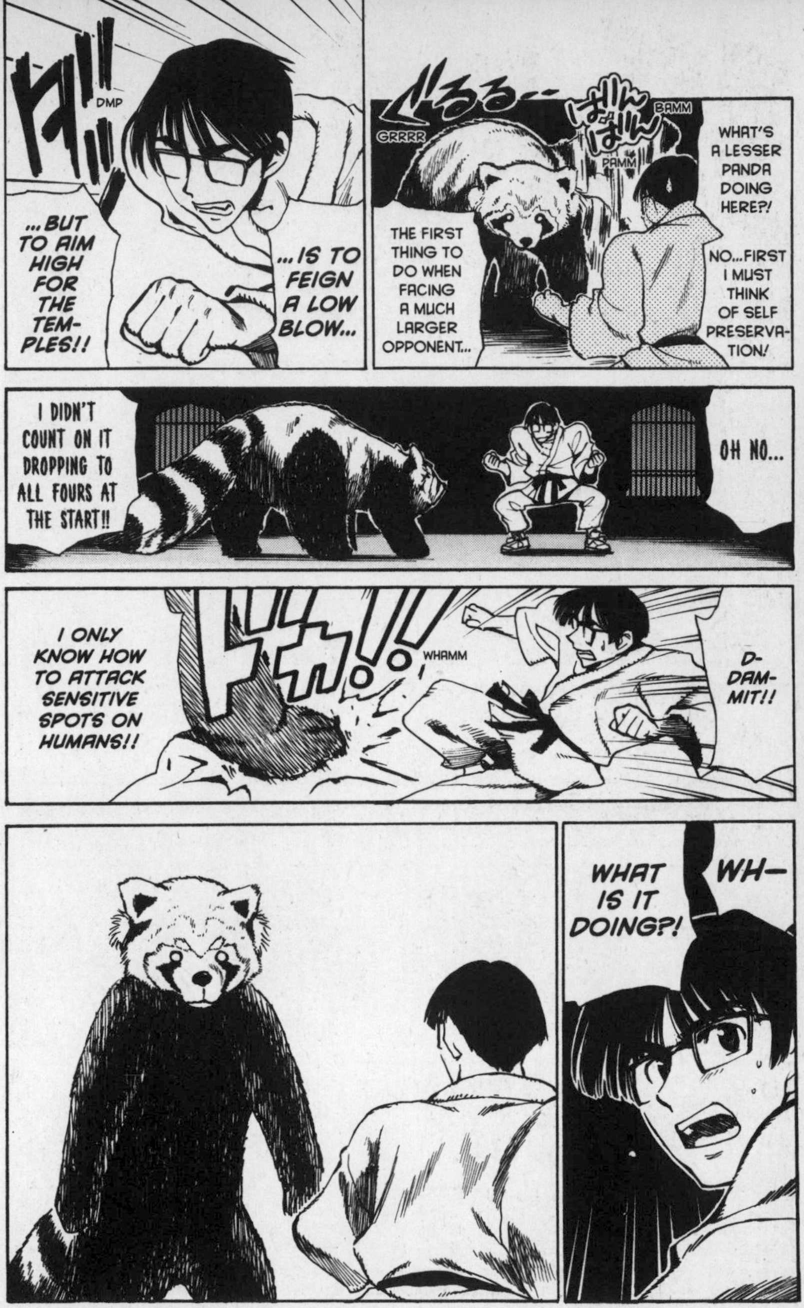
WHAT'S A LESSER PANDA DOING HERE?!
BAMM
PAMM
NO...FIRST I MUST THINK OF SELF PRESERVATION!
GRRRR
THE FIRST THING TO DO WHEN FACING A MUCH LARGER OPPONENT...
DMP
...IS TO FEIGN A LOW BLOW...
...BUT TO AIM HIGH FOR THE TEMPLES!!
OH NO...
I DIDN'T COUNT ON IT DROPPING TO ALL FOURS AT THE START!!
D-DAMMIT!!
WHAMM
I ONLY KNOW HOW TO ATTACK SENSITIVE SPOTS ON HUMANS!!
WH—
WHAT IS IT DOING?!

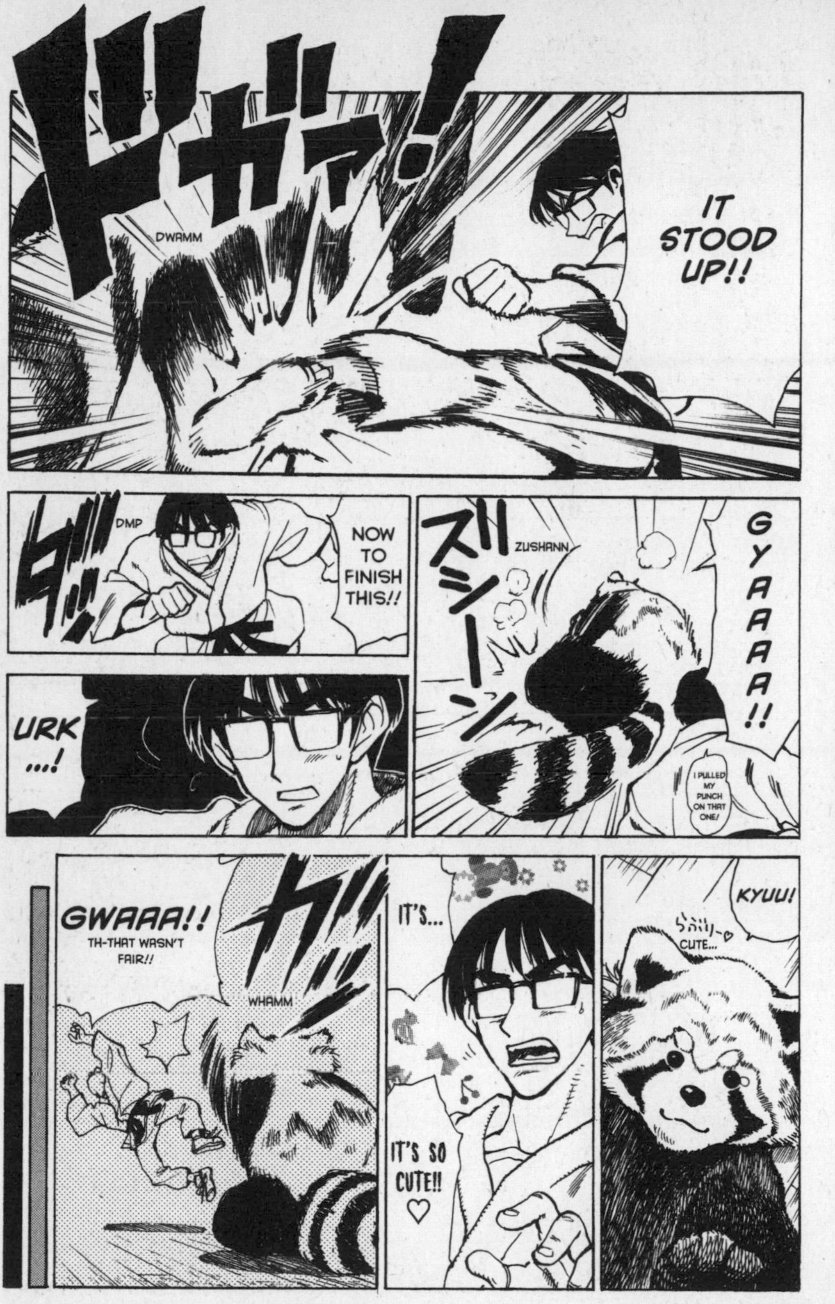
IT STOOD UP!!
DWAMM
GYAAAAA!!
ZUSHANN
I PULLED MY PUNCH ON THAT ONE!
NOW TO FINISH THIS!!
DMP
URK ...!
KYUU!
CUTE...
IT'S...
IT'S SO CUTE!! ♡
GWAAA!!
TH-THAT WASN'T FAIR!!
WHAMM

Yes, Hanai Is Truly a Nice Person.

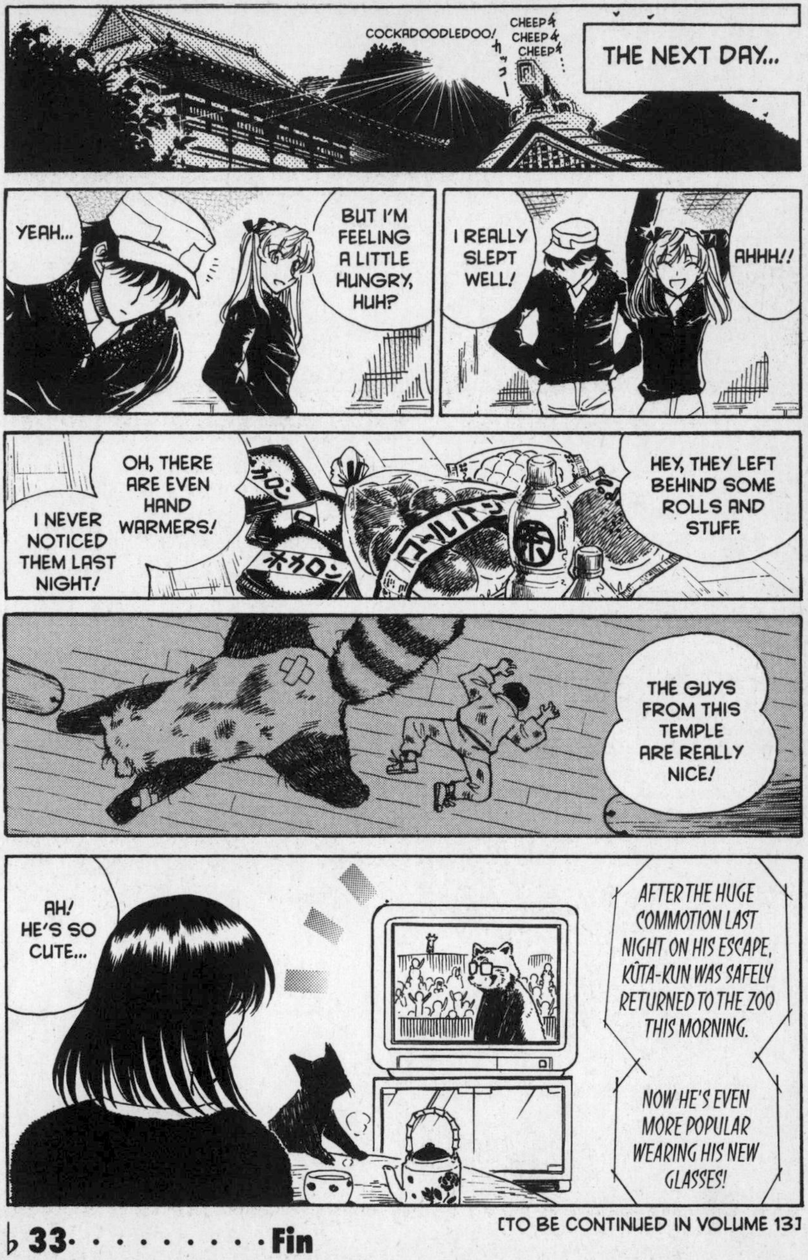
THE NEXT DAY...
CHEEP CHEEP CHEEP
COCKADOODLEDOO!
AHHH!!
I REALLY SLEPT WELL!
BUT I'M FEELING A LITTLE HUNGRY, HUH?
YEAH...
HEY, THEY LEFT BEHIND SOME ROLLS AND STUFF.
OH, THERE ARE EVEN HAND WARMERS!
I NEVER NOTICED THEM LAST NIGHT!
THE GUYS FROM THIS TEMPLE ARE REALLY NICE!
AFTER THE HUGE COMMOTION LAST NIGHT ON HIS ESCAPE, KŪTA-KUN WAS SAFELY RETURNED TO THE ZOO THIS MORNING.
NOW HE'S EVEN MORE POPULAR WEARING HIS NEW GLASSES!
AH! HE'S SO CUTE...

[TO BE CONTINUED IN VOLUME 13]

♭33·········Fin

BONUS RUMBLE

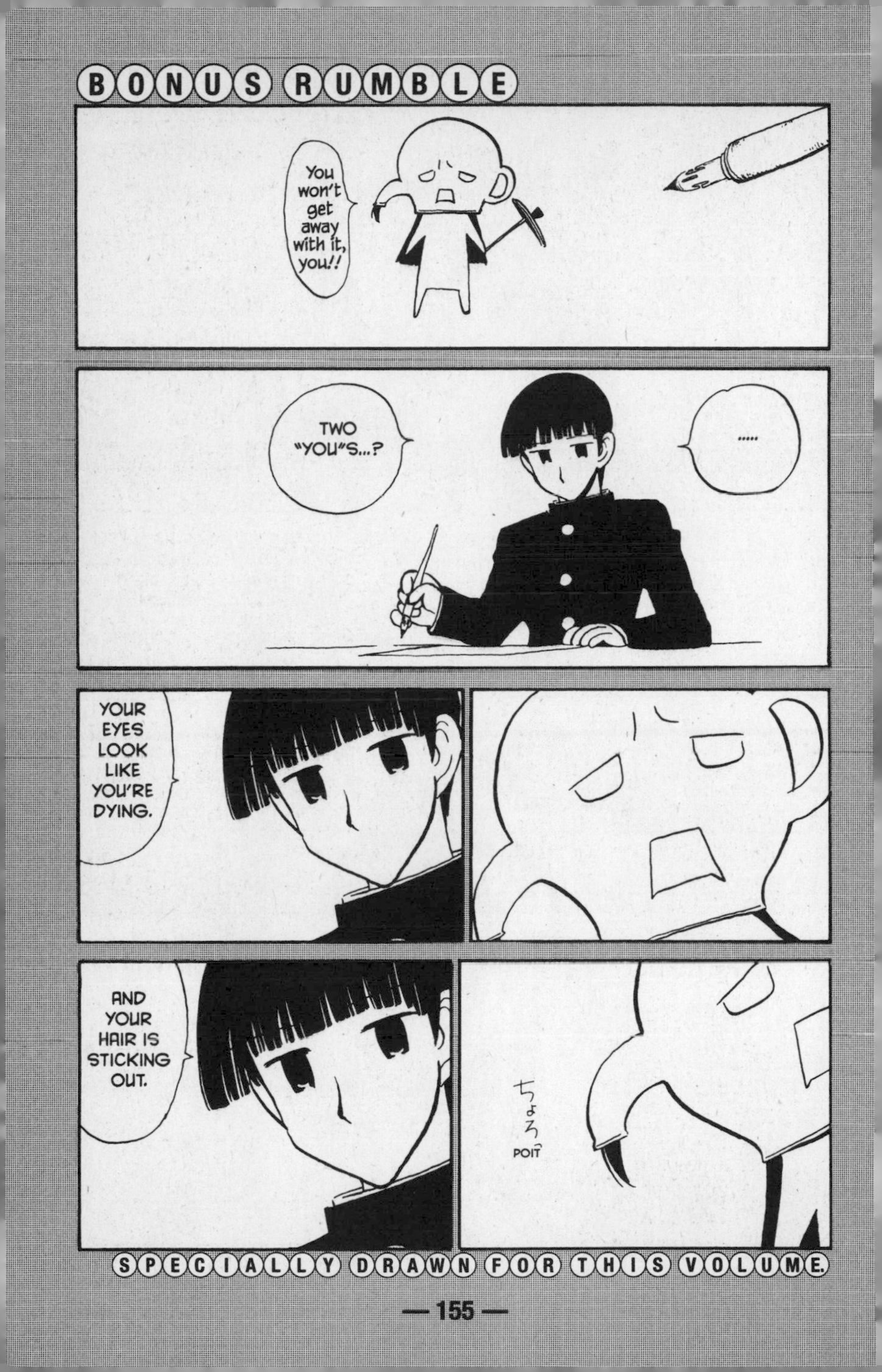

You won't get away with it, you!!
.....
TWO "YOU"S...?
YOUR EYES LOOK LIKE YOU'RE DYING.
ちょろ
POIT
AND YOUR HAIR IS STICKING OUT.

SPECIALLY DRAWN FOR THIS VOLUME.

BONUS RUMBLE

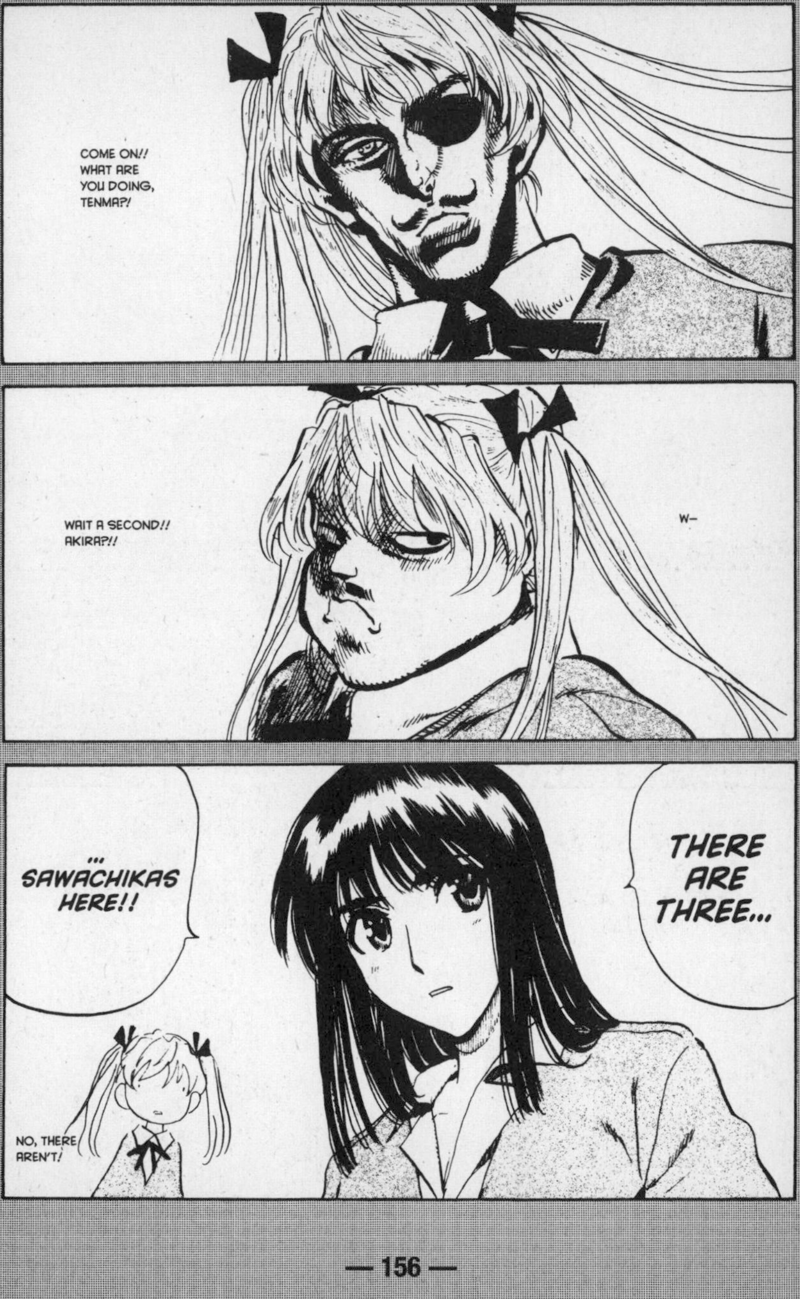
COME ON!! WHAT ARE YOU DOING, TENMA?!
W–
WAIT A SECOND!! AKIRA?!!
THERE ARE THREE...
...SAWACHIKAS HERE!!
NO, THERE AREN'T!

BONUS RUMBLE

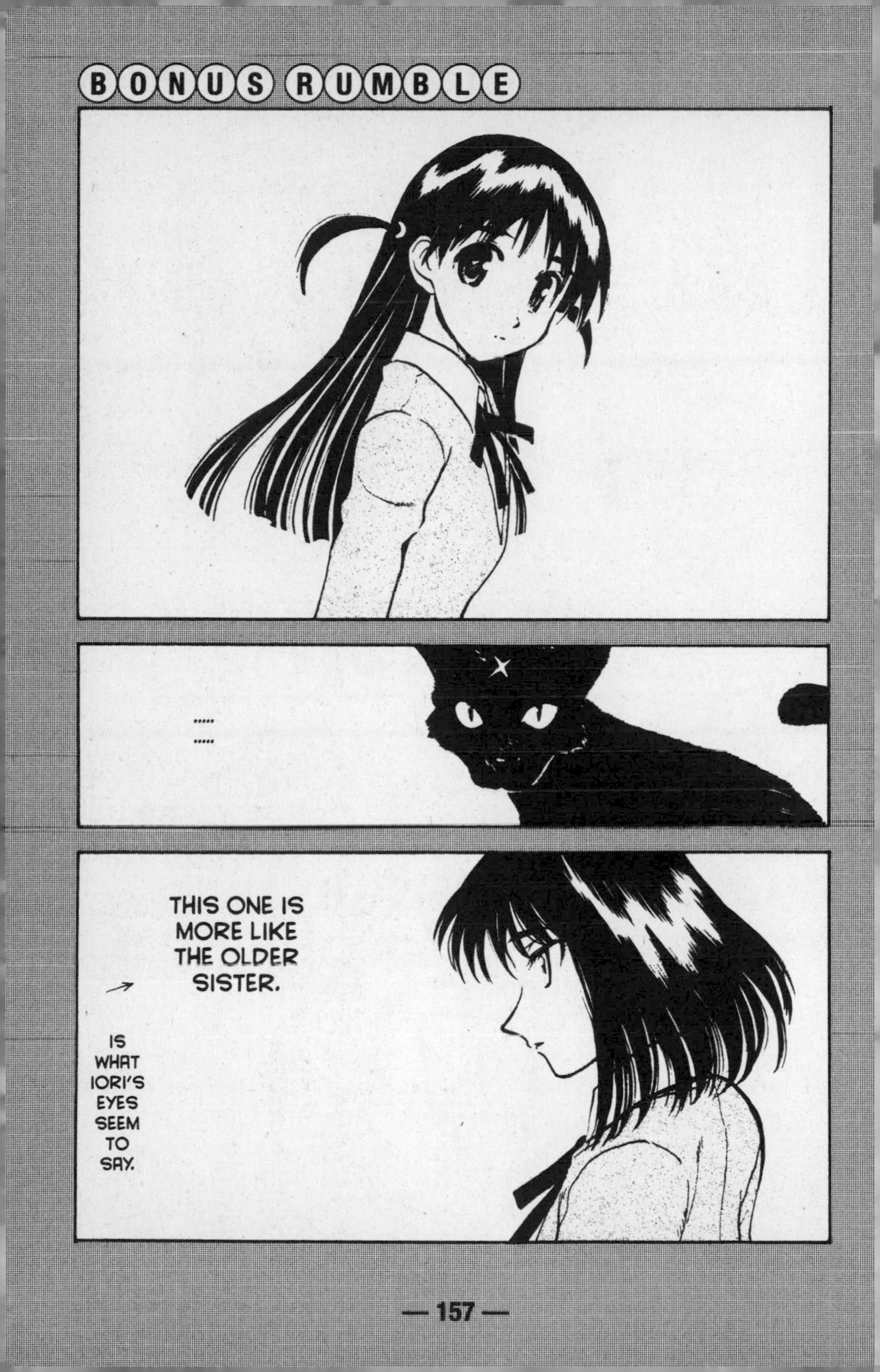
......
......
THIS ONE IS MORE LIKE THE OLDER SISTER.
IS WHAT IORI'S EYES SEEM TO SAY.

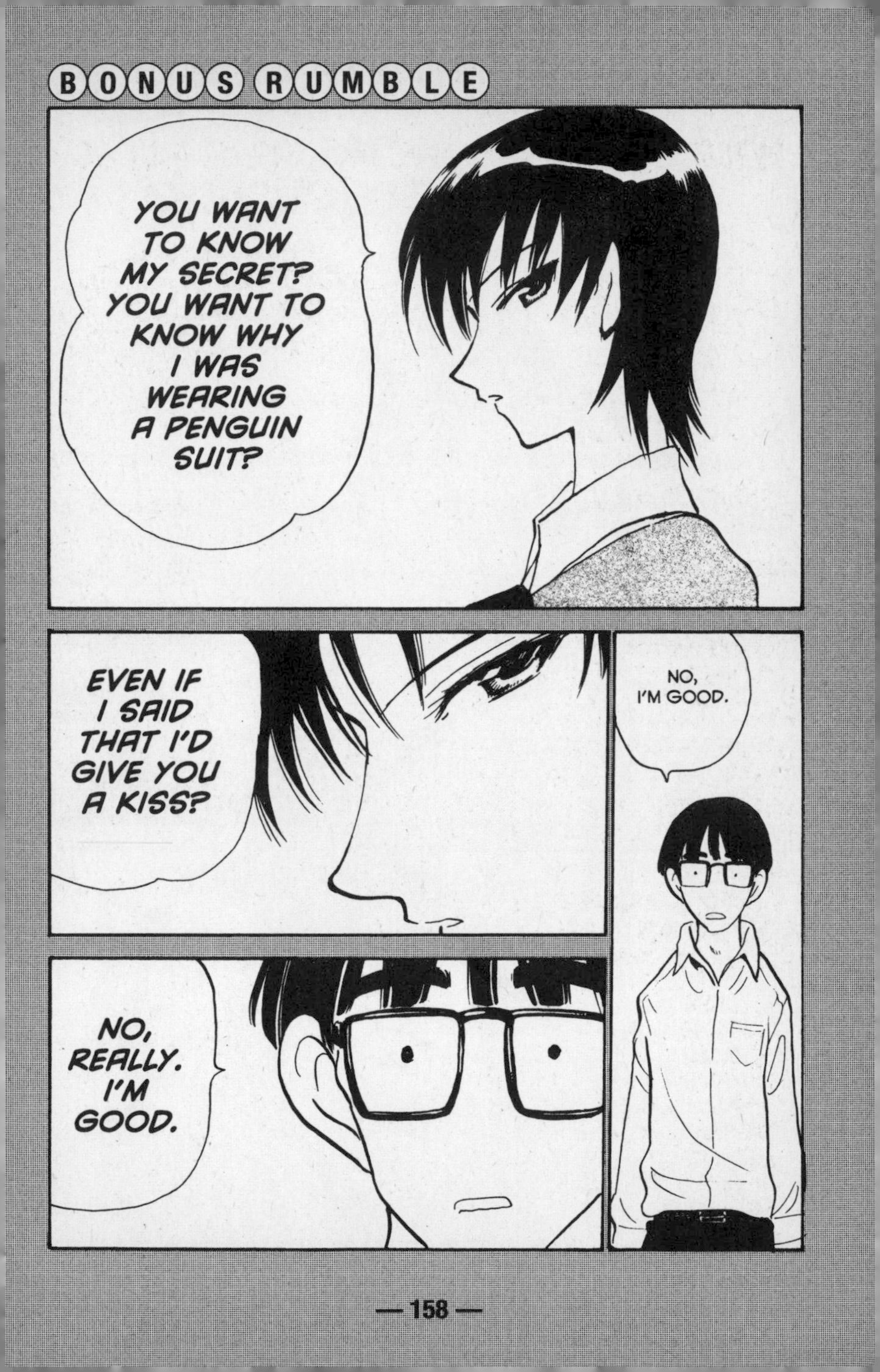
YOU WANT TO KNOW MY SECRET? YOU WANT TO KNOW WHY I WAS WEARING A PENGUIN SUIT?
NO, I'M GOOD.
EVEN IF I SAID THAT I'D GIVE YOU A KISS?
NO, REALLY. I'M GOOD.

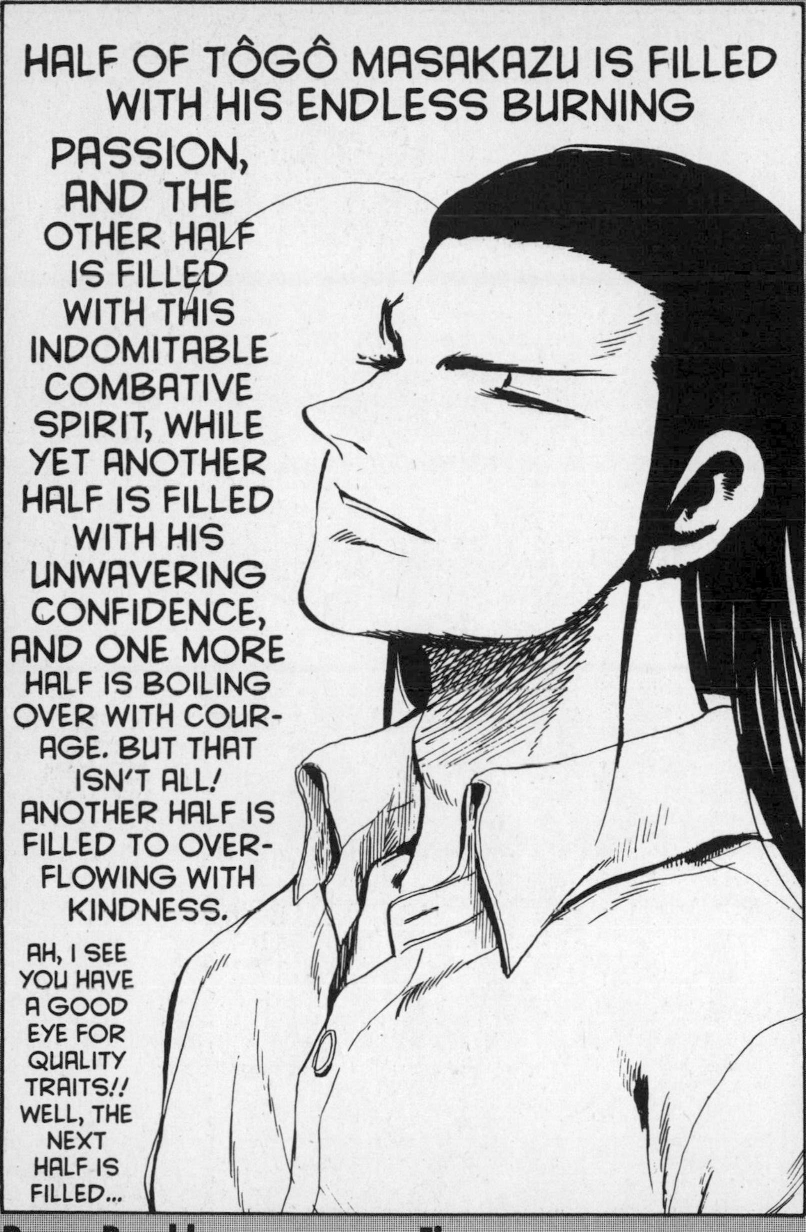
HALF OF TÔGÔ MASAKAZU IS FILLED WITH HIS ENDLESS BURNING PASSION, AND THE OTHER HALF IS FILLED WITH THIS INDOMITABLE COMBATIVE SPIRIT, WHILE YET ANOTHER HALF IS FILLED WITH HIS UNWAVERING CONFIDENCE, AND ONE MORE HALF IS BOILING OVER WITH COURAGE. BUT THAT ISN'T ALL! ANOTHER HALF IS FILLED TO OVERFLOWING WITH KINDNESS.
AH, I SEE YOU HAVE A GOOD EYE FOR QUALITY TRAITS!! WELL, THE NEXT HALF IS FILLED...

Mister, You Talk Too Much.

Bonus Rumble· · · · · · · · · ·Fin

About the Creator

Jin Kobayashi was born in Tokyo. *School Rumble* is his first manga series. He has answered these questions from his fans:

What is your hobby?
Basketball

Which manga inspired you to become a creator?
Dragon Ball

Which character in your manga do you like best?
Kenji Harima

What type of manga do you want to create in the future?
Action

Name one book, piece of music, or movie you like.
The Indiana Jones series

Translation Notes

Japanese is a tricky language for most Westerners, and translation is often more art than science. For your edification and reading pleasure, here are notes on some of the places where we could have gone in a different direction in our translation of the work, or where a Japanese cultural reference is used.

Foreigners and Eating *Nattô*, page 5

There are foods in nearly every culture that are generally loved by those within the culture and abhorred by almost anyone coming to the culture from the outside. Hawaii has poi, the Inuit have muqtuq blubber, and the Japanese have *nattô*. *Nattô* is a fermented soybean dish with a strong smell in which beans are connected by a viscous, stringy, slimy fluid (if you get the impression that this translator is one of those who dislike *nattô*, well, you're right). To play *nattô*-lover's advocate for a moment, the dish is very nutritious, and it contains nattokinase, a fibrinolytic enzyme which is said to prevent clotting in the arteries. Of course, there are Western lovers of *nattô*, and a large number of Japanese who do not eat it—in other words, there are always exceptions—but the rule is, Japanese love *nattô* and foreigners can't stand the stuff.

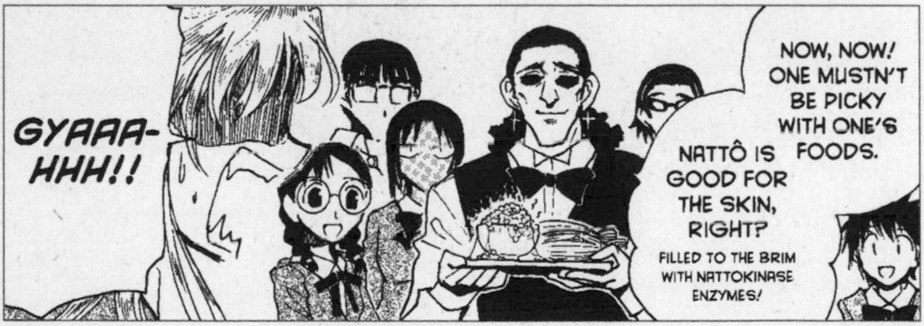
NOW, NOW! ONE MUSTN'T BE PICKY WITH ONE'S FOODS.
NATTÔ IS GOOD FOR THE SKIN, RIGHT?
FILLED TO THE BRIM WITH NATTOKINASE ENZYMES!
GYAAA-HHH!!

Not being picky with food, page 5

One of the tasks that Japanese parents set on themselves is convincing their children to eat everything served regardless of whether they like the taste or not. This becomes essential during the child's elementary school days, since it is in very bad form to refuse anything that is served in the school-provided lunches. (In some cases it's a punishable offense.) As a result, someone who is picky with his food is considered to be very childish.

Royal "We," page 6

In Western monarchies, the ruler spoke not only for his/herself, but also for the people of the land, so the monarch used what is called the royal "we." Whenever a Western monarch spoke, he/she used "we" when referring to his/herself (rather than "I"). In this panel, Tenma is acting as the ruling Shogun did in the Edo period (or at least as actors playing the Shogun do in Japanese TV period dramas). It's high and mighty enough to deserve a royal "we," so that's how I translated the line.

Kôshien, page 28

Kôshien is the name of the ballpark in which the baseball team from Osaka, the Hanshin Tigers, play. However, every year in the spring and late summer, the finals of the national high-school baseball tournament are held in Kôshien Stadium. So the tournament itself has been called Kôshien for ages. Since there is no minor-league system for Japanese baseball, the next generation of baseball stars usually comes out of Kôshien, and as a result, the tournaments are watched with as much fervor as the "March Madness" NCAA basketball tournament is viewed in the U.S. It is the dream of every high-school baseball player to go to Kôshien, and its tournament style of play makes it especially suited to manga storytelling. Countless Kôshien-themed manga have been written, and it has become something of a cliché in manga and similar entertainment.

Chi, page 30

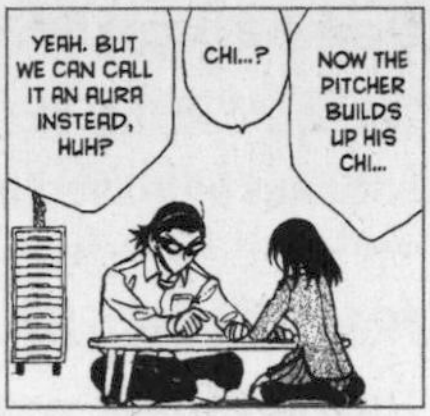
NOW THE PITCHER BUILDS UP HIS CHI...
CHI...?
YEAH. BUT WE CAN CALL IT AN AURA INSTEAD, HUH?

Pronounced *ki* by the Japanese, this flow of energy through the body is the basis of most Chinese medicine, as well as of martial-arts manga everywhere.

Writing in hiragana, page 40

The complicated Chinese characters, kanji, that are an integral part of the Japanese written language are not easily learned. The simplest characters are learned in first grade, and each additional grade adds greater numbers and more complexity until by graduation from high school, every student has learned some two thousand kanji. Since young children haven't learned kanji yet, many use the easier-to-write hiragana. How much one writes in hiragana is an indicator of how much education one has. So it would be considered very childish (or academically lazy) for a high-school-aged boy to write only in hiragana.

Hatenkô Mode, page 42

Found in the title *Hatenkô Robo Dojibiron,* Hatenkô Mode means "Heaven-Breaking" Mode. Many giant robot programs mix Japanese and English for their attacks, weapons, etc. to make for a mix that's appealing to Japanese children and anime fans.

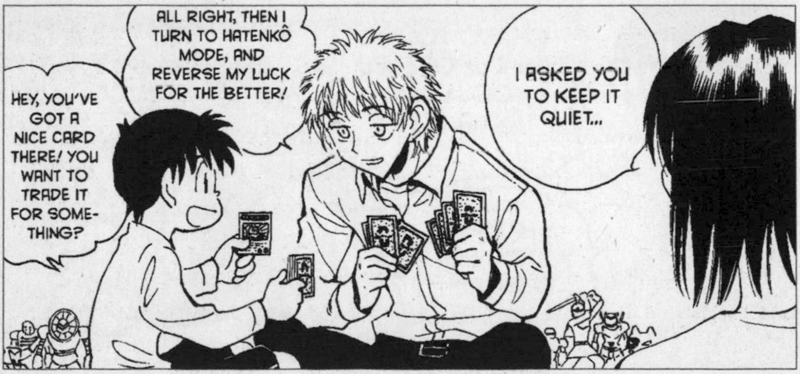
I ASKED YOU TO KEEP IT QUIET...
ALL RIGHT, THEN I TURN TO HATENKÔ MODE, AND REVERSE MY LUCK FOR THE BETTER!
HEY, YOU'VE GOT A NICE CARD THERE! YOU WANT TO TRADE IT FOR SOME-THING?

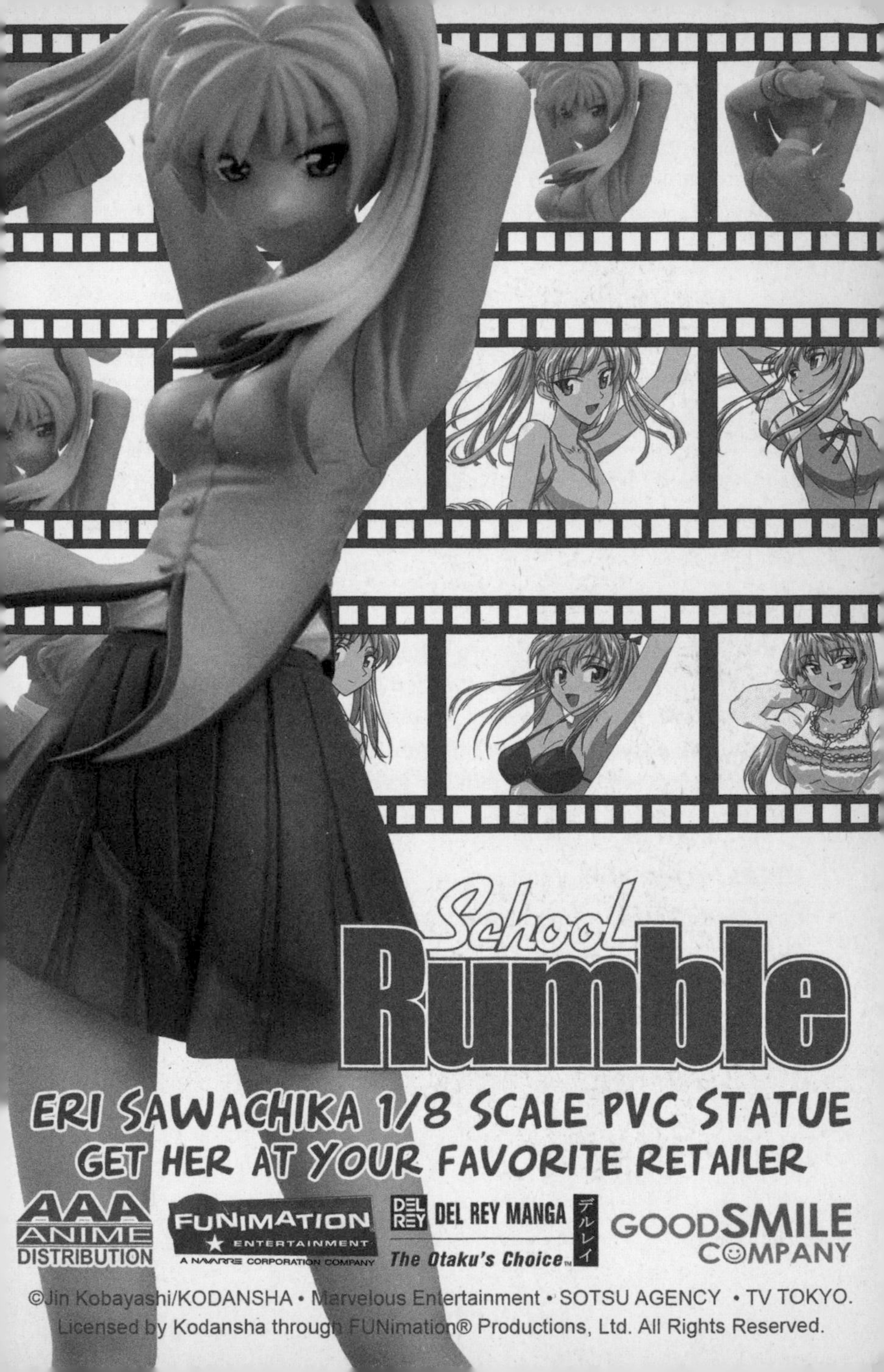
School Rumble
ERI SAWACHIKA 1/8 SCALE PVC STATUE
GET HER AT YOUR FAVORITE RETAILER
AAA ANIME DISTRIBUTION
FUNIMATION ENTERTAINMENT
A NAVARRE CORPORATION COMPANY
DEL REY
DEL REY MANGA
デルレイ
The Otaku's Choice™
GOODSMILE COMPANY
©Jin Kobayashi/KODANSHA • Marvelous Entertainment • SOTSU AGENCY • TV TOKYO.
Licensed by Kodansha through FUNimation® Productions, Ltd. All Rights Reserved.

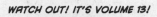

KITCHEN PRINCESS

STORY BY MIYUKI KOBAYASHI
MANGA BY NATSUMI ANDO
CREATOR OF ZODIAC P.I.

HUNGRY HEART

Najika is a great cook and likes to make meals for the people she loves. But something is missing from her life. When she was a child, she met a boy who touched her heart—and now Najika is determined to find him. The only clue she has is a silver spoon that leads her to the prestigious Seika Academy.

Attending Seika will be a challenge. Every kid at the school has a special talent, and the girls in Najika's class think she doesn't deserve to be there. But Sora and Daichi, two popular brothers who barely speak to each other, recognize Najika's cooking for what it is—magical. Could one of the boys be Najika's mysterious prince?

Special extras in each volume! Read them all!

VISIT WWW.DELREYMANGA.COM TO:
• Read sample pages
• View release date calendars for upcoming volumes
• Sign up for Del Rey's free manga e-newsletter
• Find out the latest about new Del Rey Manga series

RATING   T AGES 13+

The Otaku's Choice

TOMARE!

止まれ

[STOP!]

You're going the wrong way!

Manga is a completely different type of reading experience.

To start at the *beginning*,
go to the *end*!

That's right! Authentic manga is read the traditional Japanese way—from right to left. Exactly the *opposite* of how American books are read. It's easy to follow: Just go to the other end of the book, and read each page—and each panel—from right side to left side, starting at the top right. Now you're experiencing manga as it was meant to be!